Breaking Down the Walls of Segregation

Breaking Down the Walls of Segregation

Mexican American Grassroots Politics and Civil Rights in Orange County, California

David-James Gonzales

OXFORD
UNIVERSITY PRESS

OXFORD
UNIVERSITY PRESS

Oxford University Press is a department of the University of Oxford.
It furthers the University's objective of excellence in research, scholarship,
and education by publishing worldwide. Oxford is a registered trade mark of
Oxford University Press in the UK and in certain other countries.

Published in the United States of America by Oxford University Press
198 Madison Avenue, New York, NY 10016, United States of America.

Library of Congress Control Number: 2025030152

ISBN 9780197839454 (pbk.)
ISBN 9780197839447 (hbk.)

DOI: 10.1093/9780197839485.001.0001

Paperback printed by Marquis Book Printing, Canada
Hardback printed by Lightning Source, Inc., United States of America

The manufacturer's authorized representative in the EU for product safety is
Oxford University Press España S.A. of Parque Empresarial San Fernando de Henares,
Avenida de Castilla, 2 – 28830 Madrid (www.oup.es/en or product.safety@oup.com).
OUP España S.A. also acts as importer into Spain of products made by the manufacturer.

MIX
Paper | Supporting
responsible forestry
FSC
www.fsc.org
FSC® C103567

CONTENTS

ACKNOWLEDGMENTS

Although I was born and raised in Southern California, I have never lived in Orange County, the place that has become the focus of my scholarly work. Before then, I experienced the region like other outsiders, through theme parks, beaches, and freeways. All this changed when I stumbled upon an oral history interview as an undergraduate at the University of California, San Diego (UCSD). I was introduced to Gretchen Laue, founding director of UC San Diego's Professional Development Institute and former United Farm Workers of America (UFW) organizer, who helped organize a project to document the history and contributions of the Community Service Organization (CSO). This group, established by future US Congressman Edward Roybal and community organizer Fred Ross, trained UFW founders Cesar Chavez, Dolores Huerta, Gilbert Padilla, and several other Mexican American civil rights activists, like Herman Gallegos and California Supreme Court Justice Cruz Reynoso. Gretchen told me about her work on the CSO Project and shared oral history transcripts conducted with former members, thus introducing me to the long and deep history of ethnic Mexican grassroots organizing by unheralded individuals.

One of these individuals was Hector Tarango. Tarango was not born in Orange County, but his experiences and activism shed light on the ethnic Mexican experience in the region during the early to mid-twentieth century. In his interview, he spoke of segregation, sociopolitical marginalization, and, more importantly, how the Mexican American community organized and mobilized itself to desegregate Orange County schools. This was not the history of victimization I had become accustomed to. This was a history of community empowerment by ordinary people. Hector was not a member of the CSO, which was founded in Los Angeles in 1949, but his relationship and work with Fred Ross in Orange County before the organization's establishment were influential in its development. After working alongside Tarango to end de jure school segregation in Orange County, Ross was redbaited and run out of town by local citrus ranchers organized under the auspices of the Associated Farmers and the Catholic Church in Santa Ana. Ross later referred to his experiences in Orange County as pivotal in his approach to organizing Mexican American communities. He also never forgot about his compadre Hector Tarango, whom Ross credited with having the "huevos" to stay in Orange County and continue the fight after he left. When it came time to organize the CSO, Ross brought Tarango to the organization's founding meeting in Los Angeles, where he related the successful efforts of Mexican Americans in desegregating schools, registering voters, and electing Mexican Americans to local offices in Orange County.

The power of Hector Tarango's story and the sociopolitical conditions faced by ethnic Mexicans in the region stayed with me. There was something different about Orange County, especially the control orange growers exhibited over ethnic Mexicans in that place. There was a much longer history of community organizing and empowerment among the ethnic Mexican barrios and colonias in this unique region. This book uncovers the people and organizations that predated and led to the school desegregation movement there, culminating in the class-action lawsuit *Mendez, et al. v. Westminster School District of Orange County, et al.* (1946). It represents nearly a decade of community-engaged research and collaboration that would not have been possible without the dozens of archivists, public librarians, local historians, and longtime residents who assisted me along the way. Primary sources, generally held in "official" archives, provide the foundation of any historical work, including this one. Indeed, many of the sources that inform this book rely on federal databases, like the United States Census, and public and private records in city, county, and university archives. However, researching and writing about the ethnic Mexican experience and influence on early to mid-twentieth-century Orange County required accessing sources not contained in these archives.

During the summer of 2015, I was fortunate to connect with Lizeth Ramirez, former Archivist and Reference Librarian at the Orange Public Library and History Center (OPL), which held a series of events in 2015–16 celebrating the county's Latino (a/x/e) heritage. People from all over the county attended these gatherings, including current and former barrio/colonia residents and their families, local historians, archivists, educators, students, journalists, and public officials. In addition to introducing me to the rich history of Latinos in Orange County, these meetings facilitated numerous opportunities to locate research materials, meet with residents and families, conduct oral history interviews, collaborate with local curators and archivists, and present my research at public forums. In addition to Lizeth, I am indebted to Aida Cuevas, the current archivist and local history librarian at OPL, as well as the librarians and archivists at the Anaheim Heritage Center, Fullerton Local History Room, Placentia Local History Room, and Santa Ana History Room. I am equally grateful for the research assistance provided by Susan Berumen, Chris Jepson, and Steve Oftelie at the Orange County Archives. The knowledge and expertise of public librarians and local archivists throughout the county, as well as the materials held in these institutions, have enriched this project beyond measure. I am also greatly appreciative of the assistance of archivists and special collections staff at CSU Fullerton, UC Irvine, Chapman University, Stanford University, USC, and UCLA. I owe special thanks to archivists Abby Waldrop and Natalie Navar Garcia at the Lawrence de Graaf Center for Oral and Public History and Patricia Prestinary, Archivist and Special Collections Librarian at Cal State Fullerton's Pollack Library. Since my move to Utah in 2018, Patricia, Abby, and Natalie have aided this project in countless ways. I also thank the donors and contributors to the collections at the institutions listed above, as their generosity and commitment to preserving local and regional history have greatly facilitated the completion of this book.

While I did not meet Hector Tarango or most of the other people mentioned in this book prior to their passing, I have spoken with and interviewed many of their siblings, children, grandchildren, extended family, compadres y comadres, neighbors, and acquaintances. Getting to know these individuals and being entrusted with their stories and personal materials has been a tremendous privilege. For decades, Orange County's ethnic Mexican community has worked to preserve and pass on its history to future generations. To this end, I have been inspired by and am indebted to Gustavo Arellano, Margie de la Torre Aguirre, Yolanda Morelos Alvarez, Angelina Veyna, Mary Garcia, Manny Escamilla, and Harvey Reyes for their advice, feedback, and encouragement over the years. Much of Orange County's Latino (a/x/e) history remains in the memories and homes of the people and families who lived it. I offer my heartfelt thanks to Paul Guzman, Phil Collin, Leo Castro, Robert "Bob" Torres Jr., Dr. Albert Vela, Mimi Lozano, Zeke Hernandez, Alfredo H. Zuniga, Enrique "Kiki" Zuniga, Hon. Frederick P. Aguirre, Sam Romero, Harvey Tarango, Dr. Hector Ron Godinez, Stephanie Reyes-Tuccio, Louis Olivos Jr., Alfonso Olivos, Gay Olivos, Michael Ramirez, and Beverley Guzman Gallegos for sharing their time, stories, and personal collections with me. They are the experts and curators of the living community archive that made this book possible. As an outsider who has been welcomed into their hearts, lives, and homes, I have done my best to include as many voices and perspectives as possible. I take my responsibility as a community-engaged historian seriously to bring to light the overlooked, ignored, and underrepresented. Although many have been left out of this book, I remain committed to working with Orange County's Latino (a/x/e) community to find other avenues to preserve and disseminate their history for future generations. ¡Adelante!

My scholarly interest in Orange County began in the Department of History at UC San Diego, where David G. Gutierrez, Luis Alvarez, and Natalia Molina inspired and encouraged my budding interest in the histories of race/ethnicity, migration, and social justice movements in California and the American West. As a community college transfer student, I had no idea one could study the lived experiences and contributions of people of color in my home state, so their classes, scholarship, and mentorship were nothing short of revelatory and transformative. After UCSD, I completed my graduate training at the University of Southern California (USC) under the guidance of George Sánchez and Bill Deverell. I am most grateful for their examples as community-engaged scholars and for seeing beyond my nontraditional background to find a space for me at USC. Moreover, several others in the Department of History, like Karen Halttunen, Peter Mancall, Marjorie Becker, Sarah Gualtieri, Philip Ethington, and Lon Kurashige, welcomed me into their interdisciplinary scholarly community and made my graduate experience truly exceptional. Also, to the best office staff on campus—Lori Rogers, Sandra Hopwood, Simone Bessant, and Melissa Calderon—thank you for making me feel like family during my time at USC.

Throughout the years, several diversity programs, initiatives, and fellowships provided invaluable financial support and mentorship that facilitated and advanced my academic career and this book. Foremost among these are the Ronald E. McNair Post-Baccalaureate Achievement Programs at UCSD and USC, the EDGE-First Ph.D. Summer Institute at USC, the Summer Institute on Tenure and Professional Advancement at Duke University, the Young Scholars Program and the Institute for Latino Studies at the University of Notre Dame, and the Society for Citizens and Scholars Career Enhancement Fellowship (formerly the Woodrow Wilson National Fellowship Foundation) at Princeton University. I thank the administrators and staff of these programs, especially Thomas K. Brown, Richard Andalon, David Glasgow, Kerry L. Haynie, Mark Anthony Neal, and Luis Fraga, for their commitment to diversity, equity, and inclusion in higher education. I also express my deep appreciation for Richard Andalon, whom I first met when he was directing USC's McNair Scholars Program in 2010. Richard was the first of many BIPOC mentors who helped me feel like I belonged in academia. In recent years, Vicki L. Ruiz, Matt Garcia, Rosina Lozano, and Ana Elizabeth Rosas have become trusted advisors and colleagues who have helped me navigate the early years of my academic career. Their wisdom, encouragement, and advocacy on my behalf have meant the world to me, and I strive to emulate their examples.

Since arriving at BYU in 2018, I have felt at home in the Department of History and the College of Family, Home, and Social Sciences. I thank department chairs Eric Dursteler and Brian Cannon, and deans Ben Ogles and Laura Padilla Walker for ensuring I have everything I need to succeed at "the Y." The collegiality in my department is truly special, and I am deeply grateful to all those who have befriended and mentored me. I also thank Associate Dean Niwako Yamawaki and my department colleague, mentor, and compadre Ignacio Garcia for their commitment to building spaces of inclusion and empowerment for faculty of color on campus. Along those lines, FHSS College has provided the unique opportunity to build community among faculty and students through the establishment of the Latino (a/x/e) Civil Rights Experiential Learning Seminar. I am especially grateful to colleagues Jane Lopez, Jacob Rugh, Bryant Jensen, Eric Bybee, Kif Agustine-Adams, Ignacio Garcia, Ashley Jimenez Fraser, Daniel Becerra, Melissa Alcaraz, and our Latino CRS student alumni for joining me in this effort. Special thanks are also due to my undergraduate research assistants: Emma Chapman, Larissa Domnikov, Jena Burgess, Maya Brimhall, Kiyah Clemence, Lindsey Meza, Erick Calderon, Hunter Westbrook, Felipe Larrocha, and Logan Rodriguez. This exceptional group of young scholars poured through thousands of pages of US Census manuscripts, periodicals, local directories, voter registries, and other materials, saving me an immeasurable amount of time and energy. It has been a pleasure to mentor and learn from each of you, and I am excited to witness and applaud your many accomplishments in the years ahead.

At Oxford University Press, Susan Ferber supported and championed my book from the moment I reached out to her. I deeply appreciate her confidence and keen editorial eye throughout this journey. Thanks also to Aimee Wright, Ganga B., and the rest of the editorial and production staff for shepherding this project to completion.

Finally, and most importantly, I thank my wife, Karla, and our children, Ayiana, Belicia, Cadiz, and Joaquin, for accompanying me along the circuitous and unexpected journey that has led us to this point. They have always been and will forever remain my primary source of motivation and strength. To my parents, Anthony and Dorothy Gonzales, I am forever grateful for your examples as community-engaged bilingual educators and for being the greatest parents anyone could ask for.

Although many years of research and collaboration with Orange County's Latino (a/x/e) community have gone into this book, I am mindful of the limited reach of academic scholarship. In November 2023, I received an email from Logan Rodriguez, a student at my university who learned about *Mendez et al.* in a sociology class where a colleague assigned one of my publications. The student explained how she and her parents had spent their "whole lives in Westminster," yet "none of [them] had ever heard about this case." She shared how learning about the class-action lawsuit "was so amazing" because she "would not exist" if the case had not ended de jure school segregation in Orange County and California. Her mother is white and her father is Mexican. Had the Westminster School District remained segregated, they would not have met in junior high, dated in high school, and eventually married. I have heard countless stories like this while researching and writing this book. Every time I do, I am reminded of how little we know about the people and places we come from, and I am motivated to do what I can to rectify it.

This is not my history. It belongs to those who lived it and those now residing in Orange County whose legacy it is. I do not pretend to be detached from the people and place I have grown to love and admire. I have used the tools and methods of my profession to interpret and preserve their history to the best of my ability. While it was never my plan to write a book on Orange County, I am overjoyed by the privilege of doing so.

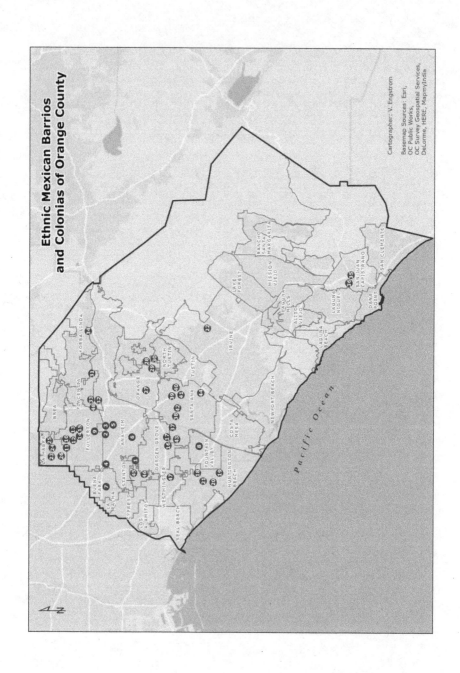

Ethnic Mexican Barrios
and Colonias of Orange County

Cartographer: V. Engstrom

Basemap Sources: Esri,
OC Public Works,
OC Survey Geospatial Services,
DeLorme, HERE, MapmyIndia

1. Colonia Independencia
2. La Conga
3. La Fábrica
4. La Palma
5. La Philadelphia
6. Tijuanita
7. Los Coyotes
8. Colonia Juarez
9. Toker Town
10. Tia Juana
11. Mexicali
12. Escondido
13. Coyote
14. Santa Fe
15. San Quintín/El Hoyo
16. Manzanillo
17. La Paz
18. Wintersburg
19. La Bolsa
20. Camp Limón
21. Chico Farms
22. Farm Labor Camp
23. Campo Colorado
24. Campo Corona
25. Campo Verde (Maravilla)
26. Alta Vista
27. Cypress
28. El Modena: El Pirripi
29. El Modena: Hollywood
30. La Paloma
31. Atwood
32. La Jolla
33. Placita Santa Fe
34. Esperanza
35. Los Rios
36. Little Hollywood
37. Santa Anita
38. Artesia
39. Logan
40. Grand & 4th Street
41. Grand & 1st Street
42. 1st Street & Bristol
43. Silver Acres
44. Delhi
45. Stanton Village
46. Crow Village
47. Olive Street
48. Pomona

Ethnic Mexican Barrios and Colonias in Orange County. Map by Vanessa Engstrom.

Introduction

The et al. Paradigm

Between the summer of 1943 and the spring of 1946, something unprecedented occurred among the ethnic Mexican neighborhoods of Orange County, CA, that changed the landscape of American public education. Over the prior thirty-three years, children of Mexican ancestry were segregated into separate "Mexican" schools across the county. As early as 1912, the Santa Ana School District began segregating Mexican children, becoming one of the first districts in California to formalize the practice.[1] By 1933, segregationist policies were in force throughout most of the county's forty-four elementary school districts with eleven districts operating at least fifteen schools with 100 percent Mexican enrollment.[2] At minimum, 68 percent of Mexican children attended a segregated school in Orange County, while the remaining 32 percent attended so-called integrated schools where they were generally placed in classrooms apart from their white peers.[3] Although ethnic Mexican families resisted school segregation from the outset, their objections fell on deaf ears for decades. Undeterred, parents, neighbors, and non-Hispanic/Latino allies built a county-wide movement to end de jure school segregation during the early 1940s. Without training or support from civil rights organizations, they mobilized parents and community members to appear before school boards, question school administrators, obtain legal counsel, organize voters, participate in elections, and dismantle the county's two-tiered educational system. This movement, made up of unheralded immigrants, citizens, parents, children,

Breaking Down the Walls of Segregation. David-James Gonzales, Oxford University Press.
© Oxford University Press 2025. DOI: 10.1093/9780197839485.003.0001

neighbors, laborers, emerging activists, and their allies, forever changed America's educational system. Shockingly, few know about them and their accomplishments.

On February 18, 1946, Federal District Court Judge Paul J. McCormick decided in favor of Gonzalo Mendez, William Guzman, Frank Palomino, Thomas Estrada, and Lorenzo Ramirez in the class-action lawsuit *Mendez, et al. v. Westminster School District of Orange County, et al.* Filed on behalf of 5,000 school children of "Mexican and Latin decent," the five plaintiff families charged the defendant Orange County school districts of Westminster, Garden Grove, Santa Ana, and El Modeno with illegally segregating their children, and thereby violating their rights to due process and equal protection as guaranteed under the Fifth and Fourteenth Amendments to the US Constitution.[4] Although Mexican Americans had previously won desegregation lawsuits in municipal, county, and state courts in Colorado, Arizona, Texas, and California, *Mendez et al.* was unprecedented in scope, as it addressed the systemic segregation of an ethnic/racial minority at a scale not previously considered by the courts.[5] Further, the case was won at the federal level and thereby provided a legal precedent that was used in future cases like *Delgado v. Bastrop Independent School District* (1948), *Gonzales v. Sheely* (1951), and *Hernandez v. Texas* (1954).[6] After the Ninth Circuit Court of Appeals upheld the decision on April 14, 1947, California became one of the first states to desegregate its public school system after Reconstruction, doing so seven years before *Brown v. Board of Education* (1954).

While *Mendez et al.* was initially championed by journalists, legal scholars, and civil rights activists, the case became a historical footnote, rarely acknowledged for its foundational role in leading to the *Brown* decision and its contributions to the Civil Rights Movement.[7] This was largely because the case occurred in an obscure part of Southern California situated between Los Angeles and San Diego. Until the mid-1950s, Orange County was a relatively unknown agricultural backwater primarily devoted to growing citrus fruits.[8] Even during the Cold War, when the population increased tenfold from 216,224 in 1950 to over 2.4 million in 1990, Orange County continued to be viewed by outsiders as little more than a suburban extension of Los Angeles. Moreover, the representation of the Civil Rights Movement in US history, memory, and culture overwhelmingly depicts the movement through a black-white binary that sidelines the experiences and contributions of Latinas/os, Asians, and Native Americans. Indeed, the dominant narrative of the Civil Rights Movement advanced by media and school curricula typically begins with the *Brown* decision in 1954 and ends with the assassination of Martin Luther King Jr. in 1968. Despite decades of scholarship challenging, lengthening, and broadening this timeline, contributions by other communities of color that fall outside the dominant narrative remain overlooked and understudied.[9] When *Mendez et al.* is acknowledged, it is largely misremembered and misunderstood. The case did not derive from one family's experience and struggle against segregation; instead, it resulted from a grassroots movement involving dozens of parents, children, and neighbors that built upon decades of ethnic Mexican community organizing in Orange County.

Breaking Down the Walls of Segregation tells the story of an improbable civil rights victory in the unlikely setting of Orange County, CA. To grasp the significance of *Mendez et al.*, requires understanding why Mexicans were segregated. Beginning in the 1880s, this book details the formative role of the citrus industry in Orange County's development and deeply segregated socioeconomic structure, which remained in place until the decisions in 1946 and 1947. The book interweaves two interrelated historical developments that recenter the history of Orange County through the perspective, experiences, and contributions of Mexican immigrants and Mexican Americans, the region's most prominent ethnic/racial minority. The first pertains to the emergence, growth, and importance of segregation in Orange County, while the second involves the people and organizations that led to its demise. Ending in the early 1960s, *Breaking Down the Walls of Segregation* illustrates Orange County's unique place in the history of California and its importance to the Civil Rights Movement. Exploring the history of this county through the lens of the grassroots movement that led to *Mendez et al.* illuminates the essential role ethnic Mexicans played in the region's social, economic, and political development from the late nineteenth century to the Cold War.

Orange County entered the American consciousness during the Cold War (1945–89), serving as the archetype of everything that was great about postwar American society. Bolstered by Disneyland, which opened in Anaheim on July 17, 1955, Orange County's abundance of well-paying jobs and affordable homes in newly built master-planned communities attracted transplants from all over the country. Massive increases in federal defense spending brought military bases, defense contractors, corporate investors, tourism, and mega churches. Orange County's postwar transformation created an enduring image of the region as ethno-racially white, affluent, and politically conservative.[10] This stereotypical view of Orange County whitewashes the region's rich and complex history of human habitation that began 10,000 years ago with the Acjachemen (Juaneño) and Tongva (Gabrieleño) people. Like most places, Orange County is full of contradictions, simultaneously cosmopolitan and progressive while also being provincial and conservative.

This book overlaps with and complements the narratives provided by prior studies of the region while focusing on two central themes that remain underexplored.[11] The first deals with the issue of segregation. While existing scholarship acknowledges that ethnic Mexicans encountered various forms of segregation in early to mid-twentieth-century Orange County, they do not stress its root causes and vital importance to the socioeconomic development of the region. This work explains who was responsible for implementing segregation in Orange County, how it spread, and who benefited from it. The second theme concerns the politicization of ethnic Mexicans as they responded to segregation and other forms of marginalization. Existing work that touches on ethnic Mexican social and political organizations leaves the impression that the push for civil rights in Orange County began during the 1940s. Connecting people and organizations that have hitherto been viewed in isolation or gone unnoticed, this book argues that ethnic Mexicans established and maintained a culture of civic engagement and grassroots civil rights activism from the late 1920s to the 1960s, resulting in the end of de jure segregation and the election of Mexican Americans to political office.

Although the book's focus is Orange County, this history mirrors much of what ethnic Mexicans experienced throughout Southern California's sprawling citrus empire, which stretched from Santa Barbara to San Diego and from Los Angeles to Riverside. Continuing the work of scholars and community members committed to historical recovery and truth-telling, it grapples with the power and tension between historical memory and narrative—what happened versus what is said to have happened—in Southern California's multilayered history.[12]

Contrary to popular belief, segregation in Orange County did not begin during the post-World War II era of mass suburbanization and white flight.[13] The practice predated the postwar years by several decades and was foundational to both the citrus industry and the region's socioeconomic development. Emerging from a constellation of profit-minded business practices during the late nineteenth century, racial segregation was a tool used by citrus capitalists in Orange County and other parts of Southern California to manage labor and secure a competitive advantage within a volatile and highly competitive industry.[14] The development and maintenance of segregation in Orange County was part of the historical process scholars describe as racial capitalism, which historians Destin Jenkins and Justin Leroy posit is not an aberration or "special application of capitalistic processes, but rather central to how it operates."[15] Examining the development of the citrus industry and the intentional use of segregation as a form of labor and social control in Orange County, *Breaking Down the Walls of Segregation* situates Latino (a/x/e) history within the literature of racial capitalism.[16] Doing so reveals the concrete material motivations undergirding the development of a regionally specific form of segregationist practices and racial ideology in Southern California that facilitated economic growth and produced a homegrown version of anti-Mexican racism and white supremacy.

The ethnic Mexican experience in Orange County provides a compelling example of ethnic studies scholar Jodi Melamed's observation that "racism enshrines the inequalities that capitalism requires," thereby making it more difficult to discern the root causes or "antinomies of accumulation."[17] The first two chapters of this book show that the practices used by citrus capitalists to access and maintain a surplus of exploitable low-wage laborers created a new social hierarchy with whites at the top and ethnic Mexicans at the bottom. Over time, the county's white residents associated their higher socioeconomic status as the result of racial/cultural differences instead of the inequities institutionalized and preserved through the partnership between the citrus industry and local governance. Consequently, segregation facilitated the production of anti-Mexican racism, which then provided cover for the very real socioeconomic disparities between the two groups. In sum, segregation, anti-Mexican racism, and socioeconomic inequality comprised the "antinomies of accumulation" produced by citrus capitalism in Orange County.

This was no accidental development, as segregation in Orange County was designed to sustain citrus capitalism. This fact was clear to Carey McWilliams, one of the foremost observers of mid-twentieth-century labor and race relations, who was among the first to document the underbelly of Southern California's "orange empire."[18] In his 1946 book *Southern California Country: An Island on the Land*, McWilliams described the "citrus belt complex" as "a world of its own" where "the orange tree itself provides the key to an understanding of the social life of the citrus belt."[19] This was a world of seeming contradictions, where "the orange tree [was] the living symbol of richness, luxury, and elegance,"[20] while the industry that sustained it produced what McWilliams later called "the colonia complex," a landscape of "physical . . . social and psychological isolation" that separated Mexicans from whites to profit from their labor and marginalized social position.[21] There were no ironies or contradictions within this system. Indeed, the colonia complex was the intended byproduct of the citrus belt complex, including its accompanying landscape of disinvestment and underdevelopment that was directly correlated to the investment and development in other parts of the citrus belt. Therefore, wealth and prosperity coexisted with poverty and inequality, not as opposites or unintended consequences but integral to citrus capitalism.

Although McWilliams did not use the term racial capitalism in his writing, it was precisely what he described to his readers in the revised edition of *Brothers Under the Skin* (1951). In the book's closing chapter, McWilliams argued that racial prejudice sustained the social order instituted by capitalism. The root cause of America's "race problem," McWilliams insisted, was capitalism's need "to find new sources of readily exploitable labor."[22] Thus, "the ideology of capitalism has always been saturated with the folklore of racial and ethnic differences," McWilliams wrote.[23] Foreshadowing the conclusions of critical race theorists and scholars of racial capitalism by several decades, McWilliams saw labor exploitation as the connective tissue that preserved racial, ethnic, and class prejudice from the British colonial system to postwar industrial capitalism.[24] Unlike the Marxists of his day, McWilliams did not dismiss racism as secondary to class conflict. Rather, he saw all forms of prejudice as central to the "strategies of dominance" employed by those seeking a competitive or profit-seeking advantage over others.[25]

Building on McWilliams, *Breaking Down the Walls of Segregation* examines the inner workings of citrus capitalism in Orange County to explain the systemic institutionalization of segregation and anti-Mexican racism. Whereas McWilliams defined the key features of the citrus belt complex stretching from Pasadena to Riverside, less is known about how the industry operated outside this region.[26] As the crown jewel of Southern California's citrus empire, Orange County provides the ideal setting to study the development of the citrus industry and its impact on people, institutions, and culture. Although portions of Los Angeles, Riverside, San Bernardino, Ventura, and San Diego counties were devoted to citrus cultivation, nowhere was it more dominant than in Orange County. Indeed, by 1925, Orange County had more land allotted to citrus than any other county in the state. At forty-six citrus acres per square mile, this was nearly four times the amount in Los Angeles County, fifteen times the amount in Riverside County, and twenty-three times the amount in San Bernardino County.[27] Moreover, by 1929, citrus accounted for two-thirds of Orange County's agricultural income, totaling $23.4 million, of which $19.5 million (or 83 percent) came from the sale of Valencia oranges.[28] All this led industry officials to designate Orange County as the home of "King Valencia."[29]

In addition to illuminating distinctions within the citrus empire, analyzing the development of the citrus industry in Orange County deepens our understanding of the broader history of racism and inequality in the United States. As with the oppressive labor systems that developed in the Caribbean and Southern states, the Valencia orange was akin to sugar, tobacco, and cotton in representing the antinomies of accumulation in Orange County. As the undisputed engine of the regional economy, citrus dictated land use patterns and social relations from the county's formation in 1889 to 1948, when the industry reached its zenith. With over fifty segregated ethnic Mexican neighborhoods and at least fifteen segregated Mexican schools, no other part of the state experienced the systemic marginalization of a minority group like Orange County during the first half of the twentieth century.

Understanding the origin and function of segregation in Orange County requires a willingness to question some basic assumptions about the history of racial inequality in the United States. People have generally been led to believe that segregation in Orange County and other parts of Southern California somehow derived from the African American experience in the Deep South. By using phrases like "Jaime Crow" and "Juan Crow," even well-meaning Latino (a/x/e) activists, educators, and public intellectuals have assumed and perpetuated such a connection. This makes sense given the constant stream of narratives through public education, media, popular culture, political discourse, and personal anecdotes that promote the myth of Southern exceptionalism. As explained by historians Matthew Lassiter and Joseph Crespino, "the notion of the exceptional South has served as a myth, one that has persistently distorted our understanding of American history."[30] Perhaps no more explicit example of this myth is seen in the presumption that Southerners and their institutions were more racist or oppressive than those in the North. Indeed, within America's national origin story, anti-Black racism and segregation are understood to have derived from the "original sin" of chattel slavery in the Southern states. While this explains a key component of America's complex history of race, it promotes a false binary of an exceptionally racist South juxtaposed to a more liberal and progressive North that erases the diverse experiences and subjectivities of other communities of color that have dealt with their own sociohistorically specific forms of racism.

However, Jim Crow did not necessarily "follow" African Americans to the North and West. In places like California, which McWilliams called "America's racial frontier," it was already there.[31] The development of segregation in Orange County did not derive from the socioeconomic order that existed in the Jim Crow South. This is not to say that white settlers and migrants from the Midwest, Northeast, and South did not bring their existing prejudices with them to Orange County, as that was certainly the case. White supremacy was the norm in late nineteenth and early twentieth-century America. One did not have to be a member of the Ku Klux Klan, although many Orange Countians were, to hold racist beliefs and create discriminatory institutions.[32] Further, citrus capitalists did not look to the South to create their system of labor management and social control; it was homegrown. As the owners of the land and institutions that sustained citrus cultivation, Orange County's citrus elite used their collective power as landowners, taxpayers, voters, bankers, elected officials, and administrators of public utilities to organize the county's social and physical landscape to ensure a return on investment.

Examining Orange County's first half-century of socioeconomic development illuminates a great deal about the intersection of race, capitalism, and inequality in twentieth-century America. It was here, outside the Jim Crow South and North, where citrus capitalists produced a regionally specific form of segregation and white supremacy without the use of segregationist statutes, thereby blurring the problematic distinction between de jure and de facto segregation.[33] It was here where the brown Mexican body became the object of socioeconomic exploitation and marginalization. It was here where land developers, real estate agents, citrus growers, and elected officials collaborated to intentionally build segregated communities to attract, maintain, and exploit Mexican family labor. And it was here where parents, educators, and social workers established a segregated and unequal educational system that placed Mexican children in "Mexican schools" while African Americans and Asians attended white schools.[34] These are just a few examples of the antinomies of accumulation produced by citrus capitalism in Orange County that illustrate the false binaries promoted by the myth of Southern exceptionalism. In sum, it was the business decisions of citrus capitalists and their allies that shaped public policy and led to the systemic segregation of Mexican families in Orange County, not some transplanted version of Jim Crow. Moreover, one did not have to be "a racist" to become a segregationist. As illustrated by Orange County and other citrus-producing regions like Ventura, Riverside, and San Bernardino counties, citrus capitalists viewed segregation as a tool that complemented the principles of scientific business management. Thus, segregation was a means to achieve the goal of increased profitability and market control, not the goal itself.

Viewing Orange County's history as part of the ongoing process of racial capitalism helps correct the distorted narratives disseminated by those seeking to hide or ignore the antinomies of accumulation. It forces the student of history to look beyond the cliches and half-truths that promote hagiographic and exceptionalist depictions of the past, challenging one to recognize that racism is not an anomaly within the development of capitalism and democracy but integral to the institutions that built and sustain them. By demonstrating how racial ideology developed to support capitalism and the social order, racial capitalism also exposes the myth that racism is merely an idea rooted in ignorance or innocence rather than an array of intentional choices, decisions, and practices that produce discriminatory outcomes for specific reasons. Finally, in addition to highlighting similarities with other forms of oppression across time and space, racial capitalism demonstrates the distinctions between them, emphasizing the malleability of ideology to fit local needs and circumstances.

Understanding the development of citrus capitalism and its influence over public and private institutions is vital to appreciating what ethnic Mexicans were up against as they began forming grassroots civil rights organizations in Orange County during the late 1920s. The social and physical barriers that constrained ethnic Mexican choice and mobility make up the walls of segregation. These included 1) workforce discrimination, 2) residential segregation, 3) educational segregation, and 4) social and political marginalization. Each wall built upon the foundation of racialized labor exploitation and worked in concert to limit the social mobility of Mexican families, thus preserving future generations of low-wage laborers. Although the foundation was set during the 1880s and 1890s, the walls of segregation were erected in Orange County over a brief period of approximately fifteen years, from 1915 to 1930. As with other oppressive systems of labor and social control, there was some permeability within citrus capitalism where a few individuals rose above or bypassed the walls of segregation. By and large, however, agricultural work and other forms of menial wage labor, segregation, and societal marginalization were the norm for ethnic Mexicans in Orange County. Indeed *Mendez et al.* co-plaintiff Felicitas Mendez recalled:

> Everybody that was a minority was treated the same. I was [an American] citizen, born in Puerto Rico. I couldn't even go to a theater [without being segregated]. In restaurants . . . nobody would wait on us. I know Orange County was the worst [place to live for Mexicans] because I had lived in San Bernardino and Los Angeles and I didn't see that bad discrimination as what was here in Orange County.[35] To this day, I still think [Orange County] is the most discriminating County there is . . . in California.[36]

Having lived in the counties of Los Angeles, San Bernardino, and Orange, Mendez's words reflect the depths of the socioracial hierarchy in Orange County, where a white-brown color line delineated subjectivity, mobility, and opportunity. By 1930, approximately 95 percent of Orange County's

ethnic Mexican population lived in a segregated neighborhood, locally referred to as colonias and barrios.[37]

To overcome the walls of segregation, ethnic Mexicans developed a
politics of mobility and used translocal organizing to transgress, disrupt,
and eventually bring down the walls of segregation.[38] The seeds for this
mobilization were sown between 1900 and 1920 as Mexicans migrated to
Orange County amidst the chaos of the Mexican Revolution. During this
period, mobility equated to survival as Mexican migrants sought jobs, stability, and safety. Lured by citrus capitalists with the promise of a job and a
place to live, Mexican families flocked to Orange County and other parts of
California's vast citrus empire. By 1930, Mexicans comprised between 15
and 21 percent of Orange County's population, making them the region's
largest ethnic/racial minority.[39] In the process of establishing homes and
communities, Mexicans became aware of the constraints placed on their
mobility by citrus capitalists as they sought better jobs, housing, and educational opportunities. Using the relationships and networks formed
through the mundane activities of work, worship, and leisure Orange
County Mexicans established grassroots organizations that articulated a
clear commitment to resisting discrimination and marginalization during
the late 1920s.

Emerging out of the segregated spaces of Orange County's "urban apartheid," ethnic Mexican grassroots organizations connected and mobilized
colonias and barrios throughout Southern California during the 1930s and
1940s.[40] Built primarily by working-class laborers that formed the largest
marginalized ethnic/racial and social class in Southern California, these
efforts to connect and mobilize ethnic Mexican communities beyond the
confines of segregated job sites and neighborhoods is what I refer to as the
politics of mobility. This was an unprecedented movement because Orange
County Mexicans had nowhere to look for help but themselves. Although
various minority groups were engaged in their own struggles against white
supremacy, racial capitalism, and settler colonialism in other parts of the
country, there was no national civil rights organization for Mexicans (or
Latinas/os) during the first half of the twentieth century. Indeed, Mexicans
had no blueprint or model for how to contend with the intersecting issues
of workplace discrimination, residential and school segregation, and sociopolitical marginalization. While African American, Native/Indigenous,
Asian, and Jewish communities faced similar challenges, "the different
axes of discrimination demanded different avenues of redress," as historian
Mark Brilliant puts it.[41] Thus, Orange County Mexicans built their own organizations that responded to the walls of segregation instituted by citrus
capitalists and partnered with ethnic Mexicans in neighboring counties to

INTRODUCTION   (11)

wage a broader translocal movement for social justice and political equality. As with most social movements, these mobilizations began with "ordinary people mak[ing] collective claims on public authorities [and] other holders of power," in the words of sociologist Charles Tilly.[42] Building a "mass movement" was not the initial goal. They simply desired to end the unequal treatment they faced and provide a better future for their children and communities. Moreover, the unheralded efforts of Orange County Mexicans during the 1930s, 40s, 50s, and 60s established a culture of civic engagement and political activism that facilitated the development of the Chicana/o and Immigrant Rights movements during the latter half of the twentieth century. Therefore, the politics of mobility exemplified by the activism of Orange County Mexicans during the early to mid-twentieth century provides a model for how the subaltern and marginalized educate, organize, and mobilize in response to local conditions across time and space.

Breaking Down the Walls of Segregation is organized into two parts. The first half details how and why segregation began, who was responsible for it, how it facilitated the socioeconomic development of Orange County, and how it impacted ethnic Mexican families. The second part reveals the grassroots organizations built by ethnic Mexicans that ended segregation in schools, private businesses, and public amenities. Connecting organizations, activists, strategies, and tactics from the 1920s to the 1960s, the second half of the book describes the formation of a regionally specific type of Latino (a/x/e) political activism that blurred the divisions of class, ethnicity, and locality to form a politics of mobility that centered on expanding civic engagement and achieving social justice for ethnic Mexican communities.

Chapter 1 explains how the systemic segregation of ethnic Mexicans in Orange County developed out of the labor practices of the Valencia orange industry and involved the decisions of industry leaders and elected officials. Starting in the 1880s, a coalition of growers, bankers, land developers, and elected officials formed that was responsible for establishing segregation. These people, whom I collectively call citrus capitalists, ran Orange County like a company town until the end of World War II. Seeking to reduce production costs and maintain a surplus labor supply, citrus capitalists implemented a system of racialized labor exploitation that became dependent upon the recruitment and management of Mexican families. Sharing the pro-growth vision promoted by citrus capitalists, civic leaders chose to invest in and develop infrastructure that facilitated the expansion of the Valencia orange industry while underdeveloping the neighborhoods and services used by Mexican families. While this solved the industry's labor problem, it created a new racial and class structure that separated and marginalized ethnic Mexicans into dozens of segregated neighborhoods (colonias and barrios).

Chapter 2 details the socioracial hierarchy that emerged in Orange County due to the citrus industry's dependence on Mexican family labor. The exploitative labor system created by citrus capitalists instituted a white-brown color line based on the surveillance, subjugation, and criminalization of Mexican bodies. While Asians, Native Americans, and African Americans experienced their own unique forms of racialization and discrimination, Orange County's socioracial hierarchy was starkly defined between whites (approximately 77% to 83% of the population) and ethnic Mexicans (approximately 15% to 21% of the population). Further, the walls of segregation erected between whites and Mexicans influenced social relations and urban development in the region into the 1960s. White journalists, social workers, and elected officials created the narrative of a "Mexican Problem" that was used to justify the segregated social and physical landscape created by citrus capitalists. With the arrival of the Great Depression, county officials weaponized the Mexican Problem as they scapegoated ethnic Mexicans for the lack of jobs and dwindling public resources. This led to increasing forms of surveillance, marginalization, criminalization, and, eventually, forced removal through an unprecedented campaign orchestrated by county, state, and federal officials.

Chapter 3 shifts the focus from what happened to ethnic Mexicans to what they did for themselves through civic engagement and political action. It details the growth of two grassroots organizations, *La Sociedad Progresista Mexicana* (Mexican Progressive Society) and the Mexican American Movement (MAM). Beginning in the 1920s, Orange County Mexicans were central in the formation of translocal organizations like *La Progresista* and MAM to educate and mobilize themselves in response to the walls of segregation. These early grassroots efforts illustrate the immediacy of ethnic Mexicans to resist marginalization and the politics of mobility adopted by ethnic Mexicans as they organized in spite of a social and physical landscape built to constrain agency and mobility. In doing so, ethnic Mexicans built a civil rights movement without help from national organizations and created a culture of grassroots civic engagement and political activism that led to future efforts to desegregate schools and influence electoral politics.

Chapter 4 illuminates the grassroots movement that led to the *Mendez, et al. v. Westminster School District of Orange County, et al.* decision in 1946. Although ethnic Mexican parents and community members resisted school segregation as soon as it began in the early 1910s, their efforts were silenced

by district officials who remained committed to upholding the segregationist system instituted by citrus capitalists. By the early 1940s, however,
ethnic Mexican grassroots organizations mobilized parents, neighbors,
and local activists into a concerted county-wide movement. Detailing the
formation of the Latin American Voters League (LAVL), the Westminster
Father's Association, the El Modena Unity League, and the Veterans and
Citizens of Placentia (VCP), this chapter details the unheralded individuals
and organizations that ended de jure segregation in Orange County. This
movement resulted from collective community action rather than the
efforts of a single family or legal strategy. This chapter puts particular emphasis on the "et al." families and community members involved in the
case, those who have been ignored, overlooked, and marginalized by prior
narratives. Together, chapters 3 and 4 illustrate that transformational
change begins with ordinary people organizing across and in spite of social
and physical barriers that seek to constrain agency and mobility.

The book concludes by connecting the grassroots efforts of Orange
County Mexicans during the 1930s and 1940s with the rapid growth of
the League of United Latin American Citizens (LULAC) in Orange County
during the 1950s. Established in San Antonio, TX, in 1929, LULAC became the country's largest Mexican American civil rights organization
by the mid-1940s. Santa Ana LULAC Council 147, the first in the county,
grew out of the school desegregation movement and was founded in
May 1946. By 1958, Orange County had ten LULAC chapters, with the
majority originating from the same barrios and colonias that formed
La Progresista, MAM, LAVL, the El Modena Unity League, and the VCP.
Mobilizing through LULAC, Orange County Mexicans elected Mexican
Americans to city councils, school boards, and mayoral offices, obtained
judicial appointments, and successfully lobbied for the appointment of
Hector Godinez by John F. Kennedy in 1961 as the first Mexican American
Postmaster General. These achievements illustrate Orange County's emergence as a hotbed of Mexican American political activism from the late
1940s to the early 1960s, thrusting Mexican Americans into national
conversations over civil rights and electoral politics.

On September 20, 2024, California Governor Gavin Newsom signed
Assembly Bill 1805 into law. The bill amends California's Education Code
to require the state board of education to review and adopt instructional
materials that will be used to teach *Mendez et al.* in kindergarten through the
eighth grade. Co-sponsored by Assemblymember Tri Ta, R-Westminster,
and Senator Tom Umberg, D-Santa Ana, the bill passed with strong bipar-
tisan support and resulted from decades of public outreach and lobbying by
community members and educators. Although the bill correctly identifies

Mendez et al. as "an integral part of the history and culture of the County of Orange" and "signifies the important role of California in the civil rights movement" its text misses the larger significance of the case by crediting the Mendez family as primarily responsible for bringing the case to trial. Moreover, the brief narrative history provided in the bill fails to mention the essential role of the co-plaintiff families or include the "et al." abbreviation in the case name and citation.[43] For decades, journalists, educators, and public officials have made the same mistake, likely due to the assumption that since the Mendez name appears first on court documents that desegregation efforts in Orange County schools began with them. This assumption is incorrect. Et al. is an abbreviation of the Latin phrases et alia and et alii, meaning "and others." It is merely a shorthand used to save space. In case law, the et al. designation is used to identify additional parties that are equal in their petition before the court. Thus, the et al. abbreviation in this case presents the families of William and Virginia Guzman, Frank and Irene Palomino, Thomas and Maria Luisa Estrada, and Lorenzo and Josephina Ramirez as equal co-plaintiff parties with Gonzalo and Felicitas Mendez in a collective class-action lawsuit against the four co-defendant school districts of Westminster, Garden Grove, Santa Ana, and El Modeno.

Moreover, et al. may be used as a metaphor or paradigm to highlight what is often missed in the writing and teaching of history. By situating *Mendez et al.* within the social and economic history of the region and illuminating the unheralded individuals and groups that were responsible for building the school desegregation movement, *Breaking Down the Walls of Segregation* provides a richer and more complete narrative of the unprecedented struggle ethnic Mexicans waged to advance the cause of social justice for themselves and others. Seen through the et al. paradigm, which highlights the overlooked, underappreciated, and lesser known "others," this story of an improbable civil rights victory in the unlikely setting of Orange County, CA, becomes less of a historical anomaly and more a microcosm of the American experience. Indeed, the ethnic Mexican experience in Orange County is representative of the struggles and contributions of African Americans, Native/Indigenous Americans, Asians, and other individuals and communities that have believed, challenged, and pushed US institutions to live up to their founding ideals. These unheralded histories are at the core of America's grand narrative. They illustrate how people of color and other marginalized populations organized to strengthen civic institutions and advance a multiethnic/racial vision of American democracy because they believed in the promise of equality and felt responsible to enact it.

CHAPTER 1

Citrus Capitalism and the Architects of Segregation

Because we were part of the community, we also were active in . . . all other public activities of all nature in the county . . . we were engulfed in all kinds of activities no matter what they were besides raising crops.

C.J. Marks, *Orange County Farm Bureau Secretary*

Orange may be the most fitting name ever devised for a California county. Indeed, it would be difficult to identify another region in the state that more aptly bears the name of a product or commodity that was more important to its social and physical development. Though only a handful of orange trees existed in the area when the name was proposed in January 1872, by the time the county formed in August 1889, Orange County was on the verge of establishing itself as one of the most important citrus-growing regions in the state. With a nod to the budding industry but more so in hopes of luring migrants and capital from states in the Midwest and Northeast, the first meeting of the County Board of Supervisors selected the name, image, and likeness of its "most promising product" as the symbol of the region's future.[1]

As with the rest of Southern California, Orange County had its share of profit-minded boosters and local stakeholders who were eager to market the region's Mediterranean climate and scenic beauty as a "Promised Land" to out-of-state investors, tourists, and potential migrants.[2] But in Orange County, the imagery and symbolism of the orange embraced by local elites were more than a mere marketing scheme. Coinciding with California's first "citrus gold rush" during the 1880s and 1890s, the formation and

Breaking Down the Walls of Segregation. David-James Gonzales, Oxford University Press.
© Oxford University Press 2025. DOI: 10.1093/9780197839485.003.0002

early development of Orange County was indebted to the prolific growth of the citrus industry.[3] Similarly, the citrus industry became increasingly dependent upon Orange County as growers and local stakeholders remade the region into the mecca of Valencia orange production during the late nineteenth and early twentieth centuries, eventually earning the county the designation of "King Valencia."[4] As an essential part of the "Orange Empire" that powered Southern California's "growth machine" from the 1880s to World War II, no region was more vital to the citrus industry or benefited more from it than Orange County.[5]

But there was an exploitative and abusive underside to the citrus industry's romance, wealth, and influence. Behind the sunbathed and exoticized images of fruit, people, and landscapes that adorned the orange crate labels accompanying Southern California oranges on their trans-continental journey to markets in Chicago and New York lay an intricate and tightly controlled system of "peoples, institutions, and relationships" that Carey McWilliams called the "citrus belt complex."[6] Among the seven counties that made up Southern California's citrus belt, Orange County particularly illuminates the citrus industry's negative consequences and abusive legacy.

Valencia orange growers and their influential networks of local, regional, and national stakeholders lay at the center of this story. Comprising citrus growers, bankers, real estate developers, elected officials, and other vested parties, the architects of segregation in Orange County were the same men and women who established the industries and institutions that governed the regional economy and shaped social life.[7] These people, whom I refer to as citrus capitalists, ran Orange County like a "company town," making the entire region dependent upon the production of Valencia oranges.[8] They owned the land, chartered the banks, formed public utilities, built local infrastructure, managed urban development, directed the educational system, and ran city and county government.[9] Rather than being concen-trated in a single town or company, the dominance and control exerted by the citrus industry extended throughout the Santa Ana Valley and was wielded by cooperative groups of citrus capitalists organized into grower associations. Whether or not one was directly involved in the citrus in-dustry, everyone was impacted by their decisions.

Originating during the 1880s and 1890s, local grower associations formed the basis of the citrus industry's organization. As they grew in number, local associations consolidated and increased their control by forming cooperative marketing exchanges like the California Fruit Growers Exchange (CFGE) and the Mutual Orange Distributors. From 1918 to 1938, these two cooperatives distributed 85 percent of all citrus fruits produced in California and Arizona.[10] Local associations and marketing cooperatives were run from the ground up by men and women committed to the principles of scientific management and corporate managerial capitalism.[11] By the end of World War I, grower associations controlled the entire means of production through their marketing cooperatives. This included land, materials, facilities, subsidiary supply companies, capital, and labor. Due to the high costs of citrus production and the unpredictability of seasonal variations, crop diseases, shipping rates, and fluctuating market prices, association leaders continuously sought ways to reduce costs and maximize returns for their member growers. Managing the supply and cost of labor was essential from the outset.

This chapter explains how the systematic segregation of ethnic Mexicans in Orange County resulted from the simultaneous development of the Valencia orange industry and the county itself. Contrary to popular belief, segregation in Orange County did not begin during the post-World War II era of mass suburbanization and white flight; it emerged from the practice of racial capitalism in the citrus industry. Driven to reduce production costs and maintain a surplus labor supply, grower associations relied on a system of racialized labor exploitation established in the 1880s.[12] After World War I, Mexicans became the preferred source of field labor in the citrus industry. While this solved the industry's labor problem, it created another issue within the broader social fabric of Orange County. Indeed, the changing social division of labor led to a "new racial class structure" with questions about where to house Mexican families and how to educate their children.[13] Finding solutions to these questions was left to the citrus capitalists who held significant influence over the County Board of Supervisors, city councils, mayoral offices, and school boards.

Sharing the pro-growth vision promoted by citrus capitalists, civic leaders chose to repeatedly invest in and develop infrastructure that facilitated the expansion of the Valencia orange industry while simultaneously underdeveloping the neighborhoods and services inhabited by Mexican laborers and their families. This occurred under the purview and direction of men like William M. McFadden, Richard H. Gilman, Albert S. Bradford, Charles C. Chapman, Willard Smith, and LeRoy Lyon, who were not only some of the most prominent citrus growers in Southern California but were also among the most esteemed businessmen and elected officials in the state. These were the architects of segregation. They succeeded in transforming Orange County into one of the most segregated regions in Southern California within the short period of fifteen years, from 1915 to 1930. Although their motives were primarily economic and not explicitly racist at first, the resulting impact of their decisions produced an

Figure 1.1 Fullerton, CA surrounded by Valencia orange groves, c. 1940s. Courtesy of Fullerton Public Library Local History Room.

apartheid-like socioeconomic and political system that profited off the isolation and marginalization of ethnic Mexican families.[14] Detailing the rise of the Valencia orange industry through the decision-making of citrus capitalists, this chapter argues that racial capitalism was foundational to Orange County's social and economic development. The segregation of ethnic Mexicans in Orange County reveals a distinct pattern that was unique to Southern California's citrus belt. Yet it highlights the myriad ways that ethnic and racial segregation developed in the United States, not according to a prescribed model emanating from the Jim Crow South but to the economic and social prerogatives of regional stakeholders.

CITRUS AND THE BEGINNINGS OF ORANGE COUNTY

Orange County and the Valencia orange industry emerged out of the same developments that spurred the prolific growth of Southern California during the last quarter of the nineteenth century. This included the demise of California's rancho economy in the mid-1860s, the subdivision and sale of Mexican land grants in the 1870s, the arrival of the Southern Pacific and Santa Fe railroads during the 1870s and 1880s, and the subsequent migration of white settlers and capital from the Midwest and Northeast.[15] Except for Anaheim, which began as a grape-growing colony in 1857 by representatives of the Los Angeles Vineyard Society, many of the towns and settlements that later comprised the principal citrus-producing regions were established during the speculative real estate booms of the 1870s and 1880s.[16] This included the future cities of Santa Ana, Orange, Fullerton, Placentia, Tustin, Irvine, La Habra, Westminster, Garden Grove, Buena Park, Villa Park, and Yorba Linda. From the outset, agriculture provided the primary engine for regional economic development. In addition to grapes, which were planted in large numbers throughout the Santa Ana Valley, local farmers harvested significant quantities of grain, alfalfa, corn, walnuts, celery, sugar beets, and several varieties of deciduous fruits.[17] Most of this was produced for export as the Santa Ana Valley quickly developed a reputation as an agricultural hub during the 1880s, shipping its products to markets along the Pacific Coast from San Diego to San Francisco and as far east as Chicago.[18] Between 1884 and 1888, a mysterious grape disease, later dubbed the "Anaheim grape disease," brought an abrupt and devastating end to viticulture in the area.[19] However, thanks to the region's agricultural diversity, especially the development of the nascent citrus industry, all was not lost.

Coinciding with the beginning of commercial citrus cultivation in Los Angeles and Riverside, white settlers began experimenting with citrus varieties in the Santa Ana Valley during the early 1870s.[20] Before switching to citrus from grapes, grains, and other agricultural products, orange and lemon growing districts began to emerge mainly in the central and northern portions of the region around Anaheim, Orange, and Santa Ana. While there has been some debate among local historians, it appears the first large planting of orange trees occurred in 1870 when Dr. William N. Hardin of Anaheim, a physician interested in horticulture, grew seedlings from two barrels of rotten Tahitian oranges that he later turned into a lucrative nursery business.[21] Shortly thereafter, a flurry of commercial groves and nurseries sprang up around the recently formed township of Orange. In 1873, less than three years after Alfred B. Chapman and Andrew Glassell platted the town, Patterson Bowers planted the first grove of Australian navels, a popular winter variety of oranges also grown along the foothills of Los Angeles and Riverside. By 1880, the area surrounding the town of Orange had a burgeoning citrus district of no less than 100,000 orange trees and 20,000 lemon trees spread over 1,100 acres. In 1881, the region's first citrus packing house was built in Orange by Andrew Cauldwell on the southwest corner of Maple Avenue. In 1883, M.A. Peters and A.D. Bishop sent the first shipment of local oranges out of state to Des Moines, Iowa, filling two train cars with over 300 boxes. This was just the beginning. After establishing his nursery, Dr. Hardin and several other Anaheim residents planted orange groves ranging in size from twenty to forty acres, a substantial and somewhat risky investment during the early years of commercial citrus cultivation when oranges remained unproven as a regional cash crop and most groves averaged less than five acres. The first commercial orange grove was planted in Anaheim around 1875 by John Knapp and Henry Brimmerman. They were followed by S. Sheffield, James Huntingdon, Dr. Hardin, and Augustus Langenberger.

While impressive, citrus farming in Anaheim and Orange eventually paled in comparison to what was developing in the area referred to as "north Anaheim." Located about six miles northeast of Anaheim in what became the city of Placentia, Gilman purchased 110 acres of farmland on behalf of the Semi-Tropic Fruit Company in 1872. Gilman and his business partners were based in Healdsburg in Sonoma County and purchased the property intent on growing oranges and other deciduous fruits. After acquiring the land, Gilman relocated to the ranch as its manager and became one of the "original white settler[s] of the Placentia district."[22] By 1875, Gilman had planted forty acres of oranges, including Australian navels, Mediterranean Sweets, and St. Michaels, and dedicated other portions of the property to walnuts, prunes, grapes, and lemons. In 1880, Gilman learned of a new type of orange from either Byron Clark, a fellow citrus rancher in Anaheim, or a visit to Alfred B. Chapman's citrus ranch in San Gabriel. The Valencia, as it was called, had been grown by Chapman since the early 1870s and was rumored to be better in quality and size than other varieties available in the Southland. Unlike the winter ripening Australian and Washington navels that required more water and favored the hotter and drier inland citrus districts stretching from Pasadena to Riverside, the Valencia was a summer ripening orange that seemed better suited to Orange County's coastal climate and soil. Recognizing the Valencia's promise, Gilman converted his existing orange crop to the untested variety between 1880 and 1890, becoming the first commercial Valencia grove in California.[23] Neither Gilman nor his neighbors would regret this decision.

One of the lesser-known aspects of Southern California's citrus history is the outsized role the small community of Placentia held in developing the Valencia industry. Placentia did not begin as a citrus-growing colony like the cities of Riverside and Corona. Still, it became a vital hub within the expansive citrus empire alongside Fullerton as the Valencia industry developed. In the 1880s, Placentia was a tight-knit farming community comprising a few dozen middle-class families that had migrated to Southern California from the Midwest and Northeast over the previous two decades.[24] Most residents lived along Placentia Avenue and farmed or raised livestock. In the early 1880s, many of Gilman's neighbors followed his lead and began replacing their existing crops with oranges and later Valencias. Such was the case with William M. McFadden, Sheldon Littlefield, Theodore Staley, Peter Hansen, Thomas McDowell, William Crowther, and John Kendall Tuffree. The trend continued in the 1890s with the arrival of Bradford and Charles C. Chapman, men, who alongside Gilman and McFadden, became notable figures for their contributions to the Valencia industry and the development of Orange County. One of the factors that led to Placentia's dominance in Valencia production was the size of the properties held by Gilman, McFadden, Tuffree, Chapman, and Bradford. Their large properties allowed them to experiment with various crops until each found success growing Valencias. Then, as Valencias proved a viable cash crop, they were well-positioned to capitalize on market demand.

Placentia also set the standard for the development of northern Orange County, which grew to include the future cities of Fullerton, Brea, La Habra, and Yorba Linda. Despite their small size, these cities became significant components of the developing citrus industry. Although it did not incorporate until 1926, Placentia produced many of the region's most influential leaders. Parlaying their success as commercial agriculturalists, men like Gilman, McFadden, Chapman, and Bradford formed the first generation of an emerging class of citrus capitalists that managed the development of local infrastructure and municipal services before Orange County's separation from Los Angeles. These men became involved in regional politics by leading efforts to develop local services, like public water projects.[25]

In 1875, farmers in Placentia and Fullerton formed Cajon Irrigation District No. 1, with Gilman as its first president. Under Gilman's direction, district commissioners imposed taxes, purchased land, and controlled water rights. Two years later, Gilman, McFadden, and six other wealthy landholders incorporated the Cajon Irrigation Company to sell shares and raise funds to complete the canal that would be essential to commercial agriculture in the region for decades. After almost a decade of delays, funding shortages, and legal battles, the Cajon developers merged their project with the Anaheim Water Company to form the Anaheim Union Water Company in 1884. By 1888, "Anaheim Union Water Company was irrigating 6,000 acres through 350 irrigators and . . . 100 miles of canals and branch lines."[26] Throughout this process, Gilman, McFadden, Tuffree, and other prominent growers emerged as public figures, gaining notoriety throughout the Santa Ana Valley as men of means, influence, and skill.[27] In the ensuing years, this first generation of citrus capitalists spearheaded the formation and early development of Orange County and the Valencia industry.

The movement to create Orange County out of the southern portion of Los Angeles County began in 1870. Initially led by Max Strobel, the divisive first mayor of Anaheim, the nearly two-decade-long process was fraught with intrigue and exposed bitter intraregional rivalries.[28] The issue was one of local control. Large landowners and capitalists like Strobel felt ignored and underrepresented by county leaders in Los Angeles. From 1870 to 1876, lobbyists from Anaheim introduced four bills in the state legislature proposing county separation, however, leaders from Anaheim, Santa Ana, and Orange disagreed on several issues. The major sticking points were the county's northern boundary and the location of the county seat, whether it should be in Anaheim or Santa Ana. These disagreements prevented separationists from forming a united front against the fierce opposition presented by the county of Los Angeles. Between late 1876 and early 1881, there was no progress on county separation until it was revived by Victor Montgomery, a prominent attorney with offices in Anaheim and Santa Ana. While much was still undecided, the 1881 bill appeared to settle the issue of the county's name. "Orange" was first proposed in 1872 to draw attention away from an earlier attempt to name the county after Anaheim and lo-cate the county seat in that city. In lobbying for his 1881 bill, Montgomery attempted to side-step the bitter rivalry between the region's two largest cities by selecting Orange as the name for the new county. He also believed this name would stand out on a map of California and "have more effect in drawing the tide of emigrants to this section than all the pamphlets, agents and other endeavors which have hitherto proved so futile."[29] Still, several issues remained unresolved, and the bill ultimately failed.

Undeterred, William Spurgeon and James McFadden of Santa Ana revived the debate in 1889. Having outgrown Anaheim by a ratio of al-most three-to-one, Santa Ana had become the clear frontrunner for the county seat and needed little help from its rival lobbying state legislators in Sacramento.[30] Although arguments for and against separation had not changed, Orange County separatists improved their position in the county of Los Angeles and the state legislature by the late 1880s. Indeed, in 1868, Augustus Langenberger, one of the first commercial orange growers in Anaheim and a founding member of the Los Angeles Vineyard Society, was elected to the Los Angeles County Board of Supervisors. William H. Spurgeon, Santa Ana's first mayor, followed Langenberger and served on the board in 1877–1878. And Sheldon Littlefield, the orange grower from Placentia, was elected to the county board in January of 1889, six months before county separation.[31] Additionally, Dr. Henry W. Head of Garden Grove, Eugene E. Edwards of Santa Ana, and William Spurgeon served in the California Assembly during the 1880s. Undoubtedly, the experience and relationships formed during their service in the state Assembly aided Edwards, Spurgeon, and McFadden, as they reintroduced and lobbied for county separation in January 1889. Employing the $10,000 war chest provided by Santa Ana donors, the trio overcame the remaining opposition, and the bill passed the Senate by a vote of 28 to 8 on March 8, 1889.[32] Three days later, Governor Waterman signed the bill to create Orange County.

With the support of state leaders secured, it was up to Orange County voters to approve county division at the ballot box. To direct this effort, Governor Waterman appointed three prominent orange growers to the five-member county organization commission, including William M. McFadden (Placentia), Andrew Cauldwell (Orange), and J.H. Kellom (Tustin). On June 4, 1889, voters overwhelmingly supported separation by a vote of 2,509 to 500. Then, on July 11, voters returned to the polls, selected Santa Ana as the county seat 1,729 to 775, and elected the county's first officers. Again, orange growers were heavily represented among those appointed to lead the county. Sheldon Littlefield (Placentia) and A. Guy Smith (Tustin) were elected to the Board of Supervisors. William B. Wall (Tustin) was elected county treasurer. George E. Foster (Santa Ana) was elected county recorder and auditor, and John P. Greeley (Placentia) was elected superintendent of schools.[33] Having led the movement to form Orange County during the 1870s and 1880s, citrus capitalists were well positioned to direct the region's early social and economic development. In subsequent decades, the power and influence of citrus capitalists grew as the Valencia orange industry became the bedrock of the regional economy.

ORIGINS OF THE ORANGE GROWER ASSOCIATION

Orange County's first half-century of economic development coincided with California's golden age of citrus production from 1890 to 1945. Indeed, between 1894 and 1968, Southern California orange growers grossed nearly three billion dollars, with almost 1.2 billion coming out of Orange County from 1923 to 1959.[34] During this period, Orange County became the crown jewel of Southern California's citrus empire and was the largest citrus producing county in the United States.[35] There was nothing natural or inevitable about this development. Citrus farming was a risky business during the 1880s and 1890s. In addition to high production costs, there was little market demand for citrus fruits, and growers lacked control over the distribution of their products. To address these problems, farmers created a novel business organization called the cooperative grower association. While farmer associations dated back to the Civil War, cooperative citrus associations were a product of a new form of capitalism known as managerial corporate capitalism.[36] Employing the principles of scientific management and business efficiency, these farmers formed associations to streamline the production, marketing, and distribution of citrus during the mid-1880s and early 1890s. By the early 1920s, the citrus industry was run by a few hundred grower associations, vertically integrated into cooperative marketing associations that controlled the entire means of production.[37] Among all forms of commercial agriculture, citrus garnered the reputation as the most organized, efficient, and profitable, with cooperative grower associations marking the characteristic feature of the industry.[38] Alongside citrus capitalists across Southern California, Orange County growers were at the forefront of this movement.

The Orange Growers' Protective Union, formed in 1885, represented the first attempt by Southern California growers to work collectively to market and distribute their crops out of state. The impetus for the union grew out of grower frustrations with the lack of regulations governing the wholesale fruit market. To sell outside of California, growers had to rely on a complex network of intermediaries that had complete control over marketing, distribution, and pricing. Initially, growers benefited from this system as fruit dealers assumed all the risk. After agreeing to a price, it was the responsibility of the fruit dealer to pick, pack, ship, and sell the crop to a wholesaler, who then distributed it to retail merchants. Under this system, the only costs incurred by growers were those directly associated with producing the crop. By the mid-1880s, however, this system began to unravel. The biggest problem was the overproduction of oranges due to the industry's explosive growth during the late 1870s and early 1880s. At this time, people viewed oranges as a specialty product consumed primarily during the winter months and holidays. By the late 1880s, production exceeded market demand, leading to massive losses for growers due to market gluts, fruit decay, and dealer price-fixing. To make matters worse, the entire wholesale market was controlled by six firms, which often functioned as dealer, shipper, and wholesaler.[39]

To this end, orange growers gathered at a meeting of the Pomological Society in Pomona on October 6, 1885. Here, it was first proposed that a "union be incorporated, representing a large majority of the producers of Southern California."[40] Six growers from Orange County sat on the organizing committee, with H. Hamilton from Orange elected as chairman.[41] During its first two years, the Orange Growers' Protective Union shipped over 1,000 carloads of oranges to thirty-two out-of-state locations, returning over one-quarter million dollars to its members.[42] Despite this initial success, the union fell apart after several years of stiff opposition from large eastern fruit dealers. After the Orange Grower's Protective Union collapsed, dealers tightened their control over the wholesale market by colluding against growers to no longer purchase oranges directly but to ship exclusively on consignment. This change shifted all costs and risks associated with production, distribution, and marketing to growers. As a result, 1890 to 1893 were known as the "red ink" years when many growers faced bankruptcy, and Southern California's citrus industry was on the verge of collapse.[43]

Facing financial ruin, more than 100 prominent growers met at the Los Angeles Chamber of Commerce on April 4, 1893, to try once more to organize a cooperative plan for handling and marketing oranges. First, growers heard from T.H.B. Chamblin, one of the founding members of the Pachappa Orange Growers Association in Riverside. Chamblin explained how his association of eleven growers packed and sold their fruit collectively using a uniform grade and brand. The association controlled the entire production and distribution process for members based on a prorated system that determined when crops were picked, packed, and shipped. The association's primary focus was to end consignments and sell all fruit at the Free On Board price (FOB), which made wholesale buyers responsible for costs and liabilities incurred once oranges were shipped. P.J. Dreher spoke of similar efforts by citrus growers in the Pomona Valley, who had recently formed the Claremont California Fruit Growers Association.[44] Following discussion, those in attendance voted to form the "committee of five" and tasked them with creating a plan to implement the recommendations of Chamblin and Dreher. The committee was composed of the most respected men in the citrus industry with varied backgrounds in law, education, medicine, marketing, and politics. Unsurprisingly, McFadden of Placentia was appointed to the committee alongside Chamblin, Dreher, J.D. Reymert from Los Angeles, and Dr. D. Hyer from Ontario.[45]

Between April and August 1893, the committee developed and implemented their plan to organize Southern California orange growers into a three-tiered vertically integrated marketing cooperative. On August 29, growers returned to the Los Angeles Chamber of Commerce building on North Main Street to formally establish the Southern California Fruit Exchange, later reorganized as the CFGE in 1905 and Sunkist Growers, Inc. in 1952. Within twenty-five years of its founding, the CFGE became the country's largest fruit-marketing agency and one of the larger national cooperative organizations.[46] The structure of the CFGE resembled a pyramid with individual growers organized into local grower associations at the base, district exchanges at the middle, and the central exchange or executive board at the top. Like the Orange Grower's Protective Union, the CFGE was a voluntary cooperative system run by and for citrus growers. But the similarities between the two ended there. The CFGE, or the Exchange as growers called it, was not a single entity but a collection of confederated nonprofit corporations run from the bottom-up.[47]

Local grower associations, also called packing house associations, formed the heart and soul of the CFGE. They were responsible for producing citrus fruits and for providing the leadership that managed the district and central exchange boards within the CFGE. Most grower associations were "nonprofit cooperative corporation[s]" with membership restricted to citrus farmers who held shares based on acreage.[48] The size of local associations varied greatly, ranging from under a dozen to over 300 individual growers. Association members agreed to pick, pack, and ship citrus fruits by pooling resources to build and operate packing houses and sell fruit through the CFGE district exchange under brands belonging to the local association. Even though they were incorporated as nonprofit entities, packing house associations existed to increase the profitability of member growers. As such, their organizational structure shared many similarities with the modern corporation. A board of directors, elected annually by shareholding growers, sat at the head of the packing house association. Members of the board held the offices of president, vice president, secretary, and treasurer and were responsible for the "governing power of the corporation in all matters of business."[49] Their responsibilities included control over the association's assets, finances, facilities, membership, and staffing. Typically, board members were prominent growers with substantial citrus holdings like McFadden, Gilman, and Augustus Langenberger. To manage the association's daily operations, the board hired a manager who ran the packing house, business office, and other facilities owned by the association. The board held monthly meetings with the manager to review market reports, crop conditions, labor needs, and packing house operations. Like the board of directors, association managers were not ordinary farmers; they were investment-minded business professionals that incorporated data, technical knowledge, and scientific innovation to maximize production and profit.

District exchanges occupied the middle tier of the exchange system and were formed by packing house associations loosely organized around a geographically defined region. The district exchange was the exclusive selling agent of its member packing house associations. Like the local association, district exchanges were nonprofit corporations run by a board of directors. Each association appointed a representative, typically a member of the board or the manager, to fill a seat on the district exchange board, ensuring local associations had full control over the district exchange.[50] Initially, the CFGE created seven district exchanges based out of Los Angeles, Orange, San Bernardino, Riverside, and San Diego counties. These five counties produced 85 percent of oranges and 97 percent of lemons in the state during the first half of the twentieth century.[51] The Orange County Fruit Exchange and the Semi-Tropic Fruit Exchange were two of the seven original district exchanges formed in 1893.[52] They marketed citrus fruits on behalf of local associations like the Santiago Orange Growers Association (SOGA) in Orange, the Placentia Orange Growers Association in Fullerton, and the Anaheim Citrus Fruit Association. Each began in 1893 and was among the first grower associations that helped organize the CFGE.

The third or top tier of the CFGE was the central exchange, which was composed of an executive board of directors chosen by the district exchanges. While it managed several other functions within the CFGE, the central exchange's most important responsibilities were to stimulate consumer demand and direct the marketing of citrus fruits sold through district exchanges. To do this, it established a network of sales offices throughout the United States, Canada, and other countries. These offices developed markets in their assigned territories and then coordinated with district exchanges to supply those regions with citrus fruit on a weekly basis.[53] This system helped prevent the disastrous gluts and shortages that had nearly bankrupted the citrus industry during the late 1880s and early 1890s. Working alongside its sales offices, the CFGE's advertising department spurred the mass consumption of its Sunkist brand of oranges and lemons through saturation advertising.[54] Partnering with railroad companies, major retail establishments, professional associations, and government agencies, the Exchange flooded magazines, billboards, streetcars, railways, storefronts, school curricula, doctor's offices, and radio airwaves with a constant barrage of messages and symbols that "transform[ed] oranges from special treasures to everyday necessities."[55]

The first of such efforts occurred in 1907 when the CFGE and the Southern Pacific Company agreed to spend up to $10,000 each on the "Oranges for Health—California for Wealth" campaign. Initially created to test the market for California oranges in Iowa, the advertising blitzkrieg was expanded to include most of the country by 1911 and cost a combined $200,000 annually. This campaign resulted in a sevenfold increase in the sale of California oranges east of the Rockies.[56] But this effort paled in comparison to the CFGE's "drink an orange" ad campaign, which began in 1916 and created America's juice-drinking habit. Using "scientific salesmanship," the Exchange funded research to convince consumers of the health benefits of drinking orange juice. The effort was so successful that by 1928, "sales of orange juice totaled $55 million at over 100,000 cafes and soda fountains, making it second only to Coca-Cola."[57]

Beginning in 1893 with seven district exchanges representing several dozen packing houses and around 2,500 individual growers, the CFGE quickly grew into a colossal organization. Through its expansive network of fifty-seven sales offices, the Exchange and its partners created year-round demand for oranges and lemons, making Sunkist a multimillion-dollar household name by the early nineteen-teens.[58] By 1917, the Exchange owned two subsidiaries, the Fruit Growers Supply Company and the Exchange By-Products Company, and had grown to include seventeen district exchanges, 117 packing house associations, and over 8,000 growers. Already the largest fruit growers cooperative by 1920, the CFGE continued to expand during the 1930s and 1940s, topping out at twenty-five district exchanges, 210 packing houses, and over 14,500 growers during World War II.[59] When the industry peaked in 1943, the Exchange shipped over 75 percent of the citrus produced in California and Arizona while supplying 60 percent of the nation's oranges and one-quarter of the global supply.[60] In fact, from 1890 to 1960, citrus revenues created many times more wealth for California than gold itself.[61]

It is tempting to think of the CFGE like other large industrial corporations of its day. But instead of being managed from the top-down like Carnegie Steel, Standard Oil, or Ford Motors, the Exchange was led by local growers from the bottom-up. As economist W.W. Cumberland emphasized in his 1917 study of the cooperative, "The [local] growers own the packing associations, the packing associations own the district exchanges, and the district exchanges own the central exchange. Therefore, the [local] growers own the entire exchange system."[62] While Cumberland's observations were correct, growers were not an undifferentiated egalitarian group. The US Senate Committee on Education and Labor confirmed as much during its investigation into the citrus industry during the Great Depression, finding that "the larger growers have a controlling voice in the direction of the local associations [and], through them, they control the district and central exchanges."[63] Thus, large local growers in Riverside, Fullerton, Pomona, Placentia, Anaheim, and Orange controlled the exchange system and the citrus industry through their outsized influence in local packing house associations. Their impact did not stop there. The same Senate committee found that grower associations amassed "wide . . . economic power [and] influence over local governing and law enforcement."[64] This was certainly the case in Orange County, where the leaders of local grower associations partnered with other regional elites to run Orange County like a company town, picking winners and losers based on a shared vision of how resources would be used to promote urban and economic development.

Figure 1.2 Citrus packing houses in Placentia, CA, c. 1940. Courtesy of Orange County Archives.

THE VALENCIA OLIGARCHY AND ORANGE COUNTY'S GROWTH MACHINE

During its first half-century, Orange County's development pattern resembled what urban historians call an "urban growth machine."[65] According to this model, "place-based elites," comprising elected officials, entrepreneurs, and other "land-related interests," cooperate to attract capital investment as the primary means of driving urban development. Viewing "place . . . as a market commodity that can produce wealth and power for its owners . . . the desire for growth creates consensus" among region elites, who then "use all resources at their disposal . . . to make great fortunes out of place."[66] Citrus capitalists led Orange County's formation and staked the region's future on the promise of the orange from the beginning. In fact, citrus was to Orange County what cotton and tobacco were to the South the driver of migration, investment, urban growth, and inequality.[67] Occupying positions of power within the citrus industry and local government, growers established a pro-growth coalition on the back of the Valencia orange industry.

As the "foundation industry" and staple export crop of the region, citrus cultivation dictated land-use patterns and social relations in the county for over two generations.[68] This was accomplished through the overwhelming support growers amassed in the halls of local government. Between 1890 and 1940, nearly 43 percent of those elected to public office in Orange County's four largest cities, Santa Ana, Anaheim, Orange, and Fullerton, had ties to the citrus industry, either as growers or through industries dependent upon its success like banking, real estate, and agriculture. Even more remarkable was the representation of the citrus industry on the County Board of Supervisors, where 67 percent of elected members were fruit farmers or citrus ranchers.[69] Dominated by citrus and agricultural interests in municipal and county government, urban planning in Orange County was essentially investor controlled.[70] This does not mean there were no disagreements among regional elites, but their shared interest in a pro-growth vision for the county outweighed any schism.[71] Such cooperation was more elusive in larger cities with diverse economies, like Los Angeles and San Francisco. However, Orange County elites built consensus around the expansion of the citrus industry because the Valencia orange was a niche commodity. Indeed, Florida was the only other region that competed with Orange County in Valencia production.[72] Still, Orange County's climate and soil were better suited for the Valencia, which ripened over the summer and could remain on the tree longer to be picked and sold when California Navels and Florida Valencias were unavailable. Further, the invention of orange juice and the Exchange's elaborate marketing campaigns made the Valencia the most recognizable orange in the world.[73] Of the six Southern California counties that made up the citrus belt, Orange County was the smallest in total area, yet it produced more than half of the Valencias in the state and surpassed Los Angeles, Riverside, and San Bernardino counties in total citrus acreage by the mid-1920s.[74] If the foothills of the San Gabriel and San Bernardino mountains were the "heart of the citrus industry," as several historians have surmised, then Orange County was its lungs.[75]

Chapman and Bradford were among those most responsible for transforming Orange County into the mecca of the Valencia orange industry. They were part of the founding generation of citrus capitalists who worked alongside Gilman, McFadden, and others to form the public-private partnership that directed Orange County's growth machine from the late nineteenth century to the early twentieth century. Like most citrus ranchers, Chapman and Bradford were transplants from the Midwest and Northeast, and neither had any experience growing oranges before they arrived in the Santa Ana Valley during the 1880s and 1890s.

Born in Shapleigh, Maine, Bradford ran away from home at age fourteen after an argument with his father. With only "three dollars and a determination to never return," he went to Boston, where he apprenticed in the nursery business and developed an interest in horticulture.[76] He began his first business in 1881, operating a nursery outside Boston, which he later turned into a successful garden produce operation in Stoneham. Bradford went west seeking health and riches during the boom of the 1880s. He arrived seven years ahead of Chapman in 1887 and became the foreman of Daniel Halliday's citrus ranch in Santa Ana, where he learned the citriculture business. While there, Bradford engaged in local politics and was involved in the movement for county separation. These activities connected him with John P. Greeley, the county's first superintendent of schools, who gave Bradford the opportunity to lease his twenty-acre property near Placentia Avenue in north Anaheim. The move placed Bradford at the epicenter of the early Valencia industry with Richard Gilman, William Crowther, William M. McFadden, and others. With the help of his neighbors, Bradford started a citrus nursery and weathered the "red ink years" with loans from friends and by working for the Anaheim Union Water Company. In 1893, he helped organize the CFGE, the Orange County Fruit Exchange, and the Placentia Orange Growers Association. Within a few years, Bradford paid back his loans, purchased both Greeley's property and an adjoining twenty acres, and was operating one of the most successful citrus ranches and packing houses in the Fullerton-Placentia district.

Born in Macomb, Illinois, in 1853, Charles C. Chapman, known as C.C., spent his first forty-one years around Chicago.[77] Like Bradford, he left home as a youth and worked as a telegraph messenger, grocery store clerk, and bricklayer before starting his first business as a produce merchant. When that business failed, the mayor of Macomb helped Chapman acquire a loan and contacts to begin publishing local histories for small towns in northern Illinois. After some initial success, Chapman opened a printing house in Chicago with his brother Frank. From 1880 to 1893, the brothers built a thriving business and were worth a combined half-million dollars until a bad investment and the failing health of C.C.'s first wife prompted the move to Southern California. Tight on cash, the Chapmans arranged a property swap, trading some of their Chicago real estate for two citrus ranches, one near Placentia and the other in Covina. C.C. chose the Placentia property, a sprawling 175-acre ranch previously owned by Sheldon Littlefield. While he had no prior experience growing oranges, Charles was a savvy investor who knew enough about the citrus industry to view it as a promising venture. Acquiring the ranch in 1894, he dedicated himself to learning everything he could about the citrus business. He made quick friends with McFadden and Bradford and spent considerable time touring their properties and picking their brains.[78]

Fitting in with the early Placentia establishment, C.C. Chapman became a key figure in the development of the Valencia industry. He was responsible for several innovations that helped popularize, standardize, and increase the profitability of Valencias. The first and perhaps most important was his realization that Valencias could be kept on trees in Orange County for months after ripening. This made it possible for local growers to pick and sell Valencias when there were no other oranges available on Eastern markets. But it also led to the year-round production and marketing of oranges through large grower cooperatives like the CFGE and Mutual Orange Distributors (MOD). He was also one of the first growers to embrace the practice of using a brand name in conjunction with attractive full-color crate labels. With the help of a Los Angeles artist, he crafted the label for his "Old Mission Brand" Valencias. Employing a mission motif that later helped popularize what Carey McWilliams called Southern California's Spanish Fantasy Past, the label depicted an idyllic-looking mission situated amidst orange groves and palm trees, with friars gazing approvingly at a table of lusciously ripe oranges.[79] In addition, Chapman was a stickler for uniformity and quality. Before most, he recognized that oranges had to be picked and packed with great care to prevent damage and decay during transportation. After studying the practices used at Chapman's Santa Ysabel Ranch, industry leaders remarked that his "Placentia orchard

Figure 1.3 Charles C. Chapman's Old Mission Brand crate label. Courtesy of Orange County Archives.

handled the fruit from tree to car 'as if it were a tender infant.'"[80] This led USDA scientist and later CFGE General Manager G. Harold Powell to invent a specialized orange clipper that reduced damage and scarring. Due to his meticulous attention to detail and standardization, Chapman's oranges became the envy of the entire citrus industry, recognized around the country for their exceptional quality and record-setting prices. These accolades earned Chapman recognition as the "Father of the Valencia Orange Industry" and the "Orange King of America."[81]

As they grew their citrus fortunes, Chapman and Bradford turned their wealth into political leverage, which they used to build the cities of Fullerton and Placentia, bringing notoriety to northern Orange County as a key player in Southern California's citrus empire.[82] Partnering with real estate developers George and Edward Amerige and fellow citrus rancher and independent fruit packer Edward K. Benchley, Chapman helped charter the city of Fullerton in 1904. Initially established in 1887 by the Amerige brothers and George Fullerton, by 1899, the unincorporated town of

Fullerton was the shipping center of Orange County. Its six packing houses, situated along the Santa Fe railroad track, were some of the largest and best equipped buildings in the state.[83] Chapman's Santa Ysabel ranch was located a few miles southeast of Fullerton.[84] Viewing it as the natural hub for the burgeoning Valencia industry and desiring "to give time and to invest money in helping to develop the town," Chapman took a keen interest in the final push for Fullerton's incorporation.[85] Working with Benchley and other citrus growers, Chapman expanded the proposed boundaries of the city to include a large agricultural area that placed his Santa Ysabel ranch within Fullerton's limits and helped farmers outnumber downtown merchants and saloon operators.[86] Local control over public services and liquor licensing were the primary political issues that led to Fullerton's incorporation, but Chapman and other citrus capitalists had bigger aims. They wanted to "build an attractive residential city" that functioned "as a business center."[87] On January 22, 1904, Fullerton residents voted for incorporation, electing Chapman, Amerige, Benchley, and two others to the city council. At its first meeting, the council elected Chapman as chairman and the city's first mayor. With citrus capitalists at the helm, Fullerton became the unofficial headquarters of the Valencia industry in Orange County. By 1916, the city housed ten of the sixteen packing houses in operation throughout the county.[88] And by the late 1930s, Fullerton was home to twenty-one packing associations and three citrus processing plants. The growth of the citrus industry in Fullerton was so great that by 1917, leaders of grower associations in Anaheim, Placentia, La Habra, Yorba Linda, and Fullerton formed the Northern Orange County Citrus Exchange. Located in the First National Bank building on W. Commonwealth Ave in downtown Fullerton, this became the second CFGE district exchange in the county.

The prolific growth of Fullerton and the Valencia industry in Orange County would not have been possible without the close ties between elected officials and bankers, who were often the same individuals.[89] Almost immediately following their election, Chapman, Benchley, and Gardiner chartered the Farmers and Merchants Bank of Fullerton, one of several local banks that "were linked inseparably with local citrus development."[90] During his time as mayor, Chapman served as the founding director of Farmers and Merchants Bank and personally financed "several large improvements" in downtown Fullerton.[91] After leaving public office, he built an extensive investment portfolio in banking and commercial real estate thanks to his combined fortunes in citrus and oil.[92] Chapman became close friends and business partners with bankers A.P. Giannini and Ora E. Monnette. In March 1923, they formed the Bank of America and housed it in Chapman's office building on Eighth and Broadway in downtown Los

Angeles. After mergers and acquisitions, the Bank of America purchased Fullerton's Farmers and Merchants Bank in 1931.[93]

In addition to his deep ties to financiers, Chapman remained an unabashed booster of the citrus industry in his public and private life. While the mayor of Fullerton, he helped form the Citrus Protective League in 1906 and served as its permanent chairman and president for many years.[94] The League was the primary lobbying arm of the citrus industry for decades and was responsible for saving growers over three million dollars in shipping charges from 1907 to 1911.[95] By far, its most significant accomplishment was preserving the tariff on citrus fruits in 1908 and 1914. Chapman was part of the initial group of Southern California citrus growers that traveled to Washington, DC, in 1897 to lobby on behalf of the Dingley Tariff Bill, which instituted heavy tariffs on agricultural products, including citrus. In public speeches, Chapman credited the tariff with almost single-handedly saving the California citrus industry from cheap imports, high freight charges, foreign labor, and poor crop yields.[96] Chapman's political connections also came in handy when Orange County boosters and citrus capitalists started the Valencia Orange Show in Anaheim. Chapman was well-known in Republican circles and was nominated to be the vice-presidential running mate to Calvin Coolidge in 1924.[97] To open the inaugural Valencia Orange Show in May 1921, Chapman called President Warren G. Harding by long-distance telephone to provide the opening remarks, which he did by praising the "glory and value of California oranges."[98]

Bradford was equally instrumental in developing Orange County's growth machine. Working with fellow citrus capitalists C.C. Chapman, William Crowther, Samuel Kraemer, and H.H. Hale, Bradford formed a committee to negotiate with the Santa Fe Railway to extend their service to Placentia from Fullerton. As the owners of the largest packing houses in the county, these men leveraged their land, capital, and influence to convince the Santa Fe to build the Richfield cutoff, which ran south of Fullerton through Chapman's Santa Ysabel Ranch and into the west side of Placentia. Shortly after completing the cutoff in the summer of 1910, Bradford purchased sixty acres near the future site of the train depot, plotted out the Placentia townsite, and formed the Orange County Investment Company to handle the sale of the town's lots.[99] He and others envisioned a prosperous residential community that would provide another hub for the Valencia industry adjacent to Fullerton. Once Placentia was surveyed and had railroad access, its founders' ambitions could be realized. Within a year, the town had a bank, newspaper, and Chamber of Commerce, all started by Bradford and his partners.[100] Although it was much smaller than neighboring citrus-producing cities like Fullerton,

Anaheim, and Orange, Placentia's six packing houses eventually "shipped more carloads of freight than any other place in the southland except Los Angeles."[101] Like Fullerton, it also acquired its own CFGE district exchange when the three largest grower associations in Placentia, Bradford Brothers, Inc., Placentia Mutual Orange Association, and Placentia Orange Growers Association, formed the Placentia Orange County Exchange in 1935.[102]

Illustrative of Orange County's dependence on the citrus growth machine, by the early 1920s, virtually every bank, public utility, and city in the Santa Ana Valley owed its existence to citrus capitalists like Chapman and Bradford.[103] Along with the McFaddens, Gilmans, Kraemers, Crowthers, and others, these families formed the vanguard of the Valencia oligarchy that ran Orange County like a company town during its initial phase of urban development from the 1890s to the 1930s. During this period, those with land-related interests benefited handsomely as county real estate values increased from $4.2 million in 1889 to $56.7 million in 1938.[104] Likewise, farm income grew apace with the development of the Valencia industry, rising from just under $6.2 million in 1910 to $51.6 million in 1930, of which 81 percent or $41.6 million came from citrus.[105] As it developed into a citrus-producing behemoth with over seventy local grower associations, forty-five packing houses, and more than two dozen citrus processing plants, Orange County became the wealthiest agricultural county in the nation and the global leader in orange production from 1925 to 1945.[106] While many benefited from the prosperity provided by the citrus economy, this tremendous growth came with costs.

RACIAL CAPITALISM AND CITRUS CAPITALISM

Orange County's dependence on the citrus growth machine led directly to labor exploitation and racial segregation. This was neither strange nor controversial as the practice of "race management" was one of the central features of US capitalist production during the nineteenth and twentieth centuries.[107] Rather than being an unintended consequence, labor contractors, factory managers, and field bosses explicitly promoted the production of difference based on race, class, gender, region, and nationality to control labor, maximize productivity, and increase profitability. While all workers were exploited to some extent by the segmentation of labor and its accompanying dual wage system, immigrants and those labeled as nonwhite faced the greatest disadvantages. Southern California's citrus industry developed within the existing structure of US labor relations that pitted immigrants against citizens, whites against nonwhites, and men against women.[108] Although citrus capitalists did not create these oppressive labor practices, they certainly manipulated them for their benefit. Indeed, Gilman, McFadden, Chapman, Bradford, and their associates were aware of and responsible for exploiting the differences in race, class, and gender as they built the Valencia orange industry during the late nineteenth and early twentieth centuries. They were the architects of the decisions, practices, and policies implemented by grower associations and local government that made Orange County into one of the most racially segregated regions in California.[109]

Citrus cultivation in Orange County was a year-round capital-intensive enterprise that required a semiskilled residential workforce completed by what industry leader J.B. Culbertson called "the cheapest labor available."[110] While the Valencia was king, many associations packed various fruits and vegetables, with citrus accounting for over two-thirds of the county's agricultural production from 1929 to 1939.[111] Despite the introduction of tractors and sorting machines during the early twentieth century, citrus required more workers per acre than almost any other agricultural product.[112] Even during their formative years, citrus growers rarely involved themselves in manual labor, opting instead to hire out the most arduous aspects of citrus production to wage laborers at the lowest cost possible.[113] When local labor proved insufficient, either due to supply issues or the unwillingness of white workers to perform menial tasks, growers brought in migrants. Such was the case with Richard Gilman, who hired 100 Chinese laborers to work for the Cajon Ditch Company and his Semi-Tropic fruit ranch during the 1870s.[114]

Gilman was neither the first nor last to exploit foreign nonwhite labor in Orange County. Chinese migrant laborers were employed alongside resident Mexicans and Native Americans in Anaheim vineyards during the 1850s and 1860s.[115] From then on, cheap labor became associated with nonwhite labor. During the late nineteenth and early twentieth centuries, Orange County's agricultural labor force was primarily composed of Chinese, Japanese, and Mexican gang labor, with Filipinos, Asian Indians, Blacks, and poor whites rounding out the supply.[116] Generally, one group dominated the labor force or was used for a particular crop until supplanted by another. For instance, Chinese laborers worked in celery fields and citrus groves from the 1870s to the 1890s.[117] Because of immigration restrictions and racial violence, growers turned to Japanese labor from the 1890s to 1910, until anti-Japanese sentiment led to another shift that saw Mexicans subsume all other ethno-racial groups as the preferred source of field labor.[118] Of course, nonwhites worked in several local industries, from construction to domestic service, but no other commercial enterprise in Orange County became as synonymous with foreign nonwhite labor as agriculture.

Building upon existing inequities within the local labor market, decisions made by growers formalized the practices and policies that segmented citrus labor as the industry took shape. Beginning with the consolidation of labor management during the 1880s, independent packers, commercial intermediaries, and grower associations played a role in this effort. In the most extensive contemporary investigation into the use of labor in California's citrus industry, economist Paul Garland Williamson found that the "concentration of employment in the functions of picking and packing" occurred "very early" when commercial middlemen assumed control over the entire process of labor recruitment and management. From this moment forward, Williamson explained, the grower "transferred . . . his customary functions" of labor recruiter and manager and "no longer labored to pick and pack his crops," neither did he "supervise the picking and packing of those crops which he sold on the trees."[119] The consolidation of labor management was so swift that "by 1890 the business was practically controlled by five or six . . . firms."[120] Then, with the formation of grower associations during the 1890s, labor management was "transferred . . . from commercial men and commercial firms to great cooperatives."[121] During their formative years, grower associations hired independent contractors to recruit and manage their workforce. Once hired, contractors provided all the labor needed to harvest and transport the fruit from the grove to the train car.[122] In their constant effort to reduce costs and consolidate control over every aspect of citrus production, associations eventually cut out intermediaries and brought labor management in-house by employing a packing house foreman. Since nearly 75 percent of California growers were members of large grower cooperatives like the CFGE and the MOD, the labor practices and policies adopted by exchanges set the standard for the entire industry.[123]

In consolidating their control over citrus labor, grower associations manipulated race, gender, and class distinctions to justify the segmentation of their workforce. Generally, white employees were assigned positions within the packing house, where they worked as graders, packers, secretaries, salespersons, and managers. Outside the packing house, a mix of white ethnic and mostly nonwhite males worked as pickers, pruners, irrigators, fumigators, and occasionally truck drivers and field bosses. To rationalize the divide between packing house and field labor, citrus capitalists circulated racialized discourses in industry publications, newspapers, and government reports that asserted nonwhite workers were better suited for field labor than their white counterparts. Citing an array of physiological and sociocultural stereotypes, growers compared Chinese, Japanese, Filipino, and Mexican laborers to "beasts of burden" and "birds of passage" that were "consigned" to stoop labor "by a mechanism of natural selection."[124] These "racial scripts" were a form of relational race-making, whereby growers promoted the inferiority of one nonwhite group by comparing them to another.[125] Whenever citrus capitalists needed to shift from one source of cheap labor to another, they simply rehashed stereotypes of foreign and nonwhite inferiority to convince stakeholders of the need and benefits of doing so. Throughout California agriculture, ideas about race, foreignness, and field labor intertwined to form a racial script that depicted Asians and Mexicans as the ideal source of stoop labor.

Of course, most growers and industry officials knew that their preference for nonwhite foreign labor was based more on cost, availability, and exploitability than on supposed innate characteristics. This was confirmed by Governor C.C. Young's Mexican Fact-Finding Committee, which studied the "use of farm labor other than white" in California after the enactment of the 1921 Emergency Quota Act. Published in 1930, the report revealed the widespread preference for employing Mexicans, Japanese, Filipinos, Chinese, and East Indians "in place of white labor" because these groups were "available," "dependable," and "work[ed] at tasks repugnant to white workers."[126] Among the 933 responses collected from grower associations, chambers of commerce, county farm bureaus, and horticultural commissioners, 76 percent preferred the "use of some group other than white labor."[127] When asked to explain why, respondents cited lower wages, cheaper housing, and lower boarding costs as their top three reasons.[128] Another finding repeatedly expressed throughout the report was that white laborers "will not, do 'stoop' labor," or "stay with the job."[129] While Governor Young's report was prompted by fears of labor shortages resulting from restrictionist immigration policy and geo-political disruptions like the Mexican Revolution (1910–1920) and World War I (1914–1918), a report by the US Senate Immigration Commission in 1911 confirmed that foreign and nonwhite workers "have been employed in citrus since [the] early days of the industry . . . chiefly because they were obtained easily at harvest time, because they would work long hours for low wages, and because they '. . . have been willing to live under conditions which proved unattractive to the white laborers with whom they competed.'"[130] Thus, the preference for nonwhite labor in citrus and other agricultural industries predated labor shortages caused by external forces and resulted from internal efforts to maximize profit by exploiting workers that had fewer opportunities to find employment elsewhere.

Chapman understood the critical role the cost of labor played in the future of the citrus industry when he spoke to an audience of prominent growers and bureaucrats at the state horticultural convention held in Los Angeles in 1914. According to Chapman, the solution to the challenges of overproduction and foreign competition was "the reduction of the cost of labor."[131] Summarizing advances made over the previous twenty years, Chapman asserted that California growers had achieved "commercial perfection" and that future improvements would have a marginal impact on the industry's ability to return "profitable prices to the producers." As the state's premier cash crop, which was projected to increase by 60,000 to 80,000 carloads over the next eight to ten years, reducing the supply of California oranges on the national market was out of the question. Unwilling to make other concessions, Chapman returned to the labor question. "The poorly paid foreign labor must be met by low priced labor here," Chapman averred, "I can see no other way that will enable us to meet this unfair competition. If the labor required to do this work is not American, then it will of necessity have to be foreign."[132] Since foreigners and nonwhites were already widely employed throughout the citrus industry, Chapman's remarks came as no surprise to growers. Instead, his comments were likely aimed at stakeholders and government officials who viewed nonwhite imported laborers as "undesirable citizens" and whose employment some believed would lead to "developing a race problem."[133] But as the "Father of the Valencia orange industry" and one of the most respected businessmen in California, Chapman's observations carried substantial weight. Not only did they reflect the thinking and business practices of citrus capitalists, but they also influenced labor and social policy at the local and national levels.

In Orange County, the widespread segregation of ethnic Mexicans did not exist before the outbreak of World War I. The practice became institutionalized between 1915 and 1930 through the decisions of growers and local officials. While Mexicans had been an essential part of Orange County's multiracial labor supply since the 1860s, they became the preferred source of citrus labor only after growers lost access to significant numbers of white and Asian workers due to the wartime draft and revisions to the Immigration and Nationality Act in 1917, 1921, and 1924.[134] These developments coincided with increased migration from Mexico after the outbreak of the Mexican Revolution in 1910. Fearing that reductions in the surplus labor supply would lead to wage increases, citrus growers joined a coalition of Southwestern agriculturalists in lobbying the Department of Labor and Congress to increase access to Mexican migrant labor. As reported in the *California Citrograph* in June and July of 1917, these efforts led to the suspension of the literacy test, head tax, and contract labor provisions of the 1917 Immigration Act for Mexican migrants.[135] Between 1917 and 1921, approximately 72,000 Mexican workers participated in the temporary labor program, which was extended after the war due to pressure from growers.[136] How many contract laborers came to Orange County during this period is unknown, but growers certainly benefited from the exemptions and began focusing on recruiting Mexican labor exclusively from this time forward.

From June 1917 to December 1919, citrus capitalists used *The California Citrograph*, published by the CFGE and distributed to over 8,000 citrus growers monthly, to promote the hiring of Mexicans as the solution to the wartime labor problem. For grower associations, the issue had more to do with increased competition for workers and fears of wage increases than shortages in personnel.[137] In seeking replacements for white and Asian workers, industry leaders developed a newfound appreciation for Mexican immigrants. Beginning in February 1918, *The Citrograph* published a five-part series by Archibald D. Shamel, a physiologist with the US Department of Agriculture and the Citrus Experiment Station in Riverside. Shamel's articles argued that Mexican families provided "the most practical source of additional labor," and if provided adequate housing and treated "like human beings," they would be "good workers . . . faithful to any trust that may be reposed in them."[138] Shamel's belief that grower-provided housing was key to attracting and retaining Mexican labor was based on his visits to some of the largest citrus ranches in Southern California. Over the prior decade, he toured the Chase Plantation in Corona and the Sespe and Limoneria ranches in Ventura County, taking copious notes on cultivation methods, employment trends, and housing accommodations. Throughout the series, Shamel presented Mexicans as capable, loyal, and readily available replacements for white and Asian workers. If provided decent permanent housing, he believed Mexican families could solve the need to continuously recruit and replace single men likely to leave for higher wages. "The main object in view," Shamel reiterated in his fifth and final article, "is to give the Mexicans a permanent home where they can find shelter for themselves and their families during the dull of the season."[139]

Shamel was not alone in advocating for Mexicans as the solution to "a more uniform supply of labor."[140] In March 1918, R.S. Vaile, Shamel's colleague at the citrus station, shared his belief that Mexicans were "content to eke out a humble, but homelike existence . . . living on small parcels of land" where they would "remain year after year, always on hand when needed, and able to care for themselves temporarily when turned off."[141] Referencing Shamel's articles, the September 1918 edition of *The Citrograph* editorialized, "the final solution of the labor problem confronting the citrus

Figure 1.4 Mexican family in front of a "typical Mexican home" on the Sespe Ranch in Ventura County, CA. The caption identifies all members of the family, including children, as "Seven Future Employees." The photograph was included in an article written by Archibald D. Shamel that was published in the *California Citrograph* in March 1918. Courtesy of BYU Harold B. Lee Library.

orchardist . . . will be found [in] the proper housing of . . . the Mexican laborer, who . . . is less likely to be attracted by the blandishments of another 25 cents a day."[142] This barrage of messaging continued in November 1919, when *The Citrograph* reported on a meeting of the Lemon Men's Club in Los Angeles where prominent growers like Charles C. Teague and stakeholders like former California State Senator Reginaldo Francisco del Valle spoke of the need for Mexican labor. Teague, the owner of the Limoneria Ranch and future president of the CFGE, considered the hiring of Mexicans "a matter of self-protection" for grower's "large investments in farmlands and orchard properties."[143] But R.F. del Valle, President Pro-Tempore of the California Senate from 1882 to 1885 and son of former Los Angeles mayor Ignacio del Valle, may have been the most persuasive speaker at the meeting.[144] "There is one class of labor on whom you must depend for your picking and . . . general ranch work and that is the Mexican," del Valle stated emphatically. "You are dependent today upon the Mexican and he can easily be made the best class of labor." Echoing Shamel, del Valle asserted that Mexicans could be trusted. He warned, "You will find that from now on you will be dependent upon the Latin race for your labor . . . they comprise the only labor available."[145] One month later, in December 1919, del Valle's claims were confirmed by *The Citrograph* when it reported that Mexicans comprised 30 percent of California's citrus workforce.[146] By 1940, Mexicans made up nearly 100 percent of pickers and 60–70 percent of the entire citrus workforce.[147]

Over the ensuing decade, grower associations responded to *The Citrograph*'s media blitz by hiring Mexicans at an astonishing rate. One of the principal findings of Governor C.C. Young's report indicated that by 1929, 86 percent of subtropical fruit growers had "a marked preference for the Mexican above any other single group."[148] This was especially true in Orange County, where according to the 1930 Census, approximately 83 percent of Mexicans listed their occupation as some form of agricultural wage labor.[149] This dramatic increase in hiring Mexicans developed alongside a newfound preference for hiring families to do the work previously performed by single men. Before World War I, single men were considered the ideal citrus workers because they "could be housed more cheaply, secured with the least complications," and were "[necessary] for holding down the costs of labor." With the tightening labor supply due to the war and growing immigration restrictions, single men acquired increased mobility and choice in the workforce. These developments led growers to give "more and more attention to the family unit as a source of labor." "Taken as a class," *The Citrograph* insisted, "the married man is more dependable than his bachelor brother . . . if comfortable housing [is] supplied," and "there is opportunity for the women and older children to obtain work a portion of the time."[150]

Following the recommendations of *The Citrograph*, citrus capitalists attracted Mexican family labor to Orange County by devising various means to house and retain them in segregated neighborhoods. Three types of housing common of housing were made available to Mexicans in Orange County. The first was the development of private subdivisions where "residence [was] restricted to Mexicans and other Spanish-speaking citizens."[151] Built by private developers in collaboration with growers and landowners, these neighborhoods provided vacant lots and scantily built homes that lacked electricity, indoor plumbing, and gas for cooking and heating. While these homes were a considerable improvement over the squatter encampments they replaced, they were built in unincorporated agricultural districts that remained cut off from basic municipal services and amenities until the 1950s. During the late 1910s and 1920s, citrus capitalists worked with land developers, bankers, and other interested parties to build dozens of these communities near La Habra (Campo Corona, Alta Vista, and Campo Verde), El Modena (El Pirripi, La Paloma, and Hollywood), Garden Grove (La Paz, Manzanillo/La Bonita), Placentia (La Jolla, Atwood, and La Esperanza), and Anaheim (Independencia, La Conga, La Fabrica, La Palma, Tijuanita, and La Philadelphia).[152]

Grower-sponsored housing provided a second option but was mostly limited to large packing house associations in Fullerton, Placentia, and La Habra, as well as independent packers like the Placentia Orchard Company owned by Charles C. Chapman, the San Joaquin Ranch owned by the Irvine family, and the massive 10,000-acre Bastanchury Ranch owned by the Bastanchury family. The La Habra Citrus Association appears to have been the first to provide housing of this type to Mexican citrus workers in Orange County. Beginning in 1915, the association built "twelve modest picker dwellings" it called Campo Colorado, which grew to include sixty-nine homes and 500 residents by the late 1940s.[153] Grower housing generally included dormitories for single men and small homes for families, like the "Mexican camp" built by the Placentia Orange Growers Association, which had three bunk houses and thirty-two family dwellings.[154] Similarly, the San Joaquin Ranch built "a hotel-like structure" to house seasonal workers and a village of seventy-five to one hundred small homes for employees with families.[155] Like the colonias that derived from private subdivisions, grower housing was built "deep in the agricultural districts" and kept far "away from the Anglo cities."[156] Because growers feared that interactions between white, Mexican, and Asian workers led to race problems, grower housing practiced intra-community segregation. This was encouraged by the CFGE through *Citrograph* articles like Shamel's series on grower housing. For example, in his March 1918 article on the Sespe Ranch, Shamel explained that the housing for "White, Mexican, and Japanese labor . . . are located at various points on the ranch convenient to the class of work performed. The camps are situated far enough apart so that they can each live according to their own customs. By this means comparatively little friction occurs between the different employees on the ranch."[157] On both the Sespe and Limoneria ranches, Mexicans lived in a "Mexican village" where the housing was clearly of a lower standard than that provided to whites.[158] Likewise, Chapman's Santa Ysabel Ranch kept whites apart from nonwhites, housing white males in bunkhouses and homes while Mexicans "liv[ed] together" in their own "village."[159]

Poor and working-class neighborhoods comprised the third option available to Mexicans and were generally located in industrial zones along the peripheries of more populated cities like Santa Ana, Anaheim, Fullerton, and Orange. Some of these neighborhoods dated back to the arrival of railroads during the boom of the 1880s, while others developed after 1900 in response to increasing demand for agricultural labor.[160] Urban barrios reflected the racial and class hiring preferences of nearby employers and were associated with lower quality housing and property values. This was true in Santa Ana, where the city had three large Mexican barrios by 1916, Artesia on the westside, Delhi on the southside, and Logan on the eastside. By 1930, these neighborhoods housed over four thousand Mexican residents working as domestics, agricultural workers, and other low-wage laborers.[161] As remembered by Artesia resident Alex Maldonado, housing covenants and other forms of racial discrimination led to the formation of Santa Ana's three barrios. "If they were Hispanic . . . If the name looked Spanish or sounded Spanish they were considered to be Mexican and not allowed" to live outside the barrio.[162] Similarly, the Cypress Street barrio in the city of Orange formed around 1918 when the SOGA built one of the largest packing houses in the world at 350 N. Cypress Street.[163] The barrio bordered the Atchison Topeka and Santa Fe railroad tracks to the west, Glassell Street to the east, and stretched north to south from Walnut Avenue to Palm Avenue.[164] By 1930, approximately 85 percent of the Mexican population in the city of Orange lived in the Cypress Street barrio, making it one of the most densely segregated urban regions in the county.[165]

Whether originating from private development, grower sponsored housing, or existing neighborhoods, barrios and colonias were spaces of "capitalist neglect" and "structural violence," in sociologist Michelle Tellez's terms.[166] The development of the La Jolla colony in Placentia provides a clear example. Initially named Colonia Villa Carlos, La Jolla began as a squatter encampment established by Mexican citrus workers employed by nearby packing houses in an unincorporated area four miles north of Anaheim and one mile south of Placentia.[167] Realizing a lucrative opportunity, the Simmons Investment Company subdivided approximately ten acres into small lots and sold almost exclusively to Mexicans for $500 on an installment plan of $10 per month.[168] Alfredo Rodriguez, a local carpenter, built many of the homes for early residents, which were small stick-built dwellings with two bedrooms and no electricity or plumbing. Surrounded by orange groves, the colonia was bound by Orangethorpe Avenue to its north, La Jolla Street on the south, Blue Gum Street to the east, and Placentia Avenue to the west. Blue Gum Street (later changed to Melrose Street) provided the northbound passage to Placentia, while Placentia Avenue led south to Anaheim.[169]

During the 1930s, the La Jolla colony had approximately seventy-five homes and between 300 and 400 residents. Several roads were named after early settlers, like the Tafolla, Gonzales, and Simmons families, while La Jolla Street served as the "main street" and featured a clothing store, two small markets, an auto repair shop, and pool hall. Until the opening of *La Nuestra Señora Virgen de Guadalupe*, a Catholic mission church located along La Jolla Street, the pool hall served as the center of community life, hosting meetings, dances, funerals, cultural celebrations, and religious services. Situated on a small hill east of Blue Gum Street, The La Jolla School was the only brick building in the colonia and was built from repurposed materials sourced from an old workshop. Opened in 1914, it was one of the first purpose-built segregated Mexican schools in Orange County and one of three Mexican schools near Placentia.[170] As remembered by former La Jolla School principal Chester Whitten, the school was evidence of the "out and out segregation" that existed in Placentia where "nearly all of the growers were school board members in one way or another."[171]

Despite their segregation from nearby Placentia, Fullerton, and Anaheim, La Jolla's residents took pride in their community, considering it "a jewel . . . in comparison to other colonies in Orange County."[172] Reflecting on the colonia years later, Edward "Eddie" Castro, recalled:

> Because Placentia to La Jolla [was] a long ways off . . . we didn't have nothing to do with downtown Placentia. Everybody was in the same boat. They were poor and the colony served as . . . a reservation for labor, like a labor camp. When the orange packing houses in the city of Placentia or Fullerton or Anaheim needed some help, they would go there and they would hire the people.[173]

Despite its rural and humble character, Castro remembered the La Jolla Colony as "a real nice neighborhood" and "a very close-knit community."[174] Yet, there were several downsides to colonia life that even the fondest memories could not dispel. "Hey, we were an unincorporated area," Castro recalled. "We didn't belong to Placentia. We only belonged to the county, and the county didn't give a damn about us."[175] Castro's reflections confirm the findings of urban historians like Jerry González, who argues: "Despite the protection they offered as culturally affirming spaces, colonias were plagued by endemic poverty, substandard housing, lack of municipal services and infrastructural improvements, public health concerns and property devaluation."[176] Throughout Southern California and especially in Orange County, "segregation [was] the rule" for virtually all Mexicans "from cradle to grave."[177] As ironic as it sounds, the isolation and marginalization of barrios and colonias were essential to the integration of ethnic Mexicans in the regional economy. These neighborhoods, which functioned as "racially segregated working-class suburbs," kept Mexicans economically central and socially marginal to the region's development throughout the first half of the twentieth century.[178]

THE ARCHITECTS

The rapid growth of Mexican barrios and colonias in Orange County from 1915 to 1930 involved the concerted actions of growers, landowners, developers, real estate agents, bankers, and elected officials, resulting in the intentional segregation of Mexican families into several dozen underserved communities.[179] This occurred during a period of investor-controlled urban development that predated the establishment of the county planning commission in 1929 and was directed by citrus capitalists using the power and influence of public and private institutions.[180] These decisions delineated land use patterns and social relations for decades, especially in the inland and northern portions of the county, which were home to the Valencia orange industry and the overwhelming majority of Mexican neighborhoods. According to the 1930 Census, nearly 80 percent of Mexicans lived in enumeration districts assigned to the cities of Brea, Anaheim, Fullerton, Orange, Santa Ana, and Tustin.[181] This region, which also included La Habra, Placentia, Villa Park, El Modena, Garden Grove, and Irvine, comprised the principal citrus growing districts in the county and was home to at least seventy grower associations and thirty-nine Mexican colonias and barrios.[182]

The Orange County Board of Supervisors presided over the prolific expansion of the citrus industry and the segregation of its Mexican workforce. From 1913 to 1934, no less than four of the five members of the Board of Supervisors were prominent growers.[183] Further, the combined tenure of the board's three longest serving members, Thomas B. Talbert (1909–1926), William Schumacher (1913–1932), and Willard Smith (1925–1955), provided growers forty-five consecutive years of representation on the county's top governing body. Spanning nearly a half-century of urban development, these men were fully aware of the Mexican population's growth and the location and conditions within their neighborhoods. Talbert, for example, was considered a "pioneer" in the sugar beet and celery industries before starting a real estate and insurance business. From their inception, both crops relied heavily on Chinese and Mexican labor. As "an active member of the Celery Growers Association" and "one of the best judges of real estate" in the county, Talbert knew better than most where and how Mexicans lived compared to others.[184] While Chairman of the Board of Supervisors from 1911 to 1926, Talbert was appointed director of both the West Whittier Oil Company in Huntington Beach and the First National Bank of Huntington Beach. In his later years, Talbert became the driving force behind a three-volume self-congratulatory work on local history that celebrated the achievements of "civic and business leaders" like himself.[185]

William Schumacher followed Talbert as chairman of the board from 1926 to 1927 and was elected president of the Citrus Orchards Association and president of Buena Park's Chamber of Commerce during his nineteen years of public service.[186] Replacing Schumacher in 1933, LeRoy Lyon was known as the "supervisor from Sunkist" due to his thirty-six years of leadership in the Olive Heights Citrus Association, Orange County Fruit Exchange, and CFGE central exchange board.[187] Prior to his time on the County Board of Supervisors, Lyon served as chairman of the Orange County Tax Commission and director of the Orange County Farm Bureau. From 1922 to 1933, he was a member of the Placentia Unified School District, holding the positions of secretary, treasurer, and president. In 1929, Lyon was elected to the CFGE-Sunkist board of directors, a position he occupied for thirty years, including eighteen years as one of the organization's three vice presidents. As vice president, Lyon sat on the citrus industry's prorate committee, where he helped set the weekly volume of rail car shipments to Eastern markets. Additionally, Lyon was the secretary, treasurer, and director of the Pilot Water Company in Anaheim, president of the Imperial Highway Association, and an eighteen-year board member of the Bank of America branch in Anaheim.

Appointed in 1925, Willard Smith became the longest-serving member of the county board and was among those most responsible for shaping Orange County's development during its first half century.[188] Born into the citrus ranching business, Smith had an eclectic professional career in fumigation, photo engraving, banking, and real estate development, but he always considered himself a farmer first and foremost. He was the founder and president of the Villa Park Orchards Association from 1913 to 1959, and like Lyon, he was elected to the Orange County Fruit Exchange and the CFGE-Sunkist central exchange board. Celebrating his selection as fourth district supervisor, *The Citrograph* called Smith "one of the best known citrus men in Orange county" and assured its readers that "Citrus growers . . . can feel gratified to know that another of their clan has filled the office." Indeed, Smith was the third consecutive citrus rancher to occupy his seat, having been preceded by Leon Whitsell and Nelson T. Edwards, both "prominent citrus men" according to *The Citrograph*.[189] "Known locally as a financial whiz," Smith held several distinguished positions in local businesses and organizations, including president of the Serrano Water Company;

director, vice president, and chairman of the board for the National Bank of Orange; board member of the Bixby Development Company; and a charter member of both the Orange County Farm Bureau and the Orange Chamber of Commerce.[190] During his thirty years on the county board, Smith served several terms as chairman, directing "the county through some of its most turbulent and transformative times."[191] While it may be tempting to think of Talbert, Schumacher, Lyon, and Smith as exceptional cases, these men were typical of those elected to the County Board of Supervisors from 1889 to 1948. They were fully invested in the citrus growth machine, but also unabashedly used the mechanisms of local and county governance to maintain its dominance.

Geographer Andrew Herod argues that "Company towns are the product of their designers' hope that shaping the built environment in particular ways will allow them to further their political, economic, and cultural goals."[192] Orange County provides a concrete example of such efforts. From county formation in 1889 to the peak of Valencia orange production in 1948, citrus capitalists used their influence over the local economy and politics to promote the unencumbered expansion of the citrus industry. During the county's first forty years, most of this development was controlled by "urban founders" and "growth entrepreneurs" like Gilman, McFadden, Bradford, and Chapman.[193] They were the "signatories" of the citrus growth machine and its attendant "racial contract."[194] In the ensuing decades, the second generation of citrus capitalists—an executive and managerial class epitomized by LeRoy Lyon and Willard Smith—continued the work of their predecessors using the newly acquired tools of professional land use planning. As the inheritors of the citrus growth machine, the second generation preserved the inland and northern portions of the county as a "space of exception" where growers maintained control over the design and function of the built environment and the people within it.[195] This occurred when the Board of Supervisors caved to pressure from the Orange County Farm Bureau by ensuring that the "interests of agriculture would be largely protected" by the county's first building codes and zoning ordinances.[196] Initially proposed in 1930, the regulations sought to modernize county buildings, alleviate urban and rural congestion, and prioritize the construction of high-quality housing, roads, and scenic highways.[197] Citrus capitalists delayed the passage and implementation of the ordinances for several years due to concerns over their potential impact on growers.[198] After months of meeting with Farm Bureau officials, the county revised the regulations so they would not apply to the county's agricultural districts. By exempting citrus growers from the county's building and zoning requirements, the board endorsed the preservation of the segregated landscape they helped establish. This is an example of what political scientist Jessica Trounstine calls "segregation by design."[199]

As the architects and purveyors of segregation in Orange County, citrus capitalists repeatedly invested in and developed infrastructure that benefited the citrus growth machine while simultaneously underdeveloping and isolating Mexican neighborhoods. Despite its seeming "banality," segregation in Orange County was not an unintended consequence of a few misguided decisions.[200] Rather it was requisite to the very mode of production that formed the basis of the regional economy. Intent on preserving their Mexican workforce, citrus capitalists built an apartheid-like social structure using the walls of residential, educational, and sociopolitical segregation and marginalization. In their efforts to solve what was purported to be a labor problem, citrus capitalists unintentionally created a social problem. Branded "the Mexican Problem" by journalists, social workers, educators, and elected officials, a new form of racism emerged from the citrus growing districts of Southern California that was not simply refashioned Jim Crowism. The so-called Mexican Problem was a homegrown version of anti-Mexican white supremacy that grew out of regional stakeholders' socioeconomic prerogatives.

CHAPTER 2

The "Mexican Problem" in Orange County

What did they [white people] know about us? They were all immigrants too! I didn't see anybody that was born here . . . So they were no different than I was . . . So I used to look at them and say, "Why do they treat us this way? They came here too, and now they're telling us what to do."

Alfred V. Aguirre, 2001

Despite a history that spanned several generations of migration, settlement, and socioeconomic development throughout California and the Southwest, Mexicans were viewed as foreigners, low-wage laborers, and unassimilated immigrants by Orange County's white majority. As longtime Placentia resident and World War II veteran Alfred V. Aguirre made clear, there was an inherent irony in the socioracial hierarchy that developed in Orange County during the early decades of the twentieth century.[1] In viewing Mexicans as foreigners and themselves as the "native" or rightful inhabitants of the region, the county's white residents conveniently ignored their own recent migration history. In fact, by 1930, only 25 percent of the region's white population were California-born. Among those arriving from elsewhere, approximately 32 percent came from the Midwest, 11 percent from the South, 5 percent from the Northeast, and 7 percent from Western states excluding California. Moreover, roughly 7 percent of whites were foreign-born, but as many as 20 percent had at least one immigrant parent. Meanwhile, nearly half of the county's Mexican population was California-born (45 percent), with the other half coming from Mexico (45 percent) or the Southwest (10 percent). Although a much

Breaking Down the Walls of Segregation. David-James Gonzales, Oxford University Press.
© Oxford University Press 2025. DOI: 10.1093/9780197839485.003.0003

larger proportion of Mexicans were born outside the United States, the number of foreign-born whites was almost equal to Mexicans (7,326 to 7,977).[2] Indeed, as Aguirre asserted, except for the Acjachemen Nation and the few remaining descendants of Californio families, virtually everyone was a newcomer to Orange County.

To mask their recent history of migration and settlement, whites fashioned an Anglo-centric worldview of Orange County that built upon the mythology of the American frontier. Inheriting the "myth consciousness" of their settler-colonial ancestors, white transplants who arrived from Midwestern, Southern, and Northeastern states viewed the Santa Ana Valley as a tabula rasa devoid of modern people, institutions, and culture.[3] Likening themselves to pioneers, they used symbols and archetypes like the independent farmer, citrus rancher, and town builder to marginalize and erase the region's Indigenous and Mexican past.[4] As in other locales throughout Southern California, white settlers imbued the region with a whitewashed version of history, locating its origins in a "Spanish Fantasy Past" that was superseded by an "Anglo Fantasy Past."[5] Continuing the so-called march of progress, domestic white migrants like the Chapmans and Bradfords replaced Spanish friars and Mexican Californios as "founders" of modern cities and industry. Providing the common ground needed to establish a collective sense of memory, history, and identity, the Spanish and Anglo Fantasy myths aided Orange County's white population in the process of "self-indigenization," wherein white settlers come to see themselves as the native or original inhabitants.[6] Despite their diverse ethnic origins, Anglo and European newcomers embraced a white ethno-racial identity that normalized their presence in a multiracial and culturally diverse region.[7]

Focusing on the 1920s and 1930s, this chapter explores the socioracial hierarchy that emerged in Orange County due to the citrus industry's dependence on Mexican family labor. It argues that the exploitative labor system created by citrus capitalists instituted a white-brown color line based on the surveillance, subjugation, and criminalization of Mexican bodies.[8] Unlike the "triracial hierarchy" that existed in Los Angeles agriculture, with Japanese tenant farmers positioned as a "middleman minority" between white landowners and Mexican laborers, Orange County's race relations were starkly defined between whites (83 percent of the population) and ethnic Mexicans (15 percent of the population).[9] While 2 percent of the county was comprised of Asians, African Americans, and Native Americans, the walls of segregation erected between whites and Mexicans influenced social relations and urban development into the Cold War era.

Citrus capitalists used the "Mexican Problem" narrative to justify and expand the county's segregated social and physical landscape. Concentrating on the perceived character flaws and cultural backwardness of Mexican immigrants, the narrative helped conceal the socioeconomic consequences of racial capitalism within the citrus industry. Until the Great Depression, this narrative succeeded in convincing most white-Orange Countians that Mexicans were a necessary nuisance who could be dealt with through physical separation and sociopolitical marginalization. As soon as it was clear that the Depression crisis threatened the long-term economic privilege and stability of white families, Mexicans were scapegoated for the lack of jobs, criminalized for seeking better wages and working conditions, denied access to public aid, and forcibly removed from the county through an unprecedented repatriation campaign. While citrus capitalists were not to blame for the economic crisis of the 1930s, they were directly responsible for instituting the apartheid-like socioeconomic system that made its impact so devastating upon Mexican families and neighborhoods. Since controlling Mexican workers was essential to keeping the industry profitable amidst fluctuating commodity prices and increased competition, segregation and low wages became the primary tools used to manage and preserve citrus labor. This chapter illustrates the devastating impact these policies had on Mexican

Figure 2.1 Mexican American boys (Harvey, Everett, Santiago, and Matt Vasquez) picking oranges c. 1940. The boys were working to buy shoes and clothes for the upcoming school year. Young orange pickers like the Vasquez boys were commonly referred to as "ratas" (rats) since they "scurried" around picking fruit from lower branches. Courtesy of the Orange Public Library Local History Room, Orange, CA.

families and communities as Orange County became one of California's most racially stratified regions.

THE MEXICAN PROBLEM

Responding to the call for citrus and other forms of manual labor, Mexicans migrated to Orange County in large numbers from domestic and international sending regions throughout the US-Mexico borderlands. El Paso, Nogales, and Albuquerque were the most common starting points for those relocating domestically, while the Mexican states of Jalisco, Guanajuato, Michoacán, Zacatecas, and Chihuahua were the top sources internationally.[10] Coinciding with the rise of King Valencia in Orange County, socio-economic and political turmoil in Mexico drove much of this migration. Whether fleeing economic dislocation before the outbreak of the Mexican Revolution in 1910 or the violence, persecution, and starvation that followed in its wake, most scholars agree that between 1 and 1.5 million Mexicans entered the United States between 1900 and 1930.[11] Traveling by foot, train, and automobile, Mexican migrants generally crossed at border checkpoints in Nogales, Arizona, and El Paso, Texas. Once at the border, experiences varied from crossing without incident to being detained and harassed by immigration officials, subjected to literacy tests, head taxes, medical examinations, and even chemical baths.[12] For those seeking to avoid this trouble, circumventing checkpoints and "crossing outside legal channels" provided an enticing but risky alternative.[13]

After crossing, Mexican migrants relied on family, extended kinship networks, and labor contractors to obtain housing and employment. Many settled near existing colonias and barrios throughout the Southwest, while others established new immigrant enclaves in the Midwest and Southeast.[14] Although most were of the working or peasant class, many were skilled artisans, former business owners, and small landholders. In general, single males were typically the first in their families to migrate; however, single females and families also made the journey.[15] This northbound procession of people, skills, and culture overlapped with and rivaled the Great Migration of African Americans out of the Jim Crow South. The Mexican Diaspora of 1900–1930 transformed the social and physical landscape of the United States.[16] Working in transportation, mining, agriculture, food processing, construction, and textiles, Mexican migrants provided the labor that fueled industrialization in the Southwest.[17]

From 1910 to 1930, Orange County's ethnic Mexican population increased thirteenfold (1,345 to 17,714) according to the Census, raising the group's proportion of county residents from 4 to 15 percent.[18] Additionally, Governor C.C. Young's Mexican Fact Finding Committee found that Mexican births accounted for 38 percent of Orange County's natural increase by 1928.[19] In response to this rapid growth, a new discourse emerged that stoked fears about the dangers of Mexico and Mexicans in the county's leading newspapers. Between 1910 and 1920, the mention of "Mexican" or "Mexicans" in the *Santa Ana Register* and *Anaheim Gazette* increased fivefold over the previous decade.[20] By 1912, a new phrase, "the Mexican Problem," was used by the local press as a shorthand for all things wrong with Mexico and its people.

On January 18, 1912, the *Santa Ana Register* published the county's annual grand jury report. Although the report primarily dealt with the county's financial affairs, the *Register's* headline, "Says Mexicans Raise Per Cent—Influx Responsible for Over Four-Fifths of the Increase in Crime," suggested that the grand jury report was about something entirely different. Quoting Orange County Superior Court Judge Z.B. West, to whom the grand jury delivered their report, the *Register* introduced its readers to the "Mexican Problem":

> You [the grand jury] have brought out some points concerning a very serious condition. There is no question but what the indigent and criminal class of Mexicans in the county is rapidly increasing. I think I am not overstating the matter when I say that fully eighty-five per cent of the increase of the criminal business of this county is due directly to the influx of a criminal class from Mexico. It is a serious problem.[21]

Reading Judge West's alarming rhetoric alongside the *Register's* provocative headline, one would think the grand jury devoted considerable attention to this newfound menace. Yet, within their extensive report, which filled six full-length columns of the *Register's* evening edition, the grand jury dedicated only a single paragraph to it, which read:

> Mexican Problem
> We desire to call the attention of the supervisors to the rapid increase of the indigents and criminals among the Mexican portion of the population of this county. It seems as if there must be some cause for the great inflow of this class of people. We recommend that you call the attention of the proper United States official to this condition. It would no doubt be found that the immigration laws are being openly violated by the criminal and indigent class being sent across the line, if so, it should and no doubt be stopped to a great extent, and thereby relieve us of an enormous expense.[22]

Notably, statistics supporting either Judge West's audacious claim or the *Register's* exaggerated headline were absent from the report. In fact, according to a 1926 survey of crimes committed in Southern California, Mexicans accounted for 25 percent of crimes in Orange County.[23] Though this was ten percentage points higher than their proportion of the population, it was far lower than the alarmist claims made by West and the *Register*. Nevertheless, the *Register* doubled down on its alarmist rhetoric in an editorial published on July 11, 1912, which began:

> The "Bad Mexican" in Orange County
> Perhaps the most serious social and economic problem and the most difficult solution, confronting Orange County is what may be termed The Mexican Problem. Without digging up statistics, it is safe to say that three-fourths of the criminal and indigent costs of the county—indeed, we believe nine-tenths would be nearer correct—are chargeable to the ignorant and vicious class of our Mexican population.[24]

After associating Mexican's supposed criminality with lax liquor laws, illegal weapons sales, and "the lack of moral sensibility," the editorialist conceded that the root of the problem might reside with growers' hiring practices. The *Register* continued:

> A wider and deeper phase of this question has to do with the labor problem in agricultural communities, which is ofttimes serious and compelling; and in a fundamental way with the racial greed for gain, which sometimes leads and sometimes forces men to employ laborers in large numbers who are not and can never become desirable citizens.[25]

This point was echoed in another *Register* editorial less than two weeks later that opined:

> Again, The Problem
> Our Mexican problem is a problem by itself. In working it out we in common with other Southern California counties cannot expect to escape some of the undesirable features that follow the presence among us of a foreign laboring class so far considered absolutely necessary for the harvesting of our crops.[26]

Alluding to the county's dependence on low-wage Mexican labor, the writer acknowledged that the Mexican Problem existed in "any Southern California city, whether it be Santa Ana, Oxnard, Ventura, San Bernardino, Corona, Riverside, or some other place." Unsurprisingly, this list included several of the most productive regions within the citrus belt, all of which experienced considerable increases in their Mexican population.

While the *Register* led its readers to believe that "bad Mexicans" were "the problem," the truth was that the social and economic challenges arising from the rapid increase of Mexican migrants were the result of labor policies instituted by citrus capitalists. Grower associations increasingly relied upon Mexican families to satisfy the industry's insatiable thirst for low-wage workers amidst labor shortages resulting from restrictionist immigration policy, workforce competition, and World War I. Thus, the solution to grower's labor problem became a social problem for cities and counties whose economies depended on the exploitation of farm labor.

This fact was clear to contemporary observers like Carey McWilliams, who exposed California grower's penchant for abusing migrant workers in his books *Factories in the Field* (1935), *Southern California Country: An Island in the Land* (1946), and *North from Mexico* (1948). In the latter, McWilliams devoted an entire chapter to "The Mexican Problem," where he affirmed that this "deceptive, catchall phrase has consistently beclouded the real issues by focusing attention on consequences rather than on causes." The "structure of the problem," as McWilliams defined it, stemmed from the social and political marginalization of ethnic Mexicans resulting from the expansion of US empire, the culture of white supremacy, and capitalist labor exploitation.[27] In Southern California, this produced what McWilliams called "the colonia complex," an intentional form of segregated urban development where "colonia residents were to live apart, work apart, play apart, worship apart, and . . . trade . . . apart" from whites.[28]

Beyond Orange County, the Mexican Problem narrative had "transnational and imperial dimensions" rooted in the "culture of empire," as historian Gilbert González put it.[29] Following US capital expansion into Mexico during the 1880s, American journalists, travel writers, missionaries, diplomats, academics, and business professionals produced a vast literature that depicted Mexico and Mexicans as a social problem requiring US intervention. Initially, this literature served the aims of American corporations, which controlled vital sectors of the Mexican economy by the early twentieth century, including its railroads, oil, and mining industries.[30] However, after the outbreak of the Mexican Revolution and the subsequent mass migration of Mexicans to the United States facilitated by American railroads and labor contractors, the discourse of empire shifted from external boosterism to internal concern over Mexicans' presumed unassimilability. "Ultimately, the 'Problem' crossed [the] border" as a part of what journalist Juan Gonzalez calls America's "harvest of empire."[31]

In Orange County, the Mexican Problem narrative became a discursive tool of self-indigenization that enabled white migrants to imagine themselves as the region's "native" and rightful inhabitants.[32] Following the settler-colonial logic of the Spanish and Anglo fantasy myths, the Mexican Problem narrative erased Mexicans from regional history and marked them as foreigners, temporary sojourners, and low-wage laborers in a land destined to belong to white settlers. While this narrative was not invented or promoted by citrus capitalists, it helped downplay the industry's role in creating the problem. As seen in the *Register*'s exaggerated commentary, Mexican migrants, not grower associations, were singled out as the source of social problems emanating from the inequities of agricultural capitalism. While editorialists implicated the "racial greed for gain" among growers and acknowledged "the absolute necessity" of "a foreign laboring class" in the regional economy, they avoided critiquing the mode of production that made Orange County's growth possible.

Not wanting to disrupt the precipitous economic growth achieved through the exploitation of Mexican labor, citrus capitalists used their influence to rebrand the Mexican Problem as an issue of social welfare and civic responsibility, between 1913 and 1932. Viewing the Mexican family paternalistically, civic groups comprising elected officials, religious leaders, employers, social workers, and educators held public forums to discuss solutions to the issues of Mexican poverty, health, morals, education, and citizenship.[33] At a countywide Parent Teacher Association meeting held at Santa Ana's City Hall on July 25, 1919, attendees listened to experts from San Francisco and Orange County speak on Americanization. At this meeting, J.A. Cranston, Superintendent of Santa Ana schools, urged, "We must show the Mexican that we need him, and that he needs us. As far as it is possible, we must make the Mexican our neighbor. If we love him at a distance we don't get very far with him. We must work with him as best we can."[34] As in other regions with high proportions of immigrant labor, Orange County's civic and commercial leaders funded and pushed Americanization programs as a solution to the social problems resulting from mass migration.[35]

Despite the inclusionary rhetoric and seeming good intentions, Americanization efforts in Orange County failed to remove the social and physical barriers erected by citrus capitalists who were more concerned with managing Mexican family labor than assimilating and transforming them into equal citizens. Consequently, the measures implemented to "Americanize" Mexican immigrants during the 1910s and 1920s, which relied on sending social workers to colonias and barrios, reinforced and expanded the pattern of ethno-racial and class segregation.[36] Already an integral component of managing Orange County's racialized labor force, segregation was also viewed as a tool to accomplish the Americanization of Mexicans, especially women and children.[37] Predictably, although ethnic Mexicans selectively incorporated aspects of Anglo-American culture, segregation ensured that the needs of citrus capitalism derailed the integrationist rhetoric of Americanization.[38]

ORANGE COUNTY'S APARTHEID-LIKE SOCIAL AND PHYSICAL LANDSCAPE

Orange County's segregated landscape was a product of citrus capitalists' intentional efforts to shape the built environment to suit their economic and political agenda. Grower associations and their allies in banking, real estate, and local government facilitated the development of barrios and colonias to attract, manage, and preserve a sizeable residential workforce centered on exploiting Mexican family labor. Located adjacent to fields, groves, packinghouses, railroads, and other forms of industry, the segregated Mexican neighborhood was a vital component of the region's "labor geography" as its proximity to the workplace and distance from white neighborhoods served explicit functions in the local economy and social relations.[39] Approximately thirty-nine of the county's fifty-three colonias and barrios fell within the northern half of the county, stretching from Santa Ana to La Habra.[40] Despite being the most densely populated region in the county, containing 77 percent of the total population, much of this area was rural and devoted to agriculture. Whites tended to live in suburban-like residential districts within municipal boundaries, while most Mexicans lived in unincorporated village-like settlements known as colonias. Although Mexicans also lived in urban neighborhoods or barrios in Santa Ana, Anaheim, and Orange, elected officials and land developers used zoning and deed restrictions to ensure residential segregation within city boundaries, keeping Mexican families in a type of spatial enclosure that sustained the regional growth machine driven by citrus capitalism.[41]

As a form of spatial apartheid, segregation in Orange County "skew[ed] opportunities and life chances along racial lines," in the words of historian George Lipsitz, creating a white-brown color line where inequities in urban space were reflected in social outcomes.[42] For Orange County Mexicans, the orange grove, the colonia/barrio, and the segregated Mexican school illustrate Lipsitz's argument that "race is produced by space" and that it "takes place for racism to take place."[43] Before the proliferation of segregated Mexican neighborhoods during the 1910s and 1920s, Orange County did not offer separate educational facilities based on race, nationality, or language. However, building on the foundation of residential segregation established by citrus capitalists, parents and educators responded to the increasing number of Mexican children in public schools by advocating for segregated schools. Between 1912 and 1913, the Santa Ana School Board established one of the first Mexican schools in the state of California by placing Mexican children in separate classrooms at the Washington school.[44] By 1915, the practice of segregating Mexicans within otherwise integrated schools was occurring at four schools in the Santa Ana district, all of which were near the city's three largest Mexican barrios (Delhi, Logan, and Artesia). By 1916, the "school-within-a-school" model of segregation failed to satisfy parents and educators who felt Mexicans and whites should not share the same school grounds.[45] In PTA meetings held between 1916 and 1918, parents demanded that the district build an entirely "separate school for the teaching of Mexican children."[46] Citing the support of parents, teachers, and administrators, the *Santa Ana Register* published an op-ed in November 1916 calling on the school board to hold a bond election to secure the needed funds.[47] This process played out in cities and school districts throughout the county until there were fifteen schools with 100 percent Mexican enrollment by the early 1930s.[48] All but one were located in the county's citrus-producing corridor.

Despite being the smallest county in Southern California, Orange was second only to San Bernardino in its number of segregated Mexican schools (fifteen and sixteen, respectively). This meant that Orange County had five more Mexican schools than Los Angeles, even though its non-English speaking student population was just 7.6 percent of its northern neighbor.[49] Further, while Orange County had just over 5 percent of the "foreign pupil population" in Southern California, it housed nearly one-quarter of the Southland's segregated Mexican schools. These figures only account for eleven of the county's forty-four school districts that opted to build separate Mexican facilities. Nineteen additional districts in the county had schools with Mexican enrollments but did not build separate facilities. Instead, they used "special classrooms" and other ad hoc arrangements.[50] To circumvent the California education code, which reserved segregation for Asians and Native Americans, Orange County school boards redrew school and district boundaries around ethnic Mexican settlements. On the off chance that a white resident lived within the boundaries of a Mexican school or district, school administrators used their discretionary power to transfer the child to another school. Hence, the creation of segregated Mexican schools solidified and institutionalized the racialization of Mexicans as second-class citizens.[51] While traveling throughout the citrus belt as the Commissioner of Immigration and Housing for the state of California from 1939 to 1943, Carey McWilliams remarked:

> The physical isolation of the colonias has naturally bred a social and psycholog-
> ical isolation. As more and more barriers were erected, the walls began to grow
> higher, to thicken, and finally coalesce on all sides. The building of the walls, as
> Mr. [Fred] Ross puts it, "went on concomitantly from without and from within
> the colonia, layer by layer, tier by tier." While the walls may have the appearance
> of being natural growths, they are really man-made.[52]

As segregation hardened, Orange County Mexicans were increasingly excluded from white society and subjected to everyday forms of what education historian David García calls "mundane racism."[53] In response, Mexicans developed vibrant community institutions and businesses that provided for the social, cultural, and material needs left unfulfilled by their marginalization.[54] For many, the colonia or barrio became a refuge from the discrimination that often resulted from contact with whites.[55] Yet, during this era of expanding segregation, whites and Mexicans interacted occasionally within the "restricted interiors" of urban space.[56] Downtown streets, stores, movie theaters, public parks, and swimming pools became contact zones, areas of cross-cultural interaction, mediated by ethno-racial and class hierarchies. As they ventured outside their segregated

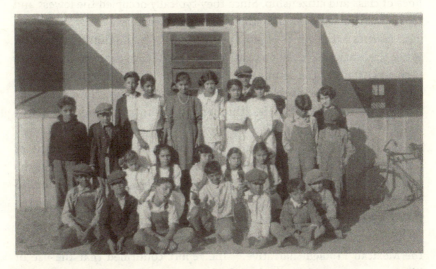

Figure 2.2 Mexican children at the segregated Sycamore School in Orange, CA, c. 1925. The Sycamore Mexican school, also known as "the barn," was in the Cypress Street Mexican barrio at West Sycamore Avenue and North Lemon Street. Courtesy of the Orange Public Library Local History Room, Orange, CA.

neighborhoods, ethnic Mexicans encountered more visible forms of segregation in the city, particularly when engaged in leisure activities at
parks, pools, and movie theaters. This was especially true for the children
of Mexican immigrants, who grew up within Orange County's segregated
landscape and rarely left the barrio unless accompanied by adults. As longtime El Modena resident Robert "Bob" Torres recalled:

> Everyone was treated right so long as you stayed in your right area . . . everybody
> had a place . . . we knew our place . . . in our society then, everybody knew where
> he belonged. Like I was telling you earlier . . . my dad said, "Don't go there, they
> don't want you there, don't go swimming. Because if they want you to go swim-
> ming in the city pool they would allow you when the Anglos are there, so there's
> evidence they don't want you so don't go there. Don't go to the theatre in Santa
> Ana because they don't want you there, if they wanted you they'd let you sit
> wherever you want." So, the same thing here, we knew our place and we kept it.[57]

Torres' experience was the norm, and most parents chose to limit their
children's mobility to safe spaces within the barrio/colonia. For others,
like Luis Olivos Sr., who grew up in Santa Ana and could be found most
Friday evenings at one of the city's five movie theaters, enduring the humiliation of segregation was a price they were willing to pay to access public
amenities.[58]

In addition to racial segregation, Orange County was divided along the
lines of class and citizenship. Since they typically occupied the lowest and
most undesirable positions within the regional economy, ethnic Mexicans
were marked in the minds of most whites as socially and culturally inferior.
While the Mexican Problem narrative fed some of this, the citrus industry's
preference for Mexican immigrant labor, especially their relegation to field
labor, was most responsible for such notions. Although ethnic Mexicans
labored in several industries throughout California, they dominated
the agricultural sector. According to California Governor C.C. Young's
Mexican Fact-Finding Committee, Mexicans held only 10.8 percent of
nonagricultural manufacturing jobs in the state by 1928.[59] Conversely, the
same report found that 84 percent of the responding farm operators in
Southern California employed Mexican labor, 65 percent of whom stated
they preferred Mexicans over all other ethno-racial groups. Published in
1930, Governor Young's study "Mexicans in California" was spurred by
the Mexican Problem narrative.[60] The report confirmed that the use of
Mexican immigrant labor had reached a tipping point, where growers had
developed a dependency on the oversupply and exploitability of Mexican
labor. Containing a thirty-three-page section prepared by the Department

of Social Welfare, complete with tables detailing birth rates, infant mortality, infectious disease, hospitalization, welfare relief, and imprisonment, the report confirmed the social costs of industrial agriculture.

Ten years later, Orange County's nascent Department of Social Welfare published "The Living Standards of Orange County Mexican Families."[61] Conducted during the height of the Depression, the Department of Social Welfare's report collected a random sample of thirty-five Mexican families comprising fourteen active relief cases and twenty-one self-sustaining households. Interviewing families, employers, Americanization workers, school authorities, immigration officers, businessmen, and "others in close contact with the Mexican population," the welfare department sought to determine "the comparative standards of living in the various income groups represented in the Mexican population of Orange County."[62] Beginning with an overview of the "Background of Mexican families," the report framed the reader's understanding of its conclusions by emphasizing the vast differences between Mexican and "American" (white) families. Referring to Mexicans in pejorative terms like "the Mexican peon," "primitive," "rural," and "superstitious," the report's authors portrayed Mexicans as accustomed to the impoverished living conditions that were "not only the way of life in his native land, but . . . the way of life in his adopted home."[63] Rather than attributing Mexican poverty to the exploitive labor conditions throughout the citrus industry, the report depicted Mexicans as lazy, stuck in tradition, and content to subsist on food, housing, and furnishings well below "American standards."[64]

Although the report's stated objective was to study variation within the living standards of Orange County Mexicans, its underlying motive was to advocate for a reduction in the amount of relief aid granted to Mexicans. In comparing self-sustaining families to those on relief, the survey found that "there was no apparent relationship between income and living standards."[65] This implied that placing Mexicans on relief was a waste of county and state aid. Yet, the primary reason for this finding was not Mexicans' attitudes and cultural preferences, as inferred by the report's authors, but rather the minimal difference in income between those on relief and those working in the citrus industry. Indeed, a comparison of the average income for families on relief and those with employment revealed that monthly incomes were nearly identical at $58 and $58.40, respectively. Such findings partially explained the "strong undercurrent of resentment among Mexicans toward current relief practices which provide higher cash allowances than the actual earnings of self-sustaining families."[66]

Rather than determining that the problems associated with "Mexican indigents" were rooted in the Depression, abusive labor practices, or the racial hierarchy of the citrus economy, the Department of Social Welfare blamed the "perversity, ignorance, . . . emotional instability [and] chronic incompetence" of Mexicans for "receiv[ing] more than its proportionate share" of relief aid and services.[67] Depicting a pathology of Mexican poverty, the report averred that "[Mexican indigent] families are not experienced in handling larger incomes," therefore "arbitrary monetary grants which are far in excess of accustomed normal requirements" created psychological and social dependency.[68] According to the welfare department's survey of Mexican families on relief, however, these conclusions failed to disclose that aid recipients comprised single-parent households with no adult male wage earner.[69]

Furthermore, by differentiating between deserving "Americans" and undeserving Mexicans, the welfare department's report stated that the "families observed clung to their Mexican traditions, customs and mores, and for that reason are not comparable to the usual American family applying for aid."[70] However, the report's conclusions contradicted its findings. According to its records, the Department of Social Welfare did indeed compare "American" (white) and Mexican families. One way they did so was by maintaining records that distinguished between the two groups. The findings of one such report were published in the *Santa Ana Register* in February 1931, in which the welfare department stated that it "expended . . . $7,957.46 . . . for assistance to white persons and $2,106.75 to Mexicans."[71] This was not a recent development implemented by the welfare department alone. Instead, it followed the decades-old practices of other county agencies, like the sheriff and health departments, conducted under the directive of the County Board of Supervisors.[72]

Not only did the County Board of Supervisors and Department of Social Welfare single out Mexicans in their reporting, but they were also aware that Mexican poverty resulted from the conditions of agricultural labor rather than a pathological condition rooted in "a significant retardation in general mental ability," or an "aptitude deficiency . . . in abstract reasoning."[73] In a report produced in May 1937 at the request of the California Senate, the Department of Social Welfare attributed fluctuations in the number of Mexican aliens on relief to work conditions within the agriculture industry. Written by Jack Snow, the Director of the Department of Social Welfare, the report found:

> The number of aliens on relief in Orange County varies widely from summer to winter due to the seasonal nature of our agricultural employment. During the five or six months in the summer there are probably 500 Mexican aliens

receiving aid, and the winter total usually reaches 2500 to 3000 for a period of some six to seven months.[74]

Although written by Director Snow, the initial request from the California Senate was sent to Willard Smith, Chairman of the Board of Supervisors, who received a copy of the welfare department's findings and response. Of course, the report's findings were no surprise to county officials, several of whom, like Smith, were leaders of grower associations or otherwise invested in the citrus industry.[75]

Comprising 90 percent of Orange County's field labor by the early 1930s, ethnic Mexicans bore the brunt of the state and county's acquiescence to abusive labor practices in the agricultural industry.[76] This resulted in impoverished living conditions, segregation, and indifference to the plight of Mexican workers and families, which was most apparent during the Depression when county officials singled out ethnic Mexicans as undeserving of relief aid and jobs. Led by the County Board of Supervisors and the newly created Department of Social Welfare, Orange County officials aimed to address both the Mexican and unemployment problems by seeking to remove Mexicans from the county through repatriation or deportation, reducing the number of Mexicans on relief cases, and blocking efforts to improve working conditions for Mexicans laboring in the citrus industry. Collaborating with grower associations, local law enforcement, and the federal immigration service, county government closed the door on previous efforts to assimilate ethnic Mexicans, instituting a new era of policing brown bodies that marked Mexicans as unassimilable, unequal, and undesirable.

As the Great Depression reached the Santa Ana Valley in January 1931, efforts to Americanize Mexican immigrants were quickly abandoned as the "Mexican Problem" intersected with an emerging unemployment crisis that drove thousands of formerly middle and working-class whites into poverty.[77] Rebranded as a social and economic crisis at the local, state, and national levels, ethnic Mexicans, along with other nonwhite immigrant groups, faced increased surveillance, criminalization, and removal.

ORANGE COUNTY ENCOUNTERS "HARD TIMES"

Orange County experienced immense growth and prosperity during the first three decades of the twentieth century. By 1930, the region had more than 200,000 acres of cultivated farmland and was the nation's leading producer of oranges, with approximately 60,000 acres devoted to Valencias and another 10,000 acres committed to other citrus varieties.[78] In all, two-thirds of Orange County's agricultural income came from citrus, of which 83 percent was attributable to Valencia sales. Although most citrus farms were modest, ranging from 10 to 15 acres, 115 (or 3.4%) of the region's 3,400 grower families were large commercial entities that reaped 28 percent of the county's $23.4 million in citrus income.[79] In addition to agriculture, oil extraction contributed substantially to regional growth during the 1920s. Riding the "twin pillars" of citrus and oil, Orange County experienced its second demographic explosion, virtually doubling in size from 61,375 persons in 1920 to 118,674 in 1930.[80] In Santa Ana alone, assessed real estate valuations soared from nearly $7.5 million in 1920 to over $21 million by 1930. The region's rapid transformation was so striking that in April 1922, the *Orange County Review* boasted, "no matter where one journeyed in the county these days, he cannot help but notice the remarkable development . . . rising everywhere. Homes, business blocks, public buildings are being constructed by the hundreds."[81] As in many other parts of the country, 1920s Orange County was booming, and both regional and national pride abounded as Orange Countians attributed their success to individualism, self-reliance, and local control.

As the early years of the Great Depression set in, Orange County appeared to be an exception to the panic and uncertainty that swept over most of the nation. At a meeting of the Orange Mutual Citrus Association on January 1, 1931, packinghouse manager L.F. Finley reported the largest net return in the association's history at $914,320.18 for the previous year's crop.[82] Representing 192 local growers, the association's 1930 profits increased by almost 9 percent from the previous year despite shipping 47 percent less fruit. Likewise, on January 20, 1931, the *Santa Ana Register* reported that the Anaheim Co-operative Orange Association netted $1,271,822.15 in 1930, a 15.6 percent increase over the prior year.[83] Like Orange Mutual, Anaheim Co-operative increased its membership and was operating at full capacity. Lauding their phenomenal success, the association's manager boasted, "It seems to us that when we read about the condition of growers of almost any other crop, and compared with the condition of the citrus growers, the latter is so far ahead of the others for 1930 that it is not a comparison, but a contrast."[84] Bolstered by similar reports featured on the front pages of the region's major newspapers from 1930 to 1932, orange growers could be excused for assuming the economic woes plaguing the rest of the nation might bypass them entirely.

Yet, the view from the middle and bottom rungs of the local economy was not so confident. Just two weeks after these glowing reports, the *Santa Ana Register* informed its readership of a meeting between the mayor, City

Council, and local clergy members to discuss the "unemployment problem" facing the city of Santa Ana. According to Mayor Frank L. Purinton, "the unemployment situation had reached such a serious and acute stage that it [could] no longer be ignored or disposed of . . . as if a passing malady."[85] Fay R. Spangler, chair of the city's municipal employment bureau, shared her concern that half of the 546 new applications for employment assistance submitted in December 1930 came from "men with families," many of them "of the old residents" who were "home-owners, reduced to a destitute condition." In her report, Spangler insisted that "none but bona fide residents had been listed in the employment office," which meant they were taxpayers who had previously participated in "the upbuilding of the community" but were "bordering on starvation." In their final assessment, attendees agreed that recent layoffs resulted from "the present depression." Therefore, measures were needed to save homes from foreclosure, put people to work, and raise relief funds.[86]

Likewise, reports from Anaheim confirmed that the unemployment problem extended beyond Santa Ana. On January 26, 1931, the *Register* reported that Anaheim's Chamber of Commerce "sent out a letter to every church, society, service club and organization in the city asking that . . . members co-operate in helping find work for men and women [in] need of jobs."[87] Stressing the gravity of conditions, the article explained, "The unemployment situation in Anaheim is just as acute as in other cities of the same size. We have in our midst men and women perfectly willing to work, who are distressed because they are idle and many are deeply chagrined because they have to seek assistance."[88] As with Santa Ana, the *Register* emphasized these were "honest and capable" persons, "bona fide residents" who had once contributed to "the upbuilding of the community" and were out of work through no fault of their own.[89]

The picture was equally grim throughout the rest of the county. During January 1930, the county's understaffed welfare department received 1076 aid requests, a 9 percent increase over the previous month. Among these, 454 cases involved work requests, while others included assistance with accidents, burials, desertion, hospitalization, death of a spouse, old age, and illness.[90] Lacking the monetary reserves and institutional framework to deal with the crisis, the county struggled to meet the desperate needs of its citizens. In general, the approach at the municipal and county level was to convene volunteer-run welfare committees that relied on churches, businesses, and the "well-to-do" to provide jobs, food, and other basic needs for the destitute.[91] Warning that "the supply of jobs has stopped almost completely," the city of Santa Ana "appeal[ed] to the sympathy and civic pride of [its] residents to supply work for those in need of it."[92]

By January 1932, unemployment was so bad that the *Santa Ana Register* declared, "No one institution, whether it be county, city, or individual, [was] able to meet the exigency of the . . . situation." Asserting that the city of Santa Ana was "warring against need, privation and hunger," the editorialist pleaded with county residents to "unite, regardless of personal opinions, politics, or prejudice."[93] This call for unity was not merely rhetorical, hinting at sharp divisions among county residents over whether a crisis existed and what should be done to address it. Responses to these questions were greatly influenced by locality and social position. Indeed, the region's three largest cities, Santa Ana, Anaheim, and Fullerton, absorbed the brunt of the unemployment crisis. Despite their more diversified economies, these cities experienced higher unemployment, particularly among working and middle-class whites. The regional economy ebbed and flowed with the seasonal nature of the citrus industry, most whites were accustomed to year-round employment in white-collar office work, retail sales, real estate, legal services, or higher-paying blue-collar positions in oil, construction, and other skilled trades. Workers in these jobs were among the first to feel the effects of the Depression as banks closed, credit dried up, sales plummeted, and local merchants went out of business. By contrast, in the more rural and agriculturally dependent regions of the county, like La Habra, Placentia, El Modena, Garden Grove, and Westminster, unemployment was mostly experienced by ethnic Mexican agricultural workers who were accustomed to periods of unemployment during the off-season months from December to April.

Divisions were also evident among elected officials who disagreed over the county's role in dealing with the Depression. At a meeting of mayors and the County Board of Supervisors on March 6, 1932, the mayor of San Clemente threatened to lead a recall effort if "the supervisors continue[d] to refuse to relieve the distress caused by unemployment."[94] Likewise, the mayor of Santa Ana suggested that "steps be taken to force the county to meet the situation if necessary." Joining this faction, the mayors of Anaheim, Fullerton, Huntington Beach, Laguna Beach, and Newport Beach felt that the county had a "moral obligation" to intervene in the crisis. To bolster their case, the mayors referred to an investigation by the Associated Chambers of Commerce that found the county had $310,000 of "uncontracted funds," disputing the board's claim that a lack of money hindered their ability to do more.[95] Yet, all were not convinced of the need for immediate action on behalf of the board. Mayor Clement of Orange didn't "believe the situation was as bad as it might be" and felt "Orange [could] take care of its own people." Moreover, the mayors of Brea, La Habra, and Seal Beach defended the county's response, claiming the board had done all it could. Despite differing opinions, all in attendance were alarmed by the number of respectable and upstanding citizens in need of aid, many of whom had "helped to build up and maintain [the county] in more prosperous times."[96]

The urgency of the matter became more apparent the next day when a mob of 300 men recently dismissed from the county employment program stormed the welfare office demanding work. Coming from all over the county, the men were at "the point of destitution and . . . desperation, because their wives and children [were] already feeling the pinch of hunger," the *Register* reported.[97] Speaking for the group, J.W. Daley said, "We don't want charity, we want work and are not specifying the amount of pay to be received for this work. All that we are asking is that we be given an opportunity to do something, no matter what, that we can earn enough money to buy food for our families."[98] In response, County Welfare Director Byron Curry told the men there was little he could do but provide them with food since the Board of Supervisors decided to terminate the jobs program.[99]

After two days of public opposition, the Board of Supervisors reluctantly took additional action on March 8, 1932. Passing Ordinance No. 298, which created the Department of Social Welfare and outlined the duties of its director, the board took the first step toward modern social service and welfare provision for Orange County residents.[100] Although the county had operated a welfare office since 1920, previous iterations were underfunded and mainly focused on providing aid to needy children.[101] With the onset of the Depression in 1929, the county increased the welfare budget to an unprecedented $81,375.13.[102] The county was unprepared for a prolonged economic downturn. As in other parts of the country, the proliferation of unemployment and poverty forced all levels of government to take extraordinary steps to relieve suffering and desperation.

While unprecedented, Ordinance 298 was a feeble attempt by the Board of Supervisors to respond to public calls for action. This was evident in the restrictive and seemingly punitive criteria established by the board to qualify for county assistance, which included excluding those with real property valued in excess of $250 or personal property worth more than $100 unless "incapacitated by old age."[103] Additionally, receiving public aid made one subject to real estate liens and the forfeiture or sale of personal property to repay the county. To ensure eligibility, the Department of Social Welfare thoroughly vetted all applicants, which included accounting for and notifying nearby relatives of the applicant's situation. Further, section five of Ordinance 298 stipulated that any "alien" applying for aid within five years of immigration would be considered a "public charge" and reported to the Bureau of Immigration for deportation.[104]

Despite these restrictions, relief cases mounted quickly, especially after August 2, 1932, when the Board of Supervisors admitted "a general depression in the citrus fruit market."[105] Between July 1933 and September 1935, Orange County's unemployment relief rolls fluctuated between 9 percent and 15 percent of the working population.[106] These rates were significantly lower than in Los Angeles and the rest of the nation, 41 percent and 33 percent respectively for 1933, but were nevertheless extraordinarily high for the region.[107] Additionally, between 1931 and 1934, city revenues plummeted by 30 percent, and delinquent taxes soared by 80 percent. By the fall of 1933, Orange County's economic situation was so bleak that it was identified as "one of nine counties in California where relief was most urgently required."[108]

With local resources nearly exhausted, on October 3, the board passed the Unemployment Relief Bond Act as an "urgent and necessary" measure for "the immediate preservation of public peace, health, and safety."[109] This measure authorized the Board of Supervisors to borrow from the State Emergency Relief Administration (SERA) to fund the county's floundering relief efforts. An initial loan for $131,706.92 was approved with an additional $70,000 requested and approved a few weeks later. These monies were intended to fund the county's relief work for six months, from December 31, 1933 to June 30, 1934. It was immediately apparent, however, that much more assistance was needed as the county requested and borrowed an additional $844,043 from SERA between January and July of 1934. Understanding that a faction remained among citrus capitalists that disapproved of their decision to involve state and federal agencies in county affairs, the Board of Supervisors released the following statement on May 3, 1934 explaining their actions:

> It is essential that adequate relief be afforded to such persons and their dependents to prevent a condition of starvation and pauperism. Such relief can be afforded only by immediate borrowing from the State of California under the provisions of the Unemployment Relief Act of 1933. If the necessary funds are not obtained . . . the unemployed persons referred to herein above and their dependents will suffer great hardship, starvation, loss of health and the deprivations which would and does immediately endanger the public peace, health and safety of the people of Orange County.[110]

Publishing their explanation along with the results of their unanimous vote in the *Santa Ana Register*, the Board of Supervisors presented a united front to the citizens of Orange County. Although they were initially slow to acknowledge and respond to the severity of the crisis, by the middle of 1934, the board appeared to reverse course and was pursuing all means of state and federal aid to mitigate the Depression. Between 1934 and 1937, the county used federal and state funds to establish four Civilian Conservation Corps work camps and two transient labor camps, provide financial aid to junior college students, and allocate $3 million for various public works projects that built and repaired roads, schools, libraries, post offices, city halls, irrigation canals, and harbors.[111] In addition to large construction projects, Works Progress Administration (WPA) funds were used to create jobs "for men and women not readily employable on ordinary projects."[112] As in other parts of the country, Orange County farmers, bankers, and homeowners also received assistance from New Deal programs like the Agricultural Adjustment Act, the Home Owners Loan Corporation, and the Federal Housing Administration. Through the relief aid, jobs, low-interest loans, and recently established industry and consumer protections provided by these programs, the crisis of pauperism and destitution slowed, and a safety net was provided for most Orange Countians.

Based on the responses of Orange County's civic and business leaders, the most alarming aspect of the Depression crisis was the overwhelming number of white working and middle-class residents who fell into poverty between 1930 and 1934. In meeting after meeting, welfare agencies, churches, and community groups stressed that most people in need of aid were upstanding citizens who helped make Orange County the crown jewel of Southern California's citrus empire.[113] Though the region had experienced brief economic downturns before, the rapid development of the citrus industry from 1880 to 1930 tempered their effects. Thus, before the Great Depression, most Orange Countians knew little of the want and desperation that became all too familiar during the 1930s. Yet underneath the veneer of pre-Depression era growth and stability, poverty and inequality had always existed among a segment of the region's population. This was most evident in the fifty-three segregated ethnic Mexican neighborhoods and fifteen segregated Mexican schools in Orange County by 1930. As they overlapped with and, for a time, overshadowed the Mexican Problem narrative, the calls to aid "bona fide" white residents built on the self-indigenizing narratives of the Spanish and Anglo fantasy pasts to mark ethnic Mexican families as unworthy of public aid.

FORCED REMOVAL

Despite posting record profits in 1929 ($30 million), 1930 ($40 million), and 1931 ($35 million), citrus revenues collapsed in 1932 and did not return to their pre-depression levels until a decade later.[114] As the depression crisis deepened in Orange County, the jobs occupied by Mexicans, once deemed deplorable to most self-respecting whites, suddenly became desirable again. Yet the problem remained: too many workers and not enough jobs. This was not an entirely new development, as grower associations orchestrated the oversupply of Mexican labor in previous decades to maintain the desired availability of field labor to meet the industry's seasonal needs and fluctuations while keeping wages low. Thus, what had been viewed as an asset to the agricultural sector between 1900 and 1930 became a liability to municipal and county governments after the industry's collapse in 1932.

Facing public pressure to provide jobs for white families, county officials embraced a federally sponsored campaign to intimidate and remove ethnic Mexicans from jobs and relief aid. This was a tricky situation for citrus capitalists enriched by the industry's dependence on Mexican family labor for nearly twenty years. However, to preserve their influence over the regional economy, county officials caved to public pressure and participated in the scapegoating and selective removal of Mexican families. From the outset, the County Board of Supervisors charged the Department of Social Welfare with working with federal immigration officials to identify and coordinate the repatriation, or "coerced removal," of Mexican nationals to Mexico.[115] Shortly after the department's establishment in March 1932, Director Byron V. Curry joined Santa Ana Postmaster Terry Stephenson and local Congressman Phil D. Swing to petition the US Immigration Service to open a regional office in Santa Ana. As the *Santa Ana Register* reported on April 26, immigration inspectors had been "working in cooperation with the county welfare department" in recent months "in connection with the return of Mexicans to their own country." The inspectors, the *Register* speculated, would "deal largely with Mexican cases" and would be "authorized to handle all kinds of matters having to do with illegal entry and residence."[116] After Curry's request was approved, the US Immigration Service stationed two inspectors in Santa Ana, housing them in the county's recently opened federal office building.

The idea of removing ethnic Mexicans to reduce county relief rolls and free up jobs for white residents did not originate in Orange County. In 1929, President Herbert Hoover, under pressure from immigration restrictionists in the US Congress and interest groups like the American Federation of Labor and the Veterans of Foreign Wars, instructed Secretary of Labor William N. Doak to institute a deportation program that targeted ethnic Mexican laborers. Working with Director of Immigration Walter

Carr, Doak initiated a series of deportation sweeps that terrorized Mexican neighborhoods from the Pacific Coast to the Great Lakes and the Rio Grande Valley.[117] The most notorious raid occurred in Los Angeles on February 26, 1931. Under Carr's direction, immigration agents gathered in Los Angeles from San Francisco, San Diego, and Nogales, Arizona. After ten days of planning and coordinating with local law enforcement, immigration agents, police officers, and sheriff's deputies descended upon La Placita—the historic plaza in the heart of downtown Los Angeles—and began summarily rounding up anyone who looked Mexican and demanding proof of legal entry and residence. In all, 400 individuals were detained, although only seventeen—including eleven Mexicans, five Chinese, and one Japanese—were arrested. Despite the low number of arrests, the raid was an act of psychological warfare intended to strike fear in ethnic Mexican communities and to encourage them to self-deport.[118]

Viewing the growing number of deportation raids at job sites, neighborhoods, and public spaces as acts of intimidation and terror, ethnic Mexicans allied with Mexican Consular officials and sympathetic civic organizations to protest the actions of immigration agents and local law enforcement. Due mainly to this groundswell of opposition, which included complaints from employers, mass public raids like the one on La Placita ended in 1931. Even so, the national deportation program instituted by Secretary Doak continued until 1934, netting 50,000 deportees before tapering off by the middle of the decade.[119] As with the raid on La Placita, the deportation dragnet that swept the country from January to September of 1931 aimed to send a clear message to Mexicans that they were no longer welcome in the United States and should choose to leave voluntarily before being forced to do so.

Taking their cues from federal agencies like the Department of Labor and the Bureau of Immigration, local and state agencies nationwide began to encourage Mexicans to repatriate to Mexico voluntarily by January 1931. Again, Los Angeles provides a striking example of the lengths local and county officials were willing to go to remove Mexicans. Rex Thomson, Superintendent of the Los Angeles Department of Charities during the early to mid-1930s, orchestrated the county's repatriation effort. Believing conservative "economics . . . was the only one cure for this extreme so-called charity situation," Thomson was determined to reduce the number of Mexicans on relief to divert funds to white "middle aged people who had been thrifty and invested their funds in stocks and bonds and mortgages" whom through no fault of their own "were left without anything."[120]

Between 1931 and 1932, Thomson made several trips to Mexico to coordinate the transportation and reception of repatriates. He recalled, "I went to Mexico City and I told them that we would like to ship these people back, not to the border but from where they came from, or where the Mexicans would send them if we agreed it was a proper place."[121] After securing the Mexican government's cooperation, Thomson acquired funds from the state of California to help pay for the four trains that left Los Angeles' Union Station twice a week full of Mexican repatriates bound for border checkpoints in El Paso and Nogales. Employing social workers fluent in Spanish, Thomson coordinated his efforts with Ricardo Hill—the Mexican Consul in Los Angeles with whom Thomson developed a close personal friendship—along with other charitable and welfare agencies throughout the county to canvass Mexican neighborhoods with the "offer [of] repatriation."[122]

Although Thompson rebuffed implications that Mexicans were tricked or forced into agreeing to repatriation, Los Angeles County Supervisor John Anson Ford remembered things differently. In a 1971 interview, Ford recalled that the Board of Supervisors was under immense pressure from the Chamber of Commerce, the "big tax paying interests," who were "afraid that our welfare loads were going to get so big that it would be unbearable." In responding to the Chamber's concerns by instituting the repatriation program, Ford felt "the material motivation was stronger than the human-itarian."[123] Commenting on the actions of the Department of Charities under Rex Thomson's leadership, Ford stated, "They went around and talked to them and made them think that they had to go back to Mexico." When asked why he felt this way, Ford responded:

> Well, that would be the natural procedure if you didn't have legal authorization. If you wanted to get rid of [Mexicans] that would be the natural procedure to make them think they were here illegally. You see, when you're dealing with poor people without much education you can, under circumstances like this, put over your program without necessarily having all the legal authority to do so.[124]

To his great regret, Ford looked upon the repatriation of Los Angeles's Mexican residents as part of "the same piece of cloth," or "mistaken psy-chology" that resulted in the "Bum Blockade" of February 1936, where destitute Dust Bowl migrants were prevented from entering the county by the LAPD, and the internment of Japanese Americans and immigrants during World War II. "It's all a part of the same philosophy," Ford explained, "the failure to recognize citizens' rights and human rights."[125] In all, Thomson estimated that "over thirty-some thousand families" were repatriated from Los Angeles County "back to their homes of origin" and that, in his estimation, "repatriation was a good thing for Mexico and a good thing for us."[126]

It is unclear to what extent developments in Los Angeles County influenced the decisions of Orange County officials regarding Mexican repatriation. Although the counties bordered each other, the conditions in Orange County differed from those in Los Angeles. Not only was the county much larger than its southern neighbor, but its economy, which was less dependent on commercial agriculture, was more adversely affected by the Depression and suffered from higher levels of unemployment. Although more ethnic Mexicans lived in Los Angeles County (167,024 to 17,714), they comprised a larger proportion of the population in Orange County (15% to Los Angeles's 7.6%).[127] This increased visibility made Mexicans more susceptible to attack and mistreatment. Differences aside, leaders of industry and county government corresponded frequently throughout the 1930s. This was particularly true for the Chamber of Commerce and Board of Supervisors, whose members formed cooperative organizations, like the Associated Chambers of Commerce and the California Supervisors Association, which held regular meetings in downtown Los Angeles.[128] Correspondence between members of these and other like-minded organizations is informative as it provides insight into the close relationship maintained by key figures within government and industry who shared similar views on Mexican repatriation.[129]

In addition to industry and county government, the Mexican Consulate provided a third connection between those most directly involved in the efforts to repatriate Mexicans in Los Angeles and Orange County. As early as 1930, the Mexican Consulate in Los Angeles worked with disenchanted Mexican nationals who wanted to return to Mexico after experiencing discrimination from employers and county relief officials.[130] As intermediaries between Mexicans and county agencies, consular officials tried to ensure that repatriation was orderly and just.[131] Due to its large expatriate community, Orange County's colonias and barrios maintained regular contact with and received occasional visits from consular representatives in Los Angeles.[132] Santa Ana resident Lucas Lucio, president of the Mexican Honorary Committee, was considered Orange County's de facto consular representative. Working from the law office of William Burke, a Santa Ana-based attorney sympathetic to the Mexican community, Lucio served as the unofficial intermediary between the Consulate and Orange County Mexicans on issues of prejudice and discrimination.[133]

With the Depression worsening in 1932, Orange County officials followed Los Angeles's lead by instituting a repatriation program. As in Los Angeles, key figures in this effort held positions of power within the Board of Supervisors, Department of Social Welfare, and Chamber of Commerce. Although opinions varied among citrus capitalists, the loudest and most influential voices favored repatriation, including some within the Chamber of Commerce who wanted to "send the dirty Mexicans home!"[134] As in Los Angeles, the Mexican Consul sought to ensure fair treatment of its citizens, so it tapped Lucas Lucio to serve as Repatriation Coordinator and to accompany "three trains, carrying approximately 2,500 people in all, to Mexico." During one trip, Lucio recalled that a train full of Mexican repatriates from Santa Ana traveled to Los Angeles, where it was "hooked to another section of cars filled with Mexicans who were also being repatriated."[135] Recalling the mood of those onboard, Lucio stated that "the majority of men were very quiet and pensive" while "most of the women and children were crying."[136] Upon reaching the border, Lucio heard a "terrible cry among the repatriates" who "did not want to cross the border because they had daughters or sons who had stayed behind."[137]

Recollections like Lucio's are essential to recovering the lost history of Orange County's efforts to remove ethnic Mexicans during the Depression. There is scant mention of repatriation in regional newspapers and county archives, but oral histories have preserved their occurrence and the trauma experienced by those who witnessed them firsthand.[138] Born in El Paso, Texas, to Mexican immigrants from Guanajuato, Alfred Munoz was between the ages of ten and eleven during the early years of the Depression. Shortly after his birth, Alfred's family moved to El Modena, CA, where his father and two brothers worked as orange pickers. During the 1930s, Alfred remembered that El Modena "was nothing but a citrus town" and that "there were very few jobs around."[139] Despite the scarcity of employment, the combined wages of Alfred's father and brothers kept the family off public relief. This, however, was not the situation for many families who struggled desperately to provide for themselves on reduced work. "People were going hungry," Alfred recalled, "so they just packed them into trains and threw them across the border."[140] The "they" Alfred referred to included county officials who viewed the removal of ethnic Mexicans—regardless of citizenship and legal status—as the easiest way to reduce the county's welfare burden. Even for those like Alfred's family, who chose to remain in Orange County—opting to ignore or refuse the persistent overtures of county officials who offered to pay for their fare back to Mexico— the image of train cars full of friends and loved ones became indelibly marked in both individual and collective memory.[141]

LOS REPATRIADOS: THE LOST MEXICANS OF ORANGE COUNTY'S BASTANCHURY RANCH

Another dark memory preserved almost entirely by oral histories was the fate of the 400 to 600 ethnic Mexicans living in six work camps on the massive 6,000-acre Bastanchury Ranch near Fullerton. Domingo Bastanchury was one of the first Europeans to settle in the hills of Fullerton during the 1870s where he worked as a sheepherder for the Stearns Rancho Company. Before he died in 1909, Domingo purchased enough property from the Stearns holdings to amass a valuable real estate portfolio of petroleum, livestock, grain, and dairy farming interests.[142] After his death, three of Domingo's sons, Gaston, Joseph, and John, formed the Bastanchury Ranch Company and leveraged their holdings to facilitate the transition from livestock and grain to citrus and tomato farming. In partnership with the Union Oil Company, the Bastanchury brothers developed 2,600 acres of Valencia oranges and lemons between Fullerton and La Habra, creating "the world's largest orange and lemon orchard."[143] By the early 1920s, the Bastanchurys were Southern California royalty, "famous" for their "beautiful orange plantation," extravagant living, and lavish weekend parties.[144]

The society pages and industry publications praising brothers Gaston, Joseph, and John for their vision and grit that generated their real estate, petroleum, and citrus empire overlooked the fact that their Mexican labor force lived in squalor. Distributed among six work camps—Tia Juana, Mexicali, Escondido, Coyote, Santa Fe, and San Quintín/El Hoyo—the Bastanchury Mexicans, as county officials and Americanization teachers referred to them, were among the most impoverished group of residents in Orange County. According to Druzilla Mackey, Director of the Department of Americanization at Fullerton High School:

> It was the policy of [the Bastanchury Ranch] company to allow any Mexican who could find sufficient scraps of sheet iron, discarded fence-posts and sign-boards to build a shelter, to establish himself on the ranch. The largest of these camps, called Little Tia Juana . . . [was] served by one lone water faucet and a few makeshift privies. And this was only one of six similar colonies scattered over the largest orange ranch in the world. Its owners had the old-world feudalistic attitude toward their farm hands. They felt generous in allowing these squatters to establish homes on their ranch and could not comprehend its danger to the health and morality of the community as a whole.[145]

Having worked as an Americanization teacher in Los Angeles and Orange counties over the previous decade, Mackey was among the most qualified in the region to make such an assessment of the Bastanchury situation. In 1920, after spending eight years teaching in the "foreign schools of Los Angeles," Mackey was selected by George Hodgkin, head of the Labor Relations Department of the California Fruit Grower's Exchange (a.k.a. Sunkist), to lead a new education program in La Habra's Mexican work camps. Known as the "La Habra Experiment," Mackey worked with the La Habra Citrus Association, Fullerton Union High School, and the La Habra Grammar School to establish an Americanization center that taught English, cooking, sewing, and other Anglo-American cultural practices to the area's three Mexican colonias, Campo Colorado, Campo Corona, and Alta Vista.[146]

By 1922, the La Habra experiment was deemed a success by local educators, civic leaders, and the heads of the La Habra Citrus Association. After two years of work, male Mexican laborers and their spouses were attending classes regularly, learning English, and adopting Anglo-American customs. By contemporary standards, La Habra's Mexicans were "assimilating" to the extent that local officials no longer viewed the Mexican population as a "problem" but "now spoke . . . with paternal pride of . . . 'Our' Mexican camp."[147] Due to the success of the La Habra experiment, Mackey was asked by Fullerton Union High School officials to expand the program to other Mexican communities within the school district's boundaries, which included most of Fullerton, La Habra, and Placentia. In addition to the La Habra Citrus Association, the Placentia Orange Grower's Association was among the largest grower cooperatives in the region. Sprawling over eight square miles, the Bastanchury Ranch comprised parts of La Habra and Fullerton and was included in the Fullerton Union High School district.

After another four years of working on expanding Americanization programs among the Maple and Truslo Mexican colonies in Fullerton and the La Jolla barrio in Placentia, Mackey recalled "discover[ing] several little-known Mexican camps far back in the hills of Bastanchury Ranch."[148] Having worked among the "model" camps provided for Mexican workers by the La Habra and Placentia grower's associations, Mackey was appalled by the site of makeshift "hovels," lacking the basics of sturdy wood framing, running water, flush toilets, and electricity.[149] Mackey was not alone in responding to the conditions Mexicans were forced to endure on Bastanchury Ranch. Elsie Carlson, another Americanization teacher who spent six years working at the Ranch School located on the Bastanchury property, remembered feeling like a "missionary" as she traveled to the secluded camps over a "winding road" that was "quite slippery during rainy weather."[150] Both Carlson and fellow Americanization teacher Arletta

Kelly confirmed Mackey's assessment of "helter-skelter"-like housing, with "dirt floors" and "poor ventilation."[151] After seven years of working with the state Commission of Immigration and Housing, Mackey and her Americanization workers were able to pressure the Bastanchury family to build "suitable homes for their laborers, provided with plenty of toilets and running water."[152]

With adequate housing in place, Mackey recalled that the work of Americanization progressed smoothly. Like La Habra and other parts of Fullerton and Placentia, "the work on Bastanchury Ranch became a genuine success."[153] To their surprise, Mackey, Carlson, and Kelly were not the only ones doing the teaching. In oral history interviews and newspaper articles, each former teacher fondly remembered the generosity and hospitality shown by the Bastanchury Mexicans. Moreover, Mackey and Kelly were entranced by the beauty of Mexican culture. "In our neighborly intercourse," Mackey recalled, "they always taught me more than I did them."[154] Similarly, in an oral history interview conducted thirty-five years after her time on the ranch, Kelly's comments revealed the two-way process of cultural exchange that occurred between Americanization teachers and Mexican households. Although hired to teach Mexicans how to speak, cook, and sew according to Anglo-American cultural norms, Kelly's favorite memories included improving her ability to speak Spanish, participating in Mexican cultural celebrations, and learning to cook traditional dishes like nopalitos and "different kinds of soup and many things that we don't think of as being particularly Mexican."[155] Ironically, while it was Mackey and Kelly whose job it was to teach "these poverty-stricken people," both remembered how their Mexican hosts discovered that they were not paid very much. In addition to being "invited to eat one good hot meal every day in some one or other of the houses," Mackey recalled years later that a group of Mexican women organized colonia residents to provide "neighborly aid until I could support myself. One brought me a quart of milk, every day, others fresh corn and one good friend brought me two fresh eggs each morning during the whole of my stay in the camp."[156]

Despite their efforts to adopt American practices and provide the labor needed to turn Fullerton's barren hills into one of the world's largest and most productive orange groves, the Bastanchury Mexicans were cast off once the Depression hit. The day of reckoning came in October of 1931 when the *Fullerton News Tribune* revealed that brothers Gaston, Joseph, and John were nearly 2 million dollars in debt and had defaulted on a $750,000-second mortgage.[157] As a result, the Bastanchury Ranch was placed into receivership, and virtually all work came to a halt as bankruptcy proceedings dragged on for two years.[158] Although theories abound about the cause of the ranch's demise, the most likely scenario appears to have resulted from a mixture of over-indebtedness and underproduction. Ignoring warnings from "old-timers," who cautioned that the property's rugged hills and somewhat steep terrain were poorly suited for the cultivation of citrus, the Bastanchury brothers buried themselves in debt to transform their barren property into the envy of citrus cultivators across the world.[159] While the Bastanchurys overestimated the property's productive capacity, the land was not necessarily bad. After emerging from bankruptcy under new management, the Bastanchury property continued to produce into the late 1940s.[160]

This last point provides essential context for the actions of county officials during the aftermath of the Bastanchurys' fall from grace. Whereas the county allowed the Bastanchurys' to run their citrus empire as they pleased, ignoring the conditions Mexicans were forced to endure, county officials decided that repatriating the entire workforce was in everybody's best interest as soon as the family was out of the way. Druzilla Mackey recalled the county's actions as follows:

> In this time of stress and strain the American community no longer spoke of "Our" Mexicans. They no longer considered that no "whiteman" could pick our oranges. Instead they felt that the jobs done so patiently by Mexicans for so many years should now be given to them. "Those" Mexicans instead of "Our" Mexicans should "all be shipped right back to Mexico where they belong." The Americanization centers in which these people had been taught how to buy homes and make themselves a part of the American community were now used for calling together assemblies in which county welfare workers explained to bewildered audiences that their small jobs would now be taken over by the white men, that they were no longer needed nor wanted in these United States. They explained that the Welfare Department no longer had money to aid them during times of unemployment, but would furnish them a free trip back to Mexico. And so—one morning we saw nine train loads of our dear friends roll away back to the windowless, dirt-floored homes we had taught them to despise.[161]

Regarding the removal of the Bastanchury Mexicans, the *Fullerton News Tribune* reported:

> Nine carloads of Mexicans, including 427 adults and children—mostly children—were deported from Orange county today to points on the Mexican border, where they were to re-enter their native country. Thus the county welfare department unburdened itself to an appreciable extent of a "relief" load. The trainload has been living in this county and their deportation represents "relief" to the taxpayers, according to Byron Curry, county welfare director.[162]

To Orange County Mexicans, the image of train cars full of friends and family members became seared into their collective memory, a painful reminder of the disdain county officials placed on their contributions to the region's growth and development before the Depression. Make no mistake, there would have been no citrus industry in Orange County, or any other part of Southern California, without Mexican labor. As illustrated by Bastanchury Ranch, citrus farming was a risky, time-consuming, and costly venture. And Mexican immigrant labor was essential to the industry's productivity and profitability. Contrary to the scornful sentiment expressed in the *Fullerton News Tribune*, unemployed Mexican laborers did nothing to justify their removal. Moreover, the newspaper erred in referring to Mexicans as being "deported." Although most Orange County Mexicans lacked US citizenship and were classified as un-naturalized "aliens" under US immigration law, most were legal residents.[163] To the chagrin of county officials and immigration officers, Mexicans who had resided in the county, state, or nation longer than five years were ineligible for deportation.[164] Repatriation, more accurately remembered by Mexican *repatriados* as "banishment" and forced removal, was a racist and unjust attempt to appease white residents and laborers.[165] It reflected the apartheid-like social and physical divisions within Orange County, where ethnic Mexicans were perpetually viewed as foreign and disposable.

Ironically, approximately six months after nine train loads of repatriated Mexicans left Santa Ana, the Bastanchury Ranch was back in business under new management. Announcing the resumption of operations under Sunnyhills Ranch Inc., the *Fullerton News Tribune* reported, "All of the Mexican camps on the ranch have been eliminated and all American labor is being used with 28 houses on the ranch now filled by regular employees, nearly all of whom have been continuously on the payroll since last April."[166] Indeed, within a month of their removal, Mexican laborers had been replaced by "American" (i.e., white) laborers doing the very same work for higher wages. Considering this gross injustice, when Druzilla Mackey was asked to reflect on the "lasting values" and influence of her time spent as an Americanization teacher, she lamented, "*Quien Sabe*" (Who knows?).[167]

POLICING BROWN BODIES DURING THE DEPRESSION

As with other accounts of Mexican repatriation, it is nearly impossible to accurately determine how many ethnic Mexicans "returned" to Mexico from Orange County during the 1930s. For some, the decision to leave did not involve government-sponsored agencies like the Mexican Consulate or county welfare officials. These individuals and families packed their belongings and left without assistance. They were not counted in consulate and county records, which placed the number of Mexican repatriates at 1,543 during the years 1930–1933.[168] However, historians believe the number of removals was much higher, between 2,000 and 2,500 (11% to 14% of the ethnic Mexican population in the county).[169] While accounts of similar efforts in Los Angeles and other parts of Southern California date county-sponsored repatriation drives as occurring primarily between 1931 and 1934, repatriation continued to be openly advocated by Orange County officials until 1939.[170] Following a sharp decline in "voluntary" repatriations, county officials worked with the Bureau of Immigration to remove Mexicans through formal deportation proceedings. After opening a field office in Santa Ana in the spring of 1932, immigration agents conducted regular sweeps of job sites in search of potential deportees. One such raid occurred in December 1932 when the Orange County sheriff's department joined immigration agents on a raid of El Modena labor contractor Gilberto Gamez. After questioning 200 persons, twelve were detained and scheduled for immigration hearings on the charge of illegal entry.[171]

Working with the Board of Supervisors and county officials in the Department of Social Welfare, immigration agents established a countywide network of informants, including residents, municipal employees, the Chamber of Commerce, and local law enforcement. This work was of such "inestimable service" to the county that in November 1935, the Board of Supervisors begged federal officials not to close the immigration office in Santa Ana, citing the agency's close "cooperation with the law enforcement officers of Orange County."[172] According to the *Santa Ana Register*, between 1933 and 1939, immigration officials acted on "rumor" and "secret information" to expand their sweeps from large-scale raids to targeted arrests at homes, public spaces, and the county jail.[173] Additionally, immigration agents received regular reports from local officials administering jobs and relief in association with WPA. This information was used to identify "foreign-born workers . . . from Mexico," who were "checked" to see if they were in the country legally. As the *Santa Ana Register* reported in January 1937, cooperation between Franklyn Davis, chief inspector for the US Immigration Service in Orange County, and Dan Mulherron, head of the WPA in Orange County, resulted in "several aliens [being] deported."[174] Between 1933 and 1938, these efforts netted an average of 100 deportations annually in Orange County.[175]

Wholly unprepared to handle the depression crisis, Orange County's citrus capitalists chose the path of least resistance by scapegoating and removing ethnic Mexicans. Seeking to deflect the desperation, criticism, and anger of "depression-frightened tax-payers" incensed over the proliferation of white poverty, county officials turned their backs on the very people they had relied on to transform Orange County into one of the most lucrative agricultural regions in the nation.[176] Why this course of action? Undoubtedly, regional boosters knew they could not remove all 18,000 to 25,000 ethnic Mexicans, most of whom were either legal residents or US citizens.[177] Since ethnic Mexicans comprised 15 percent to 21 percent of the county's population during the 1930s, not only was such a task legally, logistically, and financially impossible, but as evidenced by Governor C.C. Young's report, doing so would be detrimental to the citrus industry. Equally dubious were calls to remove the so-called illegal portion of the Mexican population. Alleged to be as much as half of all ethnic Mexicans in the region, most of this group was "not necessarily subject to deportation" and was needed for their labor in the citrus industry, which, even amidst declining revenues, remained profitable throughout the Depression.[178] Understanding that the large-scale removal of the ethnic Mexican population was impractical and improbable, county officials pursued limited removal as a form of labor control, hoping to appease white residents and reduce the county's ballooning debt burden.[179]

Although not unlike other cities and counties with high proportions of ethnic Mexicans that pursued similar courses of action, the irony within Orange County is that white, brown, or otherwise, the vast majority of residents were not native to the county or state.[180] Indeed, within one generation (1900–1930), Orange County's population had increased nearly ninefold.[181] Whether they arrived from domestic or international sending regions, virtually every Orange Countian was a "foreigner." Yet, despite sharing in this regional history of migration, settlement, and place-making, Mexicans were not included in white citizens' visions of nation, region, and community. Having migrated from predominantly white regions in the Midwest and Northeast, white Orange Countians carried predetermined notions of their "imagined communities" to the Santa Ana Valley.[182] While the early years of regional development presented moments of cultural syncretism when white migrants sought to establish themselves in an unfamiliar landscape, the actions of citrus capitalists and law enforcement during the 1920s and 1930s established an apartheid-like social and physical landscape that reflected the racial and national divisions symbolized by the US-Mexico border.

As a result, although they came from various ethnic and geographic backgrounds, Orange County's Anglo/European residents consolidated white identity, making it synonymous with notions of "Americanness" and

US citizenship, particularly as it related to claiming benefits from the New Deal state.[183] Although this was intended to exclude ethnic Mexicans, it had the unintended consequence of spurring increasing levels of civic engagement and political action among that group. Born out of their experiences with racialization and discrimination during the 1920s and 1930s, Orange County Mexicans embraced an oppositional form of ethnic identity that viewed "Mexicanness" as a source of pride while fusing it with a sense of belonging in the United States[184] Born and raised in El Modena between 1925 and 1942, Bob Torres reflected on the merging of identities, cultures, and nationalities that occurred among Orange County Mexicans during this period:

> I've always felt that I'm a Mexican. I've always felt that I can mix within any group. I think I'm flexible enough to mix with the Anglo or the Mexican in Mexico or here. I feel I carry . . . a cross etched on [my] back that says Mexican . . . everyone identifies me as a Mexican, so I feel very Mexican. If people ask me what I am I tell them I'm Mexican. And if they want to go deeper and ask me a citizen of what country . . . I tell them I'm an American.[185]

On March 21, 1939, Lucas Lucio, a leader in the ethnic Mexican community of Santa Ana, announced the formation of a "civil rights committee composed of members of 49 Orange County Mexican organizations." As the *Orange Daily News* reported, this development aimed to assist Orange County authorities in "handling problems of Mexican people."[186] Thus, it was during the 1930s that Orange County Mexicans began to express a politics of opposition that merged Mexican ethnicity and racialization with rights-based claims to belonging in the US nation-state. Whether foreign or domestic-born, the increased levels of ethnic Mexican civic engagement and political action simultaneously appropriated and transformed Orange County according to a pluralist vision of space, place, culture, and belonging.

CHAPTER 3

Mobilizing Against the Walls of Segregation

It will not be very long before politically-minded groups and individuals will attempt to appeal to the Mexican vote in the city, county, and state. Mexican Americans may someday surprise certain smug factions that are certainly not trying to avert such a possibility. Mexican candidates for public office in certain fields will offer a very uncomfortable and close competition.

Stephen Reyes, The Mexican Voice, 1940

Four days before the county general election on November 6, 1934, *El Anunciador Mexicano*, a Spanish-language newspaper serving Orange County's fifty-three barrios and colonias, appealed to "the Spanish speaking people of Santa Ana." Referring to the forthcoming election, the editorial implored:

> On November 6, you will go to the polls to vote. If you want a friend in the court, one which you can count on for counsel at any time and one who will treat you like any other American, you should vote Charles F. Mitchell for Constable. Born in Santa Ana, he knows of your problems and needs. If you deal with him you will find courtesy and kindness. There have been men in power who have abused the Mexican community's lack of knowledge of the law. If Charles Mitchell is elected, everyone will be treated fairly. Mitchell will . . . always be our friend. Vote him Constable on the 6th of November and you will not regret it.[1]

El Anunciador Mexicano call to get out the vote for Mitchell occurred amidst the peak of anti-Mexican hysteria marked by immigration raids, forced

Breaking Down the Walls of Segregation. David-James Gonzales, Oxford University Press.
© Oxford University Press 2025. DOI: 10.1093/9780197839485.003.0004

removals, and increasing labor tensions during the early to mid-1930s. Referring to the ethnic Mexican community's desire for equal treatment, the editorialist presented Mitchell as an ally who would be mindful of the county's largest demographic minority. Elected by a narrow 2.5 percent margin, Mitchell's victory was secured with the aid of an ethnic Mexican swing vote that tipped the election in his favor.[2] More importantly, voter turnout among Orange County Mexicans during the 1934 November election signaled an emerging political consciousness that viewed participation in civic matters and electoral politics as a means of responding to the walls of segregation erected by citrus capitalists.

A vital part of the increased engagement of ethnic Mexicans in civic affairs and politics included the development of nonpartisan grassroots organizations during the 1920s and 1930s. This chapter details the growth of two of these organizations, La Sociedad Progresista Mexicana (Mexican Progressive Society) and the Mexican American Movement (MAM). Established in 1929, La Progresista was like other mutual aid societies that existed in barrios and colonias throughout the Southwest. It provided life insurance, death benefits, and small loans to its membership and organized cultural and patriotic celebrations in association with the Mexican Consulate. However, unlike most of their contemporaries, Progresistas embraced a bilingual, binational, and bicultural identity, opting to conduct English and Spanish meetings and directly engage in civics and politics beyond the barrio/colonia. The second organization, MAM, began as the Mexican Youth Conference sponsored by the Young Men's Christian Association (YMCA) during the mid-1930s. Like La Progresista, MAM developed out of the ethnic Mexican experience in Southern California, with much of its membership coming from barrios and colonias throughout the citrus belt. As the first youth-led movement organized by ethnic Mexicans, MAM was comprised of high school and college students and young professionals identifying as Mexican American. While differing in age and generational experiences, La Progresista and MAM promoted education as a pathway toward racial uplift and self-improvement. Additionally, both organizations developed into translocal movements that connected ethnic Mexicans across urban, suburban, and rural spaces in Los Angeles, Orange, San Bernardino, and Riverside counties.[3] Existing scholarship in MAM's development and contributions has not fully reflected the importance of these organizations and their members in the politicization of ethnic Mexicans in Orange County and their broader contributions to Chicana/o politics and activism.

For Orange County Mexicans, grassroots organizations like La Progresista and MAM provided the space to educate and mobilize themselves in response to everyday racism and discrimination. The involvement of Orange County Mexicans in La Progresista and MAM illustrates the immediacy of ethnic Mexicans in responding to their marginalization by the racial capitalist system imposed by citrus agriculture. As this chapter shows, ethnic Mexicans mobilized across urban, rural, and suburban spaces that were built to constrain agency and mobility, and in doing so began organically to build a civil rights movement without precedence or help from national organizations. These early mobilizations established a culture of grassroots civic engagement and political activism among Orange County Mexicans that led to future efforts to desegregate schools and engage more directly in electoral politics. Their activities challenge the "conservative" representation of moderate activists and organizations like La Progresista and MAM within the generational framework of Chicana/o history. The sociohistorical context of Orange County is crucial to these civil rights claims, as the social and political landscape there differed significantly from Los Angeles. With its more diverse economy and population, Los Angeles was not dominated by a single industry, nor was it as racially stratified as Orange County. These two differences alone presented tremendous challenges for activists and organizations that dared to challenge the power and influence of citrus capitalists over the local economy and regional governance.

In assessing the early grassroots organizations that emerged in Orange County from the late 1920s to the late 1940s, this chapter interprets ethnic Mexican civic engagement and political action along a continuum of Chicana/o-Latina/o politicization that belies simplistic labeling as conservative, moderate, or radical. Regardless of age, class, citizenship status, and familiarity with US institutions, Orange County Mexicans were bold and innovative in confronting the walls of segregation through grassroots organizations like La Progresista and MAM. They did not need to "assimilate" to learn how to resist, organize, and struggle for fairness in the workplace, schoolhouse, and community. Without assistance from outside activists and organizations, Orange County Mexicans built their own unprecedented movement that responded immediately and vociferously to segregation, labor exploitation, and political marginalization. As in other parts of the country, the 1920s and 1930s marked the beginning of the "long civil rights movement" in Orange County.[4]

LA SOCIEDAD PROGRESISTA MEXICANA

At least a decade before the Mexican civil rights committee was formed in 1939 by Lucas Lucio and representatives of forty-nine local *mutualistas*,

Orange County Mexicans were central in establishing one of the oldest and largest mutual aid societies in the United States.[5] Initially formed in 1911 and reorganized in 1929, La Sociedad Progresista Mexicana spread throughout the barrios and colonias of Southern California until it reached a membership of over 10,000 individuals and sixty-seven *logias* (lodges) by 1966. According to its founders, the organization "was the product of social upheaval" and "was born of injustice."[6] While the mention of social upheaval and injustice may have referred to general conditions of poverty and marginalization experienced by ethnic Mexicans throughout the Southwest, a specific incident prompted the founding of this society.

In 1911, a group of Mexican American community leaders was walking to San Bernardino when they found a dead Mexican man lying in the street. Realizing that the body was left there intentionally and had gone unassisted by local agencies, the group formed *La Sociedad de Zaragoza* (The Zaragoza Society) to protect their members from suffering similar injustices.[7] Initially, the group operated informally, collecting donations at meetings whenever a fraternal brother or sister died. In time, divisions arose between those who desired to incorporate as a mutual society and others who were satisfied with the status quo. On April 6, 1929, the more "progressive" faction, which included approximately 300 members and the former president of the Zaragoza Society, filed articles of incorporation in Los Angeles County.[8] They called their new group La Sociedad Progresista Mexicana. Through subsequent meetings in San Bernardino, Watts, Pomona, and Colton, the group planned to grow its membership to 1000 members and launched a fundraising campaign to acquire the $20,000 necessary to formalize the society's charter with the state Department of Insurance.[9] By October 16, 1929, La Sociedad Progresista Mexicana surpassed its membership and fundraising goals and was formally "incorporated in California as a non-profit, beneficial society."[10]

The establishment of La Progresista involved hundreds of individuals from barrios and colonias throughout Southern California. Among the founding chapters established between April and November of 1929, five were in Orange County, including Lodge No. 13 in Santa Ana, Lodge No. 14 in Garden Grove, Lodge No. 16 in Placentia, Lodge No. 17 in Stanton, and Lodge No. 25 in Westminster. Over the next decade, this number expanded to eight with the additions of Lodge No. 24 in Anaheim (originally organized in West Los Angeles), Lodge No. 33 in Placentia (the second in that town), and Lodge No. 43 in El Modena.[11] Like the broader organization, the men and women who formed lodges in Orange County had previously led patriotic committees, benefit societies, church groups, and labor unions to better life within and beyond the barrio and colonia. Emerging from a rich history of ethnic Mexican community organizing, La Sociedad Progresista Mexicana established a broad agenda of social, cultural, and political goals that envisioned their full participation as equal citizens and residents in Orange County.

For its motto, La Progresista chose *Educacion, Respeto, y Patriotismo* (Education, Respect, and Patriotism), emphasizing the organization's focus on community uplift through self-education, self-respect, and collective pride in their binational and bicultural heritage. The emphasis on these "standards," as Progresistas referred to them, directly challenged the discrimination and marginalization produced by citrus capitalism. It was not coincidental then that twenty-five of the thirty-one lodges established between 1929 and 1939 were in citrus-growing districts, with the remainder near communities also dominated by commercial agriculture.[12] Housed, educated, and employed in segregated neighborhoods, schools, and work sites, Progresistas strove to transform their relationship to these spaces, refashioning them into sites of collective empowerment. Consisting of both Mexican immigrants and Mexican Americans, the organization "maintained alive within its members the beautiful and harmonious Spanish language . . . even though the majority of its associates [spoke English] the language of [their] country by adoption or birth."[13]

In contrast to contemporary Mexican-Americanist organizations, like LULAC, La Progresista conducted meetings almost entirely in Spanish and chose the Mexican flag as the basis of their logo. Further, each lodge named itself after a Mexican national hero.[14] For example, Santa Ana Lodge No. 13 "chose . . . the clear and illustrious liberal, Don Melchor Ocampo, a key figure in the War of Reformation" (Mexican War of Independence) and "the right arm of Mr. Benito Juarez from 1857–1860."[15] Placentia Lodge No. 16 named itself "La Gran Tenochtitlán" (The Great Tenochtitlán) after the Aztec capital city; Westminster Lodge No. 25 was named for "General Mariano Escobedo . . . the brilliant soldier of the Republic" during "the war against the United States, 1846–1848" and El Modeno Lodge No. 43 was named after Ezequiel Padilla, former Mexican Attorney General (1928) and Secretary of Education (1928–1930).[16]

While Progresistas "spoke two languages, respected two flags [and] gave homage to the heroes of two great brother countries," their marginalization by white society sparked a desire to learn the history and culture of Mexico as an affirmative source of ethnic pride and identity.[17] Political scientist Lisa Garcia Bedolla refers to similar actions among minoritized populations as a process of producing "affective group attachment," where members of a stigmatized group use familial and communal networks to form a collective identity infused with a sense of efficacy and personal agency.[18] She argues further that efforts to instill pride and consciousness within minority communities through education create a "mobilizing identity" that increases political participation on behalf of the community's interests.[19] This is precisely what Progresistas were doing. By promoting respect and pride in their subjectivity as ethnic Mexicans in Orange County, Progresistas fashioned an identity infused with a political ethos that led them to believe their individual and collective actions would impact the social world around them.[20] Like Chicanos/as a generation later, Progresistas used self-education to establish a sense of historical consciousness that animated civic and political action unbeholden to a single political ideology or party.

During the decade prior to the founding of La Progresista, Orange County became increasingly segregated by the imposition of a white-brown color line. Emerging during this period of intense anti-Mexicanism, the formation of Progresista lodges in Orange County was, in fact, the "product of social upheaval" and "injustice."[21] From this vantage point, Progresistas emphasis on education, respect, and patriotism was not a form of escapism, nor was it a simple nostalgic longing for *"Mexico lindo"* (beautiful Mexico). Instead, Progresistas' use of education as a method of organization and mobilization is an example of the "migrant imaginary" theorized by borderlands scholar Alicia Schmidt Camacho. As border crossers and laborers exploited by transnational capitalism, Progresistas' actions reflected a "collective desire for a different order of space and belonging" that challenged the racial capitalist order in Orange County.[22] During the 1920s and 1930s, neither Mexico nor the United States fully incorporated migrant laborers as equal social and political subjects. In truth, both nation-states failed to uphold their end of the social contract with ethnic Mexican laborers.[23] Not content to merely dream of an alternative future, Progresistas put their vision into action to "produce forms of communal life and political organization" that manifested their "expansive definition of civic life and community that defied conventions of national citizenship.[24]

One of the first arenas in which ethnic Mexicans expanded the definition of civic life and community was by challenging the county's two-tiered education system. Beginning with the Santa Ana School District in 1912, Orange County schools formalized segregation by separating Mexican children into remedial classes apart from their white peers and later moved them into separate schools. In 1919, when the Santa Ana school board expanded their segregationist policy, members of the Mexican Pro-Patria Club (a precursor to La Sociedad Progresista Mexicana) organized parents and appeared before the school board with a petition that demanded an end to segregation.[25] While local officials circumvented state law and ignored the protests of Mexican parents, this early example of civic activism illustrates the awareness and commitment ethnic Mexicans placed on the education of their youth, as well as a willingness to engage in public protest long before the New Deal reform era.

By forming grassroots organizations like the Pro-Patria Club and La Progresista, Orange County Mexicans established spaces of empowerment where they gathered publicly to take pride in and expand their knowledge of Mexican history and culture. Placing these actions within the context of anti-Mexicanism and racial stigma in Orange County during the 1910s, 1920s, and 1930s is essential to evaluating their significance. Regardless of how radical or militant their actions seemed to later generations, these early efforts laid the foundation for ethnic Mexican identity and political action in the region.[26] For many members, La Progresista meetings provided the time and space to acquire knowledge and skillsets they had missed due to the lack of educational access and opportunity resulting from segregation. Although several of the leaders in the organization were literate, possessing varying degrees of education and professional skill, most Progresistas came from rural agricultural backgrounds in Mexico and the US where access to formal education was either nonexistent or substandard. Therefore, society meetings provided an informal education in Spanish, public speaking, and organizational leadership. At the beginning of each meeting, society members participated in opening rituals, like reciting the pledge of allegiance to both the Mexican and American flags, which paid "tribute to those Mexicans on this side and the other side of the Rio Grande."[27] Next, a review of the previous meeting's minutes would be read and approved. Following strict parliamentary procedures, meetings allowed members to educate themselves on current events, discuss and debate salient issues, and determine courses of action that benefited the barrio/colonia.

As a community-centered institution, La Progresista provided services and activities that exhibited an early approach to self-determination. In addition to offering essential financial services like insurance benefits, small loans, and short-term financing, La Progresista's most significant impact on its membership included opportunities to build individual and communal self-respect and confidence. According to a survey conducted in the early 1980s with longtime members, Progresistas "were equally pleased with the instructional rewards they received through participation and attendance in the affairs of the lodges." Pedro M. Anaya, secretary of Visalia Lodge No. 47, remembered, "the organization provide[d] . . . an opportunity to hear and practice Spanish. It provide[d] a forum and an opportunity for us to speak in a crowd" and "for Mexican Americans to develop their leadership skills."[28] Within Orange County's segregated society, which intentionally denied equity in educational instruction and facilities, as well as pathways to socioeconomic integration and mobility, La Progresista helped its members develop leadership skills that empowered them to engage in civics and politics within and beyond their neighborhoods.

During the Depression, Progresistas led and served their communities by representing them to local officials and agencies intent on excluding them from public assistance. Ironically, ethnic Mexicans were seemingly more prepared to cope with the Depression since the county's intentional marginalization and underdevelopment of their communities had conditioned them to establish organizations and institutions that responded to scarcity and crisis well before the 1930s. While the County Board of Supervisors and the Department of Social Welfare portrayed Mexicans as a disproportionate drain on county services, grassroots organizations, like La Progresista, actually donated money to the welfare department from their fundraising efforts.[29] Despite facing an unemployment rate that was twice that of their white counterparts, Orange County's Mexican barrios and colonias held fiestas, benefit dances, patriotic celebrations, and other social and cultural events that raised money for those in need within their communities.[30] Moreover, grassroots organizations worked with community leaders like Lucas Lucio to combat "racial prejudice" and the "falsifying of the Mexican relief situation" by the Santa Ana Chamber of Commerce.[31] In March 1939, these groups produced a financial accounting of the Mexican community's contributions to the county. As per their report, Orange County Mexicans held $10,000,000 in personal and business valuations, earned a combined $3,200,000 in yearly wages, and paid $437,500 in taxes annually.[32] Although County officials largely ignored these efforts, they illuminate how grassroots organizations like La Progresista mobilized to provide for and defend themselves.[33]

Even during the Depression's worst moments, like the Citrus Strike of 1935–1936 and the flood of 1938, Progresistas were among the leaders of the Mexican community who responded to these crises with cool heads. In the case of the strikes that began sporadically in 1935 before erupting in full force during the summer of 1936, leaders within La Progresista and the Mexican Honorary Commission strove to ease labor tensions, working as mediators between individual workers, labor unions, and growers. Mexican community leaders appealed to growers (often working through the Mexican Consulate) to address worker grievances, including demands to increase wages and end abusive industry practices like the bonus system and charging workers for tools and transportation. Before the strike broke out, Lucas Lucio reiterated that these exploitative practices led some workers to stay on relief rather than have "a sizeable slice of each day's wages" taken from their checks.[34] Growers, county officials, and law enforcement agencies responded to reports of citrus worker discontent and labor organizing by illegally surveilling gatherings, conducting raids and mass arrests, deporting alleged agitators, and enacting other forms of violence against Mexican workers.[35] By mid-June, a massive county-wide strike ensued, effectively shutting down the citrus industry and causing irreparable damage to Mexican workers and growers.[36] Instead of resolving the conflict impartially, the County Board of Supervisors met with grower association representatives and Sheriff Logan Jackson (also a citrus rancher) behind closed doors. At the time of the strike, three of the five members of the Board of Supervisors were citrus ranchers, including LeRoy E. Lyon (the "Supervisor from Sunkist") and Willard Smith (President of Villa Park Orchards Association and founding member of the anti-labor Orange County Farm Bureau). During the meeting, Supervisor Lyon "moved that the money be spent to provide necessary shotguns, revolvers, tear gas, and other such equipment as a permanent arsenal for Orange County."[37] On the heels of Sheriff Jackson's "Shoot to Kill" order, the Board of Supervisors passed an emergency resolution granting the Sheriff a virtual blank check to shut down the strike at all costs.[38] Due largely to the collusion between growers and local officials, moderates within the Mexican community, like Lucio, had difficulty containing the more militant factions of Mexican workers. Still, the leaders of organizations like La Progresista and the Mexican Honorary Commission played an essential role throughout the conflict. As leaders of grassroots organizations that predated the citrus strikes of 1935–1936, they had a history of working with growers and local officials that kept channels of communication open even when resolution seemed unlikely. Further, they made it clear that all Mexicans could not be lumped together as radicals, agitators, and indigents and secured legal representation and concessions from local officials that protected innocent bystanders and the falsely accused.

The 1938 flood of the Santa Ana River provides another example of Mexican grassroots organizations' essential role during crises. The flood was a disaster of historic proportions and is considered the worst weather event to affect the county during the twentieth century. Over six days, from February 27 to March 3, Orange County received eleven inches of rain, as much as it usually received in a year. According to one local historian, "At the peak of the flood, shortly after midnight on March 3, the roaring waters of the river debouched from Santa Ana Canyon at an estimated rate of 100,000 cubic feet per second!"[39] When the rain finally stopped, the runoff filled the county's lowland areas with flood water, creating a temporary lake stretching from Fullerton and Yorba Linda to Newport Beach. The total loss of property in the county amounted to $21.9 million and impacted everything from orange groves and other agricultural properties to roads, bridges, utilities, businesses, and homes.[40] Although the entire Southland incurred considerable damage, the Mexican communities of Atwood and La Jolla in northern Orange County were utterly wiped out. The *Santa Ana Register* captured some of the horror witnessed by residents of these communities on the front page of its March 4 edition:

> There was death and destruction . . . for Atwood yesterday. While rescue workers were combing ruins of the devastated Mexican settlement for bodies . . . it was impossible to make an accurate check of the dead and missing in Atwood up to a late hour yesterday. Two rescue workers said that 12 or 15 bodies had been removed from the debris and that only a portion of the stricken area had been searched. They said that the majority of bodies removed from the debris were those of children. The flood struck Atwood between 2 and 2:30 a.m. and the air was filled with the screams of women and children trapped by the raging torrent that poured down through the dry wash separating the Mexican colony from Atwood proper and by the rending of wood as houses crashed about their occupants. Late yesterday the banks of the wash were lined with Mexican people waiting for rescue workers to recover more bodies. Every face had a strained and stunned expression. Mothers and fathers who found their children safe held the babies a little tighter as other tiny bodies were removed from the mud and tangled debris. At La Jolla barrio near Atwood, houses were twisted and tangled into shapeless heaps. One Mexican man, who lived in the community, said that he did not know how many were missing from the colony. He did know that three of his friends, Mrs. Mary Ritano [*sic*] and her two children were missing.[41]

By the following day, the death toll reached fifty-eight, with the Retanas counted among the missing. The bodies of Maria Retana and her seven-year-old son Rolando were later found and buried alongside each other.[42] Tragically, the Retana family was one of several, like the Montanos and Barragans (also from Atwood) and the Castros from nearby Richfield, who lost multiple family members in the flood. Among the twenty-nine names of the known dead published by the *Santa Ana Register* on March 5, 69 percent had Spanish surnames, and most resided in or near the colonias of Atwood and La Jolla.[43] The loss of life in these communities was so great that a "mass funeral service" was held for them at the Fullerton cemetery two days later.[44]

It was no coincidence that Orange County's Mexican colonias sustained the most significant losses of life. Much of the tragedy could have

Figure 3.1 La Jolla barrio after the 1938 flood. Courtesy of Orange County Archives.

been averted had the county not permitted the intentional segregation and underdevelopment of Mexican neighborhoods, which lacked sewer and drainage systems, paved roads and sidewalks, and proper home foundations. Just one of these basic improvements would have saved several lives. Additionally, because they were built next to irrigation ditches, which served as de facto socioeconomic barriers, the colonias of Atwood and La Jolla were prone to flooding during periods of heavy rain and overirrigation.[45] For this reason, homes in La Jolla were connected to a metal chain staked to the ground to prevent them from floating away when the irrigation ditch overflowed.[46] Despite these circumstances, Mexican grassroots organizations were the first to respond during and after the tragedy. They who prevented an even greater loss of life by conducting search and rescue efforts and providing food, shelter, and financial assistance to hundreds.[47]

Through its many efforts to educate, serve, and uplift ethnic Mexicans, La Sociedad Progresista Mexicana projected an emancipatory vision of Orange County that countered the exploitative and segregationist institutions built by citrus capitalists. While La Progresista was not affiliated with other civil rights organizations, their actions connected them to previous generations of "oppressed people throughout the world" that also "exercise[d] genuine self-determination." Historian Paul Ortiz argues that groups like La Progresista are connected across time and place, forming a global social movement "born of centuries of struggle against slavery, colonialism, and oppression in the Americas."[48] From the late nineteenth to the twenty-first century, ethnic Mexicans and other working-class communities of color practiced what Ortiz calls "emancipatory internationalism" as they organized across social and physical borders in response to the "reconfiguration of racial capitalism."[49] By mobilizing in response to the inequities created and perpetuated by citrus capitalism, Progresistas were akin to other emancipatory organizations and movements. Lacking a model, they taught themselves "how to execute their rights and obligations as good citizens."[50] Likewise, Progresistas practiced the "politics of empowerment" described by anthropologist Ana Aparicio. Connecting "local organizing in the present to revolutionary leaders who demanded democracy" in Mexico, Progresista activism shifted "from [a] sole emphasis on 'homeland politics' . . . to include organizing to confront local issues."[51]

Over time, La Progresista grew into the largest ethnic Mexican organization in Orange County and perhaps California, involving others in its efforts. Such was the case in March 1939, when La Progresista joined forty-eight other ethnic Mexican grassroots associations to form the "civil rights committee" headed by Lucas Lucio.[52] Although the *Orange Daily News* reported the group's purpose was to "handle the problems of the Mexican people," as its name implies, the civil rights committee was actually formed to defend and advocate on behalf of ethnic Mexicans to local authorities.[53] Alongside other ethnic Mexican grassroots organizations in the county, La Progresista helped institutionalize a culture of civic engagement and community activism that was later pursued by groups like MAM, the Latin American Voters League, the El Modena Unity League, VCP, and LULAC. Further, some of its members carried the lessons learned in Progresista lodges into the armed forces as they fought in the Second World War. Others, like co-founder of El Modeno Lodge No. 43 and co-plaintiff in the class-action lawsuit *Mendez, et al. v. Westminster School District of Orange County, et al.* (1946–1947) Lorenzo Ramirez, continued the fight against the walls of segregation in Orange County.[54] Progresistas, therefore, illustrate that Orange County Mexicans were involved in the long civil rights movement well before returning Mexican American GIs formed postwar civil rights organizations like the American GI Forum (AGIF) and the Community Service Organization (CSO).

THE MEXICAN AMERICAN MOVEMENT

Another example of Orange County Mexicans mobilizing for civil rights during the 1930s is the formation and growth of the MAM, "the first

Figure 3.2 La Sociedad Progresista Mexicana at Our Lady of Guadalupe Church, La Jolla barrio, Placentia, CA, c. 1930. Courtesy of Yolanda Alvarez.

Chicano organization formed by and for students."[55] From its beginning, Mexican American youth in Orange County were central to MAM's development, which emerged from the YMCA sponsored Mexican Youth Conference started in 1934 by Tom Garcia.[56] With the aid and leadership of Orange County residents like Stephen A. Reyes (El Modena), Luis Sandoval (Anaheim), Gualberto "Bert" Valadez (Placentia), Ross P. and Mary Anne Chavolla (Placentia), Leonel Magana (Placentia), and many others, by the mid-1940s, MAM became a translocal Mexican American grassroots organization with chapters in California, Arizona, and New Mexico. Like La Progresista, MAM is important in the history and politicization of Orange County Mexicans for several reasons. First, the participation of ethnic Mexican youth in MAM illustrates the long history of organic grassroots resistance to and mobilization against citrus capitalism in the Santa Ana Valley.[57] Second, MAM is another example of how ethnic Mexican communities organized and mobilized in a translocal fashion, practicing a politics of mobility built on kinship, sociality, and labor networks that connected barrios and colonias throughout Southern California.[58] Third, MAM cultivated affective group attachment among Mexican American youth, which led to the formation of a new mobilizing identity and political ethos as Mexican American.[59] Finally, like Progresistas, MAM's membership helped solidify a culture of civic engagement and political participation among Orange County Mexicans that impacted and foreshadowed future generations.

As a translocal organization formed by Mexican American youth from colonias and barrios throughout Southern California, MAM sought to "solve the principal problems [that] thwarted the social and economic progress of many Mexican-Americans and Mexicans residing in the United States."[60] According to MAM's Handbook, these problems included "prejudice, segregation, discrimination, social inequality, and inferiority complex."[61] To articulate their solution to what they clearly understood were larger systemic issues impacting ethnic Mexican socioeconomic mobility, MAM leaders selected the slogan "progress through education" and encouraged its members to aspire to "higher educational achievements."[62] Through *The Mexican Voice*, a monthly newsletter begun in July 1938, Mexican Youth Conference leaders Felix Gutierrez, Manuel Ceja, and Jesse Aguirre kept conference participants informed of the group's activities throughout the year. The newsletter served as both a "forum for their ideas and opinions on the issues facing Mexican youth and the Mexican population in general" and as an organizational tool that led to the founding of MAM in 1942.[63] In addition to keeping readers abreast of regional gatherings and conference proceedings, *The Mexican Voice* circulated inspirational messages of high-achieving Mexican American youth in sports, education, and the arts, while engaging them in a translocal dialogue.

Writing under the pen name Manuel De La Raza (de la raza meaning "of the race"), editor Felix Gutierrez explained, "One of the purposes of 'The Mexican Voice' is to build up 'Pride in Our Race.'" He continued, "We the Mexicans, are as good a race as any other—artistically, mentally and physically!"[64] In the same August 1938 issue, Manuel Ceja asked readers, "Are We Proud of Being Mexicans?" He posed a series of self-reflective questions: "Why are we afraid to tell people that we are Mexicans? Are we ashamed of the color of our skin, the shape and build of our bodies, or the background from which we have descended?"[65] Of course, Ceja knew that many Mexican Americans struggled with these questions daily. His solution for Mexican youth was to take pride in their bicultural, bilingual, and binational heritage. "You have two cultures . . . two languages," Ceja reminded them. "Mexican Youth comes [sic] from a background of the highest type of Aztec and Spanish cultures. Take the best of our background, and the best of the present one we are now living under." Ceja's advice sounds somewhat similar to Jose Vasconcelos' musings on the benefits of *mestizaje* (racial mixture in Latin America) advanced in the essay *La Raza Cosmica: Misión de la raza iberoamericana* published in 1925.[66] Ceja, Gutierrez, and other contributors to *The Mexican Voice* likely read Vasconcelos and other Latin American intellectuals in college or came into contact with their ideas on racial and cultural hybridity through Spanish-language newspapers like the Los Angeles-based *La Opinion* or the Santa Ana-based *El Anunciador Mexicano*. Despite its internalized racism and philosophical contradictions, the discourse of *mestizaje* provided an intellectual foundation for Mexican American intellectuals that challenged white supremacist discourses like the "Mexican Problem" and affirmed their presence and contributions in the United States.

Coming of age during an era of intense nativism, xenophobia, and anti-Mexicanism, Mexican American youth were subjected to various forms of race-based traumatic stress that influenced the development of their identity and worldview.[67] Indeed, many had witnessed or heard of family and friends being forcibly removed during the repatriation campaigns of the early 1930s while also experiencing the daily humiliation of second-class treatment in segregated schools, movie theaters, parks, and private establishments. Such was the case with Virginia Vargas, born in Fullerton, CA, in 1921:

> When I was going to school I always wished that there was a place for me and my kind, my Mexican kids . . . it was pretty bad then. There was a lot of prejudice.

We were left out. In the first place, they didn't like people that weren't white, you know. I remember when we used to go to the theater in Anaheim, we always had to sit to the rear. That was where we sat. And then at the city plunge [swimming pool], if we wanted to go there at all we had to go on Mondays, because that was the day they changed the water. And my mother would never allow us to go there. We grew up with this atmosphere.[68]

Similarly, Lucy Cornejo Duran remembered what it was like to live in the segregated Cypress Street barrio and attend the Cypress Mexican School in Orange, CA during the 1930s:

I think that we were treated, maybe not idyllic. We went to the movies and we were aware of the people around us that said all of you have to sit upstairs . . . you can't sit downstairs. At the Orange [Hart] park swimming pool [we] were not allowed to go unless it was Monday because they would change the water Monday evening. We were kind of, I can't say the word, I'm sorry, we were kind of segregated. You know I never gave it very much thought, while I was going to school, about any of this [discrimination]. I accepted everything like it was a natural thing . . . it was just acceptable at the time.[69]

These experiences left a lasting impact. However, as much as they understood they were not fully accepted by Anglo-American society, Mexican American youth envisioned a day when they would have equal rights in the nation of their birth regardless of race, culture, and ancestry. While MAM leaders have faced criticism by scholars for their naivete in suggesting that Mexican youth could overcome structural racism through individual hard work, education, and good citizenship, their optimism exemplifies the migrant imaginary.[70] Despite their acceptance of American individualism and seemingly unfounded faith in its institutions, MAM pushed to redefine the nation's racial, cultural, and institutional boundaries to include Mexican Americans as equal citizens. Gutierrez illustrated this point in the September 1938 issue of *The Mexican Voice*:

So, next time anyone asks you what you are, say, "I'm an American." If he questions further, say, "I'm an American of Mexican descent." Let's discard at once and for all that outworn saying, "A Mexican hasn't a chance." It's up to us to show other people that our brains are just as good, our bodies just as strong as the best! All we need do is to develop and train them. And only WE can do it! Let's start NOW, not twenty years hence![71]

By encouraging their readers to claim an American identity, Gutierrez and other MAM leaders articulated a pluralist vision of US social and political belonging that did not exist in the late 1930s. This was bold and brash but not naïve. Mexican American youth had some idea of what they were up against. They had seen family, friends, and neighbors profiled, detained, and expelled by the racial capitalist system that marked them as a caste of "alien citizens."[72] Nevertheless, despite all the evidence to the contrary, they chose to believe in, work toward, and promote an inclusive vision of what US society could be.

Like La Progresista, MAM built affective group attachment among Mexican American youth by encouraging them to proudly identify as bicultural Americans with equal rights. It was both an affirmation of a lived experience and a rallying cry for social and political action that formed organically in the colonias and barrios of Southern California. From their beginning as an outgrowth of the Mexican Youth Conference, MAM organizers planned to build a movement that served Mexican American youth throughout the Southwest. In its third issue, published in August 1938, *The Mexican Voice* printed a letter from El Modena resident and past president of the Mexican Youth Conference Stephen A. Reyes. In the letter, Reyes discussed organizing "The El Modeno Latin-American Club" and provided a diagram that outlined his vision for a "confederation" of clubs "with the same laws and purposes."[73] After discussing his club's achievements, Reyes shared a plan for a much larger organization that would "unite" like-minded Mexican American youth groups across Southern California. At the top of the organization, Reyes envisioned an executive committee or "confederation" with a president, vice president, treasurer, and secretary elected by affiliated clubs throughout Los Angeles and Orange counties. Local clubs were modeled after the confederation's executive committee, each electing officers and sharing the same constitution, allowing "changes to be made according to conditions of locality."[74] Dues from local clubs would be collected by the confederation and used for communication and activities. Each year, local chapters would send delegates to an annual conference where reports would be made on the progress of their clubs, followed by an election for the new confederation president and officers. Reyes explained the "aims and purposes" of the confederation and affiliated clubs with the following outline:

I. **Social.** To engage in social functions for the benefit of community and members, such as outdoor parties [and] orderly dances.

II. **Recreational.** To participate in clean sports, competitive or otherwise, for physical improvement as well as to provide interest in sports. To keep fellows interest away from activities detrimental to ourselves and the community.

III. **Civic.** To help in the community activities and in that way acquaint city officials with our problems. By being citizens, to participate in elections and other doings of American citizens.[75]

He then concluded his proposal by adding one condition regarding membership:

One Provision of our club constitution allows only American born or naturalized citizens, eighteen years or over. Inside of five years we shall be able to elect a local official to the school board to represent the Mexican colony. We may then be in a position to employ Mexican teachers in our school.[76]

In the same August 1938 issue of the *Mexican Voice*, Felix Gutierrez embraced Reyes' vision, writing, "Stephen has a marvelous plan which will someday exist."[77] As evidenced by MAM's founding documents, Reyes' plan provided the organizational model for the movement's growth from a loose collection of Mexican Y clubs in the late 1930s to its formal incorporation and expansion during the early 1940s.[78] Further, the plan envisioned an organization that transcended the purpose of a social club primarily concerned with recreational activities. His ultimate goal was to mobilize Mexican Americans to vote and increase the representation of ethnic Mexicans in local schools and public office. While the provision to reserve membership for US citizens may sound discriminatory, it was a strategic and pragmatic move reflecting the integrationist goals of an organization that sought to fight discrimination through the ballot box. In this way, MAM was like LULAC and other Mexican American organizations from the 1930s to 1960s that believed the best approach to fighting discrimination was through social and economic integration.[79] Despite Reyes' suggestion, MAM did not limit membership to US citizens when the organization incorporated in 1945. According to Article XV of the By-Laws for the Supreme Council and Article III of the Constitution for subordinate councils, membership was open to "Any person of Mexican ancestry born in the United States or lawfully resident therein, over the age of fifteen years, of good moral character and favorably disposed towards the aims and purposes of the Mexican-American Movement."[80] This change was quite progressive for the time, departing from the policies of larger organizations like LULAC and AGIF which reserved membership for US citizens.

Further, the revised membership provision better suited MAM's "chief purpose . . . to improve conditions among the Mexican-American and Mexican people living in the United States."[81]

Like La Progresista, MAM viewed education as the means to attaining "economic security" and "social equality."[82] Indeed, both Reyes' proposal and MAM's official *Handbook* encouraged local councils to promote activities that improved the educational attainment and empowerment of the entire ethnic Mexican community. These included sponsoring youth programs and the facilities to support them, leadership training, night school and English-language classes for adults, a scholarship fund for college students, and participation "in all Civic endeavors such as service clubs, veterans organizations, P.T.A., church activities, interracial councils, etc."[83] For both organizations, culturally affirming and community-centered education was vital to overcoming the inequity of segregated schools and developing civically engaged leaders. Despite these shared values and objectives, there appears to have been little interaction between MAM and La Progresista.

In the January 1940 issue of the *Mexican Voice*, Stephen Reyes asserted, "the greatest problem effecting [*sic*] the Mexican population in the United States is the problem of leadership."[84] To what extent Reyes and other MAM leaders were aware of La Progresista's contributions is uncertain. Although their organizations were contemporaries with members living in the same colonias and barrios, they appealed to different facets of the ethnic Mexican community. MAM was not only much younger, with a membership that ranged in age from fifteen to thirty-five, but they were also almost entirely US-born and educated. Progresistas, on the other hand, were older, married, mostly Mexican-born, and established in their professions. In short, there was a sharp generational difference in perspective and experience between the organizations. Perhaps this is why Reyes and other Mexican American youth felt there was a leadership void they had to fill within the ethnic Mexican community. In his study on the development of Mexican American ethnicity and culture in East Los Angeles, historian George Sánchez emphasizes the role of the Depression in creating this vacuum. The disruptions of the 1930s, he argues, sowed the seeds for a generational shift in leadership, with US-born children of Mexican immigrants becoming community leaders and more likely to engage in labor unions and civil rights organizations.[85] Orange County, however, did not appear to have such a clean break from one generation to another. As evidenced by their shared focus on education, leadership, and civic engagement, La Progresista and MAM had much in common. Yet, like the youth movements that followed in the mid-to-late-1960s, MAM was anxious to distinguish itself from the previous generation, whom it felt had not developed the necessary social and material capital to facilitate the integration of ethnic Mexicans into Anglo-American society. Whereas La Progresista engaged in local politics, they did not identify integration and transformation of the US political system as tantamount to achieving their goals.[86] This shift in orientation, method, and tactics reflected the lived experience and bicultural upbringing of Mexican American youth.[87] In fact, for many, like Reyes, MAM provided the gateway to a lifetime of community activism and public service.

THE ARCHITECTS OF MEXICAN AMERICAN ACTIVISM AND LEADERSHIP IN ORANGE COUNTY

Stephen Anthony Reyes was born in Etiwanda, CA, in 1910 to Encarnacion Reyes and Teresa de Jesus Amador. The couple came to San Bernardino, CA, from Jalisco, Mexico, in 1900 as migrant farmworkers. During his early childhood, Reyes' family moved frequently as they followed the harvesting seasons of various crops throughout Southern California. By 1918, the family was living in northwest Orange County near Garden Grove and Westminster where Encarnacion thinned sugar beets and picked walnuts and chili peppers.[88] Tragically, Encarnacion died in 1921, the victim of a robbery and murder. With five children ranging in age from one to twelve years old, Teresa had little choice but to move the family to El Modena to live with her oldest daughter who had recently married. To support the family, Teresa took on domestic work, washing clothes and providing meals for single men in the area. Due to their frequent moves, Reyes did not begin kindergarten until the family settled in Orange County. By this time, he was eight years old and unable to speak English. Reyes attended the segregated Hoover (Mexican) School in Garden Grove from kindergarten through third grade and recalled "There was no such thing as teaching English. You just studied your books and talked and recited."[89] When the family moved to El Modena's El Pirripi barrio in 1921 after the death of his father, Reyes stayed in the third grade but attended the integrated Lincoln School. This was short-lived, however, because the El Modena School District began segregating Mexican children in April 1923 when they opened the newly built Roosevelt School next to Lincoln.[90] From this time forward, Lincoln became the de facto Mexican school while Roosevelt was reserved for white children. What was done in El Modena was simply standard practice for the rest of the county. As the Mexican population grew rapidly during the 1910s and 1920s, districts used the issue of overcrowding to build new schools for white children without fanfare or pretense of equality. By the early 1930s, Orange County had at least "fifteen schools with one hundred per cent Mexican enrollment."[91] This practice was common throughout Southern California's citrus belt as it allowed school boards to segregate Mexican children without running afoul of the State Education Code, which permitted the segregation of Native Americans and Asians, but was unclear on Mexicans.[92]

Despite the two-tiered educational system that intentionally underserved Mexican children and sought to keep them from advancing beyond the primary grades, Reyes developed a love for learning and was chosen co-valedictorian at his eighth-grade graduation.[93] Had he not lost his right arm in a hunting accident at age fifteen, Reyes would have left school to pick oranges full-time like most other Mexican youth. "We were not supposed to know anything," he recalled. "Mexicans were supposed to have a good back, fast hands, no brains."[94] Realizing there was "no other way out . . . it was either the academic track or you dropped out," Reyes graduated from Orange Union High School in 1931, earned an associate's degree from Santa Ana College in 1933, and a bachelor's from UCLA in 1936. While he still picked oranges during the summer, Stephen's academic accomplishments opened the door to new economic opportunities. After graduating from UCLA, Reyes returned to El Modena where he found work as a playground supervisor and later as a Spanish teacher in Orange and Santa Ana. "When I saw my first hourly wage after I started teaching night school . . . then I knew I had made the right choice of going to school be- cause . . . in two hours of work . . . I made more than a whole day of picking oranges at 6 cents a box."[95]

Shortly after returning to El Modena, Reyes became one of the lead organizers of the YMCA-affiliated Mexican Youth Conference and was elected president of the organization's third annual meeting in 1937.[96] He was a frequent contributor to *The Mexican Voice*, where his accomplishments provided an example of the new generation of youth MAM sought to cultivate. This included the organization of the El Modeno Latin American Club in 1936, which Reyes insisted "was really a political club because nobody could be a member unless they could vote." "Before any election," he recalled, "I'd go house to house and tell them how to vote so that we would get things our way for a change."[97] In the summer of 1938, Reyes met with the El Modeno School Board to establish an evening recreational program on the fields that adjoined the Lincoln and Roosevelt schools. Aware that he had enough "political clout" to "swing an election," the board approved Reyes' request and even provided money to help him install lights on the playground.[98] It was likely this experience that helped Reyes envision new opportunities for Mexican Americans in the fields of public service, education, and social service. As he opined in the March 1940 issue of *The Mexican Voice*:

> It will not be very long before politically-minded groups and individuals will attempt to appeal to the Mexican vote in the city, county, and state. Mexican Americans may someday surprise certain smug factions that are certainly not trying to avert such a possibility. Mexican candidates for public office in certain fields will offer a very uncomfortable and close competition . . .

> It will not be long before the value of Mexican teachers in the Mexican districts will be appreciated. Now enough pressure can be put on some school boards so that selections of teachers will not always be from one group. Appointment of teachers of Latin extraction will be good diplomacy . . .

> Under the present social and economic conditions of the Mexican population in the United States, it is almost indispensable that we put Mexicans in charge of the work done with them. I feel that workers in the social field who are working with Mexicans know where and how to act in certain situations because of the basic and intimate knowledge of Mexican behavior, tendencies, or psychology. Social service is the field of opportunity for both the professional and the people in general.[99]

As with other MAM leaders, Reyes' optimism stemmed from his lived experience that confirmed that hard work, education, and community organization were keys to achieving social and political equality for the rising generation of Mexican Americans. Shortly after marrying Lydia Escobosa in November 1938, Reyes was hired as the new Director of the Pasadena Settlement House in Pasadena, CA. Opened in 1914 as a maternal facility for Mexican immigrants, the Settlement House grew into a community center over the ensuing decades, providing social, educational, recreational, and job programs for Mexican, African American, and Japanese families in Pasadena and Altadena.[100] Learning of the position through YMCA contacts, Reyes interviewed with the settlement association's board of directors and was chosen for the job amongst thirteen other applicants. His combination of personal experience overcoming poverty alongside his college education, extensive work with Mexican youth, and intimate understanding of immigrant and working-class communities made him uniquely qualified for the directorship. Further, the board was also impressed with Lydia's experience, which included volunteer work at the Methodist Mission in El Modena and the Goodwill in Anaheim. As Director of the Settlement House, Reyes expanded youth programs, instituted revolving student loan and scholarship funds, partnered with faith and community organizations by founding the Mexican Central Council, and created the Mutual Aid Society to provide death benefits to those without life insurance.

Amidst his new responsibilities, Reyes continued to serve as business manager of the Mexican Youth Conference, printer of *The Mexican Voice*, and co-founder of MAM. After much deliberation, Paul Coronel, Felix Gutierrez, and Stephen Reyes decided in 1942 that the Mexican Youth Conference "could not depend on the Y forever" and that it was time for their movement to become an independent nonprofit organization.[101] While they did not entirely sever ties with the YMCA and its leadership remained virtually unchanged, MAM became independent to facilitate partnerships with other entities.[102] This included the formation of an interracial advisory board with prominent Mexican Americans like Ernesto Galarza and Bert Corona and white progressives in business and education. The name change was also significant as "It was the first time the word Mexican-American had been used," signaling the organization's commitment to "go one step further" to show they were not "embarrassed or ashamed to admit their origin."[103] As with the Mexican Youth Conference, Reyes' contributions were vital to MAM's growth and development. As a member of the Board of Directors and Supreme Council and Constitutional Committee, Reyes helped develop MAM's organizational structure and draft its constitution and by-laws.[104] Additionally, he served two stints as treasurer and chaired MAM's education and membership committees from 1943 to 1947. Amidst his many contributions, Reyes was particularly proud that his position at the Settlement House helped further MAM's work. In 1942, he opened the doors of the Settlement House to the organization, giving MAM its first headquarters at 864 Raymond Avenue.[105] This he felt was mutually beneficial to both organizations, providing "the central place for the Mexican-American Movement" and helping the Settlement House gain recognition as a center for Mexican American activity in Pasadena.[106]

After nine-and-a-half years at the Settlement House, Reyes resigned as director in 1948 to pursue his lifelong dream of becoming an educator. Despite his extensive experience and qualifications, securing a teaching position was difficult. Anti-Mexican discrimination "was a fact [of life]" Reyes recalled, referring to his experiences being segregated in movie theaters and parks and refused service at barber shops and restaurants that "did not cater to Mexican trade."[107] Nevertheless, Reyes was determined to try. Fortunately, relationships with local educators and school board members, fostered through MAM and the Settlement House, helped Reyes secure a job teaching Spanish at John Muir Junior College in 1948, where he became "one of the first Latinos to teach in the Pasadena schools."[108] While teaching Spanish, Latin, and English grammar at John Muir, Reyes continued his education and earned a master's degree in Spanish at the University of Southern California. In 1955, he co-founded the Pasadena Scholarship Committee for Americans of Mexican Descent, which awarded scholarships to high school seniors. In addition to writing its constitution and by-laws, Reyes established partnerships with local business leaders and helped overcome the opposition of district officials. In 1960, he accepted a faculty position in the Foreign Language Department at Pasadena City College where he spent the remainder of his career teaching Spanish, advising student clubs, and assisting in faculty government until he retired in 1976. Throughout his life, Reyes worked as a "cultural broker," operating between white and Mexican communities to expand educational access and public services for Mexican American youth. To him, "progress through education" was more than a slogan; it was a mantra he embodied through word and deed.

Luis Sandoval was another MAM leader who dedicated much of his adult life to improving social conditions for Mexican Americans. Although little is known about him before he came to Orange County, public records confirm Luis was born in Juchipila, Zacatecas, Mexico, in 1915, migrated to the United States with his family in 1916, lived in Clarkdale, Yavapai County, Arizona, in 1920, registered with the Selective Service in Placentia, CA, in 1940, and married Charlotte Negrette of Los Angeles in Maricopa County, Arizona, in 1941.[109] According to *The Mexican Voice*, Sandoval's involvement in the Mexican Youth Conference began while attending Arizona State Teacher's College in Tempe during the late 1930s.[110] Shortly after moving to Placentia, Luis helped organize two Mexican American youth clubs. The first, Los Guadalupanos, formed during the summer of 1939 at St. Joseph's Catholic Church, while the second, a YMCA club, began at La Jolla Mexican School in the spring of 1940. Sandoval's involvement in these groups connected him with Gualberto Valadez, Ted and Lupe Duran, Alfred and Joe Aguirre, Mary Anne and Ross Chavolla, Leonel Magana, and several other Mexican Americans who got their start in civil rights activism through MAM.[111] In 1942, this group formed MAM's first local council, the Orange County MAM Council, with Luis Sandoval as its president.[112] During its first three years, the Orange County MAM Council operated out of Anaheim with members in Santa Ana, Westminster, Orange, and Huntington Beach. Since the bulk of its membership lived in Placentia, the larger Orange County MAM Council later split into two local councils with one in Anaheim led by Sandoval and the second in Placentia led by Valadez. When MAM formally incorporated on December 19, 1945, Placentia and Anaheim were two of the six subordinate councils that made up the organization's core. In addition to Stephen Reyes, Luis Sandoval, Gualberto

Valadez, and Mary Anne and Ross Chavolla were founding members of MAM's Supreme Council and board of directors.[113]

As evidenced by his selection as president of both the Orange County and Anaheim MAM councils, Sandoval quickly gained the respect of his peers after moving to Placentia in 1939. At the time of the move, Sandoval was attending Arizona State Teachers College in Tempe, where he completed four terms between 1936 and 1938.[114] It is unclear why Sandoval chose to move to Orange County prior to completing his degree since public records suggest he lived in Arizona continuously from 1916 to 1938. But considering the people he surrounded himself with in Placentia, all of whom participated in youth organizing, it is very likely the move was facilitated by contacts made through the Mexican Youth Conference. While Sandoval returned to Arizona off and on between 1940 and 1941, he maintained a permanent address at 504 East Adele in Anaheim from 1940 to 1947 and 837 South Olive from 1948 to 1966.[115] Living at these addresses situated Luis and Charlotte near Anaheim's La Philadelphia barrio, which was one of six Mexican neighborhoods in the city. Despite his short time in Orange County, Sandoval quickly became familiar with the discrimination experienced by Mexican Americans in the area. In 1941, he was "asked to leave the tennis court in the Anaheim City Park . . . because [the] facilities were not to be used by Mexican-Americans."[116] This experience echoed that of other Mexican Americans like Celia Salas, who was raised in Colonia Independencia on Anaheim's westside. Recalling what it was like to interact with white people during the 1930s, Salas said:

> Anaheim was different then. I know. When I was going up the stairs if I saw a white person coming down I would move out of the way. Especially some of the men. There were a few women that treated me equally, but when we were in school it was very, very different than it is now. I remember this teacher stopped me in the hall and called me into her office. She said Celia, I'd give you an "A" if you just stayed away from those Mexicans.[117]

Because she studied hard and wanted to "get out of the colonia," some white teachers saw Salas as different from her ethnic Mexican peers. However, her good grades and infectious personality did not shield her from experiencing racism. "I wouldn't go where I wasn't welcome" and "I would never think of dating anybody that was white," Salas remembered.[118]

One of the places Salas avoided was the public swimming pool at Anaheim City Park, which only allowed Mexicans to swim on Mondays, the day before it was cleaned.[119] For Celia Salas and Virginia Vargas, the segregation of the Anaheim plunge was too much to bear, so they avoided it entirely.[120] But during the summer of 1945, the pool was suddenly integrated, thanks to the work of Sandoval:

> There was a man, not from the school, he was just a Mexican-American man, and when we were teenagers, he started what they call the MAM, the Mexican-American Movement in Anaheim. And it lived for a very short while. But it did accomplish something because we were allowed to go to the city plunge anytime we felt like it, and we could sit at the theater almost anywhere we wanted also.[121]

Sandoval was the man Vargas and others credited with desegregating the pool. As reported in *Accion*, a Spanish-language newspaper published by Francisco Moreno in Fullerton, and *Forward*, MAM's official newspaper published in Los Angeles, Sandoval brokered the deal that ended segregation at the city pool. Believing the municipal code that restricted Mexicans' use of the pool to one day a week to be "unconstitutional," Sandoval built a coalition of community members to overturn the policy during the summer of 1945. As reported in *Accion* and reprinted in *Forward*:

> [Luis] personally contacted the clergy of different denominations, members of the Chamber of Commerce, representatives of packing houses, publishers of local newspapers and explained the unconstitutionality of such a regulation. As a result of those meetings . . . the pain and injury inflicted upon our youth was exposed, which was a shame to the city where so many were affected. For the cause of justice, the Members of the City Council met and agreed to nullify the order to segregate.[122]

Accion praised Sandoval's efforts as a model for others to follow:

> This triumph attained by Luis Sandoval must be deemed as an incentive and example for all Mexicans. In a cordial but energetic manner he asked for what was just. He was able to hit the mark by going through proper channels and asked for justice from those who could give justice, and his work has been crowned with success, because from now on, Mexicans will have access to municipal pools on any day of the week.[123]

Sandoval's success was partly due to the compelling nature of his argument, which connected the city's discriminatory policies with the country's ongoing struggle against authoritarianism during the Cold War. According to *Accion*, Luis argued that the city's segregationist policy was "unworthy of democratic principles" and violated the "good neighbor policy" between the United States and its Latin American allies.[124] Celia Salas also remembered

Sandoval appealing to postwar patriotism due to the service rendered by Mexican American GIs:

> After the war, there was a man that came from Arizona, his name was Luis Sandoval. He came and started passing out a petition that stated the blood flowed equally during the war on the battlefield [so] why weren't we allowed to go in the pool? So I helped him pass out some of those petitions. I remember we got so many signatures and then it was changed.[125]

MAM leaders developed this approach to civil rights and social justice far earlier than civil rights activists during World War II and the Cold War.[126] This was evident during the summer of 1938 when the Mexican Youth Conference sent a delegation to the Monrovia city council to protest the city's segregated swimming pool.[127] While their action proved unsuccessful, experiences like these, coupled with programs, activities, and networks facilitated by the Mexican Youth Conference and MAM, helped Mexican Americans acquire the skills and confidence to become civically engaged. Indeed, during the 1930s and 1940s, Mexican American youth utilized their time in YMCA-affiliated clubs to train and mobilize each other to overcome systemic inequality. In Orange County between the spring of 1936 and the fall of 1939, Mexican American youth organized at least eight clubs stretching from Fullerton to Costa Mesa. Evidence of their strength and popularity was covered by *The Mexican Voice*, which regularly featured the efforts of Mexican American youth in Santa Ana, Fullerton, Placentia, and Anaheim.[128]

Another aspect of Sandoval's success that went unmentioned by *Accion* was the recent decision in the *Mendez, et al. v. Westminster School District of Orange County, et al.* desegregation case. *Mendez et al.* was decided on February 18, 1946, several months before the agreement to desegregate the pool in Anaheim. Some have speculated that the Anaheim School District was not listed as a defendant in the case because its formal "administrative policy" of segregating Mexican children ended in 1925.[129] Nevertheless, Anaheim schools were not fully integrated as a result of the policy change and Mexican children continued to be segregated on the basis of language in Anaheim for at least another twenty years. Indeed, led by Superintendent Melbourne A. Gauer, the Anaheim School District opened the La Palma Mexican School on October 11, 1926, to serve Mexican students from kindergarten through the sixth grade until they could speak and understand English.[130] Likewise, west of Anaheim, the Magnolia School District also maintained separate schools, Magnolia #1 for white students and Magnolia #2 for Mexicans.[131] Despite Gauer's claim that this "was the way [Anaheim schools] integrated," by the time of the *Mendez et al.* hearings, the La Palma and Magnolia #2 schools had 100 percent Mexican enrollments. Further, according to Superintendent Gauer, attempts to transfer Mexican students to white schools were met with strong resistance:

> When we tried to put the Mexican in the American school we had a terrific problem with American mothers. They weren't going to have those Mexican Americans in their school. They came before the school board and before me in September when I'd try to transfer some of them over and said, "We're not going to send our kids to school if they are going to be in the same grade with Mexican children."[132]

Intolerance of this sort led to the persistence of anti-Mexican discrimination in housing, education, employment, and public amenities well into the postwar years.[133] Due to the city's proximity to the defendant districts and the widespread press coverage garnered by the case, residents and city officials followed the *Mendez et al.* proceedings closely. While *Accion* did not mention the case, the paper applauded Sandoval's efforts to resolve the issue "without boastings, commotion, or judicial intervention and by demonstrating to our community that more can be done by using reason instead of force."[134] This statement implies the paper's editors were not only aware of *Mendez et al.* but that they feared further "commotion" resulting from additional court action.

Although MAM's leadership supported *Mendez et al.*, they chose not to involve the organization in the case. This decision was primarily based on the recommendation of MAM's Placentia Council led by Gualberto Valadez, who was concerned about the repercussions if MAM were to entangle itself in a "controversial issue" that "should be settled by the courts."[135] In a letter to MAM's Supreme Council, Valadez asserted, "Our work is to be done through cooperation and not thru [sic] antagonism. We feel that our work is overcoming many prejudices and we are beginning to receive cooperation from people that we never dreamed would cooperate."[136] Indeed, the cooperation Valadez referred to was essential to MAM's success and it included numerous public, educational, religious, and business leaders who had partnered with the organization's leadership since the late 1930s to facilitate conferences, fund programs, and provide scholarships to Mexican American youth.[137] While La Progresista and other grassroots organizations had previously worked with attorneys and religious leaders who were sympathetic to the plight of ethnic Mexicans in Orange County, MAM made interracial alliances a pillar of their organizational strategy.[138] The success experienced by Sandoval instilled confidence in the strategy of interracial cooperation and signaled that the walls of segregation in Orange County were beginning to fall.

During the 1940s and 1950s, no other person had a greater impact on improving the social conditions of Mexican Americans in Anaheim than Sandoval. In just six short years after his arrival to Orange County, he led successful campaigns to end segregation in public and private establishments and built one of MAM's largest and most influential local councils with approximately eighty members by 1946.[139] Like Stephen Reyes, Sandoval was a "cultural broker" who helped renegotiate and break down the socioeconomic barriers erected by citrus capitalists in prior decades.[140] His life illustrated the vast social distance Mexican Americans traversed in a single generation. Born to working-class Mexican immigrant parents, Sandoval graduated from high school, attended college, and eventually worked his way into an emergent Mexican American middle-class as a department store manager at J.C. Penney during the day and an adult education teacher at Fullerton High School and Fullerton Junior College at night.[141] By 1950, his commitment to Mexican American youth, public service, and civic engagement garnered him the respect and appreciation of individuals, businesses, and associations throughout the city, including the *Anaheim Gazette*, which referred to him as a "well-known" and "prominent" civic leader.[142] This was a tremendous turnaround from the representation of ethnic Mexicans in local papers during the 1920s and 1930s when virtually every mention of a Mexican included derogatory and threatening language. This change in the public representation of Mexicans was secured by the actions of people like Reyes, Sandoval, Valadez, and several others. It was their belief in and commitment to grassroots activism and civic engagement that fueled a rising generation of Mexican Americans to envision and realize different spatial and social relations.

Like Reyes and Sandoval, Gualberto "Bert" Valadez joined the Mexican Conference during the late 1930s and became an influential leader within MAM and the Mexican American community in Orange County during the 1940s and 1950s. Born in Jerome, Arizona in 1913, Valadez moved to San Francisco at the age of five when his mother relocated the family in search of better employment opportunities.[143] After graduating from Mission High School, Valadez worked as a janitor for the YMCA while pursuing his bachelor's degree at San Francisco State University where he majored in physical education and minored in Spanish and biological sciences. Valadez received a scholarship from the *San Francisco Chronicle* to attend the University of California at Berkeley, where he obtained a secondary teaching credential in 1938. Valadez began working with youth sports programs at the San Francisco YMCA while attending college and transferred to the Los Angeles YMCA after graduating, believing that opportunities for Mexican Americans were better in the Southland.[144]

The move to the Los Angeles YMCA was momentous for Valadez as it brought him into close contact with Mexican Youth Conference leaders Paul Coronel, Felix Gutierrez, Bert Corona, and Stephen Reyes, among others.[145] While working for the Los Angeles YMCA in 1939, Valadez sent his resume to Stephen Reyes asking him "to keep [his] eyes and ears open for a teaching position." The request surprised Reyes, who thought Valadez had "a lot of guts, trying to land a job . . . as a school teacher in Southern California." "I wondered where he thought he could get a job, being of Mexican descent," Reyes recalled.[146] After learning of an opening at the segregated La Jolla School near Placentia, Valadez spoke with Anaheim YMCA Secretary J.B. Wilburg to inquire about the position. Wilburg introduced Valadez to the superintendent and members of the Placentia Unified School Board. Because of Valadez's work with the YMCA, Wilburg vouched for his character and Valadez started at the La Jolla School in the fall of 1939. Reflecting on how he became one of the first Mexican teachers hired by the Placentia School Board, Valadez stated it would have been "impossible" for him to obtain the position on his own. The YMCA, he asserted, "got me the job."[147]

At the time of Valadez's arrival in 1939, the La Jolla School (also known as La Jolla Junior High) was one of three Mexican schools in the district, including Chapman (originally Baker Street) and Richfield.[148] It provided instruction for Mexican American children from kindergarten through the tenth grade and was in the Mexican barrio of the same name situated a few miles south of Placentia. However, as the "pet project" of UCLA Professor J.L. Meriam, the La Jolla School was unlike any other segregated Mexican school in the county. Considered a "model school" that experimented with "progressive instructional methods," it had more funding and better facilities, although neither put it on par with white schools in the region.[149] Despite its progressive mission and methods, the La Jolla School existed to keep Mexicans apart from whites. Indeed, Valadez believed that district officials maintained grades seven through ten at La Jolla in order to "prevent integration for the handful of Mexicans that made it past the eighth grade."[150] Although he acknowledged that segregation in the Placentia Unified School District was not as rigidly enforced as in other parts of the county like Westminster, El Modena, Garden Grove, and Santa Ana, Valadez was convinced that district officials favored segregation and did little to encourage Mexican students to continue their studies beyond the eighth grade.[151] This view was shared by Chester Whitten, principal at the La Jolla School, who confirmed the district practiced "out and out segregation."[152]

Valadez was hired to establish a physical education program and teach social studies and Spanish to students in grades seven through ten. Prior to his arrival, physical education at La Jolla was virtually nonexistent and consisted of the "shop teacher" handing "a bat and ball" to students and telling them to "go out and play."[153] As former captain of the track team at San Francisco State with a degree in physical education, Valadez was certainly qualified for the position. Further, both his personal experience and involvement in the YMCA and Mexican Youth Conference convinced him that athletic programs aided in the social and intellectual development of Mexican American youth. Indeed, one of MAM's primary objectives was to increase the participation of ethnic Mexican youth in athletic and recreational programs to keep them off the streets and out of trouble. Yet, MAM's emphasis on social and recreational activities was more than an anti-delinquency program pushed by white progressives in the YMCA. Participation in school athletics helped Mexican American youth develop confidence, discipline, and other skills that were transferrable to scholastic success, while also aiding in the formation of positive relationships with faculty and administrators that broke down negative stereotypes. Buttressed by these experiences, many of Valadez's students, like Ervie Peña, Bobby Garcia, Lee Esperes, and Jim Segovia, became the first in their family to graduate from high school, enter college, and pursue professional careers in medicine, law, and education.[154]

Participation in school athletics also aided in the development of Mexican American youth by expanding their social world beyond the real and perceived boundaries of Orange County's segregated landscape. Prior to traveling to regional tournaments in Los Angeles and coastal Orange County, most of Valadez's students had never ventured beyond the cities adjacent to their segregated barrios in Placentia, Anaheim, and Fullerton. Combining his work with local YMCA groups and the development of La Jolla's athletic program, Valadez recalled the impact of having a lighted softball field in Placentia:

> I had a club. Young men who were called the volunteers solicited funds from the community. Mr. Whitten was able to get some used light poles from the Edison Company. They came in and these volunteers dug the holes. The company came in and put the poles in and covered them up. Then we paid an electrician to wire the poles and put up the lights. We were one of the few . . . Hispanic communities to have lights. We immediately organized softball teams; these softball teams played there at night. They'd invite teams from other cities to come and play under the lights . . . [and] we had big crowds come out at night and watch the girls play.[155]

As with the yearly patriotic and cultural celebrations put on by local *mutualistas* and religious groups, the development of a regional sports culture strengthened ties between ethnic Mexican communities across the Santa Ana Valley. While exposing Mexican American youth to "another world outside . . . the local colony," athletics helped build bridges with members of the white community, most of whom had never set foot inside the barrio or witnessed ethnic Mexicans excel at anything other than picking oranges and walnuts.

In addition to his teaching and coaching at the La Jolla School, Valadez remained active in the YMCA and was elected president of the seventh annual Mexican Youth Conference held in San Pedro, CA in March 1940.[156] Like Stephen Reyes before him, Valadez's selection as president of the annual conference confirmed Orange County's importance in the Mexican youth movement that was building throughout Southern California during the late 1930s and early 1940s. Indeed, because of the influence of Reyes, Sandoval, and Valadez, Orange County hosted several regional gatherings sponsored by the YMCA and the Mexican Youth Conference. The first of these occurred in March 1939, when "a large gathering . . . of Mexican youth from Irwindale, Azusa, Monrovia, Pasadena, Orange, and Santa Ana" were "hosted by the Santa Ana Mexican boys clubs" for a day of sporting events and motivational speeches.[157] This "rally," as *The Mexican Voice* referred to it, was held within a few weeks of the sixth annual Mexican Youth Conference, where boys basketball teams from Santa Ana and Orange competed for the conference championship.[158] Nine months later, Mexican American youth gathered again in Orange County at a regional conference sponsored by the Fullerton High School and Junior College's El Dorado Club. Approximately 150 youth delegates from Los Angeles, Orange, and San Diego counties attended the conference, which was presided over by Valadez and included messages from Stephen Reyes, who spoke on the "Need of Social Work Among Mexican People," Mary Anne Gonzalez (later Chavolla), who discussed "The Problems of Young American Girls of Mexican Descent," and J.B. Wilburg, who shared "several stories about successful Mexican youths."[159]

Between 1940 and 1942, the Mexican Youth Conference held at least four more district and regional conferences in Orange County.[160] These gatherings were organized and run by local Mexican clubs, led by individuals including Gualberto Valadez, Luis Sandoval, Pete Partida, Joseph Frias, Mary Anne and Ross Chavolla, Ina Gerritt, Ted Duran, Leonel Magana, and Joe and Alfred Aguirre. While the YMCA, which operated local branches in Anaheim, Santa Ana, Fullerton, Orange, and Placentia, provided the facilities and initial funding for what was referred to colloquially as

"Mexican boys [and girls] work," Orange County Mexicans were the driving force behind the youth movement in the region. Reflecting on the importance of the work in local clubs, Valadez stated:

> These boys [and girls] really learned to express themselves and how to conduct formal meetings; secretaries, how to take minutes; treasurer, how to account for money and so on. Afterwards many of them went on to other organizations where they knew how to conduct themselves in formal meetings.[161]

The experience of Tillie Arias, a student at Fullerton High School, supports Valadez's assertions. After hearing about the Fullerton regional conference from "every Mexican student at Fullerton High School," Tillie approached El Dorado Club advisor Ina Gerritt to inquire about the conference that everyone was buzzing about. Gerritt told Tillie "all about the Mexican Youth Conference" and invited her to attend. Tillie agreed and was assigned by Gerritt to chair the registration committee, where she worked with peers to organize the December 1939 regional conference at Fullerton Junior College. In a letter to *The Mexican Voice*, titled "What the Regional Conference Meant to Me," Tillie enthusiastically reported on the proceedings, which included talks and workshops on forming Mexican clubs in schools, churches, and the YMCA; mental and physical wellbeing; dressing and grooming standards; attending college; and overcoming poverty. Tillie also related how the conference was attended by teachers, principals, and the superintendent, all of whom "agreed that there is a brighter future for us than there has ever been before."[162] Tillie closed her report by affirming, "speaking for myself and the 'El Dorado Club,' we received so much encouragement and inspiration from the Conference that we are looking forward with a great deal of enthusiasm to the next."[163] The significance of these clubs and conferences to the development of Mexican American youth in Orange County and the Mexican youth movement throughout Southern California cannot be overstated. Organized from the ground up, by and for Mexican Americans, these gatherings trained and mobilized a generation of leaders who truly believed they had a future and could make a difference in their communities and nation.

The importance of Orange County within the Mexican youth movement was also manifest in the composition of MAM's Supreme Council, which began to take shape in 1942 and was formally organized in December of 1945.[164] At the time of its charter, MAM had six "subordinate councils" or local chapters, two of which were in Orange County. Placentia was listed as the first subordinate council, followed by Santa Barbara, Chaffey District, Los Angeles Metropolitan Area, San Bernardino, and Anaheim, respectively.[165] As suggested by Stephen Reyes, the subordinate councils nominated the delegates that elected the organization's Supreme Council, which also functioned as the organization's board of directors. The fact that six of the fifteen members of MAM's Supreme Council from Orange County illustrates the importance of the region to the organization. This is even more impressive when one considers that Orange County had as many members on the Supreme Council as Los Angeles County, despite being one-twenty-fifth the size in population. Further, Mexican Americans from Orange County held half the positions of the organization's elected officers, including Gualberto Valadez as President, Mary Anne Chavolla as Secretary, and Stephen Reyes as Treasurer.[166]

As had been the case with Stephen Reyes' Latin American club in El Modena, Placentia's local chapter, also presided over by Valadez, provided the prototypical model for MAM's vision of how its subordinate councils should operate. In the first edition of *Forward*, the monthly newspaper published by MAM alongside its "official magazine" *The Mexican Voice*, MAM highlighted the pivotal work of the Placentia Council. Evolving out of the "Orange County M.A.M. Council" formed by Sandoval, Valadez, Mary Anne Chavolla, and Ted Duran in 1942, the Placentia Council was considered a "pioneer" for being "the first community M.A.M. council to be organized." Further, the Placentia group was praised for "doing for several years what has now become a national movement."[167] Notably working "to improve social, educational, economic and spiritual conditions among Mexican-Americans and Mexican people living in the United States."[168] Placentia MAM did so by building coalitions between ethnic Mexicans and whites. As reported by *Forward*, the Placentia group formed a local "Advisory Board" primarily comprising white educators. Among those elected to this board were Louis Simmons, superintendent of the Placentia School District; Mrs. B. Twombley, principal of the Chapman School; Mr. Addy, principal of the La Jolla School (who replaced Chester Whitten after his retirement); and Walt Taylor, secretary of the North Orange County YMCA.[169]

Working with the advisory board, the Placentia MAM Council set the following goals for 1944: 1) establish a recreation center for Mexican American youth to engage them in after school activities; 2) organize an instructional education program for the recreation center; 3) "solicit the cooperation of the Anglo-American mothers," whom the group hoped would help to reduce prejudice and discrimination against Mexican American youth; 4) establish a library; 5) build a club house; 6) organize evening programs and social functions; 7) form a service club for teenage girls; and 8) "establish a revolving scholarship fund for worthy Mexican-American students."[170] Applauding the Placentia Council's work at interracial collaboration, *Forward* connected these efforts with MAM's central mission and purpose:

> In our movement that is the essence of our work: Cooperation and under-standing between people of different national and cultural backgrounds. But, our impetus is different. Ours is not solely to prevent riots or keep down juve-nile delinquency, ours is to raise the social standing of a people. The people: our Mexican-Americans or Mexicans residing in the United States.[171]

This focus on interracial cooperation signaled a key shift in ethnic Mexican civic activism and politics in the region. This strategy not only reflected the binational and bicultural experience of Mexican Americans, it also revealed an increasing awareness that progress on issues of racial discrimination had to be achieved through interracial coalitions. Mexican Americans in Orange County led MAM's efforts on this front. As Valadez saw it, MAM stepped into a "leadership vacuum" that bridged the chasm between whites and ethnic Mexicans in the region. Arriving in Orange County just a few years after the citrus strikes of 1935–1936, Valadez was warned by Principal Chester Whitten to "keep his nose clean" and that it was not uncommon for Mexicans to get "beat up" if they "stepped out of line."[172] Valadez understood Whitten's caution to include any beha-vior that could be perceived as "antagonistic" or uppity, like speaking out against the prevailing socioeconomic order that sanctioned racism and discrimination.[173]

Within this climate of hostile race relations, Valadez, Sandoval, Reyes, and other MAM leaders recognized that if something was to be done to improve the social, economic, and political position of ethnic Mexicans in the region, it would have to be led by Mexican Americans, since "the Anglo community wasn't doing anything about it."[174] However, they also understood that Mexican Americans lacked the social and political power to act alone, so their efforts had to involve white allies. This necessitated mobilizing around an issue both sides could agree on, had knowledge of, and had a shared interest in improving. Drawing from his YMCA network, Valadez engaged white educators, members of law enforcement, religious, business, and community leaders in the work of MAM "to encourage [Mexican American] youth to . . . make something of themselves."[175] This work also had the dual purpose of educating white allies. Through their interactions with MAM leaders and high achieving Mexican American youth, white allies saw Mexicans in a new light. Such was the case with the secretary of Fullerton High School, who admitted to Valadez, "When I was a boy, I didn't think Mexicans could do anything except pick oranges."[176]

MAM's focus on building an interracial grassroots movement led by Mexican Americans clarifies the organization's reluctance to engage in direct action or public protests that threatened their relationships with white allies. Despite their seeming moderation, MAM did not acquiesce to racial injustice, and they often worked with other minorities to lobby elected officials to end systemic racism. According to Valadez, MAM used its publications to show solidarity with groups engaged in similar struggles. Such was the case in the May 8, 1947, issue of *Forward* when MAM reported on the proceedings of a civic unity conference:

> Delegates from more than thirty community interracial and civic unity groups in all sections of California wound up a two day convention last February at Asilomar of the California council for civic unity. The program called for: Statewide action to bring to an end "the illegal use of force and violence on the part of police officers" against Negroes, Mexican-Americans and members of other minority groups.[177]

MAM's coverage of the conference also included a series of resolutions endorsed at the meeting. These called for "the creation of a [statewide] commission on political and economic equality," and the establishment of a US Congressional commission "to adjudicate the accountable and measurable losses suffered by lawfully resident Japanese aliens and their citizen children as a result of government imposed wartime evacuation."[178] Not only did MAM publish such articles to inform their readership and champion efforts that promoted interracial cooperation, but they also participated in a national network of organizations that corresponded and strategized over issues affecting minority youth and communities.[179]

A MOVEMENT WITHOUT PRECEDENCE

From the earliest issues of *The Mexican Voice*, the founders of the Mexican Youth Conference and MAM clearly envisioned their movement as a translocal effort to connect and mobilize Mexican American youth from rural, suburban, and urban communities across the Southwest. As Paul Coronel asserted in the February 1940 issue of *The Mexican Voice*, "Our youth movement is using several powerful weapons through which we are now reaching more of our youth in various Mexican communities in this state and lately, in the state of Arizona."[180] Foremost among the "weapons" used by MAM to reach this vast audience were its publications, conferences, leadership trainings, and social gatherings. Through them, MAM created spaces that empowered Mexican American youth to organize, educate, train, and mobilize themselves as leaders of their communities and an emerging multicultural-racial society.[181] Emerging from underserved communities throughout Southern California, these spaces and networks did not exist for ethnic Mexican youth prior to the establishment of the Mexican Youth Conference and MAM. Formed by and for the benefit of Mexican American youth, MAM arose organically from barrios and colonias throughout Southern California's citrus belt without help or precedence from outside civil rights organizations.

Encumbered with the responsibilities of working and raising families, MAM's leaders disbanded the organization during the early 1950s. As Valadez recalled, "After the war we were going strong . . . but what happened was that the old leaders got tied up. I just didn't have the time, I was trying to exist."[182] The end of MAM did not result in the termination of the movement started by the Mexican Youth Conference in 1934. In fact, MAM's ideals, goals, strategies, aspirations, and networks lived on in other Mexican American organizations like LULAC, CSO, Mexican American Political Association (MAPA), and the Chicana/o student movement.[183] Alongside La Progresista, which maintained a presence in Orange County into the 1970s, the Mexican Youth Conference and MAM established a culture of civic engagement and political activism among Orange County Mexicans and provided a blue print for the development of grassroots organizations in the region. This is most clearly seen in the desegregation movement that led to the *Mendez et al.* decision in 1946 and the rapid growth of LULAC in Orange County during the 1950s and 1960s.

For Valadez, teaching and mentoring youth remained the primary focus of his activism. Although he participated in LULAC and MAPA, he is primarily remembered by those he taught and mentored during his nearly fifty-year career as an educator at the La Jolla School and Valencia High School. Valadez's impact was so great that in 2005, forty-two of his former students lobbied the Placentia-Yorba Linda School Board to name a school in his honor. Organizing themselves under the name "The Septuagenarian Tigers of Placentia-Yorba Linda," the group collected dozens of petitions supporting their cause. In a letter submitted to the school board the group wrote:

> We are former students of La Jolla Jr. High School, and Valencia High School. Most of us are in our 70s, we all are U.S. born citizens, and most of us are from Mexican American ancestry. The majority of us are retired or semi-retired, and still live within a 50-mile radius of the communities where we grew up (Placentia, La Jolla, Atwood, Esperanza, Yorba Linda, and Rancho Santa Ana).

We unanimously share a strong loyalty toward the schools where we received our early education, and many still attend civic and sports events that take place in Placentia and Yorba Linda. Several of us are former city and school district employees, and a few are parents, grandparents, and even, great grand parents of children who have attended or who are presently enrolled in the district's schools. Most importantly, all are former students of Mr. Gualberto Valadez when he taught at La Jolla Jr. High School or at Valencia High School.

For the past year, we have met for breakfast once a month in Placentia. At some point in our informal conversations, we always end up discussing the great influence that our former Spanish teacher, coach, advisor, and most importantly our friend, Mr. Gualberto J. Valadez, who is 92 years old, and is a longtime resident of Yorba Linda. We know that there are countless number of friends and ex-students who feel as indebted to him as we do, and who would like to pay special tribute to him for dedicating 45 years of his life to the education of several generations of children from the Placentia-Yorba Linda Unified School District.

Our group therefore formally requests as a voice of one that either the high school in Yorba Linda be named, "Valadez (Gualberto J.) High School" or that the future middle school in Placentia be named, "Valadez (Gualberto J.) Middle School."[184]

Among the letters' signatories were teachers, school administrators, engineers, professors, doctors, business owners, military veterans, and elected public officials. Most of them, like Valadez, were the first in their family to graduate from high school and attend college. In their letters, Valadez's students credited his example, professionalism, and guidance for inspiring them to stick with their education and to pursue careers that were previously outside the reach of most ethnic Mexicans in Orange County. In December of 2008, the Placentia-Yorba Linda Unified School District named their new state-of-the-art middle school after Gualberto J. Valadez, known today as Valadez Middle School Academy.[185]

As the formative contributions of Orange County Mexicans to La Progresista and MAM show, residents actively played an early role in the politicization of Mexican Americans in Southern California, a truth obscured by the tendency of scholars to overemphasize people, organizations, and institutions emanating from Los Angeles. As with the development of racial capitalism, civil rights struggles had local and translocal origins. Hence, organizations like La Progresista and MAM did not have a single place of origin. They were multinodal grassroots organizations that relied on a network of activists and places connected by a shared experience and subjectivity. The reliance of commercial agriculture, and citrus capitalism more particularly, on ethnic Mexican family labor in Southern

California provided the backdrop for the formation and growth of La Progresista and MAM. Given the region's centrality in the development of citrus capitalism, it should be of no surprise that Orange County's citrus communities proved such fertile and essential ground for the development of ethnic Mexican grassroots organizations during the 1920s, 1930s, and 1940s.

The significance of what was achieved by so-called moderate organizations like La Progresista and MAM stemmed from the unique sociohistorical moment in which they arose. Prior to the development of these translocal organizations, Orange County Mexicans lacked any semblance of social, economic, and political influence in the region. Arising out of the "Mexican Problem" era, when they were racialized, marginalized, criminalized, and removed for being Mexican, those involved in La Progresista and MAM initiated the movement that began to break down the walls of segregation established by citrus capitalists in Orange County and other locales throughout Southern California. By all measures this was extraordinary. Their actions preceded, foreshadowed, and mirrored the work of other emancipatory struggles that challenged the social, economic, and political institutions that supported racial capitalism. The particular pattern of ethnic Mexican grassroots organizing established by La Progresista and the Mexican Youth Conference/MAM involved building affective group attachment through community centered education; creating spaces for the development of leadership through the formation of lodges, clubs, and organizations; and collaborating and mobilizing translocally across urban, rural, and suburban space.[186] This pattern which developed organically out of Orange County Mexicans daily experiences with the abuses of citrus capitalism, provided a model for future mobilizations to adapt and improve. Collectively, the actions of Progresistas and Mexican American youth instilled hope and confidence in a rising generation of activists who imagined and fought for a reordering of space and social relations in Orange County. As a result, Mexican Americans entered the 1940s primed to end de jure segregation in Orange County schools and push for increased participation in electoral politics.

CHAPTER 4

Mendez, et al. v. Westminster School District of Orange County, et al.

I didn't want other children to go through what we went through . . . I said no I'm not
going to let our kids go to those schools because I was there and knew what was going on.

Virginia Guzman, *2011*

On a Sunday afternoon in 1932, Hector Tarango attended worship services at a Methodist congregation in El Modena, near Orange, CA. On
his way to the chapel, the teenager noticed the peculiar sight of two elementary schools standing adjacent to each other, albeit separated by an open
field. Tarango observed that one of the schools, Roosevelt Elementary, was
noticeably newer, featuring a clean stucco exterior, large commons areas,
and a row of palm trees. The other school, Lincoln Elementary, was in dis-
repair, having a much older exterior and less inviting landscaping. After
learning that the pristine-looking school was for white students only,
while Lincoln was reserved for Mexican students, Hector recalled, "That
shook me up tremendously, because I didn't realize they were doing that
[segregating Mexican American school children]."[1]

Born into an ethnic Mexican working-class family and raised in multiracial communities outside of Orange County, Hector developed interethnic
relationships with peers and neighbors. Hector's multicultural worldview
was abruptly challenged that Sunday afternoon with the realization that
one's language, culture, and skin tone justified second-class treatment.
Running counter to his lived experience, Hector was politicized at an early
age by the segregated landscape of Orange County. Although he lacked a college education and professional training, Hector drew on his multicultural

Breaking Down the Walls of Segregation. David-James Gonzales, Oxford University Press.
© Oxford University Press 2025. DOI: 10.1093/9780197839485.003.0005

experiences and hybridized Mexican American identity in his lifelong community service and social activism to curtail civil injustice. A decade after learning of Orange County's segregated school system, Hector became a crucial figure in the grassroots efforts that led to the landmark *Mendez, et al. v. Westminster School District of Orange County, et al.* (1947) decision, which ended de jure segregation in California's public schools and "served as a dry run" for *Brown v. Board of Education* (1954) seven years later.[2]

On February 18, 1946, Senior District Court Judge of Los Angeles, Paul J. McCormick, ruled in favor of plaintiffs Gonzalo Mendez, William Guzman, Frank Palomino, Thomas Estrada, and Lorenzo Ramirez in the class action lawsuit *Mendez, et al. v. Westminster School District of Orange County, et al.* Sending shockwaves throughout the country, *Mendez et al.* was a watershed case that extended the Fourteenth Amendment's equal protection clause to the educational rights of Mexican Americans and other communities of color in California and led to additional civil rights victories through the courts and legislative actions in ensuing decades.[3] Despite its transformative impact on American law and society, *Mendez et al.* is relatively unknown, especially compared to *Brown v. Board of Education* (1954).[4] Even those familiar with the case are often unaware about how it developed, who was involved, and when and how the movement to desegregate Orange County schools began. In particular, other accounts diminish the central role of grassroots community organizing in bringing the case to trial, which overlooks the structural violence inflicted upon ethnic Mexicans and the dozens of local citizens, community activists, and parents who courageously stood up to the power of citrus capitalists in Orange County.

A host of unheralded, ordinary, and mostly unrecognized individuals from the Mexican colonias and barrios of Orange County were responsible for change on the ground that led to the more celebrated headlines, courtroom drama, and legislative successes of the Civil Rights Movement in Southern California. These men and women, while seemingly lacking great political influence and power, made significant contributions to the trajectory of civil rights through their everyday experiences, conversations, and actions.

Examining *Mendez et al.* outside the local context of ethnic Mexican social struggle and political activism in Orange County, as has been the case in previous studies, has resulted in silencing important historical actors like the co-plaintiff "et al." families of William and Virginia Guzman, Frank and Irene Palomino, Lorenzo and Josefina Ramirez, and Thomas and Maria Luisa Estrada who were equally essential to bringing the case to trial. Previous accounts stressing the Gonzalo and Felicitas Mendez family's version of events produced a master narrative detached from the legacy of social relations and social struggle in the region.[5] By basing the region's economic well-being on citrus and racial capitalism, regional boosters exploited ethnic Mexican family labor by isolating them in segregated neighborhoods and schools. Ethnic Mexicans, whether immigrant or domestically born, had a long history of challenging racial discrimination and social marginalization through individual and collective action. These circumstances are key to situating *Mendez et al.* and providing a fuller understanding of how the case made it to trial and the impact of its legacy on the region, state, and nation.

Employing the experiences and activism of Hector Tarango and the unheralded grassroots efforts of many others leading up to the *Mendez et al.* decision, this chapter illustrates how Orange County Mexicans built a translocal civil rights movement in Southern California. With a particular focus on the county's socioeconomic dynamics, it adds a spatial dimension to the identity formation and political mobilization of Mexican Americans.[6] Viewing public spaces, like streets, convenience stores, classrooms, the workplace, and the courtroom, as contact zones in which members of various ethnoracial and cultural groups express competing identities, politics, and visions of society, this chapter demonstrates how public space served as a social and political borderland in the politicization of Mexican Americans. In doing so, it establishes Mexican American political activism as a vital component of the Civil Rights Movement that has for too long been predicated on a black-white binary of race relations.[7] The early civil rights activities of Mexican American individuals and organizations established the framework for overturning segregation within American public schools and led to the more widely recognized Chicano/a movement of the sixties and seventies.

THE ROLE OF PLACE IN THE ACTIVISM OF HECTOR TARANGO

Hector Ruben Tarango was born in the small, isolated mining town of Clifton, AZ, in 1919. His parents, Ponciano Tarango and Maria Parades, emigrated from Mexico in 1911 and 1910, respectively, and settled in the Clifton precinct's Shannon Hill Spanish Section. Ponciano, who Hector later described as "traditionally Mexican," worked as a laborer in the adjacent Clifton-Morenci copper mines, an industrial magnet for the thousands of migrant laborers that came to the region from Europe, Latin America, and Asia. Maria, a "nontraditional Mexican" according to Hector, was a college graduate, former Baptist missionary, and schoolteacher who chose to stay home and care for Hector and his younger sister, Ethel.[8] By age six, Hector developed a severe hip infection, later identified as a rare form of skeletal tuberculosis. Receiving a medical sponsorship from their local Baptist congregation, the Tarangos moved to Los Angeles to seek treatment for their young son. While Hector went through a long and arduous recovery, his family settled in the ethnically diverse East Los Angeles community of Boyle Heights. Although the effects of the disease left him permanently disabled, Hector was determined that it would not hold him back.[9]

Arriving in Boyle Heights during the early 1920s, the Tarangos encountered a cultural landscape quite different from the one they left in Arizona. Indeed, after experiencing the deep-seated racial discrimination and segregation of the Clifton-Morenci region, Los Angeles' Eastside may have seemed like a multicultural paradise due to the prevalence of spaces in which ethnic Mexicans, Japanese immigrants, African Americans, Jews, and other ethnic Europeans coexisted in neighborhood streets, schools, churches, parks, and businesses.[10] Renting a small house on the eleven hundredth block of South Dacotah Street, the Tarangos immediate neighbors comprised a cross-section of the broader demographics of Boyle Heights. Directly to their left resided the Rodriguez family and, on their right, the Merona family. According to the 1930 census, both households were listed as "Mexican," whether "alien," native-born, or naturalized citizen. Moving southwest along S. Dacotah St., most of the homes were occupied by ethnic Mexicans, with the exceptions of a "Syrian" family (the Abdeors) twelve houses down, a "Russian" family (the Massopeans) nine houses down, and an Anglo-American family from Colorado (the Hayes) two houses down. To the rear of the Tarango property was a block of homes facing Euclid St. Moving southwest along Euclid were three Russian families (Gaukman, Rosenberg, and Bogdonoff), three Armenian families (Abajian, Abajian, and Arzorian), two Anglo-American families (Provant and Gamble), and one Italian (Coulette), Austrian (Hoff), and Mexican (Martinez) family. To the west or front of the Tarango property was South Fresno Street. Heading south on Fresno lived three Chinese families (Poon, Shuey, and Ng), one Irish family (Kelly), another from New Zealand (Chalk), and two ethnic Mexican families (Silvestre and Delarosa).[11]

As residents of the city's "most ethnically diverse neighborhood," the Tarangos had ample opportunity to interact with people from various races and cultures in public spaces like Hollenbeck Park or the movie theatres, groceries, barbershops, delis, and other businesses along Brooklyn Ave. Additionally, fraternal organizations, religious institutions, and the YWCA's International Institute of Los Angeles sponsored cultural events that celebrated notions of cultural pluralism amidst the nativism of the interwar era. By encouraging "the American-born children of immigrants to retain the language and distinct cultural traditions of their parents," the residents of Boyle Heights promoted a multicultural vision of society that contrasted with the repatriation drives and residential restrictive covenants of their day.[12] Further, popular music, like jazz and swing, echoed across dance halls, ballrooms, music stores, homes, and schools, promoting cross-cultural community interaction. Bringing youth and adults of various races together in Boyle Heights's public and private spaces, broke down the barriers of racial stereotypes and challenged the segregated landscape of the greater Los Angeles region.[13] Despite its multicultural composition, life in Los Angeles' Eastside was far from ideal. Studies of the predominantly working-class immigrant populations in the area have addressed the prevalence of dilapidated housing, poor health, demanding labor conditions, and cultural struggles against assimilation that permeated the lives of many ethnic Mexicans, Asians, Blacks, and ethnic Europeans.[14]

In the case of Hector Tarango, however, growing up in such a multiracial community shielded him from more blatant experiences with racial discrimination, like the entrenched forms of housing and workplace segregation that existed in Orange, Riverside, and San Bernardino counties.[15] Arriving in Boyle Heights in time to begin his primary education, Tarango attended integrated schools where he made friends with white, Jewish, Japanese, Chinese, and African-American children. Unhindered by feelings of inferiority resulting from the humiliation and degradation of school segregation, his early experiences at school and within the community formed his views of societal membership, social justice, and politics long before he became politically active.[16]

PLACE AND THE SEGREGATION OF
MEXICAN CHILDREN IN ORANGE COUNTY

Offered an opportunity by family friend and later LULAC organizer William "Henry" Wheat, the Tarango family took over the management of a small grocery store in Orange, CA. As they moved into the Cypress Street Mexican barrio in 1932, they experienced an entirely different sociocultural landscape than Boyle Heights. Thirteen years old at the time of his family's move to Orange, Tarango may have noticed subtle differences in his new environment's sociocultural landscape. Whereas his previous neighborhood exemplified a cultural polyglot, Orange was more clearly stratified along lines of race and class.

A product of the region's dependence upon industrial citrus agriculture, the Cypress Street barrio developed in the shadow of the packinghouse owned by the SOGA at 350 North Cypress Street. Located about a block south of the Tarangos' grocery and residence, the SOGA packinghouse was situated along the Atchison, Topeka, and Santa Fe Railroad line. In addition to forming the barrio's western boundary, the railroad tracks were the economic artery of the regional economy as they provided the means for the distribution of the county's most lucrative crop, Sunkist brand Valencia oranges. Located at the corner of North Cypress and West Palm Avenue, the packinghouse solidified the barrio's southwestern edge. Heading east of the packinghouse along West Palm, the barrio extended two blocks until it reached Olive Street and then moved north two blocks to its northeastern limit at Walnut Avenue. Heading west along Walnut back toward the Tarango grocery, the North Cypress barrio formed a two-by-two-block rectangle. Occupied almost entirely by ethnic Mexicans, the barrio was effectively cordoned off socially, culturally, and physically from the white population east of Glassell.[17]

Hector Tarango became abruptly aware of Orange County's apartheid-like society shortly after his family arrived in the city of Orange. By the 1930s, each of the county's major cities, including Santa Ana, Anaheim, Fullerton, and Orange, maintained segregated public schools, parks, swimming pools, and movie theaters. Due to his age and physical handicap, Tarango did not attend the segregated Cypress Street Mexican school, although it was located a few blocks from his family's store. Soon enough he encountered the humiliation of segregation firsthand. This occurred unexpectedly while the family attended church services in El Modena on a Sunday morning. Recalling his initial experience with racial discrimination, Hector stated, "I was only in [my] teens then" but "from then on, I started realizing that they were discriminating against [us]." Devastated by the scene of run-down Lincoln Elementary (Mexican school) contrasted by the elegance of Roosevelt Elementary, Tarango struggled to make sense of a reality that contrasted so sharply with his lived experience. He thought, "in Los Angeles, we didn't have any segregation."[18] While he may not have been aware of school segregation as a child, "by 1930, eighty-five percent of Mexican children in the Southwest were attending either separate classrooms or entirely separate schools."[19]

Contemporary accounts and court transcripts described the stark differences between "Mexican" and "American" schools throughout Orange County during the 1930s and 1940s. In El Modena, Roosevelt (white school) was styled after the old California missions, having a white stucco exterior, columns, and a row of palm trees, while Lincoln (Mexican school) was an old dark brick building. The two schools were located on the same property, albeit separated by baseball diamonds that placed them 120 yards apart.[20]

Figure 4.1 Roosevelt "White" School (left) Lincoln "Mexican" School (right), El Modena, CA, c. 1940. Courtesy of Margie Aguirre.

Although Lincoln was integrated during its first decade from 1913 to 1923, the El Modeno School Board began segregating Mexican children after Roosevelt Elementary opened on April 4, 1923.[21] Attending Lincoln during the era of segregation, Dan Gomez recalled, "We'd always seem to end up with the leftovers or stuff that wasn't quite right . . . we went through a lot of that."[22] Also attending Lincoln was Rudy Hernandez, who remembered, "I noticed [Roosevelt] had a library . . . and we did not . . . If we wanted to borrow a book to read, we had to go over there. So we hardly never went."[23]

About thirteen miles southwest of El Modena was the city of Westminster, which also began segregating Mexicans during the 1920s. Prior to 1929, Westminster Main (also known as the 17th Street School) was the city's only public elementary school and was attended by white, Mexican, and Asian children. As in El Modena, Mexican children attended alongside white children at Westminster Main for over a decade until the Westminster School District opened the Hoover School and required all Mexican children to go there. As in El Modena, the Hoover Mexican school was inferior to the school white children attended.[24] Parents noted that Hoover and other Mexican schools lacked a cafeteria, tables, or benches for children to eat lunch, so they had to eat outside the school building sitting on the ground or go home.[25] Describing the disparities between white and Mexican schools in Westminster, journalist and social activist Carey McWilliams stated, "There were two schools in Westminster: a handsomely equipped school with green lawns and shrubs for the Anglo-Americans;

and a Mexican school whose meager equipment matches the inelegance of its surroundings."[26]

East of Westminster was the city of Santa Ana, the county seat, which had practiced segregation among the primary grades since 1912. In 1943, the Santa Ana Board of Education hired University of Southern California professors Osman Hull and Willard Ford to evaluate the facilities within the district to assist in formulating a comprehensive building program. Hull and Ford described the condition of the Mexican schools in Delhi, Fremont, and Artesia as a "fire hazard," "poorly constructed," and having "less than one-third of the required amount of light." Further, the buildings were "entirely unsuited to school use . . . condemned for years [with] no interior finish." Summing up their report, Hull and Ford noted that "the temperature in many of the rooms is almost unbearable [and since] no artificial light is provided in the building, it is impossible to do satisfactory reading without serious eye strain on many days of the year."[27]

In addition to the striking physical differences between facilities, the curriculum, pedagogy, and treatment of students differed significantly between Mexican and white schools. For the most part, the curriculum and instruction of Mexican American children supported the socioeconomic system in the surrounding agricultural communities.[28] This meant that, while white children were taught academic subjects that would prepare them for further educational advancement, Mexican children were taught a mixture of basic grammar and arithmetic with heavy doses of vocational training to prepare them to fill low-wage, labor-intensive occupations.[29] Further, several districts structured their curriculum to ensure it took Mexicans twice as long to complete the primary grades.[30] Longtime El Modena resident Annie Quintana remembered Mexican children being tracked into "retarded classes" (due to difficulties with the English language) as well as "manual arts for boys and homemaking . . . for girls."[31] Dan Gomez also remembered differences in how white teachers treated Mexican children at Mexican schools as opposed to how their white peers were treated at their schools. "There was some feeling," Gomez recalled, "that the teachers were a little harder on the Mexican kids. Discipline wise, they'd really come down on us."[32] Clarence Peralta, resident of the Mexican colonia of Atwood near Placentia, also recalled the use of corporal punishment on Mexican children at the Richfield School. "There were mean and nice teachers," said Peralta, "but there was discipline. They would get a strap or ruler or anything and would really work you over. If you couldn't get a problem . . . you got a whuppin."[33] School districts also worked with local agribusinesses to adjust the schedules of Mexican children to coincide with their need for low-wage seasonal labor.

In Orange County, Mexican schools started a few weeks later than white schools so Mexican children could help their parents with the walnut harvest. Once in session, Mexican schools typically began and ended an hour earlier than white schools. This prevented intermixing with white children and permitted Mexican children to join their parents in the fields by early afternoon.[34]

Segregation existed along the lines of gender as well as race. According to historian Gilbert González, "the pattern of segregation tended to reinforce the traditional sexual division of labor within the Mexican family and to add and develop those divisions peculiar to an advanced capitalist society."[35] The education of Mexican girls presented a particular area of concern for educators, administrators, and social scientists, as there was a dual function in their education. Like boys, Mexican girls were trained vocationally to prepare them for menial service occupations such as laundry workers, domestic servants, and seamstresses. Unlike boys, girls were also instructed in homemaking to teach them how to be good housewives and mothers.[36] The educational curriculum and instruction of Mexican children thus attempted to assimilate and "Americanize" them into certain aspects of white society as hired help. Hence, the treatment of Mexican American girls exemplified the intertwined relationship between the social constructions of race and gender in American capitalism. These practices survived Reconstruction as racial capitalism evolved in response to the termination of slavery and the expansion of constitutional protections to African Americans. They later expanded to the Southwest as a system of social controls that supported industrial capitalism and maintained white supremacy.[37]

As seen in the lives of Stephen Reyes, Luis Sandoval, Gualberto Valadez, and others, many Mexican Americans overcame the structural inequities segregation strove to produce. Yet, these were exceptions to the norm. Indeed, Orange County's unequal and discriminatory school system worked in tandem with the other walls of segregation, including inequities in labor, housing, social integration, and political representation, to enclose ethnic Mexicans in spaces of disadvantage that served the citrus economy. In education, this resulted in only 4 percent of ethnic Mexican children advancing to high school, an intentional outcome of policies implemented by citrus capitalists to preserve the next generation of low-wage labor.[38] While Hector Tarango was not subjected to the injustice of a segregated school system until his family's move to Orange County in 1932, his disgust with the spectacle of racial discrimination, coupled with his multiracial view of society, served as the foundation for his future activism. For others like Tarango, the indelible impression of daily humiliation and

Figure 4.2 Fourth-grade class photo of Arthur (third row, second from left) and Bobby (bottom right) Palomino. Fremont Mexican School in Santa Ana, CA, May 2, 1946. Courtesy of Chapman University Frank Mt. Pleasant Library of Special Collections and Archives.

disgrace resulting from an inherently unequal educational system dramatically shaped the future politicization of Mexican Americans.

MOBILIZING IDENTITIES

Although Tarango did not attend segregated schools himself, his reaction to the segregation of Mexican American schoolchildren fueled his political activism. His response to the injustice of racial discrimination resulted from a hybridized Mexican American identity was forged in Orange County's segregated landscape.[39] Neither his Mexican heritage nor his American birthright alone could adequately explain his repulsion to the contrasts of Lincoln and Roosevelt Elementary, but rather the union of these identities within a particular place and time motivated him to respond. Representative of the second-class position ethnic Mexicans retained during the first half of the twentieth century, the sight of Lincoln Elementary separated from Roosevelt by a mere hundred yards or so crystalized the terrain of Orange County's social, cultural, and political landscape. For Hector Tarango and

Mexican Americans in Orange County, the struggle to break down the walls of segregation played a central role in solidifying their identity and spurring their political mobilization.

Living in and managing their grocery store in the Cypress Street barrio introduced the Tarangos to various community members. In addition to the network of contacts made through the family business, as an adult, Tarango developed relationships with Santa Ana business owners Cruz Barrios and Manuel Veiga Jr. In a conversation with Barrios during the early forties, Hector mentioned the disturbing scene of racial segregation he witnessed in El Modena as a child. Barrios responded, "Yeah, I know all about it. We were very disturbed . . . because our fighting group is coming home . . . and their kids are being segregated, and that isn't right."[40] Tarango and Barrios decided that it was time to do something about the injustice of school segregation. They enlisted the support of Isadore Gonzales, a department store clerk at J.C. Penny, and Manuel Veiga Jr., owner of Veiga's Mortuary, in forming the Latin American Voters League (LAVL) between 1942 and 1943.[41] This was the first of three grassroots organizations formed by Tarango, Barrios, Veiga, Gonzales, and others in Orange County during the 1940s.[42] Their aim was to build a movement within the ethnic Mexican community to desegregate the school system and attack the broader system of ethno-racial apartheid.

While the broader context of World War II played some role in motivating Tarango and his nascent cohort of Orange County activists to form the LAVL, ethnic Mexicans had a rich prewar history of resistance, civic engagement, and grassroots mobilization. Like the mutualistas, honorary societies, and religious organizations formed by their immigrant parents, Mexican Americans built ethno-racial solidarity as they mobilized their community against the second-class treatment of their children by Orange County school districts.[43] Developing out of the homegrown culture of ethnic Mexican civic engagement and political activism illustrated by *La Progresista* and MAM, the LAVL organized a more assertive campaign that demanded equal protection in the United States, based on their constitutional rights. While some Mexican American activists and organizations used citizenship-based rights claims to appeal for inclusion within white middle-class America, Orange County ethnic Mexicans did not make these claims in exchange for or at the "sacrifice" of their bicultural and binational heritage.[44] Their activism and tactics were rooted in their subjectivity and lived experiences as Mexican and American. Claiming one did not necessarily come at the expense of another.

Once their initial conversations led to a shared desire for direct action and organization, the first order of business for the LAVL was to raise

Figure 4.3 Hector Tarango, c. 1950. Courtesy of Tarango family personal collection.

awareness against this gross violation of Mexican American rights. This was an essential step in the Orange County desegregation movement, but it was not the first. In 1919, responding to the Santa Ana School District's plans to expand segregation by removing all Mexican children from the Logan School, ethnic Mexican parents and members of the Mexican Pro-Patria Club "presented a petition to the school board which demanded that all children subject to segregation be returned to 'their respective schools.' "[45] Santa Ana's city attorney attended the meeting at the request of the school board to discuss the legal ramifications of segregating Mexican children. In response to the parents' protest, the district attorney argued that "it is entirely proper and legal to classify [students] according to the regularity of attendance, ability to understand the English language and their aptness to advance in the grades to which they shall be assigned."[46] To avoid running afoul of state law, which permitted the segregation of Chinese and Native American students, but not Mexicans, the district followed the advice of the city attorney to implement the policy "regardless of race or color."[47] In practice, however, the district's segregationist policy targeted ethnic Mexican children exclusively. Indeed, all four defendant school districts named in *Mendez et al.*, Westminster, Garden Grove, Santa Ana, and El Modeno, permitted African American and Asian children to attend white schools while Mexican Americans were segregated by themselves.[48] This fact attests to the homegrown system of ethno-racial apartheid that specifically targeted ethnic Mexicans in Orange County.

As they began their campaign against segregation, the LAVL had to educate some parents and community members about the injustice of segregation and their children's rights as US citizens. In a 1991 interview, former El Modena resident, World War II veteran, and Lincoln Elementary student Bob Torres explained the indifference among some in the ethnic Mexican community. Referring to segregation in El Modena, Torres stated, "I myself . . . wasn't aware of it, because I felt comfortable with it. Nobody was hurting me. I never felt that they were depriving me of anything, until later I learned that they did. Once we found out that we had been wronged, then we wanted to do something about it."[49] Another resident of El Modena at the time, Dan Gomez, echoed a similar sentiment. "There was just very little involvement. There was really no concern about it . . . it was like well, if no one says anything about it, it's not really happening. And that's really the way it was handled. Nobody says anything, it doesn't exist."[50] While some families were either ignorant, apprehensive, or discouraged by previous failures to mount another challenge to the system directly, they did not necessarily remain silent, but chose their own forms of individual protest. Those who could afford it, like Annie Quintana and *Mendez et al.* co-plaintiffs Frank and Irene Palomino, enrolled their children in private Catholic schools where segregation did not exist.[51] And some, like Felicitas Fuentes and William and Virginia Guzman, kept their children at home, refusing to enroll them in school until the district changed its policy.[52]

While keeping children out of school and away from other segregated facilities, like public parks, swimming pools, and movie theaters, may seem ineffective or counterproductive to overturning a segregated society, such practices sowed the seeds of future activism and politicization. This kind of silent resistance, which often followed unsuccessful attempts at public intervention, was fundamentally political and important groundwork for what is often the more recognized and lauded forms of political activism.[53] Others, like Bob Torres and Dan Gomez, felt there was a void of leadership within the community before the efforts of Tarango, the LAVL, and the *Mendez et al.* plaintiff families. "I think that was one of the things that got us going," Gomez reflected, "because you needed someone . . . outspoken. Someone who wasn't afraid to start making a few waves and afraid that the establishment would come back and pound him."[54] Likewise, Carol Torres, one of two minors who testified during the trial, remembered that many ethnic Mexicans were "leery" of getting involved due to fear of reprisals from employers and district officials.[55] While there certainly were groups like *La Progresista* and MAM that provided leadership and worked to address forms of discrimination at the time, neither were focused, as LAVL was, on building a grassroots movement with the specific intent of ending school segregation. Moreover, as Gomez commented, perhaps community members were waiting for a leader. In conversations between Tarango and his associates, it became increasingly evident that a more assertive type of action, one based on ethnic identity and the mobilization of organic community leadership, was necessary if something was to be done about the second-class treatment of Orange County's Mexican Americans.[56]

THE FORMATION OF ORANGE COUNTY'S DESEGREGATION MOVEMENT

Several individuals began their own personal battles with segregation before uniting to file the class action suit against Orange County schools in March 1945. Such was the case with Felicitas Fuentes, who recalled that "a lot of . . . mothers," including herself, Virginia Guzman, Manuela Ochoa, Jane Sianez, Mabel Mendez, and others, had either spoken with individual school administrators and district officials or appeared before the defendant school boards over the previous four years to request an end to segregation. As with earlier efforts in 1919, these initial protests were rebuffed. As historian Nadine Bermudez detailed in her study of the fifteen women whose families' names are recorded in the *Mendez et al.* court transcripts, Mexican American mothers were often the first in their families and communities to confront school and district officials over the policy of segregation.[57] During these early and recurring interactions with school administrators, the protests of Mexican American women anticipated the arguments made by attorney David C. Marcus years before the lawsuit was filed.[58] They complained that school zones and district boundaries were enforced arbitrarily, that the system of segregating Mexican children was discriminatory and racially motivated, and that Mexican school facilities, materials, and instruction were unequal to those provided to white children.

For Frank and Irene Palomino, also plaintiffs in *Mendez et al.*, their struggle began during the fall of 1941. In court testimony, Frank Palomino explained that after moving to Santa Ana, he visited with the Superintendent of Orange County Schools to inquire about the district his children should attend. After being informed that his children were assigned to the Garden Grove School District, Palomino visited with Superintendent Emley, who told him his children had to attend the Hoover School. Knowing Hoover was reserved for Spanish-speaking Mexican children, Palomino asked if he could enroll his English-speaking children, Arthur and Sally, at Lincoln Elementary. Superintendent Emley denied Palomino's request, stating that since his children were of "Mexican descent" they would not be permitted to attend Lincoln "until they were in the sixth grade."[59] Refusing to submit to the district's overtly segregationist policy, the Palominos enrolled eleven-year-old Arthur at the Fremont School in Santa Ana, and eight-year-old Sally at St. Joseph's Catholic school, also in Santa Ana.

Likewise, Felicitas Fuentes met with school officials in September 1942 to enroll her son Roberto "Bobbie" in the Franklin School in Santa Ana. Franklin was only a block and a half from the Fuentes home, but district officials made Bobbie attend the segregated Fremont School. This was a clear example of "segregation by design" as the city of Santa Ana divided itself into fourteen zones with a schoolhouse in each.[60] Three of the zones and their corresponding schools were placed directly inside the city's three Mexican barrios, Logan, Delhi, and Artesia. These schools were "attended exclusively by persons of Mexican descent," where "complete segrega-tion" was practiced.[61] In her conversation with Assistant Superintendent Reinhard, Felicitas explained that not only did she live three blocks closer to Franklin than Fremont, but also that a few non-Mexican children in her neighborhood attended Franklin while her son could not. Reinhard insisted that Bobbie attend the school within her boundary and then changed the subject by asking her "why the Mexican people were so dirty."[62] Unfazed, Fuentes pressed Reinhard for over an hour until he asked her why she wanted Bobbie to go to Franklin. "I told him in the Franklin School he had more privileges, he would learn more, and he would not be held be-hind," said Fuentes. She then asked if he had children, to which Reinhard answered he did not. "If you had a child, would you send him to the Fremont School?" Fuentes probed. Reinhard admitted he would not, "Because they didn't have any privileges and I would want the best for my child," he confessed.[63] Despite her valiant effort, Reinhard did not allow Bobbie to attend Franklin, saying it was the school board's policy and that "there was nothing he could do." In protest, Fuentes refused to enroll Bobbie in school until he was eight years old, though she returned to the district office in the fall of 1943 and 1944 to petition the school board to change their minds.

Immediately following the formation of the LAVL in 1943, Tarango and his associates began working with families like the Fuentes, Ochoas, Guzmans, and Palominos.[64] Driving from one barrio/colonia to another, the LAVL searched for families willing to speak out against segregation and assisted them in their entreaties before school administrators. Between the fall of 1943 and the spring of 1945, all five plaintiff families worked with the LAVL to organize and train parents to meet with district officials and attend school board meetings.[65] Such was the case on October 25, 1943, when Mrs. Leonides Sanchez and Mrs. Frank Garcia appeared before the Santa Ana Board of Education to "protest the denial of a request to send their children" to the nearby Franklin (white) School. Per the board's minutes, the women "wished to have their children educated in an American School so that they would have all the advantages of American children and learn to speak English as Americans do." The mothers also alleged, "it is a matter of discrimination when Mexican children are forced to go to the Mexican School."[66] Although the board denied their requests, Sanchez and Garcia temporarily circumvented Santa Ana's gerrymandered school zones by enrolling their children at Franklin under falsified addresses the following year. After discovering the ruse, the district promptly returned the children to the Fremont school.[67] As evidenced by the actions of Sanchez and Garcia, the protests and resistance of ethnic Mexican parents against the segregated school system were becoming more frequent and insistent.

Between the summer of 1943 and 1944, Gonzalo and Felicitas Mendez moved their family from the Artesia Mexican barrio in Santa Ana to Westminster to lease the forty-acre asparagus farm owned by Japanese immigrants Seima and Masako Munemitsu.[68] The California Alien Land Laws of 1913 and 1920 barred "aliens ineligible for citizenship" from owning agricultural land in the state, so the family placed the title of their property in the name of their oldest son, Seiko Lincoln "Tad" Munemitsu.[69] Because of the infamous Japanese internment order issued by President Franklin D. Roosevelt on February 19, 1942, the Munemitsu family faced an uncertain future. How long would internment last, they wondered, and what to do with the family farm in the meantime? As fate would have it, the Mendez and Munemitsu families shared the same banker, Mr. Frank Monroe of First Western Bank in Garden Grove. Knowing the Munemitsu's dire situation and Gonzalo Mendez's desire to operate his own farm, Monroe arranged a meeting between the two families and a lease was signed on December 20, 1944.[70] While seemingly unrelated, the internment of Japanese families and the segregation of Mexican school children resulted from overlapping policies of white supremacist ideology manifest not just in Orange County, but throughout mid-twentieth century American society.[71]

Westminster Main, also referred to as Seventeenth Street, was the closest school to the Munemitsu property. After their move to the farm, Gonzalo's sister Soledad Vidaurri took the Mendez children, including Sylvia, Gonzalo Jr., and Jerome, along with her two daughters, Alice and

Virginia, to enroll at the school. While her lighter-skinned daughters were admitted to Westminster Main, Vidaurri was told that the darker-skinned Mendez children had to attend the Hoover Mexican School.[72] The rejection shocked the Mendez family, especially Gonzalo, who attended the fifth grade at Westminster Main in 1927 or 1928 when his family lived in the nearby Olive Street Mexican barrio.[73] Although the Hoover Mexican school had not yet been built, segregation was practiced in the Westminster District during the 1920s. After opening the Hoover Mexican school in the "La Garra" section of the Olive Street barrio in 1929, the district hardened its segregationist policy.[74] Despite the fact that Sylvia had attended the segregated Fremont Mexican school when the family lived in Santa Ana, which was the same school attended by Billy Guzman and Bobbie Fuentes, the Mendezes did not become involved in the desegregation movement until the summer of 1944. Nevertheless, following the denial, Gonzalo Mendez met with school and district officials individually before uniting with others, like the Pena and Bermudez families, to form the Westminster Fathers' Association.[75] Per his court testimony, the purpose of this group, which formed about a year after the LAVL in the fall of 1944, was to organize parents whose children were forced to attend the Hoover Mexican School.[76]

It did not take long for Tarango's LAVL and Mendez's Father's Association to begin working together.[77] On the evening of September 19, 1944, Cruz Barrios, Manuel Veiga, and Hector Tarango attended the monthly meeting of the Westminster School Board as representatives of "the Latin American Voters Counsel [sic]." The minutes from this meeting provide some of the earliest documentation of the fruit born by the grassroots activity spearheaded by Tarango, Mendez, and their associates. According to the record:

> Representatives of the Hoover school Mexican colony were present, and accompanied by Messrs. Barrios, Vega [sic], and Diago [sic misspelling of Tarango], of the Latin American Voters Counsel. The Group presented a petition to the school board in which it called attention to the fact of the segregation of the American children, of Mexican descent, and children of non-Mexican descent. A definite request that the Mexican school at Hoover be unified with the Westminster school was made.[78]

The petition presented to the school board contained the signatures of twenty-six parents, all of whom had children attending the Hoover Mexican School, several of whom were members of Mendez's Father's Association. The petition stated that half of the parents were "American born" and that their "American born" children were victims of "racial discrimination." In a united voice, the parents of Westminster called for an immediate "doing away with . . . segregation."[79] In response, the board claimed "that the system of segregation had been inherited by them and that they had considered the problem before that date."[80] The board's comments were misleading, as the minutes before September 19, 1944, did not indicate that any such discussion ever took place. While the Westminster board attempted to pass a school bond to raise funds for the construction of new facilities, the improvements were to be made to Westminster Main and did not appear to be of any benefit to the Mexican children attending Hoover.

On October 23, 1944, at the encouragement of the LAVL, a coalition of twenty-five to thirty Mexican American parents and community members attended a meeting of the Santa Ana Board of Education. For some, like the Guzman, Sanchez, and Garcia families, this was their second or third time appearing before the board over the previous three years.[81] By the time of this meeting, William and Virginia Guzman had hired Los Angeles attorney Charles Martin to represent them.[82] Speaking for the group, Martin charged the board with racial discrimination for not permitting Mexican American children to attend Fremont even though they allowed Anglo/white children living out of the district to do so. In their court testimonies, William and Virginia Guzman remembered the board as dismissive: "they wouldn't pay any attention to him."[83] Seeing that such accusations had little effect, Martin noted that the Guzmans lived closer to Franklin and that their son Billy encountered dangerous traffic conditions as he walked to Fremont. Defiantly, the school board refuted these claims and stated that, since Billy had experienced no problems arriving at school safely in prior years, any danger posed to him should be mitigated as he grew older. Sensing they had failed to pacify the group of Mexican parents, the board requested an additional ninety days to determine how to respond.[84] Because of the district's obstinance, the Guzmans kept Billie at home until the following school year when they enrolled him in St. Anne's Catholic school. No Guzman child ever attended Santa Ana Schools again.[85] For Virginia Guzman, this decision was rooted in her own traumatic experience attending Fremont as a child. "I didn't want my son to go there [Fremont Mexican School]," Virginia explained. "The White schools were better. I wanted my son to get a better education than what I got there. I knew what was going on, and I knew what I went through, so I said No!"[86]

While Tarango's LAVL and Mendez's Father's Association initiated the desegregation movement against the districts of Westminster, Santa Ana, and Garden Grove, the Lorenzo and Josefina Ramirez family began a similar process in El Modena. Although Ramirez had lived and attended school in El Modena from the age of thirteen, he spent the previous eleven years prior to the *Mendez et al.* filing (1933–1944) working on the 370-acre Murphy Ranch in Whittier, CA. During this time, Ramirez was quickly promoted from general laborer to fumigator, tractor operator, and field-worker foreman. While in this position, he represented the ranch in its dealings with the Mexican Consulate in Los Angeles. After the institution of the Bracero Program in August of 1942, he became involved in the process of requesting and securing Mexican contract laborers (braceros).[87] This put Ramirez in frequent contact with Los Angeles attorney David C. Marcus, who had worked with the Mexican Consulate since passing the bar in the 1920s.[88] Due to his extensive knowledge of the living and working conditions of braceros on Murphy Ranch, Ramirez was asked to accompany Mexican Secretary of Foreign Affairs Ezequiel Padilla to San Francisco in 1943 as he participated in a series of Congressional hearings addressing abuses against Mexican contract laborers.[89]

When he moved his family back to El Modena during the fall of 1944, Ramirez was aghast to discover that the very school he attended as an adolescent, Lincoln Elementary, had become a segregated school for Mexican children. In his meeting with Principal Hammarsten (principal for both Lincoln and Roosevelt), Lorenzo requested that his sons (Ignacio, Silverio, and Jose) be transferred to Roosevelt since they spoke English and attended integrated schools in Whittier. Hammarsten denied Ramirez's request, informing him that "there was no seats for them in there." When Ramirez pressed Hammarsten, adding that he knew that some Mexican children had been granted waivers to attend Roosevelt, the principal again denied the request, stating, "I am sorry, but they have to go to the Lincoln School, because that is the school for them. That is where they have to go."[90] Although he relented and enrolled his sons, and eventually his daughter Phyllis, at Lincoln, Lorenzo immediately began to organize other parents in the barrio. While it is uncertain when he joined the LAVL in their efforts, Ramirez was credited by Dan Gomez as being one of the "instigators of the movement" to desegregate the El Modeno School District.[91]

A few months later, the coalition comprising the LAVL and the Westminster Father's Association acquired the services of attorney David C. Marcus.[92] On January 9, 1945, Mendez and Marcus went to the office of the Westminster School District as representatives of "the Mexican speaking peoples." In their meeting with board member Harris, Marcus alleged "there was discrimination being practiced in the district."[93] This conversation was reported in the minutes of "a special meeting" of the Westminster School Board held on January 10, 1945. Coming from legal counsel rather than a group of Mexican parents, the accusation of discrimination, coupled with

the implication of litigation, jolted the school board into seriously considering the Mexican American community's protests as more than harmless
disturbances to their weekly meetings. As the minutes of this emergency
meeting indicate, the school board "discussed at length . . . the complaint
from the Mexican speaking peoples" and was seeking legal advice to determine their official position on the segregation of Mexican children.[94]

A week later, on January 16, 1945, Gonzalo Mendez reappeared in
front of the school board with Mr. Youngyoung [*sic*] as representatives
of the Mexican community.[95] Facing inquiries about their inaction over
the requests of the Mexican American parents to integrate the Main and
Hoover schools, the board continued to insist that it had inherited the
problem from the previous school board and that funding, housing, and
construction limitations prevented integration.[96] Tellingly, in the months
between the board meetings of January 16 and March 12, neither the
Westminster nor the Santa Ana school boards discussed the integration
issue until their notification of the *Mendez et al.* filing in federal district
court.[97] Despite the repeated protests of the Mexican American community, the Westminster, Santa Ana, El Modeno, and Garden Grove districts
persisted in the segregation of Mexican American children.

Unsuccessful in their attempts to avoid litigation by appealing to school
districts directly, on March 2, 1945, the Mendez, Guzman, Palomino,
Estrada, and Ramirez families filed a class action suit in federal district court on behalf of 5,000 Mexican American children in the Orange
County school system.[98] By the time of the filing, there were at least fifteen
segregated Mexican schools distributed throughout eleven of the fifty-two
school districts in the county. *Mendez et al.* involved only four of those
districts: Westminster, Garden Grove, El Modeno, and Santa Ana. These
defendant districts operated six schools with 100 percent Mexican enrollment. Unnamed in the suit were school districts in Anaheim, Placentia,
La Habra, Orange, Costa Mesa, and other cities that also maintained
segregated Mexican schools. The fact that they were not named in the case
did not imply that segregation did not exist in these districts, as it most
certainly did.[99] However, Judge McCormick determined in pretrial proceedings that it was unnecessary to name every school practicing segregation
at the time as this would have made for a much lengthier trial. Instead, the
defendant districts in *Mendez et al.* were selected for being representative
of the types of segregation practiced in the county to determine if it was
discriminatory and thereby illegal.[100] Although unsuccessful in getting the
school boards to integrate without legal action, a small number of seemingly inconsequential Mexican communities throughout Orange County
took a significant step forward in the battle to desegregate public schools

throughout California and the nation. This was not a battle that began in Orange County or even Southern California.[101] Still, *Mendez et al.* rose to such national prominence that the desegregation movement sparked by the early yet forgotten victories of *Maestas et al. v. Shone et al.* (1914), *Romo v. Laird* (1925), *Del Rio Independent School District v. Salvatierra* (1930), and *Alvarez v. Lemon Grove* (1931) was reawakened with heightened vigor and determination.

THE TRIAL

The *Mendez et al.* trial was held from July 5 to 11, 1945. In the weeks leading up to it, the LAVL and Westminster Father's Association were crucial in finding, encouraging, and preparing witnesses. They also assisted in arranging transportation for parents and community members to attend the trial in Los Angeles at the US Courthouse building at 312 N. Spring Street. The case hinged on whether the districts had acted in a discriminatory manner in implementing their segregationist policies, thereby denying Mexican students the equal protection of the laws. Because the courts had previously upheld racial segregation under the "separate but equal" doctrine established by the Supreme Court of the United States in *Plessy v. Ferguson* (1896), segregation itself was not on trial.[102] Moreover, neither was race, as the courts had determined that Mexicans were "legally white" nearly fifty years earlier in *In re Rodriguez* (1897).[103] At issue, was whether the defendant districts were illegally discriminating against Mexican students by segregating them on the basis of ethnic prejudice, instead of for language deficiency, as the districts claimed. Although the burden of proof rested with Marcus and the et al. plaintiffs, Judge McCormick viewed the suit as an unprecedented "civil rights case" with potentially significant ramifications.[104]

In light of existing case law, Marcus was careful to narrowly construct his argument as an issue of ethnic, not racial, discrimination. He and the plaintiff families alleged that the districts had "conspired" to "design" a "common plan" of segregation "based solely upon the fact that the petitioners were of Mexican and/or Latin descent" in violation of the "Fifth and Fourteenth Amendments" to the US Constitution.[105] As citizens of the United States, the students' rights to due process and equal protection were being violated by the defendant districts, who segregated them arbitrarily and without statutory authority. Indeed, neither the state's Constitution nor its Education Code permitted the segregation of Mexicans. In their defense, the districts denied there was any conspiracy between them to segregate Mexican students "solely" on the basis of descent. The children were segregated, they claimed, "for [their own] benefit" because "they are all in a class that speaks the Spanish language . . . and are unfamiliar with the English language." In the districts' view, the children were "handicapped by their deficiency in the English language," thus segregation had a pedagogical purpose that was protected by the power delegated to them by the state to educate the population as they saw fit.[106]

Over the five-day trial, Marcus called upon sixteen Latino witnesses, fourteen of whom were of Mexican descent, while the remaining two, including Felicitas Mendez and John Marval, were Puerto Rican. Manuela Ochoa, Frank Palomino, Jane Sianez, and Juan Munoz of Garden Grove testified on day one. Felicitas Fuentes, who also spoke on day one, testified again alongside fellow Santa Ana residents William and Virginia Guzman and Mabel Mendez on day two, with El Modena residents Lorenzo Ramirez, Mrs. Nieves Pena, and the only two minors to testify in the case: fourteen-year-old Carol Torres and seventeen-year-old Robert Perez.[107] Gonzalo Mendez of Westminster testified on days three and five, followed by Felicitas Mendez of Westminster and John Marval of Santa Ana on day four, and Isabel Ayala of Garden Grove on day five. Throughout the trial, plaintiff testimonies, which were all delivered in English, rejected the districts' claims that their children were segregated because of a language handicap, claiming instead that segregation was based on whether someone looked Mexican. Parents recounted their experiences with district officials dating back to 1939, claiming that school principals and superintendents repeatedly emphasized that their children were required to attend the Mexican schools as a matter of well-established school board policy. They also testified that none of their children had ever been tested to determine English proficiency and that school administrators like Garden Groven Grove Superintendents Mr. Emley and James L. Kent and Westminster Superintendent Richard Harris had made discriminatory remarks about Mexicans being dirty, lazy, and mentally inferior.

Marcus also called on superintendents James L. Kent of Garden Grove, Frank A. Henderson of Santa Ana, Harold Hammarsten of El Modena, and Richard F. Harris of Westminster to explain their district's segregationist policies. In his examination of the superintendents, Marcus demonstrated that the districts of Garden Grove, El Modena, and Westminster segregated Mexican students regardless of English language proficiency, undermining their claims that language deficiency was the primary reason for segregation. The superintendents' testimonies also revealed that none of the districts regularly tested Mexican students to determine if they were ready to advance to white schools. When pressed on this discrepancy, the superintendents claimed their districts provided equal facilities and specialized instruction to Mexican students, negating the need for transfer to white schools. Furthermore, Superintendent Kent asserted that segregation facilitated the Americanization process, as Mexican students needed to be taught "American standards of cleanliness, morality, and socialization."[108] Compared to his peers, Kent's testimony proved most damning to the districts' defense as his contempt for Mexicans was clear when he acknowledged his belief that Mexicans were "socially," "mentally," "scholastically," and "economically" "inferior to the white race."[109] Although the other superintendents did not vocalize the same level of racial/ethnic prejudice, it became clear that their districts had no intention of ever integrating the Mexican and white student populations. This fact was confirmed during the testimony of Superintendent Hammarsten of El Modena, who admitted that Carol Torres was "one of our best students" and "has an I.Q. that is very high." When asked by Marcus why he never suggested she transfer to Roosevelt from Lincoln, Hammarsten admitted, "I don't think it was necessary."[110]

On the last day of the trial, Marcus invited Dr. Ralph L. Beals and Marie H. Hughes to provide expert testimony on the harmful effects of segregation, an inspired move that shaped the trajectory of civil rights litigation from *Mendez et al.* to *Brown v. Board*. Throughout the trial, Marcus had established that the "systematic segregation" of Mexican students was occurring among the defendant districts.[111] The question remained, however, had he and his witnesses done enough to convince the court that the motive for segregation was harming and infringing upon the rights of ethnic Mexican children. Beals, an anthropologist at UCLA, had spent the previous twenty-five years researching Indigenous and ethnic Mexican communities in Mexico, New Mexico, and Los Angeles.[112] At the time of the trial, he was conducting research on minorities in Los Angeles, including the experiences of Mexicans in segregated schools. When questioned by Marcus about whether segregation supported the districts' claims that it facilitated English language proficiency and Americanization, Beals responded:

> As a matter of fact, the learning of adequate English, it seems to me, would be interfered with by a program of segregation. I think it is a widely known fact, that if you want to learn a foreign language you immerse yourself among people that speak that language, and do not stay among speakers of your own language. In other words, keeping Mexican and Spanish-speaking children together simply means they talk Spanish together and do not learn English as rapidly as if they were associating with English-speaking people.[113]

Then, responding to the issue of Americanization, Beals asserted:

> There is no question but what segregation slows up . . . Americanization [and] would definitely retard the assimilation of the child to American customs and ways. In terms of making the children familiar with the whole body of customs . . . there can be no substitute in my opinion, for the actual contact with Anglo-speaking people, and rather intimate contact.[114]

Over his career, Beals had developed a progressive view of Americanization that departed from the classic or straight-line assimilation model popularized by early to mid-twentieth-century sociologists. Based on his extensive research in Mexico and the Southwest, Beals viewed the project of Americanization as more of a two-way process of cultural exchange, or what he called acculturation, not simply the adoption of Anglo-American customs and norms by minorities.[115] Judge McCormick took great interest in Beal's testimony and even interjected his own opinion of the role public schools played in the Americanization process when he stated:

> In the concept of the public school system . . . there is supposed to be an ad-mixture of all types of children. I conceive . . . the fundamental principle of public school education in the United States, the general comingling of children of all ancestries and descents for the purpose of building up a culture of our own. That is what I conceive to be the Americanization aspect of public school instruction.[116]

Seizing the opportunity to expose segregation as an impediment to the pluralistic view of Americanization advocated by the judge, Marcus said, "Your Honor is in entire accord with my views in the matter." He then asked Beals if segregation posed any potential harm to the white children who were kept apart from Mexicans. Beals replied affirmatively:

> The disadvantage of segregation, it would seem to me, would come primarily from the reinforcing of stereotypes of inferiority-superiority, which exists in the population as a whole. The advantages, properly handled, would come, then, in the breaking down of those stereotypes and in the broadening of understanding of people of different cultural background and the understanding of different cultures.[117]

Before concluding his testimony, Beals provocatively asserted that segregation not only "retard[ed]" the development of Mexican children, but it had the same effect on white children in terms of achieving the type of

Americanization expressed by Judge McCormick.[118] Hearing this, Marcus must have been thrilled. He had skillfully built his case over the previous four days of the trial to prove this very claim. Segregation not only harmed all those involved, but it was also un-American and anti-democratic.[119]

Marie Hughes was the last witness to testify in the trial. Like Beals, she was a respected social scientist who had spent the prior fourteen years as a field worker at the University of New Mexico's San Jose Experimental School and conducting her doctoral research at the Pio Pico School in Los Angeles County.[120] Hughes specialized in the "education of minority groups," particularly among the "children of Mexican descent."[121] Echoing Beals' testimony, Hughes emphatically confirmed that segregation was counterproductive to English language acquisition among Spanish-speaking children and hindered the project of Americanization for Mexicans and Anglos. "It is not to the best interests of children in America, Orange County or not, to work and play together and go to school together under segregated conditions. Segregation, by its very nature, is a reminder constantly of inferiority, of not being wanted, of not being part of the community," Hughes declared. Responding to amici council Robert F. Christopher's explanation of the type of segregation practiced in the El Modeno School District where the Lincoln and Roosevelt schools were separated by a mere 120 yards, Hughes stressed "any separation of children which prevents free communication among them, on an equal basis . . . would be bad because . . . segregation tends to give an aura of inferiority." Then referring to the five years she spent observing Anglo-Mexican interactions within Los Angeles' Ranchito School District, Hughes explained that segregation led to "frequent . . . fights and other demonstrations of unfriendly feeling, because the children are not together on a normal basis."[122] Like the testimony of her colleague, Judge McCormick appeared intrigued by Hughes' conclusions. Seeking further clarification, the judge inquired as to which "authorities" sponsored her research and how representative it was to the situation in Orange County. Hughes confirmed that her research was "a project of the Los Angeles County School office, in cooperation with the office of Inter-American Affairs," and that the Pio Pico School and Ranchito School District were "chosen as a typical segregated school situation."[123]

After Hughes' testimony, McCormick instructed Marcus and Deputy County Counsel George F. Holden to focus their closing briefs on three questions. The first pertained to the issue of jurisdiction, which McCormick considered the most important. Did the Federal District Court have jurisdiction to hear the case? The question had perplexed the judge since the pre-trial hearing and was the basis of Holden's repeated calls for dismissal. Believing "education [was] a state matter," McCormick thought it necessary to settle this question first before proceeding with the others.[124] Second, considering that segregation was, in fact, occurring among the defendant districts, was the "extent" of said segregation "unjust discrimination"? Finally, the last question considered whether the plaintiffs were justified in seeking redress as a "class action," and if so, "what form of relief" were they entitled to?

The opinion handed down by Judge Paul J. McCormick on February 18, 1946, delivered a tremendous blow against the segregated society that existed throughout California's Citrus Belt and established a legal precedent that shook the foundations of Jim Crow America. Addressing the question of jurisdiction, McCormick acknowledged that "While education is a state matter, it is not so absolutely or exclusively." Citing *Cumming v. Richmond County Board of Education* (1899), *Missouri ex rel. Gaines v. Canada* (1938), and *Meyer v. Nebraska* (1923), the judge confirmed that states and municipalities acting under the "color of law" fell under the jurisdiction of the federal courts if their appointed actors (superintendents and school boards) violated "a personal right or privilege protected by the Fourteenth Amendment."[125] Regarding the issue of Mexican students forming a protected class, McCormick affirmed that the actions of the defendant districts had "singled out" "pupils of Mexican ancestry" "as a class for segregation," and that this was done in violation of the state's Constitution and Education Code.[126] Then, elaborating on the constitutionality of school segregation in California, McCormick declared:

> Our conclusions in this action, however, do not rest solely upon what we conceive to be the utter irreconcilability of the segregation practices in the defendant school districts with the public educational system authorized and sanctioned by the laws of the State of California. We think such practices clearly and unmistakably disregard rights secured by the supreme law of the land. "The equal protection of the laws" pertaining to the public school system in California is not provided by furnishing in separate schools the same technical facilities, text books and courses of instruction to children of Mexican ancestry that are available to the other public school children regardless of their ancestry. A paramount requisite in the American system of public education is social equality. It must be open to all children by unified school association regardless of lineage.[127]

Concluding that the defendant districts "arbitrarily discriminate[d] against the pupils of Mexican ancestry and deni[ed] them the equal protection of the laws," McCormick granted the plaintiffs "injunctive relief against all defendants, restraining further discriminatory practices against the pupils of Mexican descent in the public schools of defendant school districts."[128]

Although McCormick's opinion was limited to the districts of Westminster, Garden Grove, Santa Ana, and El Modeno, it established the foundation for undermining the very premise of the "separate but equal" doctrine established fifty years earlier. Indeed, the Supreme Court's underlying assumption in *Plessy* was that segregation did not automatically infer social inferiority. The testimonies in *Mendez et al.*, however, proved otherwise. McCormick confirmed this truth by stating emphatically: "It is established by the record that the methods of segregation prevalent in the defendant school districts foster antagonisms in the children and suggest inferiority among them where none exists." One "flagrant example" cited by the judge was the El Modeno district where the Lincoln and Roosevelt schools were located on the same grounds but were clearly "not uniform" in methods of instruction and operation.[129] This was the same scene that disturbed Hector Tarango a decade earlier and later spurred the grassroots movement to end segregation. Like the Hoover and Lincoln schools in Garden Grove and the Hoover and Main/Seventeenth Street schools in Westminster, El Modeno's Lincoln and Roosevelt schools were supposed to provide equal facilities and specialized instruction, thereby negating the need for integrated schools in the first through sixth grades. In their attempts to dismiss the plaintiffs' claims as unfounded and without merit, county counsel leaned on the "separate but equal" doctrine by asserting the federal court lacked jurisdiction since there was no violation of state or federal law by merely practicing segregation.[130] While race was technically not an issue in *Mendez et al.*, trial proceedings revealed that Mexicans constituted a separate class established by the "regulations, customs, usages, and practices" of the defendant districts. Thus, if ethnic Mexicans, who were supposedly included in the white race, could be denied the equal protection of the laws, what did this imply for other nonwhite populations? Illustrating that segregation inevitably led to unequal treatment and social inferiority, witness testimonies compelled McCormick to question whether any form of segregation was justified under the Equal Protection Clause of the United States Constitution.[131] Although it would take eight more years for the courts to answer this question decisively in *Brown v. Board* (1954), *Mendez et al.* provided the legal rationale for the demise of de jure segregation throughout the nation.

SOLIDIFYING VICTORY IN *MENDEZ, ET AL. V. WESTMINSTER, ET AL.*

Judge McCormick's ruling caught everyone by surprise, especially the defendant districts who responded by filing an appeal to the Ninth Circuit

Court of Appeals on March 30, 1946.[132] The Appellate Court would not hear the case for several months, so in the meantime, the districts faced the uncertainty of how to proceed in light of the injunction. While the Westminster district agreed to integrate by the beginning of the 1946–1947 school year, Santa Ana, Garden Grove, and El Modeno refused to desegregate until the appeals process was complete.[133] Despite McCormick's unequivocal denunciation of segregation, citrus capitalists resisted the broader social, economic, and political repercussions of his ruling. Subsequently, the Farm Bureau, Chamber of Commerce, District Attorney, Deputy Registrar of Voters, and other public officials, business owners, and residents mounted a counterattack to prevent the integration of Orange County schools.[134] As this backlash intensified, the efforts of Hector Tarango and the coalition of community activists became even more vital as they used the *Mendez et al.* victory to push for an expansion of Mexican American social and political rights.

Caught off guard by McCormick's decision, national civil rights leaders and organizations flocked to Orange County when they received word of the improbable victory achieved by Mexican Americans and their Jewish attorney.[135] Seeing *Mendez et al.* as a "test case" to challenge segregation and other forms of racial injustice, the National Association for the Advancement of Colored People (NAACP), American Civil Liberties Union (ACLU), Japanese American Citizens League (JACL), and the American Jewish Congress (AJC) filed amicus curiae "friend of the court" briefs in support of McCormick's opinion.[136] In their brief, NAACP counsel Thurgood Marshall, Robert L. Carter, and Loren Miller, seized the opportunity to attack race-based school segregation as unconstitutional. Holding to McCormick's categorical denunciation of school segregation, the attorneys affirmed that while the Fourteenth Amendment "was designed to primarily benefit the newly freed Negro . . . its protection has been extended to all persons within the reach of our laws. From its adoption to the present, [Supreme Court] decisions have almost uniformly considered classifications and discriminations on the basis of race as contrary to its provisions."[137] Citing the recently established United Nations Charter (1945) alongside the Act of Chapultepec (1945), the NAACP asserted:

> Segregation on a racial basis in the public school system is a type of arbitrary
> and unreasonable discrimination which should be forbidden under our laws.
> Both our national constitution and the terms of our international commitments
> demand that this Court invalidate the acts of defendants in setting aside in
> their respective jurisdictions separate schools for children of Mexican or Latin
> origin.[138]

Supporting the expert witness testimony of Dr. Beals and Marie Hughes, the NAACP's brief masterfully incorporated the findings of several scholarly studies that proved "social bias" and inferiority were the intentional byproducts of school segregation, and that racial segregation writ large, including the types practiced among the defendant districts, was a "social weapon" wielded against minority groups to keep them in an inferior social status.[139]

Even Latino civil rights leaders like George I. Sánchez and LULAC, the nation's most prominent Mexican American civil rights organization at the time, were entirely unaware of *Mendez et al.* prior to McCormick's decision.[140] LULAC had been litigating school desegregation cases in Texas since the early 1930s with limited success. Seeing *Mendez et al.* as a prime opportunity to reenergize the school desegregation movement, LULAC leaders met with Tarango and his LAVL associates in Orange County after receiving news of the ruling. During these discussions, LAVL leaders became convinced that affiliating with LULAC would assist in their efforts

Figure 4.4 Founding of Santa Ana LULAC Council No. 147, May 8, 1946. The Latin American Voters League (LAVL) was the precursor to this organization. Left to right: Tony Luna, Ray Carrasco, David Ortiz, Manuel Veiga Jr., Isadore Gonzales, Cruz Barrios, Hector Godinez, and Alex Maldonado. Hector Tarango, not pictured, took the photo and was also a founding member of the LAVL and LULAC Council 147. Courtesy of Margie Aguirre.

to end segregation and other forms of discrimination in Orange County. Subsequently, on May 8, 1946, Manuel Veiga Jr. (President), Phillip Mendez (Vice President), Hector Tarango (Secretary), and Cruz Barrios (Treasurer) were elected as the founding officers of Santa Ana LULAC Council 147.[141] Although a late addition to the grassroots movement begun three years earlier, the backing of LULAC during the appeals process provided much needed financial support and publicity. Indeed, in the December 1946 issue of *LULAC NEWS*, Vice President General John O. Gonzales called upon all LULAC members to support Santa Ana Council 147 as they fundraised for the *Mendez et al.* appeal.[142] Continuing the work of the LAVL, Santa Ana LULAC members canvassed Orange County barrios/colonias for donations, raffled off a refrigerator, held fundraising dinners, and even enlisted Luis Sandoval and MAM's Anaheim Chapter to help organize a community cultural performance entitled "Mexico en Fantasia."[143]

After the formation of Santa Ana LULAC Council 147, Fred Ross, an organizer with the American Council on Race Relations, came to Orange County to help mobilize the Mexican American community amidst the *Mendez et al.* appeal. As a young and aspiring social activist, Ross was enamored with the challenge of bringing democracy to the Mexican barrios and colonias of Southern California's Citrus Belt. Having spent the previous three months investigating conditions in Pomona, Chino, Ontario, San Bernardino, and Redlands, Ross had become acquainted with the plight of Mexican communities while he cut his teeth on the basics of grassroots organizing. Mentored by local activists Ruth Tuck and Ignacio Lopez, Ross experienced considerable success in the Riverside barrios of Bell Town and Casablanca. Inspired by the *Mendez et al.* decision, Ross and Lopez harnessed the energy and frustration of residents like Blossie Adams and Claudia Maldonado to pressure the West Riverside School District to desegregate during the summer of 1946.[144]

Tarango met Ross at a Santa Ana LULAC meeting in August 1946. After hearing about Ross's success organizing barrio residents into Unity Leagues that registered voters and influenced local elections, Tarango was eager to do the same in Orange County.[145] Targeting the resistant school districts of Santa Ana and El Modeno, Ross and Tarango began registering voters in the Santa Ana barrios of Delhi, Logan, and Artesia.[146] According to Tarango's estimate, by August 1946, 90 percent of Orange County Mexican Americans were not registered to vote.[147] Those who were registered were scattered so thin throughout the county that, even if they did vote together, their voices would be drowned out by the majority white population. Tarango's fellow LULAC officers were less enthusiastic about this more assertive strategy. Following the lead of Manuel Veiga Jr., they doubted the dependability of barrio residents and felt their time would be better spent by increasing the membership of the Santa Ana LULAC Council, which operated at the county level.[148] Undeterred, Tarango, Ross, and other barrio residents like Alex Maldonado and Matt Lujan registered hundreds of new voters and started Unity Leagues in Santa Ana and El Modena. Once established, Ross and Tarango believed the more activist-oriented Unity Leagues would work alongside Santa Ana LULAC to keep the larger organization informed of conditions and activities in the barrios.[149]

With local leadership in place, barrio residents mobilized to solve other problems afflicting their neighborhoods. In house meetings and community gatherings, local leaders, such as Lujan and Maldonado, held open forums to identify issues of importance to barrio residents and then formed committees tasked with finding solutions. In Delhi, for example, Unity League members fought a zoning ordinance and lobbied for community improvements like the installation of streetlights. Meanwhile, Unity Leagues in Artesia and El Modena joined forces to contest the persistent segregation of their children in the Santa Ana and El Modeno districts while also supporting a statewide Fair Employment Practices bill (Prop 11) in the upcoming November 1946 election.[150] Having achieved their goal of empowering local barrios to wage their own battles against the marginalization of their specific communities, Ross and Tarango succeeded in mobilizing the most oppressed and forgotten neighborhoods of Orange County. Armed with an increasingly unified and determined coalition of Mexican American voters, Orange County barrios were prepared to make their final push to desegregate schools in Santa Ana and El Modena. To do this, the communities of Delhi, Artesia, and El Modena used the political process that had previously allowed for their marginalization. Speaking with a unified collective voice, Mexican Americans resolved to end school segregation for good.

With the opening of the 1946–1947 school year, the Santa Ana and El Modeno districts persisted in segregating Mexican American children, in defiance of McCormick's decision. Citing teacher shortages, space limitations, and financial issues as reasons for not adhering to McCormick's injunction, the boards of education attempted to stall integration until the appeals process was completed.[151] In response, Tarango and Ross organized parents and local activists to keep the pressure on school board officials. On the evening of September 12, 1946, Ross and Tarango appeared before the Santa Ana Board of Education. The minutes of that meeting record Ross as being "antagonistic and belligerent concerning the matter of Mexican American children." Further, the minutes recorded Ross' advice to Mexican American parents that they should take their "children to the school of their choice on the opening day of school and if they were not admitted, the Board of Education would be cited for contempt." In the discussion that followed, board members learned that "there were a number of Mexican students who appeared at the McKinley school for enrollment and were sent back to their former school." While neither the children nor their parents objected, school officials "feared that they might have been sent purposely to see what action the schools would take."[152]

Attempting to ease tensions, Tarango arranged for further negotiations between four school board members and four Mexican American community leaders to take place over dinner. The minutes of the following board meeting on November 14, 1946, show that the dinner was successful in gaining concessions from the board. First, the board acknowledged that it was important "to permit the Mexican-American Committee to report progress to their contingency." Second, it decided that "in order to show the good faith of this administration and an appreciation and understanding of their problem, it was proposed that under certain restrictive conditions the Mexican-American people may . . . transfer Mexican-Americans to other districts in the same proportion as Anglo-Americans are transferred out of their district."[153] While this fell short of complete and immediate integration, the concessions attest to the effective pressure Mexican American grassroots organizers placed on the school board. Indeed, the fact that the Santa Ana board found itself in the awkward position of being forced to accommodate the demands of the Mexican American community was in and of itself a tremendous victory considering that the district had refused to do so over the previous thirty-five years.

While the Santa Ana School Board was willing to compromise, El Modeno remained obstinate. In spite of McCormick's ruling, administrators at the Roosevelt school refused to admit Mexican American children when classes began in September 1946. Outraged, parents refused to send their children to Lincoln, which led to "rumors of a mass boycott."[154] True to its word, the El Modena Unity League, with the assistance of Ross and Tarango, filed contempt charges against the district and collected an anti-segregation petition with 500 signatures.[155] Emboldened by these actions, Unity League leadership called a special executive committee meeting during the first week of October 1946 to discuss how to maintain pressure on the El Modeno School Board. With the *Mendez et al.* appeal dragging on, parents and activists were unwilling to wait for and rely on the Ninth Circuit's decision. Considering their increasing membership, then at over 100 members, and their recent success in registering 300 new voters, league leadership decided it was time to start brandishing the Mexican American vote, which they did at the next school board meeting.[156]

Both the official minutes and recollections of those present at the October 9, 1946, El Modeno School Board meeting attest to the emerging strength of the Mexican American community and the pressure felt by school administrators to respond to their demands for equal treatment. According to the board's minutes, a contingent of Mexican American activists and parents attended the meeting, including Fred Ross, Hector Tarango, and Manuel Veiga Jr., as representatives of the "Latin American Council" (LULAC), Alex Llevanos, as a representative of the El Modeno Unity League, and two others, Mr. Seijas and Mrs. Perez. Speaking for the group, Llevanos related their commitment to "cooperate in any way to eliminate segregation and to keep from having any hard feelings on either side." Speaking for the district, Henry Campbell replied that since "the school board and Mr. Hammarsten have been cited before the federal court and . . . has to appear . . . on October 14 to answer charges," the decision was up to the judge. He then spitefully added, "[the solution] should have been decided before the contempt charges were issued." In response, Seijas reminded the board that he and several others tried to find a solution to the integration issue at the previous board meeting but "Mr. Hammarsten just laughed at us." This led Campbell, board member Nieger, and Superintendent Hammarsten to defensively rehash the district's challenges in implementing integration. Because of budget and staffing constraints, the board claimed it was not possible to fully integrate the schools at the present time. Instead, they proposed a testing program to identify Mexican children that would be allowed to transfer to Roosevelt if they were proficient in English. Beyond this, the board refused to provide a specific timeline or process for how and when full integration would be achieved. This was unacceptable to the Mexican American community leaders at the meeting. Although Tarango, Ross, and Llevanos proposed several ideas for how integration could be accomplished, the board remained defiant and abruptly ended what was clearly becoming a heated debate. As he closed the meeting, Campbell restated there was nothing the district could do. "We can only wait and see what the court decides next Monday."[157]

There was more to the October 9th meeting than what the official minutes recorded. According to Fred Ross, the Mexican American contingent "launched the attack . . . badgering board members for over an hour on the patent unfairness and illegality" of the district's segregationist policy, which the board continued to base on false claims of limited English proficiency and intellectual inferiority. Prior to the meeting Tarango aided Unity League leadership in devising a plan to expose the board's prejudice against Mexican American children. Anticipating that the board would reject their request for full and immediate integration, Tarango, Llevanos prepared a list of "the 20 top [Mexican American] students in Lincoln School" which the group acquired by "check[ing] with their teachers."[158] Considering the board's claim that they formed classes based on language and intellectual ability, this proposal should have been embraced as a first step toward integration. Instead, the board rejected the offer, claiming there was no room at Roosevelt to admit new students. What the board failed to acknowledge, however, is that two Mexican American children were admitted to Roosevelt a few weeks prior to the meeting.[159] To Mexican Americans, this proved that the claims of budget and space limitations at Roosevelt were as bogus as the board's testing plan. Unsurprisingly, there was no mention of this conversation in the board's official minutes. Moreover, it was the Mexican American contingent that ended the meeting by abruptly walking out after the board refused to admit any Mexican children to Roosevelt regardless of language and intellectual ability. Surprised by this move, board member Campbell quickly adjourned the meeting and "called out, 'Goodnight, gentlemen.'" On his way out, Tarango paused at the door, looked back at Campbell, who was up for reelection, and said, "Good night, Mr. Candidate. See you at the polls!"[160]

Three days after the board meeting, the *Orange Daily News* reported on a "new class setup" adopted by the El Modeno district that would immediately integrate the Roosevelt and Lincoln schools:

Under the new arrangement, which was worked out by the board of trustees, recently cited into federal court on charges of contempt, all elementary school children, grades one to four inclusive, both of American and Mexican parentage, will be taught in the Roosevelt school house. Formerly the Roosevelt school house was used only in instructing pupils of American parentage. The Lincoln school house, used originally for pupils of Mexican parentage, will be used hereafter as the intermediate school house, housing both Mexican and American extraction students in grades five to eight, inclusive.[161]

Unbeknownst to the *Orange Daily News*, the district's integration plan was actually proposed by Tarango during the October 9 meeting, which the board rejected.[162] With their scheduled court appearance just two days away, the board apparently had a change of heart. But this "different arrangement" was merely a last-ditch effort to save face in front of Judge McCormick. Following Ross's return to Orange County after spending the weekend with family in Long Beach, Tarango informed him that the district "integrated the schools, but not the kids." Although white and Mexican students attended school under the same roof, the classes remained segregated within the buildings.[163]

Following through on their promise, the El Modena Unity League formed a Political Action Committee and selected neighborhood barber Grant Baggott to challenge the well-connected citrus grower, Henry S. Campbell, for his seat on the El Modeno School Board. In addition to being chairman of the school board, Campbell was a member of the Orange County Farm Bureau and sat on the board of directors for both the Bank of Orange and the Villa Park Orchards Association. According to Unity League President Alex Maldonado, Baggott's selection was strategic, as he was supportive of the Mexican American community in their struggle against segregation and could also attract the support of white voters. There were some, Maldonado included, who preferred running a Mexican American candidate, but Baggott was seen as the safer choice by those in fear of a "backlash" against the Mexican American community.[164] In preparation for the election, Tarango and Ross helped the El Modena Unity League conduct a voter registration campaign during the winter of 1947. With the school board election scheduled for May 16, League members had only a few months to deputize registrars and sign-up new voters before the April 16 deadline. This task was made more difficult by Lilian Engle, the County Registrar of Voters, who refused to deputize more than one Mexican American registrar at a time.[165] To overcome this obstruction, Unity League leadership selected Pete Hernandez, Nate Serrato, and Adolph Lemos to rotate as registrars so they could "go like heck," as Maldonado recalled, and register voters nonstop.[166] As they canvassed El Modeno's three barrios, Unity League members passed out flyers with the headline "The un-American Way," which blamed Campbell and other members of the El Modeno School Board for maintaining segregation. After getting wind of the campaign, Superintendent Hammarsten barged into every classroom at Lincoln to show Mexican children the flyer and mock the efforts of their parents.[167]

Within weeks of the election, Hector Tarango, Manuel Veiga Jr., Isadore Gonzales, Cruz Barrios, Eddie Valenzuela, and Hector Godinez were "rounded up" by Sheriff's deputies and hauled into the District Attorney's office where they were "issued stern warnings" by the DA and representatives of the Associated Farmers to stop engaging in communist activities. As recalled by Santa Ana LULAC co-founder and future LULAC National President Hector Godinez, Tarango was the only one in the room bold enough to respond to the charges.[168] "Have you got any more proof?" Tarango retorted. "Isn't that enough?" asked the representative of the Associated Farmers. Pulling out his own clippings from the *Reader's Digest*, *Riverside Press Enterprise*, and the *San Francisco Chronicle*, Tarango explained that Ross had merely been involved in fighting forms of racial discrimination throughout Southern California. Then, addressing the DA directly,

Tarango said, "So far all we've done is recruit voters. Is that illegal, is that anti-American, is that communist?" To which the DA responded, "Oh no-not recruiting voters." Tarango then asked, "Well, we're fighting the school system [against segregation] for better relationships in the school for our children, is that communism?" Again, the DA responded, "Oh no, no, that's fine." Hector persisted, "Well the other thing we're doing is we're trying to improve the benefits of workers by having better housing and things like that. Is that bad?" Shocked by Tarango's bold and impassioned response, the DA again confirmed there was nothing un-American or communist about these activities. "What are we doing here then?" Tarango inquired. "You're wasting our time . . . we're busy."[169] Tarango then demanded that, unless the DA planned to file charges, he better let them go. Caught off guard, the DA "uttered a few words . . . and told the Associated Farmers' representatives, 'You don't have a case.'" Reflecting on the experience, Godinez later recalled "We had just [started] something they didn't want. They were afraid of it. They didn't want us to organize. They did everything to block us from organizing."[170]

Despite these obstacles, Mexican Americans flooded the polls on May 16, 1947.

Driven by the voter registration campaign led by Tarango, Maldonado, and the El Modena Unity League, Mexican Americans proved the deciding factor in Grant Baggott's unexpected defeat of Henry Campbell, trouncing the incumbent by a vote of 193 to 117. As reported by the *Orange Daily News* on the day after the election:

> At El Modena there was such a steady stream of voters throughout the afternoon that the election officials were completely swamped. Some voters were forced to stand in line for more than an hour before being able to vote, so heavy was the rush. One of the heaviest votes in El Modena's history was cast, with 310 voting. An unprecedentedly heavy Latin-American vote was cast, inspired by the student segregation issue which was injected into the election campaigning here.[171]

One month after the election, the El Modeno School Board voted to comply with Judge McCormick's decision, asking Orange County Counsel Joel Ogle to drop further litigation.[172] In subsequent years, Mexican Americans elected Jess Martinez and Primo Rodriguez to the school board, effectively controlling that body from 1947 to 1953, when the district was incorporated into the newly formed Orange Unified School District.[173] Decades later, Tarango and Maldonado reflected on the 1947 school board election with great pride and as a turning point for Mexican Americans in Orange County.[174] Indeed, while Mexican Americans had participated in local elections previously, this time they did much more than merely help swing an election. Mexican Americans choose their own candidate and turned what was supposed to be an ordinary school board election into a referendum on the segregation issue. In the process, they galvanized and mobilized Mexican Americans into a unified voting bloc that followed through on Tarango's promise to hold elected officials accountable for their neglect and marginalization of barrio and colonia residents.

One month before the election, the Ninth Circuit Court of Appeals finally affirmed McCormick's decision on April 14, 1947. As penned by Justice Stephens, the Ninth Circuit ruled:

> By enforcing the segregation of school children of Mexican descent against their will and contrary to the laws of California, respondents have violated the federal law as provided in the Fourteenth Amendment to the Federal Constitution by depriving them of liberty and property without due process of law and by denying to them the equal protection of the laws.[175]

Declining to rule on the broader issue of "separate but equal" raised by McCormick's decision and several amicus briefs submitted by civil rights organizations, the Ninth Circuit Appellate Court ruled on the narrower grounds that, since California law did not allow for the segregation of "children of Mexican descent," their separation from white peers was "arbitrary and discriminating."[176] Immediately following the Ninth Circuit's decision to uphold McCormick's ruling, California Governor Earl Warren asked the state legislature to send him a bill repealing sections 8003 and 8004 of the state Education Code, which had previously allowed for the segregation of "Indians under certain conditions and children of Chinese, Japanese, or Mongolian parentage."[177] Warren signed the bill shortly after that on June 14, 1947, officially ending de jure segregation in California's public schools. Seven years later, as Chief Justice of the Supreme Court of the United States, Earl Warren presided over the very court that overturned the doctrine of "separate but equal" enshrined by *Plessy v. Ferguson* (1896) in the 1954 ruling of *Brown v. Board of Education of Topeka*. Hearkening back to McCormick's decision in *Mendez et al.* the Warren Court ruled unanimously (nine to zero) that "separate educational facilities are inherently unequal."[178]

ENFORCING DESEGREGATION IN ORANGE COUNTY

Despite the Ninth Circuit's validation of *Mendez et al.*, it was up to Mexican Americans and their allies to enforce desegregation in Orange County.

Indeed, some districts not named in *Mendez et al.* continued segregating Mexican American children into the 1950s.[179] Placentia Unified and La Habra were two of these districts. Like Anaheim, El Modena, and La Habra, approximately 1,000 ethnic Mexicans lived within the boundaries of the Placentia Unified School District, where Mexican children comprised roughly 25 percent of the district's enrollment.[180] Like other districts in Orange County, citrus capitalists were well represented on the school board. Despite *Mendez et al.*, Placentia Unified maintained its policy of segregating children of Mexican descent into two schools, Chapman Hill Elementary and La Jolla Junior High. Following the model of grassroots organizing implemented by MAM, LAVL, the Westminster Father's Association, and the El Modena Unity League, Mexican American parents and community members in La Jolla, Placentia, and Richfield organized themselves to pressure the Placentia Unified School District to integrate or face a legal battle they would surely lose in the wake of the Ninth Circuit's decision.

Born and raised in Placentia, Alfred V. Aguirre joined MAM after serving in the Army Air Corps as an Aviation Engineer during World War II.[181] As a member of MAM, Alfred, and his brother Joe, worked with Luis Sandoval, Gualberto Valadez, and Ted Duran on organizing after school programs and leadership conferences for Mexican American youth in La Jolla, Placentia, and Anaheim. Politicized by encounters with racist police officers and the persistence of school segregation, the Aguirre brothers joined Duran, Jack Gomez, Gabino Taboada, and eleven others to form the VCP in late 1946.[182] From the outset, VCP had two goals: end school segregation in Placentia Unified and stop police harassment in ethnic Mexican communities.

Like the LAVL, the VCP originated from conversations between friends and neighbors who felt it was their civic duty to end discrimination against ethnic Mexicans. According to Alfred Aguirre, Ted Duran called him one day and said, "Freddy, we're getting tired of being discriminated and . . . treated like second-class citizens and we think it's about time . . . we start getting involved in politics and demand that they close [the La Jolla Mexican School]."[183] While Aguirre and Duran were involved in MAM at the time of this conversation, the organization's leadership preferred to retain its focus on youth programs and education as opposed to confrontational political issues like desegregation. Considering the large number of Mexican American World War II veterans in Placentia, Aguirre and Duran reasoned that their new organization could capitalize on the experience, contributions, and public support of this population. Shortly after their conversation, Duran suggested they meet with Reverend Gabino Taboada, the pastor at St. Joseph's Catholic Church in Placentia and Our Lady of Guadalupe Catholic Church in La Jolla. The "small but energetic" Taboada occasionally spoke against the ongoing segregation of Mexican children during sermons and offered to help Duran organize Mexican Americans "for the purpose of desegregating Placentia's schools."[184] In late 1946, Taboada hosted fourteen men in his rectory at St. Joseph's as they organized the VCP, electing Lucas Raya as president, Vincent Raya as vice president, Joe V. Aguirre as secretary, Robert Moreno as treasurer, and Ismael Vargas as sergeant-at-arms. In all, nine of the original fifteen VCP members were World War II veterans, while others like Duran and Alfred Aguirre, were also active in the Catholic Youth Organization, MAM, and other community organizations.[185]

Over the ensuing months, the VCP's membership swelled to thirty-five men, most of whom were born and raised near Placentia, attended segregated schools in Placentia Unified, picked Valencia oranges in nearby groves, and served in the US Armed Forces during World War II. Born in 1920 to parents who immigrated to Placentia from Mexico in 1919, Alfred began attending the Baker Street (Mexican) School in 1925. Since the Aguirres lived on the corner of Baker and Walnut near the center of Placentia, they saw no problem in sending their children to the nearby Baker Street School. Although they lived within the municipal boundaries of Placentia, as opposed to the nearby Mexican colonies in La Jolla and Richfield, the Aguirres and their neighbors were essentially segregated within the city.[186] Drawn to Placentia through a network of relatives and friends that had migrated to the area between 1913 and 1917, the Aguirres settled on Walnut Street along with several other recent Mexican immigrant families like the Rayas, Negretes, Vargases, Martinezes, Guerreros, and Solorzanos.[187] Prior to the rapid increase of Mexican migrants during the 1910s and 1920s, Walnut and Baker streets were not known as a Mexican barrio. But by the early 1940s, whites began referring to the area south of Santa Fe Avenue as "Mexican Town" due to the prevalence of Mexican owned residences and businesses, and the segregation of Mexican children in the Baker Street School.[188] Like Cypress Street in Orange, and the Logan, Delhi, and Fremont barrios in Santa Ana, the transition of south Placentia into "Mexican Town" further illustrates how the "spatial imaginary" of white Orange Countians ascribed racial meaning to space, leading to disinvestment and marginalization.[189]

During the winter of 1946–1947, the VCP met in Reverend Taboada's rectory and at La Jolla Junior High. Although not a member of VCP, Gualberto Valadez supported the organization by opening the gym and allowing them to meet there when needed. This was short lived, however, for as soon as the school board discovered the VCP was organizing to end segregation, they revoked the group's use of the gym and attempted to pressure Valadez into spying on the organization. Unsurprisingly, Valadez refused.[190] Turning to Taboada, who served as the group's "unofficial, behind-the-scenes advisor," the VCP met at St. Joseph's until a group of influential growers discovered his involvement and pressured the diocese to transfer Taboada to Our Lady of Guadalupe in Pasadena.[191] Before his removal, Taboada suggested VCP leaders meet with C.W. Marshall, attorney for the Archdiocese of Los Angeles. In their forty-five-minute meeting with Marshall, Aguirre and Duran explained the situation in Placentia, how citrus ranchers ran the town, controlled the school board, and kept their children segregated despite *Mendez et al*. Marshall offered to represent the VCP if needed and encouraged the group to meet with the school board and threaten them with a lawsuit.[192]

After returning to Placentia, Aguirre and Duran decided to involve Santa Ana's recently formed LULAC Council 147 in their struggle. Knowing of their success in leading the *Mendez et al*. movement, Aguirre asked President Manuel Veiga Jr. if the council would accompany them to their meeting with the school board. "We need good speakers, speakers that are not afraid to get up and speak," Aguirre told Veiga.[193] Choosing three of their best, Veiga tapped Alex Maldonado, Ralph Perez, and Manuel Esqueda to assist the VCP. During the spring of 1947, VCP and LULAC leaders appeared before the Placentia Unified School Board. At this initial encounter, Warren Bradford, son of Alfred S. Bradford, was obstinate in rejecting the VCP's call for integration. "But we're just trying to help you," Aguirre recalled Bradford saying, "because mentally you're not as smart as Anglos. That's why we keep you in different schools. You're too slow."[194] Relating his experiences in the Civilian Conservation Corps and military, Alfred argued that segregation was to blame for academic deficiencies between white and Mexican American children. "If I got your children and put them in a box and kept them there for twenty years," Aguirre asserted, "they're not going to know any more than what they did when they put them in there. The mind won't develop." Aguirre continued, "Give them a chance, and they'll be as smart as I am or smarter."[195] Surprised by the assertiveness of LULAC and VCP leaders, the school board put off a decision until their next meeting. Unrelenting, Aguirre responded, "Hey, either way we're not going to lose because we already have professional help. We already have attorneys."[196]

Throughout the remainder of 1947, the VCP pressured board members with letters and visits to school board meetings. Seeing the board's obstinance, Santa Ana LULAC leaders suggested the VCP conduct a voter registration campaign. Referring to their success in El Modena, LULAC leaders encouraged the VCP to present the board with a "show [of] force" by registering voters.[197] Once again, the county registrar attempted to block

Mexican Americans from serving as deputy registrars. Having previously threatened the county with a lawsuit for obstruction, Santa Ana LULAC leaders aided the VCP in overcoming the registrar's objections. Over the ensuing months, the VCP canvassed every inch of Placentia, spending considerable time in the nearby colonias of La Jolla and Atwood. Mirroring the success of Tarango and Unity League members in El Modena, the VCP registered 300 to 400 first-time Mexican American voters.[198]

In early 1948, the VCP appeared before the school board accompanied by C.W. Marshall and forty community members. At the meeting, Marshall threatened the board with legal action citing their refusal to comply with *Mendez et al.*[199] Alfred Aguirre also warned, "Either you do something about closing the [Mexican schools], or we're going to have to get involved with politics and start changing the school board."[200] Realizing they would surely lose a lawsuit, the board finally acquiesced. Although the *Placentia Courier* failed to report on VCP's efforts to force integration, a series of articles published from July 1948 to May 1949 covered the school board's decisions to increase funding to build additional facilities and phase out the use of the Chapman Hill (Mexican) School.[201] True to their word, the VCP ran founding member Jack Gomez for a seat on the Placentia Unified School Board in the May 1949 election. While Gomez was unsuccessful in this initial attempt, receiving 195 votes to John Hamilton's 500, this was only the beginning of Mexican American attempts to flex their collective voice at the ballot box.[202] With the opening of Bradford Elementary to Mexican American children at the beginning of the 1950–1951 school year, Placentia Unified was finally integrated. Alfred's eldest son, Frederick Aguirre, was among the first children of Mexican descent to attend all integrated schools in Placentia. After graduating from Valencia High School, Frederick received an alumni scholarship to the University of Southern California, where he earned his BA, and then a UC Regents Fellowship to UCLA, where he earned his JD. After passing the bar exam, Frederick became a civil rights attorney working on fair housing, legal aid, and anti-discrimination suits. In 1974, Frederick founded the Hispanic Bar Association of Orange County and in 2002 was appointed to the Orange County Superior Court by California Governor Gray Davis.[203]

ORANGE COUNTY'S UNHERALDED DESEGREGATION MOVEMENT

The movement to desegregate Orange County schools was built from the bottom up by parents, neighbors, and community leaders dedicated to

Figure 4.5 Founding of Placentia LULAC Council 174, January 1949. The Veterans and Citizens of Placentia (VCP) was the precursor to this organization. LULAC Council 174 represented Mexican neighborhoods in Placentia, La Jolla, and Atwood. Hector Tarango (not pictured) took the photo and was instrumental in forming the council along with Jack Gomez, Robert Moreno, Alfred V. Aguirre (first three seated on row left to right), and Joe V. Aguirre (back row on left). Courtesy of Margie Aguirre.

achieving educational equality for their children. Viewing the segregated school system as the primary impediment to the social mobility of ethnic Mexicans in Orange County, untrained activists like Hector Tarango, Manuel Veiga Jr., Cruz Barrios, Alex Maldonado, Alfred Aguirre, Ted Duran, Reverend Taboada, and of course, the et al. families of William and Virginia Guzman, Frank and Irene Palomino, Lorenzo and Josefina Ramirez, and Thomas and Maria Luisa Estrada, built a grassroots movement that transformed educational opportunities for ethnic Mexicans across the country. To this day, *Mendez et al.* remains one of the most consequential court decisions pertaining to the rights of Mexican Americans and other communities of color.[204] It became one of the first in a series of state and federal court decisions that expanded the interpretation of the Fourteenth Amendment's Equal Protection Clause to secure the civil rights of ethnic/racial minorities since Reconstruction.[205] Indeed, the *Columbia Law Review* affirmed that prior to *Mendez et al.*, "Attacks on segregation based on the equal protection clause of the 14th Amendment have been equally unsuccessful." Stressing Judge McCormick's precedence setting decision, the *Columbia Law Review* continued, "The court in the instant case breaks sharply with this approach and finds that the 14th Amendment requires 'social equality' rather than equal facilities."[206] Further, referring to *Mendez et al.*, Robert L. Carter, counsel for the NAACP Legal Defense and Education Fund, said the case provided a "model" for the brief he wrote in *Brown v. Board* and brought "the American courts closer to a decision on the whole question of segregation."[207]

For decades, legal scholars and historians have either dismissed, misunderstood, or failed to recognize the significance of *Mendez et al.* Beyond the precedent it set for future civil rights victories, *Mendez et al.* demonstrated the emerging political strength of ethnic Mexicans in Orange County. Developing out of the previous two decades of intense anti-Mexican racism, Mexican Americans built a grassroots civil rights movement that ended de jure segregation in schools and public accommodations seven years before *Brown v. Board* and nearly two decades before the 1964 Civil Rights Act. Such a development was not an inevitable or natural outcome of World War II, and it was without a doubt, virtually unthinkable a generation earlier. Although Orange County's desegregation movement did not end all forms of discrimination against ethnic Mexicans, it was nevertheless a monumental achievement by a community and people that had little to no social or political power. Understanding how, why, and by whom this victory was achieved is essential to the history of the long Civil Rights Movement and the development of ethnic politics in California and the nation. Resulting from sustained grassroots organizing and mobilization, Orange County's unheralded desegregation movement brought ethnic Mexicans out of the shadows of the citrus economy. No longer could they be ignored by citrus capitalists and their allies in local government.

Conclusion

The fight for civil rights is one with no beginning and no end.

Hector G. Godinez, *1996*

In February 1977, the *Los Angeles Times* published a multipage article on the emerging political strength of Mexican Americans in Orange County. Citing the recent success of grassroots organizations in conducting "intensive voter registration drives" and turning out the vote for the November 2, 1976, election, political staff writer Bud Lembke asserted, "Mexican American barrios . . . are beginning to play a part in the political process."[1] Indeed, with an estimated 78 percent voter turnout, Mexican American participation in the general election was something of note. Bucking county trends, Orange County Mexicans overwhelmingly supported Democratic presidential candidate Jimmy Carter (77.4%) over the incumbent Republican Gerald Ford, who won the countywide vote by a ratio of two to one. While these results surprised Lembke, Mexican Americans had been active in county politics for some time. In fact, by the time this article was published, Mexican Americans had been elected to city councils, mayoral offices, and school boards throughout the county.[2] Moreover, Hector Godinez (Southern California District Manager for the US Postal Service), James O. Perez (Orange County Superior Court Judge), Luis Cardenas (West Municipal Court Judge), Rick Orozco (Central Municipal Court Judge), and Cruz Reynoso (CA Appellate Court Judge) had secured prominent political and judicial appointments. Unbeknownst to Lembke, the politicization of Orange County barrios was achieved through half a century of grassroots organizing. By the mid-1970s, Mexican Americans

Breaking Down the Walls of Segregation. David-James Gonzales, Oxford University Press.
© Oxford University Press 2025. DOI: 10.1093/9780197839485.003.0006

had proven they were a consequential social and political force vital to the region's history and future.

Viewing the history of Orange County through the lens of *Mendez et al.* makes visible Mexican Americans' vital contributions to the social and physical development of not only their communities but also of the county, state, and nation they are a part of. While this book has focused on local and regional developments, the accomplishments of ethnic Mexicans in Orange County reverberated nationally. This is evident in their outsized and overlooked contributions to the Civil Rights Movement as well as in the development of Chicano-Latino (a/x/e) politics. Despite all the attention paid to the religious, entrepreneurial, and "kitchen-table" activists who formed the vanguard of postwar American political conservatism in the region, Orange County Latinos played an important role in the emerging liberal consensus that developed alongside "the rise of the new Right."[3] The grassroots organizations founded by barrio and colonia residents during the 1930s and 1940s provided the foundation for the exponential growth of LULAC in California during the 1950s and 1960s. In fact, before the formation of Santa Ana Council 147, LULAC was virtually nonexistent in California. Although LULAC councils were established in Sacramento, San Bernardino, and Los Angeles during the 1930s, they were in a stage of "rigor mortis" by the mid-1940s.[4] *Mendez et al.* and the creation of Santa Ana Council 147 injected new life into LULAC's efforts to expand the organization into Southern California as it sought to achieve a national footprint.[5]

Referring to *Mendez et al.* as "the greatest opportunity which has ever come to us" LULAC National Vice President John O. Gonzales of Los Angeles foreshadowed Martin Luther King Jr.'s famous "I Have a Dream" speech when he urged "every member of LULAC" to support Santa Ana Council 147 as they awaited the 9th Circuit Court's ruling in December 1946:

> I begin to feel the magnitude of the task that lies before all of us who hold hopes for a day when all persons regardless of former ancestry, color or creed shall have the right to equal educational and economic opportunities and the equal protection of our laws. When all persons may meet on common ground as educated and intelligent human beings, forgetting those stupid and utterly false prejudices, mothered and nurtured by ignorance and handed down from the dark ages to poison the minds of gullible and moronic individuals who presume to be sane and who willingly accept and practice them for the sole purpose of furthering their own selfish ends.[6]

In the decade after *Mendez et al.*, Mexican Americans established eight additional LULAC chapters throughout the county. El Modena Council

179 (1949), Placentia Council 174 (1950), Stanton Council 245 (1954), La Habra Council 259 (1955), Buena Park Council 269 (1955), Fullerton Council 278 (1956), Orange Council 292 (1956), and Anaheim Council 316 (1958). Orange County LULAC leaders such as Hector Tarango, Isadore Gonzales, Alex Maldonado, Danny Olivas, Joe O'Campo, Stephen Lara, Nash Garcia, and Hector Godinez were pivotal in organizing dozens of LULAC councils throughout the state.[7] Each of these men held prominent positions within LULAC at the state and national levels, including Hector Tarango as National Trustee, Isadore Gonzales as Regional Governor, Alex Maldonado as Regional Organizer and District Governor, Danny Olivas as Regional Governor and State Director, Nash Garcia as National Treasurer, Stephen Lara as Regional Governor, Victor Zuniga as District Governor, Joe O'Campo as Regional Governor, National Organizer for West Coast, and First National Vice President, and Hector Godinez as District Governor, Regional Governor, First National Vice President, and LULAC National President from 1960 to 1961.[8]

Figure C.1 LULAC women at the home of Hector and Mary Godinez, April 1956. Seated front row left to right: Josefina Magdaleno, Ruth Rodriguez, Julia Aguirre, Luisa Roman, Gloria Cruz, Ruth Hernandez, and Gloria Campos. Standing left to right: Ruth Cruz, Mary Godinez, Mary Garcia, Vickie Magdaleno, Rosina Mendoza, and Dora O'Campo. Courtesy of Margie Aguirre.

Men were not the only ones engaging in LULAC activities and leadership.[9] According to Joe O'Campo, women's involvement in LULAC was crucial to its success as they encouraged men and children to become more active in the organization.[10] Throughout the county, Mexican American women and youth formed Ladies and Junior LULAC councils that worked alongside men to grow the organization.[11] Together, Mexican American men, women, and youth ran LULAC meetings and conferences, held fundraisers and social gatherings, awarded scholarships, sponsored youth activities and sports programs, operated health clinics, and participated in local politics and all manner of civic affairs. These efforts established Orange County as the hotbed of LULAC activity in California during the 1950s and 1960s. This led to Placentia Council 174's selection as the host of the organization's 1957 national convention at the Disneyland Hotel in Anaheim, Fullerton Council 278 as host of the 1963 national convention, and Stanton Council 245 as host of the 1969 national convention.[12] Thanks to the work of Orange County LULACers Danny Olivas, Joe O'Campo, and Hector Godinez, California Governor Goodwin J. Knight officially recognized National LULAC Week during his time in office, 1953–1959, signaling the organization's elevated profile in state politics.[13] According to Alex Maldonado, "[LULAC] took off like wildfire from here in Orange County it spread into Riverside and LA County and just kept on moving. But [it started here] because we had a reason that gets people excited." That reason was the success of the school desegregation movement, as Maldonado explained:

> We had Councils throughout Orange County because . . . LULAC had something
> to grow with, especially because we had segregated schools, everybody had been
> touched by it in Orange County. So, it was something that people [could] look
> back on, what happened, what they had been through. It was a community ef-
> fort where they did something for themselves.[14]

Having achieved their goal to end de jure school segregation, Mexican Americans continued their push for full social and political equality in Orange County by engaging more directly in electoral politics.[15] Building on their success in the May 1947 El Modena school board election, Mexican Americans used local LULAC Councils to educate and mobilize their communities to elect candidates (white and ethnic Mexican) that represented their interests.[16] These efforts resulted in the elections of Victor Zuniga to the Stanton City Council and as the city's first mayor in 1956, Sal Zavala to the Placentia school board (1956–1977), Alfred Aguirre to the Placentia City Council (1958–1962) and later as mayor pro-tempore,

Welcome 28th National Lulac Convention

YOUR CONVENTION COMMITTEE: (L. to R., seated) Blas Marron, Rudy Rodriguez, Aileen Olivas, Danny Olivas, Sara Miranda, Julia Aguirre, Mike Mena; (Standing), Ray Aparicio, Ted Duran, Fred Aguirre, Ray Castillo.   (Photo by Ray Pound.)

YOUR HOSTS, The Placentia Council No. 174, welcome delegates to this, the largest LULAC convention in history, and the first to be held in historic Southern California.

WE ARE HONORED to have been selected to host this convention and assure you that everything possible has been done to make this not only a fruitful convention, but an enjoyable stay as well.

IT IS OUR hope that this California convention will not only mark a milestone in the advance of LULAC as an organization, but as an expanding and influential positive force throughout the nation.

DANNY OLIVAS,
Convention Chairman
Placentia LULAC Council No. 174

Figure C.2 Placentia LULAC Council 174 hosted the 1957 National LULAC Convention at the Disneyland Hotel in Anaheim, CA. Courtesy of Margie Aguirre.

Jack Gomez to the Placentia City Council (1962–1978) and mayor in 1968, Edmund Ponce as Placentia city clerk in 1969, and Jess Perez to the Orange City Council in 1968 and as mayor in 1972.[17] These and several other electoral victories resonated beyond the barrio, illustrating Mexican Americans' emergence as a potent political force in the county.

To accomplish all this, Mexican Americans did more than mobilize the barrios; they built multiethnic coalitions with labor, civil rights organizations, and other interested parties across the political spectrum.[18] Lifelong El Modena and city of Orange resident Bob Torres alluded to this point when reflecting on Mexican American's impact on regional politics years later:

> One thing I know that we have done . . . is make the Anglo community aware that we are [here] and that we mean well and mean to work with them as close as possible providing everything is fair. The city of Orange is very aware of that. The City of Orange has a lot of respect for Latinos. I think it's evident, for instance, in . . . the election of Jess Perez, where he broke state recordings . . . and this was not a Mexican vote so there is this respect. They have respect for the Latino because they know we do well. Give us the opportunity and we can do well.[19]

Indeed, part of the significance of Perez's election as the city's first Latino (a/x/e) city councilman and mayor was that "it took a lot of Anglos throughout the city" to elect him.[20] This point was not missed by the *Anaheim Bulletin*, which remarked, "Up to 1927, Orange's 'mayors' were presidents. After 1927, Orange's 'presidents' became mayors. Now a long list of Anglo-Saxon and German names is topped by that of Perez."[21] While the writer hinted that Perez's election was a sign of the times, there was nothing inevitable about a Mexican American being elected to lead a predominantly white city in Orange County in 1972. In fact, because of the massive influx of white residents into the county driven by postwar suburbanization, the Latino (a/x/e) population in the county decreased from a high of 15 to 20 percent during the 1930s to approximately 10 percent by the late 1960s.[22] Perez's election was even more unlikely considering the county's history of racial capitalism and white supremacy. Thus, Perez's election was only possible through the multiethnic grassroots coalition built by Mexican Americans over the preceding decades.

Mirroring the translocal activism practiced by *La Progresista* and MAM, Orange County LULACers helped form the liberal coalition that elected Edmund "Pat" Brown as California Governor in 1958 and John F. Kennedy as President of the United States in 1960. As in other communities throughout the Southwest, Mexican Americans in Orange County organized Viva Kennedy clubs that built on the prior success of voter registration drives led by the LAVL, El Modena Unity League, VCP, and LULAC. These efforts were monitored by the local press, which covered the rapid growth of the Viva Kennedy movement in the county during the last month of the 1960 general election.[23] As with Lembke's *LA Times* article seventeen years later, the *Register* failed to connect the "political activity" within "the Mexican-American colony" with the desegregation movement that led to *Mendez et al.* Still, LULACers Hector Godinez, Victor Zuniga Sr.,

and David Ortiz were listed among those leading the "movement to organize the Mexican-American Colony throughout Southern California into
a 'powerful, politically-important minority group.'"[24] Although Kennedy
lost Orange County to native son Richard Nixon, Mexican Americans were
recognized and rewarded for their strong support of the president-elect
in the ensuing years. As former National LULAC Vice President turned
Democratic Party organizer Joe O'Campo remembered:

> It was about 1959 that we thought we would truly show the power of the
> Hispano vote, and someone came up with a Viva Kennedy club. Here in Orange
> County, I was elected chairman of the Viva Kennedy club. Never met the man,
> but we worked our buns off. When he was elected president, we were, of course,
> right smack dab in the middle of it. We had all kinds of friends in the Democratic
> Party. We also worked in the first [Edmund] Brown campaign.[25]

Scholars acknowledge that, despite its limitations, the Viva Kennedy
campaign "catapulted Latinos to national prominence," providing an origin of sorts for "the birth of national Latino politics."[26] While this is true,
Mexican Americans in Orange County have been almost entirely left out
of this narrative. One prominent example is Hector Godinez's ascent to
the position of Santa Ana Postmaster. As the National President of LULAC
during the Viva Kennedy campaign, Godinez worked alongside Mexican
American activists and politicians including Los Angeles City Councilman
Edward R. Roybal, Texas State Senator Henry B. González, US Senator
Dennis Chávez, American G.I. Forum President Héctor P. García, and
Kennedy campaign advisor James Carlos McCormick.[27] Six months after
the election, the Kennedy administration appointed Godinez acting postmaster despite significant opposition from the Orange County Chamber
of Commerce and Republican Congressman James B. Utt.[28] Godinez was
confirmed by the US Senate in July of 1962 and served a distinguished
career in the postal service.[29] As one of few Latinos to secure a patronage
appointment from the Kennedy administration, the selection of Hector
Godinez as the first Mexican American postmaster in the nation's history marked a significant milestone for the emergence of Latino (a/x/e)
politics in Orange County and the nation. In addition to Godinez, Orange
County residents Joe O'Campo, James O. Perez, Cruz Reynoso, and several
others helped raise the profile of Mexican Americans in local, statewide,
and national political circles as they received patronage appointments by
Governor Edmund Brown during the early to mid-1960s.[30]

Remarkably, three decades after the *Santa Ana Register*'s alarmist coverage of the so-called Mexican Problem, the paper unwittingly admitted

that Mexican Americans had so thoroughly integrated into American society that they were in the process of creating a "political machine." In an
article headlined "Mexican-Americans Spur County Political Machine,"
published on October 31, 1963, the *Register* detailed "A major county-
wide movement" comprising "Mexican-American leaders . . . geared to
sponsoring candidates for public office."[31] While the article had alarmist
undertones, referring to a meeting in Santa Ana as evidence of "the formation of the new political front," the writer listed prominent Mexican
American professionals alongside labor and community leaders who were
organizing "not to create any new problems, but rather to solve problems
that already exist in our community by uniting ourselves to help ourselves."
According to a source, the group's purpose was "to prepare and groom qualified leaders to seek public office." Although the leaders of this "movement"
favored the Democratic Party, there were similar efforts at work within local
Republican circles. The chairman of the Republican Central Committee of
Orange County, who was also interviewed by the *Register*, noted that "An
organization of Republicans of Latin Extraction (ROLE) was formed several months" earlier.[32]

ROLE was not the first attempt to organize Mexican Americans in the
county to elect Republicans and gain influence within the party. That
"movement" was well underway at least one year prior with the formation of the Committee of Mexican Americans for Nixon. Established by
newspaper publisher Francisco Moreno, union organizer Lino Tinajero,
movie theater owner Luis Olivos, Santa Ana LULAC Council 147 co-
founder Cruz Barrios, and Gil Lujan, Mexican Americans for Nixon illustrated the divisions and multiple efforts among Orange County Latinos
as they organized for greater political recognition and representation
during the 1950s and 1960s.[33] In the first issue of *Despertar* (Awaken),
the official newspaper of the Mexican Americans for Nixon movement in
Orange County, Moreno explained that the purpose of the organization
was to "awaken the Sleeping Giant" (the Mexican American electorate)
to reexamine their loyalty to the Democratic Party and make Democrats
and Republicans realize they could neither take for granted nor ignore the power of the Mexican American vote. "Currently, Democratic
Leaders do not recognize us because they . . . know we are going to vote
for them," Moreno asserted. Likewise, "Republican Leaders do not take
us into account because they know we are registered as Democrats." "In
this state of affairs," he concluded, "we are the ones losing."[34] Mexican
Americans for Nixon represented a growing faction within the Mexican
American electorate who felt their efforts to elect Governor Pat Brown
and other Democrats were not adequately reciprocated with patronage appointments and specific policies that addressed their needs.

Registered Democrat and labor organizer Lino Tinajero raised this very point, stating, "I am like many of you Democrats are, disenchanted, discontented, displeased and completely disgusted with [the] present Governor's policies."[35] After four years of diligently campaigning for and

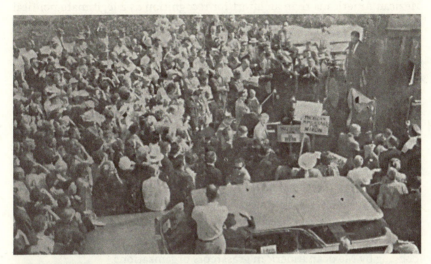

Figure C.3a, b Under the heading "Las Fotos No Mienten" (Photos Don't Lie), *Despertar* printed pictures of Mexican Americans among the crowd of Nixon supporters at a campaign rally in Orange County, CA, in October 1962. (a) Signs reading "Mexican Americans por Nixon" (Mexican Americans for Nixon) and "Yo Estoy con Nixon" (I am with Nixon) are visible. (b) Abigail Olivos, daughter of Mexican Americans for Nixon Committee President Luis Olivos, presents Nixon with flowers and wishes him good health. In return, Nixon embraced Abigail and kissed her on the cheek. Courtesy of Special Collections and Archives, University of California, Irvine.

electing Democrats, Mexican Americans legitimately asked, what have you done for us lately?[36]

Viewed alongside the *Register*'s reporting of the emerging Mexican American "political machine," support for Nixon during the 1962 guber-natorial election was less a sign of significant partisan division among Mexican Americans than an effort for recognition as a legitimate political constituency. Democrat or Republican, Orange County Latinos desired to make it known that they had "been neglected too long by . . . politicians"[37] and were confident they had "the votes to bring State and National leaders from both Parties to [their] doorstep."[38] Through grassroots efforts like the unnamed Democratic "political front" and Mexican Americans for Nixon, Orange County Latinos forced politicians to respond to their demands for recognition and representation. By all accounts, Mexican Americans fared far better under Pat Brown's two terms as California Governor than the previous four Republican administrations of Frank Merriam, Culbert Olson, Earl Warren, and Goodwin Knight. Moreover, Brown appointed approximately sixty-five Mexican Americans as staff, judges, and commissioners, while dozens more were elected to municipal, county, and state offices.[39] None of this would have been possible without persistent organizing and lobbying by Mexican American grassroots organizations.

From the early 1930s to the mid-1960s, Mexican Americans raised the profile of their communities as an emerging political constituency that was not going away. Without assistance from established civil rights organizations, they built a movement that broke down the walls of segregation in Orange County and helped establish the liberal coalition that forever transformed American society and politics. Even by modest assessments, they achieved much of what they set out to accomplish within a single generation. This point was highlighted in an interview with Hector Godinez published by the Long Beach *Press-Telegram* in January of 1964:

> [I] was just another "dirty Mexican" then—"lazy, mentally retarded, unworthy of this country." When I was a kid, I couldn't even sit downstairs in a movie house because I was Mexican. One time my mother walked into a department store and was told by the saleslady that she couldn't wait on Mexicans. My ambition was throttled. My opportunity was nil. The only future I had was in truck farming or picking oranges.[40]

Twenty-five years later, Godinez had worked his way up from letter carrier to postmaster and went on to serve as Southern California District Manager, Los Angeles Postmaster, and Chief Operations Executive in Orange County. Further, Godinez served on the boards of Rancho Santiago Community

College, Western Community Medical Center, The Development and Disability Center of Orange County, the City of Santa Ana Redevelopment Commission, Orange County Health Planning Council, Orange County Boy Scouts of America, KOCE-TV Channel 50, and the Orange County YMCA. In addition, he helped co-found El Banco del Pueblo with Santa Ana businessman and Mexican Americans for Nixon co-founder Luis Olivos and actor Anthony Quinn.[41]

While Godinez was exceptional in some respects, he and others like Hector and Lupe Tarango, Stephen and Lydia Reyes, Luis and Charlotte Sandoval, Ross and Mary Anne Chavolla, Gualberto and Cecelia Valadez, Alfred and Julia Aguirre, and the et al. families of Lorenzo and Josefina Ramirez, William and Virginia Guzman, Thomas and Maria Luisa Estrada, Frank and Irene Palomino, and Gonzalo and Felicitas Mendez represented the vast socioeconomic gulf that many Mexican Americans overcame during the first half of the twentieth century. The change was so remarkable that the *Press-Telegram* wondered, "Has the millennium arrived for Mexican-Americans in Orange County?"[42] Considering that within twenty years Orange County went from being one of Southern California's most

Figure C.4 Orange County LULAC leaders attend national conference in Texas, c. 1950s. Back row: Hector Godinez (far left), Joe O'campo (next to Godinez), Nash Garcia (center). Front row standing: Danny Olivas (second from left). Courtesy of Margie Aguirre.

segregated regions to a space of Mexican American social mobility, this was not simply bluster.

Individual Mexicans and Mexican Americans were the primary reason for this incredible transformation in Orange County, and their contributions must be recognized and taught alongside the many other freedom struggles that comprise the Long Civil Rights Movement. Virtually unknown and grossly underappreciated, the movement to desegregate schools and establish ethnoracial equality in Orange County was unprecedented. It was built by ordinary men and women, immigrants and citizens, country folk and city-dwellers, and the poor and working class. None of them had any formal training in or knowledge of other civil rights struggles before their involvement in Orange County's desegregation movement. Influenced by their own subjectivities, lived experiences, morality, and sense of justice, they formed grassroots organizations in the late 1920s and early 1930s with the explicit purpose of fighting the anti-Mexican discrimination that stemmed from citrus capitalism. Promoting education, civic engagement, and political participation, organizations like *La Progresista*, MAM, LAVL, El Modena Unity League, VCP, and LULAC established a politics of mobility. Built on kinship, social relations, labor networks, and an emerging ethnoracial identity, the politics of mobility connected and mobilized ethnic Mexican communities across Southern California into a concerted movement for social justice. Emerging from the most evident spaces of capitalist neglect, disinvestment, and underdevelopment, these individuals and organizations imagined and fought for a new ordering of space and social relations that only they thought possible.

While some scholars and activists interpret this generation of Chicano (a/x/e) and Latino (a/x/e) politics as moderate, accommodationist, and even conservative, *Breaking Down the Walls of Segregation* contextualizes Mexican and Mexican American responses to systemic racism and marginalization in Orange County during the early to mid-twentieth century, arguing that what they achieved, however limited, was nothing short of incredible. Beyond seeking an increase in status and recognition, those practicing the politics of mobility desegregated schools, businesses, and public accommodations and ushered Latinos into the electoral arena years before the boycotts, sit-ins, and marches that led to the 1964 Civil Rights Act and the 1965 Voting Rights Act.[43] Along the way, they transcended the social and geographic barriers that limited their full and equal incorporation into American society. Moreover, as they broke down and removed these barriers for themselves, they provided a path for others to follow. That tens of thousands of Latinos integrated into American society and politics during the 1940s, 1950s, and 1960s is evidence of their remarkable and improbable success amidst tremendous odds. In addition to providing the groundwork for later generations of Chicano (a/x/e) and Latino (a/x/e) activists, Orange County's unheralded civil rights movement illustrates how minoritized groups have historically pushed US social, economic, and political institutions to live up to the nation's founding ideals.

In *These Truths: A History of the United States*, historian Jill Lepore contemplates whether a thorough accounting of the nation's history will "prove" the validity of its founding principles ("truths") or "belie them."[44] Viewing the history of Orange County through the lens of *Mendez et al.* provides one way of testing Lepore's thesis. As with Native/Indigenous nations, enslaved individuals, women, migrants/immigrants, and other marginalized communities, ethnic Mexicans had to organize and fight to gain access to America's "self-evident" truths of political equality, natural rights, and sovereignty. They believed in and were inspired by the American creed despite being denied the protections it claimed to offer. Like *Brown v. Board* seven years later, *Mendez et al.* illustrated that Americans and their institutions were subject to change, even if that change occurred gradually and reluctantly. If American history affirms "these truths," it does so on the backs of those who secured them for others who were left out of its founding charter.[45] Thus, American history is as much about the people who struggled to expand access to its founding principles and institutions as those who articulated them in the first place. By interweaving these seemingly conflicting and competing narrative threads, the nation's history provides a source of unity, not separation, illustrating the ongoing project of becoming America.

NOTES

INTRODUCTION

1. "P.T. Association Meeting," *Santa Ana Register*, November 12, 1913; Gilbert G. González, *Chicano Education in the Era of Segregation* (Denton: University of North Texas Press, 2013), 177–79.
2. Simon Ludwig Treff, "The Education of Mexican Children in Orange County," MS thesis (University of Southern California, 1934), 23.
3. Treff, "The Education of Mexican Children in Orange County," 24–26.
4. *Mendez et al.* Petition, No. 4292-M, March 2, 1945.
5. Judge McCormick concluded during pretrial hearings that *Mendez et al.* was *sui generis* (unprecedented in American case law). Reporter's Transcript, June 26, 1945, 84–86.
6. Mexican American school desegregation cases that predate *Mendez et al.* include *Francisco Maestas et al. v. George H. Shone et al.* (1914), *Romo v. Laird* (1925), *Del Rio ISD v. Salvatierra* (1930), and *Alvarez v. Lemon Grove* (1931). None of these cases were cited as legal precedent in *Mendez et al.* However, one year before representing the *Mendez et al.* plaintiffs, attorney David C. Marcus represented Mexican American residents in San Bernardino, CA in their successful petition to end the segregation of the Perris Hill Park public swimming pool. Although *Lopez v. Seccombe* (1944) was not cited as legal precedent in McCormick's opinion, it was discussed as such by Marcus during pretrial proceedings and was later used in the Ninth Circuit Court's decision to uphold *Mendez et al.* See *Westminster School District of Orange County et al. v. Mendez et al.*, 161 F.2d 774 (9th Cir. 1947).
7. Contemporaneous accounts affirm *Mendez et al.* was seen as a very real threat to overturning the "separate but equal" doctrine enshrined in *Plessy v. Ferguson* (1897). See "Minorities Jim Crow Attacked," *The Weekly Review*, December 7, 1947; "Separate School Law Violates Constitution," *Afro-American*, December 14, 1946; Ignacio Lopez, "El Caso De Segregacion En Orange County Toma Proporciones Nacionales," *El Espectador*, November 15, 1956; Carey McWilliams, "Is Your Name Gonzales," *The Nation*, April 8, 1947; "Segregation in Schools as a Violation of the XIVTH Amendment (Mendez v. Westminster School District, S.D. Cal. 1946)," *Columbia Law Review* 47, No. 2 (March 1947): 325–27; "Segregation in Public Schools: A Violation of 'Equal Protection of the Laws,'" *Yale Law Journal* 56, No. 6 (June 1947): 1059–67; "Constitutional Law-Equal Protection of the Laws-Schools-Requirement That Children of Mexican or Latin Descent Attend Separate Schools Held Invalid," *Minnesota Law Review* 30 (1945–1946): 646–47; "Segregation of Races in Public Schools and Its Relation to the

Fourteenth Amendment," *Illinois Law Review* 42 (1947–1948): 545–49; Lester H. Phillips, "Segregation in Education: A California Case Study," *Phylon* 10, No. 4 (1949): 407–13.

On the influence of *Mendez et al.* on *Brown v. Board* see Gilbert G. González, *Chicano Education in the Era of Segregation* (Cranbury, NJ: Associated University Presses, 1990), 28; Christopher Arriola, "Knocking on the Schoolhouse Door: Mendez v. Westminster, Equal Protection, Public Education, and Mexican Americans in the 1940's," *Berkeley La Raza Law Journal* 8, No. 2 (1995): 166–207; Vicki L. Ruiz, "South by Southwest: Mexican Americans and Segregated Schooling, 1900–1950," *OAH Magazine of History* 15, No. 2 (Winter 2001): 23–27; Frederick P. Aguirre, "*Mendez v. Westminster School District*: How It Affected *Brown v. Board of Education*," *Journal of Hispanic Higher Education* 4, No. 4 (October 2005): 231–332; Joy C. Shaw, "Foreshadowing *Brown v. Board*: The 1946 Case of Mendez v. Westminster," *The California Supreme Court Historical Society Newsletter* (Autumn/Winter 2004): 1–12; Lisa Y. Ramos, "Dismantling Segregation Together: Interconnections between *Mendez v. Westminster* (1946) and *Brown v. Board of Education* (1954) School Segregation Cases," *Equity & Excellence in Education* 37 (2004): 247–54; Jeanne M. Powers and Lirio Patton, "Between Mendez and Brown: Gonzales v. Sheely (1951) and the Legal Campaign Against Segregation," *Law & Social Inquiry* 33, No. 1 (Winter 2008): 127–71; Richard R. Valencia, *Chicano Students and the Courts: The Mexican American Legal Struggle for Educational Equality* (New York: New York University Press, 2008), 36–42; Carlos R. Moreno, "*Mendez v. Westminster* and School Desegregation," *California Legal History* 14 (2019): 93–104; David-James Gonzales, "Mendez v. Westminster, 1945–1947," in Lilia Fernandez ed., *50 Events that Shaped Latino History: An Encyclopedia of the American Mosaic*, 2 vol. (Goleta, CA: Greenwood, 2018), 417–34; Jose Luis Castro Padilla, "Before *Brown v. Board of Education*: Paul J. McCormick, the *Mendez v. Westminster* Decision, and Its Religious-Social Context, *U.S. Catholic Historian* 41, No. 4 (Fall 2023): 79–98.

8. Rob Kling, Spencer Olin, Mark Poster eds., *Postsuburban California: The Transformation of Orange County Since World War II* (Berkeley: University of California Press, 1991), 1–3; Lisa McGirr, *Suburban Warriors: The Origins of the New American Right* (Princeton: Princeton University Press, 2001), 21–29; Elaine Lewinnek, Gustavo Arellano, and Thuy Vo Dang, *A People's Guide to Orange County* (Oakland: University of California Press, 2022), 7–8.

9. For critiques of the dominant CRM narrative see F. Arturo Rosales, *Chicano: The History of the Mexican American Civil Rights Movement* (Houston: Arte Público Press, 1997), xv–xix; Jacquelyn Dowd Hall, "The Long Civil Rights Movement and the Political Uses of the Past," *Journal of American History*, 91, No. 4 (March 2005): 1233–63; Thomas J. Sugrue, *Sweet Land of Liberty: The Forgotten Struggle for Civil Rights in the North* (New York: Random House, 2008), xvi–xxiii; Cynthia E. Orozco, *No Mexicans Women or Dogs Allowed: The Rise of the Mexican American Civil Rights Movement* (Austin: University of Texas Press, 2009), 185–88; Jeanne Theoharis, *A More Beautiful and Terrible History: The Uses and Misuses of Civil Rights History* (Boston: Beacon Press, 2018).

10. Kling et al., *Postsuburban California*, 20–21, 48–51, 55–88; McGirr, *Suburban Warriors*, 26–52; Eric Avila, *Popular Culture in the Age of White Flight: Fear and Fantasy in Suburban Los Angeles* (Berkeley: University of California Press, 2004), 47–49, 106–20, 144; Darren Dochuk, *From Bible Belt to Sun Belt: Plain-Folk Religion, Grassroots Politics, and the Rise of Evangelical Conservatism* (New York: W.W. Norton, 2011), 19–20, 277, 341–43, 379, 401–4.

11. Gilbert G. González, *Labor and Community: Mexican Citrus Worker Villages in a Southern California County, 1900–1950* (Urbana: University of Illinois Press, 1994); Lisbeth Haas, *Conquests and Historical Identities in California, 1769–1936* (Berkeley: University of California Press, 1995). González and Haas were the first scholars to shed light on the underbelly of Orange County's history, disrupting the anesthetized booster narrative promoted by local elites while also documenting the contributions of ethnic Mexican and Native/Indigenous communities in the region's development. In her groundbreaking book on the origins of the conservative movement in Orange County, Lisa McGirr overlooks the work of González and Haas by characterizing the region as "lack[ing] a large organized working class," having a "near absence of racial minorities," and as "remarkably racially homogenous." Likewise, Eric Avila's consequential book on postwar mass culture and the growing inequality between cities and suburbs in Greater Los Angeles views Orange County as little more than a "vanilla suburb" devoid of racial and class distinctions. These surface-level depictions of Orange County as homogenously white and middle-class fail to see beyond the façade constructed by white settlers, boosters, conservative activists, and local historians. McGirr, *Suburban Warriors*, 43; Avila, *Popular Culture in the Age of White Flight*, 6, 106–44.

    Examples of Orange County's booster narrative include Samuel Armor ed., *The History of Orange County, California with Biographical Sketches* (Los Angeles: Historic Record Company, 1921); Thomas B. Talbert ed., *The Historical Volume and Reference Works: Including Biographical Sketches of Leading Citizens*, 3 vols. (Whittier: Historical Publishers, 1963); Leo J. Friis, *Orange County Through Four Centuries* (Santa Ana: Pioneer Press, 1965); Virginia L. Carpenter, *Placentia, A Pleasant Place* (Santa Ana: Pioneer Press, 1977); Esther R. Cramer ed., *A Hundred Years of Yesterdays: A Centennial History of the People of Orange County and Their Communities* (Santa Ana: The Orange County Centennial, 1988); Doris Walker, *Orange County: A Centennial Celebration* (Houston: Pioneer Publications, 1989); Richard H. Barker, *Citrus Powered the Economy of Orange County for over a Half Century Induced by "a Romance": An Illustrated History* (Balboa, CA: Citrus Roots, Preserving Citrus Heritage Foundation, 2009); Phil Brigandi, *Orange County Chronicles* (Charleston: The History Press, 2013); Charles Epting ed., *Orange County Pioneers: Oral Histories from the Works Progress Administration* (Charleston: The History Press, 2014).

    More recently, community members, journalists, and scholars have added depth and color to Orange County's multifaceted history. See Mary Garcia, *Santa Ana's Logan Barrio: Its History, Stories, and Families* (Santa Ana: Santa Ana Historical Society, 2007); Gustavo Arellano, *Orange County: A Personal History* (New York: Scribner, 2008); Richard A. Santillán, Susan C. Luévano, Luis F. Fernández, and Angelina F. Veyna, *Mexican American Baseball in Orange County* (Charleston: Arcadia Publishing, 2013); Phuong Tran Nguyen, *Becoming Refugee American: The Politics of Rescue in Little Saigon* (Urbana: University of Illinois Press, 2017); Erualdo R. González, *Latino City: Urban Planning, Politics, and the Grassroots* (New York: Routledge, 2017); Albert V. Vela, *Tracks to the Westminster Barrio: 1902–1960s* (East Hampton: Diocito Publishing Company, 2017).

12. On the tension between memory, history, and narrative see Hayden White, *The Content of the Form: Narrative Discourse and Historical Representation* (Baltimore: Johns Hopkins University Press, 1987); Michel-Rolph Trouillot, *Silencing the Past: Power and the Production of History* (Boston: Beacon Press, 1995); Sarah Maza, *Thinking About History* (Chicago: University of Chicago Press,

2017); John Lewis Gaddis, *The Landscape of History: How Historians Map the Past* (New York: Oxford University Press, 2022).

13. White flight was part of the larger processes of post-World War II deindustrialization, urban disinvestment, and suburban expansion. See Arnold R. Hirsch, *Making the Second Ghetto: Race and Housing in Chicago, 1940–1960* (Cambridge: Cambridge University Press, 1983); Kenneth T. Jackson, *Crabgrass Frontier: The Suburbanization of the United States* (New York: Oxford University Press, 1985); Thomas J. Sugrue, *The Origins of the Urban Crisis: Race and Inequality in Postwar Detroit* (Princeton: Princeton University Press, 1996); Robert O. Self, *American Babylon: Race and the Struggle for Postwar Oakland* (Princeton: Princeton University Press, 2003); Avila, *Popular Culture in the Age of White Flight*; Kevin M. Kruse, *White Flight: Atlanta and the Making of Modern Conservatism* (Princeton: Princeton University Press, 2005); Matthew D. Lassiter, *The Silent Majority: Suburban Politics in the Sunbelt South* (Princeton: Princeton University Press, 2006); Leah Platt Boustan, *Competition in the Promised Land: Black Migrants in Northern Cities and Labor Markets* (Princeton: Princeton University Press, 2017).

14. The crusading attorney and journalist Carey McWilliams was among the first to document the widespread practice of segregation within the citrus industry. See Carey McWilliams, *Southern California Country: An Island on the Land* (New York: Duell, Sloan, and Pearce, 1947).

15. Destin Jenkins and Justin Leroy eds., *Histories of Racial Capitalism* (New York: Columbia University Press, 2021), xvii.

16. Key works on racial capitalism include Carey McWilliams, *Factories in the Field: The Story of Migratory Farm Labor in California* (Boston: Little, Brown, 1939); McWilliams, *Southern California*; Carey McWilliams, *Brothers Under the Skin*, Revised Edition (Boston: Little, Brown, 1951); Oliver Cromwell Cox, *Caste, Class, & Race: A Study in Social Dynamics* (New York: Doubleday, 1948); Walter Rodney, *How Europe Underdeveloped Africa* (London: Bogle-L'Ouverture Publications, 1972); Cedric Robinson, *Black Marxism: The Making of the Black Radical Tradition* (London: Zed Press, 1983); Manning Marable, *How Capitalism Underdeveloped Black America* (Cambridge: South End Press, 1983); David Montejano, *Anglos and Mexicans in the Making of Texas* (Austin: University of Texas Press, 1987); Cheryl I. Harris, "Whiteness as Property," *Harvard Law Review* 106 (June 1993): 1707–91; Robin D.G. Kelley, *Race Rebels: Culture, Politics, and the Black Working Class* (New York: The Free Press, 1994); Charles W. Mills, *The Racial Contract* (Ithaca: Cornell University Press, 1997); George Lipsitz, *The Possessive Investment in Whiteness: How White People Profit from Identity Politics* (Philadelphia: Temple University Press, 2006); Ruth Wilson Gilmore, *Golden Gulag: Prisons, Surplus, Crisis, and Opposition in a Globalizing California* (Berkeley: University of California Press, 2007); David R. Roediger, *The Wages of Whiteness: Race and the Making of the American Working Class*, New Edition (New York: Verso, 2001 and 2007); David R. Roediger and Elizabeth D. Esch, *The Production of Difference: Race and the Management of Labor in U.S. History* (New York: Oxford University Press, 2012); Nancy Leong, "Racial Capitalism," *Harvard Law Review* 126, No. 8 (June 2013): 2151–226; Natalia Molina, *How Race Is Made in America: Immigration, Citizenship, and the Historical Power of Racial Scripts* (Berkeley: University of California Press, 2014); Jodi Melamed, "Racial Capitalism," *Critical Ethnic Studies* 1, No. 1 (Spring 2015): 76–85; Paul Ortiz, *An African American and Latinx History of the United States* (Boston: Beacon Press, 2018); Keeanga-Yamahtta Taylor, *Race for Profit: How Banks and the Real Estate Industry Undermined Black*

Homeownership (Chapel Hill: University of North Carolina Press, 2019); Walter Johnson, *The Broken Heart of America: St. Louis and the Violent History of the United States* (New York: Basic Books, 2020); Jenkins and Leroy eds., *Histories of Racial Capitalism*.

17. Melamed, "Racial Capitalism," 77.
18. McWilliams, *Southern California*, 216. On McWilliams' life and intellectual contributions see Carey McWilliams, *The Education of Carey McWilliams* (New York: Simon & Schuster, 1979); Peter Richardson, *American Prophet: The Life and Work of Carey McWilliams* (Oakland: University of California Press, 2019).
19. McWilliams, *Southern California*, 207.
20. McWilliams, *Southern California*, 207.
21. Carey McWilliams, *North from Mexico: The Spanish-Speaking People of the United States* (New York: Greenwood Press, 1968), 217. See also Matt Garcia, *A World of Its Own: Race, Labor, and Citrus in the Making of Greater Los Angeles, 1900–1970* (Chapel Hill: University of North Carolina Press, 2001), 47–78.
22. McWilliams, *Brothers Under the Skin*, 324.
23. McWilliams, *Brothers Under the Skin*, 320.
24. McWilliams, *Brothers Under the Skin*, 323–42.
25. McWilliams, *Brothers Under the Skin*, 327, 345–46.
26. Exploring the themes of labor, migration, urbanization, boosterism, and cultural production, most of the scholarly literature on California's citrus industry has followed McWilliams definition of the citrus belt proper, focusing primarily on the inland valleys of Los Angeles and Riverside counties. See Garcia, *A World of Its Own*; Douglas Cazaux Sackman, *Orange Empire: California and the Fruits of Eden* (Berkeley: University of California Press, 2005); José Alamillo, *Making Lemonade out of Lemons: Mexican American Labor and Leisure in a California Town, 1880–1960* (Champaign: University of Illinois Press, 2006); Benjamin T. Jenkins, *Octopus's Garden: How Railroads and Citrus Transformed Southern California* (Lawrence: University of Kansas Press, 2023).

    Examinations of the citrus industry outside the citrus belt proper include González, *Labor and Community*; Paul J. Sandul, *California Dreaming: Boosterism, Memory, and Rural Suburbs in the Golden State* (Morgantown: West Virginia University Press, 2014); David-James Gonzales, "Battling Mexican Apartheid in Orange County, California: Race, Place, and Politics, 1920–1950," PhD diss. (University of Southern California, 2017); Mark Anthony Ocegueda, "Sol y Sombra: San Bernardino's Mexican Community, 1880–1960," PhD diss. (University of California, Irvine, 2017).
27. "270,162 Acres Now Planted to Citrus Crop Report Shows," *California Citrograph*, September 1925. See also Edward J. Bachus, "Who Took the Oranges out of Orange County?: The Southern California Citrus Industry in Transition," *Southern California Quarterly* 63, No. 2 (Summer 1981): 161; "Orange Leads all Counties in Oranges," *California Citrograph*, October 1943.
28. "Two-thirds of Orange County's Agricultural Wealth from Citrus," *California Citrograph*, August 1929.
29. Jim Sleeper, "Oranges Helped County Get Its Start," *Santa Ana Register,* November 17, 1968.
30. Matthew D. Lassiter and Joseph Crespino eds., *The Myth of Southern Exceptionalism* (New York: Oxford University Press, 2010), 7. See also Sugrue, *Sweet Land of Liberty*, xiii–xv.
31. Mark Brilliant, *The Color of America Has Changed: How Racial Diversity Shaped Civil Rights Reform in California, 1941–1978* (New York: Oxford University Press, 2010),

3. The literature on racism and segregation outside the Jim Crow South is extensive. California provides an especially convincing foil to the myth of southern exceptionalism as Natives, Latinos, Asians, Jews, and African Americans faced various forms of homegrown discrimination throughout the state's history that were not simply rebranded Jim Crowism. For examples of this literature see McWilliams, *Southern California*; Carey McWilliams, *Prejudice Japanese-Americans: Symbol of Racial Intolerance* (Boston: Little, Brown, 1944); Carey McWilliams, *A Mask for Privilege: Anti-Semitism in America* (Boston: Little, Brown, 1948); Alexander Saxton, *The Indispensable Enemy: Labor and the Anti-Chinese Movement in California* (Berkeley: University of California Press, 1975); Albert Camarillo, *Chicanos in a Changing Society* (Cambridge: Harvard University Press, 1979); Ricardo Romo, *East Los Angeles: History of a Barrio* (Austin: Texas University Press, 1983); Albert L. Hurtado, *Indian Survival on the California Frontier* (New Haven: Yale University Press, 1988); George J. Sánchez, *Becoming Mexican American: Ethnicity, Identity, and Culture in Chicano Los Angeles, 1900–1940* (New York: Oxford University Press, 1993); Tomás Almaguer, *Racial Fault Lines: The Historical Origins of White Supremacy in California* (Berkeley: University of California Press, 1994); Nyan Shah, *Contagious Divides: Epidemics and Race in San Francisco's Chinatown* (Berkeley: University of California Press, 2001); Natalia Molina, *Fit to Be Citizens?: Public Health and Race in Los Angeles, 1879–1939* (Berkeley: University of California Press, 2006); Allison Varzally, *Making a Non-White America: Californians Coloring Outside Ethnic Lines, 1925–1955* (Berkeley: University of California Press, 2008); Scott Kurashige, *The Shifting Grounds of Race: Black and Japanese Americans in the Making of Multiethnic Los Angeles* (Princeton: Princeton University Press, 2008); George J. Sánchez ed., *Beyond Alliances: The Jewish Role in Reshaping the Racial Landscape of Southern California* (West Lafayette: Purdue University Press, 2012); Benjamin Madley, *An American Genocide: The United States and the California Indian Catastrophe* (New Haven: Yale University Press, 2017); David G. García, *Strategies of Segregation: Race, Residence, and the Struggle for Educational Equality* (Berkeley: University of California Press, 2018); Genevieve Carpio, *Collisions at the Crossroads: How Place and Mobility Make Race* (Oakland: University of California Press, 2019); Damon B. Akins and William J. Bauer Jr., *We Are the Land: A History of Native California* (Oakland: University of California Press, 2021); Jean Pelzer, *California a Slave State* (New Haven: Yale University Press, 2023).

32. The history of the Klan in Orange County is well documented in local archives, newspapers, oral histories, and the publications of local historians. See "Ku Klux Klan file" in the Anaheim Heritage Center, which includes a list of over 1400 Klan members throughout the county during the early 1920s. See also KKK folder, Box 41, Folder 8 in Don Meadows Papers, UC Irvine Special Collections and Archives, Irvine, CA; KKK folder, Box 13 in Jim Sleeper Papers, UC Irvine Special Collections and Archives, Irvine, CA.

Examples of the secondary literature include Galal Kernahan, "The Travail of Klanheim," *Orange County Illustrated*, July 1965; Richard Melching, "The Activities of the Ku Klux Klan in Anaheim, California, 1923–1925," *Southern California Quarterly* 56, No. 2 (Summer 1974): 175–96; Alan Trudell, "'White Power' Returns: KKK Makes New Bid to Regain Past OC Reign," *Orange County News*, August 30, 1979; Christopher Nicholas Cocoltchos, "The Invisible Government and the Viable Community: The Ku Klux Klan in Orange County, California During the 1920s," PhD diss. (University of California, Los Angeles, 1979); "Out of the Past: Ku Klux Klan," *Orange Coast Magazine*, February 1990;

John Westcott, "Adolph Tuma Resisted the Klan," *Orange County Register*, July 31, 1999; Cristopher N. Cocoltchos, "The Invisible Empire and the Search for the Orderly Community: The Ku Klux Klan in Anaheim, California," in Shawn Lay ed., *The Invisible Empire in the West: Toward a New Historical Appraisal of the Ku Klux Klan of the 1920s* (Urbana: University of Illinois Press, 2004); Gustavo Arellano, "Profiles in OC Pioneers Who Were Klan Members," *OC Weekly*, March 15, 2011; Gustavo Arellano, "Alexander P. Nelson Was the Klanbuster," *OC Weekly*, January 12, 2012; Gustavo Arellano, "Yes, Brea: Your Founding Fathers Were Mostly KKK Members. Get Over It," *OC Weekly*, June 12, 2017; Jesse La Tour, "A Brief History of the Ku Klux Klan in Orange County: Notes on the Banality of Evil," *Fullerton Observer*, January 7, 2019.

33. On the problematic distinction between de jure and de facto segregation see Lassiter and Crespino, *Myth of Southern Exceptionalism*, 25–44; Sugrue, *Sweet Land of Liberty*, xv–xvi; Richard Rothstein, *The Color of Law: A Forgotten History of How Our Government Segregated America* (New York: Liveright, 2017), vii–xv; Jessica Trounstine, *Segregation by Design: Local Politics and Inequality in American Cities* (Cambridge: Cambridge University Press, 2018), 1–3, 23–40; Arnold R. Hirsch, "Containment on the Home Front: Race and Federal Housing Policy from the New Deal to the Cold War," *Journal of Urban History* 26, No. 2 (January 2000): 158–89; Arnold R. Hirsch, "With or Without Jim Crow: Black Residential Segregation in the United States," in Hirsch and Raymond A. Mohl eds., *Urban Policy in Twentieth-Century America* (New Brunswick, NJ: Rutgers University Press, 1993), 65–99; Jeanne Theoharis, "Introduction," in Theoharis and Komozi Woodard eds., *Freedom North: Black Freedom Struggles Outside the South, 1940–1980* (New York: Palgrave Macmillan, 2003), 8.

34. Treff, "The Education of Mexican Children in Orange County," 23. See also supra notes 46–52 in Chapter 2 and Rubén Donato, *The Other Struggle for Equal Schools: Mexican Americans During the Civil Rights Era* (Albany: State University of New York Press, 1997), 12–14.

35. Gilbert G. González interview with Felicitas Mendez, 1987, Box 2, A046-U, UCI Libraries Special Collections and Archives, Irvine, CA.

36. Alfredo H. Zúñiga interview with Felicitas Mendez, September 10, 1975, Box 2, A048-U, UCI Libraries Special Collections and Archives, Irvine, CA.

37. This figure was tabulated by a team of researchers led by the author and is based on associating the place of residence with those identified as "Mexican," or having a Spanish surname, and/or having a parent born in Latin America in the 1930 Census.

38. Here I build on migration studies scholar Vicki Squire's notion of "mobilizing politics." Squire defines mobilizing politics in two ways. First, the phrase refers to how the "movement of people" is politicized through the prism of "irregularity" (or illegality), as in the case of undocumented immigrants. Second, it illustrates "how the irregular movements and activities of people entail a shift in what it means to be political." See Vicki Squire ed., *The Contested Politics of Mobility: Borderzones and Irregularity* (New York: Routledge, 2011), 5. Similarly, urban studies scholar Genevieve Carpio employs the concept of mobility to illustrate how communities of color were racialized in Southern California's Inland Empire through municipal codes that limited their freedom of movement. See Carpio, *Collisions at the Crossroads*, 3–6.

39. Calculating the Mexican (and later Hispanic/Latino) descended population in the United States has always been fraught with methodological inconsistencies and

disputes over terminology and identity. Between 1850 and 1920, the US Census Bureau did not distinguish Mexicans from non-Hispanic whites, thereby including them in the white racial category. While there were some attempts to estimate the "Spanish-speaking" or "Latin" population during this period, figures are unreliable. Due in large part to the mass migrations spurred by the Mexican Revolution (1910–1920), in 1930, the Census Bureau created the racial category of "Mexican" and tasked Census enumerators with the job of "classifying all persons born in Mexico, or having parents born in Mexico, who are not definitely white, Negro, Indian, Chinese, or Japanese." See Elizabeth Broadbent, "The Distribution of Mexican Population in the United States," PhD diss. (University of Chicago, 1941), 1. This comprised "the first and only time 'Mexican' appeared as a separate racial category" on the US Census. See Laura A. Gómez, *Manifest Destinies: The Making of the Mexican American Race* (New York: New York University Press, 2007), 152. As such, the 1930 Census provides an imperfect, but nonetheless helpful estimate of the Mexican descended population in the US by 1930. Using the 1930 Census, Broadbent calculated the Mexican population in the US at 1,422,533, which she also broke down by state, county, and city. Thus, the most conservative estimate of the ethnic Mexican population in Orange County by 1930 is provided by Broadbent, who put the figure at 16,536. My own analysis of the 1930 manuscript Census forms for Orange County identified an additional 1,178 persons of ethnic Mexican/Hispanic/Latino descent placing the figure at 17,741 or 15 percent of the county's population. However, contemporaneous newspaper accounts provide even larger estimates ranging from a low 18,000 to a high of 25,000 persons of Mexican ethnicity in the county during the 1930s. These larger estimates increase the size of the ethnic Mexican population to just over 21 percent of the county's population. See "Los Mexicanos Del Condado Conmemoran El Dia De La Independencia, *La Prensa*, September 16, 1938; "Cites Mexican Relief Status," *Santa Ana Register*, March 15, 1939. On the creation of Hispanic/Latino identity, categorization, and the US Census see Clara E. Rodríguez, *Changing Race: Latinos, the Census, and the History of Ethnicity in the United States* (New York: New York University Press, 2000); Arlene Dávila, *Latinos Inc.: The Marketing and Making of a People* (Berkeley: University of California Press, 2001); G. Cristina Mora, *Making Hispanics: How Activists, Bureaucrats and Media Constructed a New American* (Chicago: Chicago University Press, 2014); Laura E. Gómez, *Inventing Latinos: A New History of American Racism* (New York: The New Press, 2020).

40. On urban apartheid see George J. Sánchez, *Boyle Heights: How a Los Angeles Neighborhood Became the Future of American Democracy* (Oakland: University of California Press, 2021), 8–10; Douglas S. Massey and Nancy A. Denton, *American Apartheid: Segregation and the Making of the Underclass* (Cambridge: Harvard University Press, 1993), 9–16; Robert Chao Romero and Luis Fernando Fernandez, "Doss v. Bernal: Ending Mexican Apartheid in Orange County, CSRC Research Report, No. 14 (February 2012). Other studies that apply the apartheid concept to Jim Crow America include Garrett Power, "Apartheid Baltimore Style: The Residential Segregation Ordinances of 1910–1913," *Maryland Law Review* 42, No. 2 (1982); 289–328; Bobby Wilson, *America's Johannesburg: Industrialization and Racial Transformation in Birmingham* (Lanham, MD: Rowman & Littlefield, 2000).

41. Brilliant, *The Color of America Has Changed*, 9. See also Frances Fox Piven and Richard A. Cloward, *Poor People's Movements: Why They Succeed, How They Fail* (New York: Vintage Books, 1979).

42. Charles Tilly and Lesley J. Wood, *Social Movements, 1768–2012*, Third Edition (Boulder: Paradigm Publishers, 2013), ix.

43. Instructional materials: history-social science: Mendez v. Westminster School District of Orange County, AB1805, California Legislature, Assembly (2023–2024), https://leginfo.legislature.ca.gov/faces/billNavClient.xhtml?bill_id= 202320240AB1805. See also Kaitlyn Schallhorn, "California Legislators Want Public Schools to Teach Mendez v. Westminster," *Orange County Register*, August 30, 2024; Hanna Kang and Kaitlyn Schallhorn, "Newsom Signs Law to Teach Mendez v. Westminster in California Schools," *Orange County Register*, September 23, 2024.

CHAPTER 1

1. On the naming of Orange County see Sleeper, "Oranges Helped County Get Its Start," *Santa Ana Register*, November 17, 1968, and Jim Sleeper, "How Orange County Got Its Name," in Esther R. Cramer ed., *A Hundred Years of Yesterdays: A Centennial History of The People of Orange County and Their Communities* (Santa Ana: The Orange County Centennial, 1988), 38–41; Brigandi, *Orange County Chronicles*, 42, 46. Sleeper's November 17 article was later reprinted by the *Santa Ana Register* as "A Century of Citrus: The Story of Orange County's Golden Harvest."

2. Harry Ellington Brook, *Land of Sunshine: Southern California an Authentic Description of Its Natural Features, Resources, and Prospects* (Los Angeles: Southern California World's Fair Association and Bureau of Information, 1893), 7, 73–75. See also McWilliams, *Southern California*, 114–28.

3. Barker, *Citrus Powered the Economy*, 10–11.

4. Sleeper, "Oranges Helped County Get Its Start."

5. Sackman, *Orange Empire*, 5–7. On the importance of citrus to California's economy see special issue "Citriculture and Southern California," *California History* 74, No. 1 (Spring 1995): 6–111; David Boulé, *The Orange and the Dream of California* (Santa Monica: Angel City Press, 2013).

6. McWilliams, *Southern California*, 207.

7. González, *Labor and Community*, 12.

8. "In Biz: Orange knows its business history," *The Orange County Register*, April 3, 2013.

9. Oliver J. Dinius and Angela Vergara eds., *Company Towns in the Americas: Landscape, Power, and Working-Class Communities* (Athens: University of Georgia Press, 2011), 6. An apt description of how citrus communities functioned as company towns is in Alamillo, *Making Lemonade out of Lemons*, 15–32.

10. Farm Credit Administration, *The Citrus Industry and the California Fruit Growers Exchange*, 13, 20; Sunkist Growers, *The Story of California Oranges and Lemons* (Los Angeles: California Fruit Growers Exchange, 1932), 12.

11. Ronald Tobey and Charles Wetherell, "The Citrus Industry and the Revolution of Corporate Capitalism in Southern California," *California History* 74, No. 1 (Spring 1995): 7–10; H. Vincent Moses, "'The Orange-Grower Is Not a Farmer': G. Harold Powell, Riverside Orchardists, and the Coming of Industrial Agriculture, 1893–1930," *California History* 74, No. 1 (Spring 1995): 22–37; G. Harold Powell, Riverside Orchardists, and the Coming of Industrial Agriculture, 1893–1930," *California History* 74, No. 1 (Spring 1995): 22–37; Pierre Laszlo, *Citrus: A History* (Chicago: University of Chicago Press, 2007), 74–76.

12. Paul Garland Williamson, "Labor in the California Citrus Industry," MA thesis (University of California, 1947), 3–4, 31–38; González, *Labor and Community*, 41–48; Garcia, *A World of Its Own*, 50–53; Sackman, *Orange Empire*, 126–27; McWilliams, *Southern California*, 218–19.

13. González, *Labor and Community*, 28.

14. My use of the apartheid concept builds on the work of apartheid scholar Nyasha Mboti who views apartheid as a global paradigm to analyze the persistence of "socioeconomic, sociohistorical, and sociocultural problems" across time and space. Mboti argues apartheid is more than the "hardware," for example, South African passport system or Jim Crow laws in the United States, used to "keep things apart," it is rooted in the motivations that undergird the practice of "telling apart." Establishing apartheid first requires creating new knowledge to discriminate or "tell things apart." This knowledge is then used to keep things apart through various forms of social and physical separation and marginalization. Telling things apart involves creating notions of racial, gendered, religious, or national difference and integrating them into unequal and exploitative systems of socioeconomic and political organization for a specific purpose like capitalist production or political governance. Illuminating the various forms of apartheid beyond its "narrow technical application" (as in the case of South Africa) is what Apartheid Studies seeks to accomplish. See Nyasha Mboti, "Circuits of Apartheid: A Plea for Apartheid Studies," *Glimpse* 20 (2019): 15–70; *Apartheid Studies: A Manifesto* (Trenton, NJ: Africa World Press, 2023), xii–xxii, 359–61.

15. Harold E. Wahlberg, "Progress of County Traced Through Agriculture," *Santa Ana Register* (November 22, 1939); Works Progress Administration, "Commerce," *Orange County Historical Research Project #3105* (Santa Ana: WPA, 1936), 58–59, Box 4, Folder 11, Works Progress Administration Collection on Orange County, California, University of California, Irvine Libraries Special Collections and Archives; Richard Dale Batman, "Orange County, California: A Comprehensive History—Part I: Anaheim Was an Oasis in a Wilderness," *Journal of the West* 4, No. 1 (January 1965): 1–5, 15–17; Haas, *Conquests and Historical Identities*, 45–137; Richard H. Barker, "Citrus Roots: California Citrus Spurred Colonization," *Citrograph Magazine* (March/April 2013), 60–64, https://citrusroots.com/wp-content/uploads/sites/3/March-April-2013.pdf.

16. On the early history of Anaheim see Armor, *History of Orange County*, 53–56; Works Progress Administration, "The Rise and Fall of the Grape Industry," *Orange County Historical Research Project #3105* (Santa Ana: WPA, 1936), 78–90, Box 6, Folder 12, Works Progress Administration Collection on Orange County, California, University of California, Irvine Libraries Special Collections and Archives; Talbert, *The Historical Volume and Reference Works*, Vol. 2, 104–11; Friis, *Orange County*, 45–54; Batman, "Orange County, California—Part I: Anaheim," 5–7; Barbara Ann Milkovich, "Townbuilders of Orange County: A Study of Four Southern California Cities, 1857–1931," PhD diss. (University of California, Riverside, 1995), 24–41; Gonzales, "Battling Mexican Apartheid in Orange County," 4–20; Julia Ornelas-Higdon, *The Grapes of Conquest: Race, Labor, and the Industrialization of California Wine, 1769–1920* (Lincoln: University of Nebraska Press, 2023), 105–30.

17. Armor, *History of Orange County*, 151–67, 173–77; Wahlberg, "Progress of County Traced Through Agriculture"; Works Progress Administration, "Agriculture," *Orange County Historical Research Project #3105* (Santa Ana: WPA, 1936), 1–115, Box 4, Folders 5–6, Works Progress Administration Collection on Orange County,

California, University of California, Irvine Libraries Special Collections and Archives.

18. Batman, "Orange County, California: A Comprehensive History—Part II: 'Gospel Swamp . . . The Land of Hog and Hominy,'" *Journal of the West* 4, No. 2 (April 1965): 235; Milkovich, "Townbuilders of Orange County," 6–9, 16.

19. Batman, "Orange County," 235–36; Talbert, *Historical Volume and Reference Works*, Vol. 2, 109–11; Gonzales, "Battling Mexican Apartheid," 30–31.

20. A.D. Shamel, "Early History of Orange Growing in California," *The California Citrograph*, October 1926; Byron O. Clark, "Introduction of the Valencia Orange into California," *The California Citrograph*, September 1937; Works Progress Administration, "Agriculture," *Orange County Historical Research Project #3105* (Santa Ana: WPA, 1936), 83–88, Box 4, Folder 6, Works Progress Administration Collection on Orange County, California, University of California, Irvine Libraries Special Collections and Archives; Boulé, *The Orange and the Dream of California*, 31–47; Farmer, *Trees in Paradise: A California History* (New York: W.W. Norton, 2013), 227–49.

21. On the beginnings of the citrus industry in Orange County see Sleeper, "Oranges Helped County Get Its Start"; Pulley, "Early Citrus Culture in Orange County," *County Courier: Official Publication of the Orange County Historical Society* 36, No. 4 (April 2006): 2–4; Armor, *History of Orange County*, 147–57; Roy K. Bishop, "History of Citrus in Orange County," *The California Citrograph*, October 1943; Batman, "Orange County, California: A Comprehensive History—Part II," 237–38; Friis, *Orange County*, 79–80.

22. "Those Who Have Achieved in the Citrus Industry: Richard H. Gilman, Placentia Grower, First to Raise Valencias on a Commercial Scale," *The California Citrograph*, December 1925. See also "First Commercial Planting of Valencia Oranges Commemorated: Citrus Industry and Native Daughters of the Golden West Do Honors to R.H. Gilman at Placentia," *The California Citrograph*, March 1935; WPA, "Agriculture," *Orange County Historical Research Project #3105*, 86–87; Helen Bowen interview with Kay Heil, October 28, 1973, transcript, Center for Oral and Public History, California State University, Fullerton, Fullerton, CA; Shamel, "Early History of Orange Growing in California"; Clark, "Introduction of the Valencia Orange into California"; Sleeper, "Oranges Helped County Get Its Start"; Friis, *Orange County*, 84; González, *Labor and Community*, 52.

23. "Those Who Have Achieved: Richard H. Gilman"; Virginia L. Carpenter, "The Valencia in Placentia," *Biblio-Cal Notes* 8, No. 1 (Spring 1975): 13–17.

24. Carpenter, *Placentia*, 26–40.

25. Barker, *Citrus Powered the Economy*, 113–27; Laszlo, *Citrus*, 72–74; Col. S.H. Finley, "Limited Annual Rainfall Spurred Interest of County in Huge Colorado River Project," *Santa Ana Register*, November 22, 1939.

26. Barker, *Citrus Powered the Economy*, 117; Patricia Lin, "Perspectives on the Chinese in Nineteenth-Century Orange County," *Journal of Orange County Studies* 3, No. 4 (Fall 1989/ Spring 1990): 29. On the water wars of the 1870s and 1880s see Barker, *Citrus Powered the Economy*, 115–21; Carpenter, *Placentia*, 42–44, 52–55, 59–60, 75–77, 81–83; Friis, *Orange County*, 84–85.

27. Talbot Bielefeldt, "Placentians Led in Fight to Establish County Separation," *Santa Ana Register*, November 22, 1939.

28. On the formation of Orange County see Works Progress Administration, "County Division and Organization," *Orange County Historical Research Project #3105* (Santa Ana: WPA, 1936), 1–46, Box 7, Folder 1, Works Progress Administration

Collection on Orange County, California, University of California, Irvine Libraries Special Collections and Archives; Brigandi, *Orange County Chronicles*, 38–52; Armor, *History of Orange County*, 33–36; Friis, *Orange County*, 96–103; Carpenter, *Placentia*, 103–4.

29. Brigandi, *Orange County Chronicles*, 46. On citrus tourism see: Boulé, *The Orange and the Dream of California*, 147–55.

30. California Department of Finance, "Historical Census Populations: 1850–2020," accessed March 10, 2022, https://dof.ca.gov/reports/demographic-reports/; Armor, *History of Orange County*, 33.

31. Board of Supervisors County of Los Angeles, "Board Member Biographies," accessed March 10, 2022, https://bos.lacounty.gov/executive-office/about-us/board-of-supervisors/board-member-biographies/.

32. Brigandi, *Orange County Chronicles*, 50–52; Armor, *History of Orange County*, 33; Friis, *Orange County*, 96–97.

33. Armor, *History of Orange County*, 33–34; Friis, *Orange County*, 98–100; Carpenter, *Placentia*, 103–4; Cramer, *A Hundred Years of Yesterdays*, 36–37.

34. Sleeper, "Oranges Helped County Get Its Start"; Baker, *Citrus Powered the Economy*, 30–32.

35. Inter-office Memorandum from W.L. Aldrich, Irvine Ranch Agriculture Division, to W.J. Williams, Irvine Ranch Public Relations, October 8, 1969, Box 4, Folder "Citrus - 1A," Jim Sleeper Papers, University of California, Irvine Libraries Special Collections and Archives. From the early 1920s to the late 1960s Orange County maintained the largest acreage of bearing and nonbearing orange trees in California. See "270,162 Acres Now Planted to Citrus Crop Report Shows," *The California Citrograph*, September 1925; "Orange Leads All Counties in Oranges," *The California Citrograph*, October 1943; Bachus, "Who Took the Oranges out of Orange County?," 161.

36. Quotes taken from Moses, "The Orange-Grower Is Not a Farmer," 25. See also Alfred D. Chandler Jr., *Scale and Scope: The Dynamics of Industrial Capitalism* (Cambridge: The Belknap Press of the Harvard University Press, 1990); Alfred D. Chandler Jr., *The Visible Hand: The Managerial Revolution in American Business* (Cambridge: The Belknap Press of the Harvard University Press, 1977); Martin J. Sklar, *The Corporate Reconstruction of American Capitalism, 1890–1916: The Market, the Law, and Politics* (Cambridge: Cambridge University Press, 1988); Olivier Zunz, *Making America Corporate, 1870–1920* (Chicago: University of Chicago Press, 1990). On the uniqueness of cooperative citrus grower associations see G. Harold Powell, "Principles and Practice in Cooperation," *The California Citrograph*, February 1920; G. Harold Powell, *Cooperation in Agriculture* (New York: The Macmillan Company, 1921); W.W. Cumberland, *Cooperative Marketing: Its Advantages as Exemplified in the California Fruit Growers Exchange* (Princeton: Princeton University Press, 1917); Farm Credit Administration US Department of Agriculture, *The Citrus Industry and the California Fruit Growers Exchange System*, by Nephtune Fogelberg and A.W. McKay, Circular C-121 (Washington, D.C.: Farm Credit Administration, 1940). Moreover, Julia Ornelas-Higdon argues that the wine industry served as precursor to the development of agricultural capitalism in Orange County. See Ornelas-Higdon, *Grapes of Conquest*, 107.

37. The Sunkist Growers, *The Story of California Oranges and Lemons: By the Sunkist Growers* (Los Angeles: California Fruit Growers Exchange, 1932), 21–23; Barker, *Citrus Powered the Economy*, 34–86.

38. Cumberland, *Cooperative Marketing*, iii; Powell, *Cooperation in Agriculture*, v; González, *Labor and Community*, 21–24. See also Gilbert G. González interview with C.J. Marks, November 12, 1986, Box 1, A035-U, UCI Libraries Special Collections and Archives, Irvine, CA.

39. Cumberland, *Cooperative Marketing*, 41–46; Fogelberg and McKay, *The Citrus Industry and the California Fruit Growers Exchange System*, 13–14; Powell, *Cooperation in Agriculture*, 198–212.

40. "Pomological: Address of Hon. J. de Barth Shorb on 'Marketing Fruit,'" *Los Angeles Times*, October 6, 1885.

41. "Fruit Growers: They Meet to Form a Protective Union," *Los Angeles Times*, October 18, 1885"; "Incorporated," *Los Angeles Times*, November 28, 1885.

42. Rahno Mabel MacCurdy, *The History of the California Fruit Growers Exchange* (Los Angeles: [G. Rice & Sons], 1925), 13; Sleeper, "Oranges Helped County Get Its Start."

43. MacCurdy, *History of the California Fruit Growers Exchange*, 15.

44. MacCurdy, *History of the California Fruit Growers Exchange*, 16–26; Sunkist Growers, *Heritage of Gold: The First 100 Years of Sunkist Growers, Inc. 1893–1993* (Los Angeles: Sunkist Growers, 1994), 17–29; Cumberland, *Cooperative Marketing*, 47–48.

45. MacCurdy, *History of the California Fruit Growers Exchange*, 26; "Committee of Five Laid Foundation for Successful Exchange Operation," *The California Citrograph*, October 1943.

46. Fogelberg and McKay, *The Citrus Industry and the California Fruit Growers Exchange System*, 1.

47. Charles C. Teague, *Fifty Years a Rancher* (Los Angeles: The Ward Ritchie Press, 1944), 82.

48. Placentia Mutual Orange Association, *Articles of Incorporation Code of By-laws Revolving Fund Agreement and Growers Agreement* (Placentia: Placentia Mutual Orange Association, 1910), Box 1, Folder 1, Placentia Mutual Orange Association records, LA-CA-03, University Archives and Special Collection, Pollak Library, California State University, Fullerton. See also Cumberland, *Cooperative Marketing*, 59; Fogelberg and McKay, *The Citrus Industry and the California Fruit Growers Exchange System*, 22; Sunkist Growers Inc., *Fifty Golden Years, 1893–1943*.

49. Cumberland, *Cooperative Marketing*, 64; Teague, *Fifty Years a Rancher*, 82–84.

50. Cumberland, *Cooperative Marketing*, 115; Sunkist Growers, *Fifty Golden Years*.

51. Sunkist Growers, *Story of California Oranges and Lemons*, 8.

52. MacCurdy, *History of the California Fruit Growers Exchange*, 67.

53. MacCurdy, *History of the California Fruit Growers Exchange*, 33–34, 56–58; Cumberland, *Cooperative Marketing*, 134–35; Sunkist Growers, *Fifty Golden Years*; Teague, *Fifty Years a Rancher*, 94–96.

54. MacCurdy, *History of the California Fruit Growers Exchange*, 59–64; Sackman, *Orange Empire*, 86–87; Farmer, *Trees in Paradise*, 255–56.

55. Sackman, *Orange Empire*, 89, 96, 107–14; Sunkist Growers, *Heritage of Gold*, 42–58; Brook, *Land of Sunshine*, 3; A.J. Cook, *California Citrus Culture* (Sacramento: California State Printing Office, 1913).

56. Barker, *Citrus Powered the Economy*, 8–9; MacCurdy, *History of the California Fruit Growers Exchange*, 59–64; Laszlo, *Citrus*, 94–96.

57. Sackman, *Orange Empire*, 86, 101; Sunkist Growers, *Fifty Golden Years*. See also "Free Sunkist Oranges for the Ladies," *Santa Ana Register*, March 9, 1917; "Santa

Ana And Orange County Merchants Join in Drive to Impress Public with Orange Juice Benefits," *Santa Ana Register*, November 24, 1939.

58. Don Francisco, "Increasing the Consumption of Citrus Fruits," *The California Citrograph*, April 1921; "How Many Millions Is Sunkist Worth?," *The California Citrograph*, November 1924; Teague, *Fifty Years a Rancher*, 85–88; Boulé, *The Orange and the Dream of California*, 56–73.

59. MacCurdy, *History of the California Fruit Growers Exchange*, 29, 67–68; Cumberland, *Cooperative Marketing*, 134; Sunkist Growers, *Story of California Oranges and Lemons*, 21; Fogelberg and McKay, *The Citrus Industry and the California Fruit Growers Exchange System*, 21–22.

60. MacCurdy, *History of the California Fruit Growers Exchange*, 21; "C.C. Teague Speaks on Co-operative Marketing of Farm Products," *The California Citrograph*, January 1920; United States Congress, Senate Committee on Education and Labor, *Violations of Free Speech and Rights of Labor*, Hearings Before a Subcommittee of the Committee on Education and Labor, Part 56 (Washington, D.C.: Government Printing Office, 1940), 20357.

61. Sleeper, "Oranges Helped County Get Its Start"; González, *Labor and Community*, 6; Barker, *Citrus Powered the Economy*, 4; Richard H. Barker, "Citrus Roots: How Important Was California's Citrus Industry?," *Citrograph Magazine* (Winter 2014), 76–78, https://citrus-research-board static.sfo2.digitaloceanspaces.com/citrograph/pdf/CRB-Citrograph-Mag-Q1-Winter2014-Web.pdf; Farmer, *Trees in Paradise*, 276; Tobey and Wetherell, "The Citrus Industry and the Revolution of Corporate Capitalism," 6–19; McWilliams, *Southern California*, 209.

62. Cumberland, *Cooperative Marketing*, 146.

63. United States Congress, Senate Committee on Education and Labor, *Violations of Free Speech and Rights of Labor*, Report of the Committee on Education and Labor, Part I (Washington, D.C.: Government Printing Office, 1942), 57.

64. United States Congress, Senate Committee on Education and Labor, *Violations of Free Speech and Rights of Labor*, Report of the Committee on Education and Labor, Part IV (Washington, D.C.: Government Printing Office, 1942), 539. See also C.J. Marks interview.

65. Harvey Molotch, "The City as a Growth Machine: Toward a Political Economy of Place," *American Journal of Sociology* 82, No. 2 (September 1976): 309–22; John R. Logan and Harvey Molotch, *Urban Fortunes: The Political Economy of Place* (Berkeley: University of California Press, 1987); Kevin R. Cox, "Revisiting 'the City as a Growth Machine,'" *Cambridge Journal of Regions, Economy and Society* 10, No. 3 (November 2017): 391–405. For alternatives to the growth machine model see Mark Gottdiener, *The Social Production of Urban Space*, Second Edition (Austin: University of Texas Press, 1985), 222–26; Mark Gottdiener, Ray Hutchison, and Michael T. Ryan, *The New Urban Sociology*, Fifth Edition (New York: Routledge, 2015), 44; Eric H. Monkkonen, *America Becomes Urban: The Development of U.S. Cities and Towns, 1780–1980* (Berkeley: University of California Press, 1988).

66. Logan and Molotch, *Urban Futures*, 50. See also Monkkonen, *America Becomes Urban*, 125–30, 141–44, 212–14.

67. Wahlberg, "Progress of County Traced Through Agriculture"; George Hart, "Value of Land Shows Growth," *Santa Ana Register*, November 22, 1939; Neil Stanley, "County's Major Crop of Oranges Grows from Two Acres Planted in 1873 to 75,000 in Area Today, *Santa Ana Register*, November 22, 1939: Dixson W. Tubbs, "Transition in County's Agricultural Activity Colorfully Recorded for More than Half-Century," *Santa Ana Register*, November 22, 1939; Floyd McCracken,

"Prosperity of Anaheim Founded on Oranges," *Santa Ana Register*, November 22, 1939.

68. Tobey and Wetherell, "The Citrus Industry and the Revolution of Corporate Capitalism," 6; Molotch, "City as a Growth Machine," 312; Gabriele Gonder Carey, "From Hinterland to Metropolis: The Origins of Land Use Planning in Orange County, California, 1925–1950," PhD diss. (University of California, Riverside, 1997), 1–6, 12–14.

69. These figures are based on the analysis of publicly available information obtained through city and county directories, US Census records, and state voter registration records between 1890 and 1940.

70. Carey, "From Hinterland to Metropolis," 13–14; McGirr, *Suburban Warriors*, 39. In his interview with Gilbert González, C.J. Marks repeatedly emphasized growers influence on all aspects of county governance, commerce, and politics through the lobbying efforts of the Farm Bureau. C.J. Marks was the Executive Secretary of the Orange County Farm Bureau, the lobbying arm of growers, and editor of the *Orange County Farm Bureau News*. He was involved with the OC Farm Bureau for over thirty years (1930s to 1960s), ran for the OC Board of Supervisors, served as tax consultant for the County Chamber of Commerce, and was elected president of the OC Fair and Exposition Board. See also "The Fourth District Means All of the Fourth District," *Santa Ana Register*, November 1, 1954 and "Tustinite C.J. Marks New Fair and Exposition Board President," *The Tustin News*, February 6, 1969.

71. Monkkonen, *America Becomes Urban*, 127.

72. Sunkist Growers, *The Story of California Oranges and Lemons*, 7–9; Fogelberg and McKay, *The Citrus Industry and the California Fruit Growers Exchange System*, 7–11; D.D. Waynick, "Growth Rates of Valencia Oranges," *The California Citrograph*, April 1925; Clark, "Introduction of the Valencia Orange into California."

73. Sleeper, "Oranges Helped County Get Its Start." On the rise and dominance of the Valencia orange among other citrus varieties see Fogelberg and McKay, *The Citrus Industry and the California Fruit Growers Exchange System*, 7–13; Bishop, "History of Citrus in Orange County"; "Orange Leads All Counties in Oranges," *The California Citrograph*, October 1943; J.A. Prizer, "Early History of the Placentia Orange Growers Association," *Manager's Annual Report: Placentia Orange Growers Association, Season of 1945*, Box 2, Folder 5, Placentia Orange Growers Association records, LA-CA-02, University Archives and Special Collection, Pollak Library, California State University, Fullerton. See also "CA-Citrus-Stats_compressed" and "OC-Citrus-Production-Stats" in "Citrus Roots Presenting the Story-The Story Told from Statistics," Citrus Roots, Preserving Citrus Heritage Foundation, accessed November 30, 2021, https://citrusroots.com/citrus-fruits-story/.

74. Williamson, "Labor in the California Citrus Industry," 13; "270,162 Acres Now Planted to Citrus Crop Report Shows," *The California Citrograph*, September 1925; Bachus, "Who Took the Oranges out of Orange County," 161; Richard H. Barker, "The Building Boom of 1925–26 caused a relinquishment of citrus acreage," *Citrograph Magazine* (May/June 2013).

75. Moses, "The Orange-Grower Is Not a Farmer," 25; McWilliams, *Southern California*, 216; Sackman, *Orange Empire*, 7; Garcia, *A World of Its Own*, 19.

76. Bielefeldt, "Placentians Led in Fight to Establish County." See also biographic profiles of A.S. Bradford in Armor, *History of Orange County*, 224–26 and Wayne Goble, "Those Who Have Achieved in the Citrus Industry: A.S. Bradford, Orchardist, Banker, Industrial Financer, Who Started with a $5 Gold Piece and Attained Success," *The California Citrograph*, September 1921.

77. Biographical information on C.C. Chapman gathered from: Armor, *History of Orange County*, 211–15; J.L. Mathews, "Sentiment and Beauty in Fruit Raising: Capitalizing a Reputation for a Brand and the Industry—Good Oranges and Good Citizenship," *The California Citrograph*, April 1918; Merle Crowell, "Wiped out at Forty," *The American Magazine* 29, No. 4 (April 1921): 14–15 and 108–10; "C.C. Chapman, Capitalist, Philanthropist, Builder," *Orange County Review* 2, No. 12 (November 1923): 19–22; "Those Who Have Achieved in the Citrus Industry: C.C. Chapman of Fullerton, a Grower Who Uses His Wealth to Help Mankind," *The California Citrograph*, April 1921; C. Stanley Chapman interview with Arlene R. Sayre, February 14 and March 29, 1968, transcript, Center for Oral and Public History, California State University, Fullerton, Fullerton, CA; C. Stanley Chapman interview with Nita June Busby, October 16 and November 18, 1975, transcript, Center for Oral and Public History, California State University, Fullerton, Fullerton, CA; Maureen McClintock Rischard, "Charles C. Chapman: Father of the Valencia Orange Industry in Orange County," *Orange County California Genealogical Society Quarterly* 7, No. 2 (June 1970): 69–70; Donald H. Pflueger, *Charles C. Chapman: The Career of a Creative Californian, 1853–1944* (Los Angeles: Anderson, Ritchie, and Simon, 1976).
78. Pflueger, *Charles C. Chapman*, 79–84.
79. Pflueger, *Charles C. Chapman*, 88–91; Charles C. Chapman, "Citrus Talks-The Value of an Orange Brand," (1915), *Charles C. Chapman Citrus Speeches*, 25, https://digitalcommons.chapman.edu/chapman_citrus_speeches/25/; Sunkist Growers, *Heritage of Gold*, 13–14; Boulé, *The Orange and the Dream of California*, 116–25. On the Spanish Fantasy Past see McWilliams, *Southern California*, 70–83.
80. Richard G. Lillard editor, *Letters from the Orange Empire by G. Harold Powell* (Los Angeles: Historical Society of Southern California, 1990), 29, 59.
81. Lillard, *Letters from the Orange Empire*, 91–95; Cramer, *A Hundred Years of Yesterdays*, 46; Crowell, "Wiped out at Forty," "Those Who Have Achieved: C.C. Chapman of Fullerton"; Rischard, "Charles C. Chapman: Father of the Valencia"; Sleeper, "Oranges Helped County Get Its Start."
82. Logan and Molotch, *Urban Futures*, 54; Pflueger, *Charles C. Chapman*, 101.
83. Milkovich, "Townbuilders of Orange County," 61; Barbara Ann Milkovich, "Fullerton, Orange County, California: The Struggle for Local Control," *Southern California Quarterly* 78, No. 4 (Winter 1996): 301–22; Cramer, *A Hundred Years of Yesterdays*, 108–11; Works Progress Administration, "Outline of Early History of Fullerton," *Orange County Historical Research Project #3105* (Santa Ana: WPA, 1936), 51–53, Box 2, Folder 2, Works Progress Administration Collection on Orange County, California, University of California, Irvine Libraries Special Collections and Archives.
84. Charles C. Chapman, "Citrus Notes-The Santa Ysabel Ranch," (1912), *Charles C. Chapman Citrus Speeches*, 33, https://digitalcommons.chapman.edu/chapman_citrus_speeches/33; Pflueger, *Charles C. Chapman*, 77–78.
85. Pflueger, *Charles C. Chapman*, 101.
86. Pflueger, *Charles C. Chapman*, 101; Milkovich, "Fullerton," 308–11; Milkovich, "Townbuilders of Orange County," 62–69; Chapman interview with Busby, November 18, 1975; C. Stanley Chapman, Sr. interview with C. Stanley Chapman Jr., January 6, 1979, transcript, Center for Oral and Public History, California State University, Fullerton, Fullerton, CA.
87. Pflueger, *Charles C. Chapman*, 103; Carey, "From Hinterland to Metropolis," 98–101.

88. Milkovich, "Townbuilders of Orange County," 61; Sleeper, "Oranges Helped County Get Its Start."

89. Tomás Almaguer found a similar relationship between "grower elites" and the banking industry in Ventura County. See Almaguer, *Racial Fault Lines*, 96–98.

90. Baker, *Citrus Powered the Economy*, 107–12; Chapman, Sr. interview with Chapman Jr., January 6, 1979.

91. Pflueger, *Charles C. Chapman*, 107–8.

92. In March 1919, the Union Oil Company opened several oil wells in the Placentia-Richfield section of the county. The most valuable of these was found on C.C. Chapman's Santa Ysabel Ranch. By April 1919, Chapman's well became known as "the wonder of all Southern California," and the "best producer in the state," responsible for over 1.5 million barrels of oil in its first seven months of operation. Armor, *History of Orange County*, 145.

93. Pflueger, *Charles C. Chapman*, 152–58; Rischard, "Charles C. Chapman." Using his wealth and connections, Chapman was the lead donor and founder of California Christian College in Los Angeles (also known as California School of Christianity) in 1918. The college was renamed Chapman College in 1934 and moved to its current location in Orange, CA twenty years later. In 1991, Chapman College became Chapman University. See Arlene Reasoner Sayre, "Chapman Remembers: A History of Chapman College," LD.C466 S29 1969, Frank Mt. Pleasant Library of Special Collections and Archives, Chapman University; "Our Story," Chapman University, accessed January 10, 2022, https://www.chapman.edu/about/our-story/index.aspx.

94. Pflueger, *Charles C. Chapman*, 119–28; "Fruit Growers Are Organized," *Los Angeles Express*, March 15, 1906; Charles C. Chapman, "Citrus Talks-Citrus League," (1914), *Charles C. Chapman Citrus Speeches*, 35, https://digitalcommons.chapman.edu/chapman_citrus_speeches/35/; Cook, *California Citrus Culture*, 6, 104.

95. Pflueger, *Charles C. Chapman*, 120.

96. Pflueger, *Charles C. Chapman*, 118–19; Charles C. Chapman, "Citrus Notes-The Value of the Tariff to Citrus," *Charles C. Chapman Citrus Speeches*, 22, https://digitalcommons.chapman.edu/chapman_citrus_speeches/22/; Chapman interview with Busby, November 18, 1975; "The Citrus Protective League," *Pacific Rural Press*, Vol. 76, No. 3, July 18, 1908; "Why the Citrus Industry Needs a Protective Tariff," *The California Citrograph*, August 1918. See also Tariff of 1897 (Dingley Tariff), July 24, 1897, accessed January 10, 2022, https://fraser.stlouisfed.org/title/5862.

97. Pflueger, *Charles C. Chapman*, 184–85; Charles C. Chapman, "Strong Appeal for Support of the Coolidge Ticket for Delegates to the Convention," *Santa Ana Register*, May 1, 1924; "The Two Tickets," *Santa Ana Register*, May 3, 1923; "Chapman Boom for V.P. in Cleveland," *Santa Ana Register*, June 9, 1924; "Chapman Back from G.O.P. Sessions," *Santa Ana Register*, July 7, 1924.

98. Pflueger, *Charles C. Chapman*, 128–31; Wayne Goble, "Valencia Orange Show at Anaheim Attracts Fruit and Visitors," *The California Citrograph*, June 1921; "Valencia Orange Has Show All of Its Own at Anaheim," *The California Citrograph*, July 1921; Boulé, *The Orange and the Dream of California*, 77–85.

99. Carpenter, *Placentia*, 135–38; Bielefeldt, "Placentians Led in Fight to Establish County"; Cramer, *A Hundred Years of Yesterdays*, 156–57.

100. Banks started by Bradford and his associates include Placentia National Bank in 1911, Placentia Savings Bank in 1916, and American Savings Bank of Anaheim in 1924. Bradford also held several prominent positions in many public and

private organizations including director of the Anaheim Union Water Company, chairman of the County Board of Foresters, commissioner of the county harbor, V.P. and director of the Southern Counties Gas Company, director of the Orange County Automobile Association, and president of the Republican Petroleum Corporation. Carpenter, *Placentia*, 138–39, 194, 203; Armor, *Orange County*, 225–26; Bielefeldt, "Placentians Led in Fight to Establish County"; Barker, *Citrus Powered the Economy*, 110.

101. Carpenter, *Placentia*, 136, 150–51.

102. Barker, *Citrus Powered the Economy*, 62–67; "Placentia Mutual Has Best Season: Is Largest Orange Packing House in the World," *Placentia Courier*, January 2, 1931.

103. "Citrus Fruits," *Santa Ana Register*, February 8, 1921. See also Almaguer, *Racial Fault Lines*, 96–97.

104. Wahlberg, "Progress of County Traced Through Agriculture"; Barker, *Citrus Powered the Economy*, 30–34.

105. Hart, "Value of Land Shows Growth."

106. "270,162 Acres Now Planted to Citrus Crop Report Shows," *The California Citrograph*, September 1925; "198,729 Acres Southern California Citrus Estimate," *The California Citrograph*, July 1926; J.M. Thompson, "Economic Study of Orange Industry Throughout the World," *The California Citrograph*, November 1938; Neil Stanley, "County's Major Crop of Oranges Grows from Two Acres Planted in 1873 to 75,000 in Area Today," *Santa Ana Register*, November 22, 1939; "Orange County Leads All Counties in Oranges," *The California Citrograph*, October 1943; "Valencia Orange Acreage as Reported by California Cooperative Reporting Service and Orange County Department of Agriculture," Box FR-3, Folder 12, Don Meadows Collection, University of California, Irvine Libraries Special Collections and Archives; "Santiago Orange Growers Association, 1893–1967," Box 4, Folder "Citrus (Photographs)," Jim Sleeper Papers, University of California, Irvine Libraries Special Collections and Archives; "Barbeque List," August 13, 1938, Box 1, Folder 12, Willard Smith Papers, 1880–1965, Orange County Archives, Santa Ana, CA; Louis Reccow, "The Orange County Citrus Strike of 1935–1936: The "Forgotten People in Revolt," PhD diss. (University of Southern California, 1972), 5, 10, 13, 257–59; Bachus, "Who Took the Oranges out of Orange County," 161; United States Department of Agriculture, "Florida Citrus Fruit: Acreage, Production, Utilization, Prices and Tree Numbers," 6, accessed February 8, 2022, https://www.nass.usda.gov/Statistics_by_State/ Florida/Publications/Historical_Summaries/citrus/cs/acreage,%20product ion%20%20utilization-1948.pdf.

107. This argument was first articulated by John R. Commons in 1907, when he attributed the practice of "playing one race against the other" as a defining feature of US labor management. John R. Commons, *Race and Immigrants in America* (New York: The Macmillan Company, 1907). See also Roediger and Esch, *The Production of Difference*, 5–16.

108. For a survey of these practices in California agriculture from the Spanish mission system to the rise of industrial agriculture see Richard Steven Street, *Beasts of the Field: A Narrative History of California Farmworkers, 1769–1913* (Stanford: Stanford University Press, 2004). Various forms of coerced and unfree labor predated the rise of commercial agriculture in California and the West. See Hurtado, *Indian Survival on the California Frontier*; Haas, *Conquests and Historical Identities*, chapters 1–3; Andrés Resendez, *The Other Slavery: The Uncovered Story*

of Indian Enslavement in America (New York: Houghton Mifflin Harcourt, 2016); Pfaelzer, *California, A Slave* (New Haven: Yale University Press, 2023).

109. González, *Labor and Community*, 12, 36–39, 48–49, 103–6, 169–73; Gilbert G. González, *Chicano Education in the Era of Segregation* (Denton: University of North Texas Press, 2013), 11–19, 175–202; Haas, *Conquests and Historical Identities*, 165–66, 174–84, 190–95.

110. J.B. Culbertson, "Housing of Ranch Labor," *The California Citrograph*, May 1920.

111. Wahlberg, "Progress of County Traced Through Agriculture"; Stanley, "County's Major Crop of Oranges Grows."

112. Culbertson, "Housing of Ranch Labor."

113. According to C.J. Marks, secretary with the OC Farm Bureau, "Farmers . . . in Orange County didn't particularly care to get out and stoop in the field. They felt like they were beyond that." See C.J. Marks interview.

114. Carpenter, *Placentia*, 42–43; Helen Bowen interview.

115. Armor, *History of Orange County*, 166; Lin, "Perspectives on the Chinese in Nineteenth-Century Orange County," 28–29; Works Progress Administration, "Anaheim's China Town," *Orange County Historical Research Project #3105* (Santa Ana: WPA, 1936), 15–19, Box 2, Folder 1, Works Progress Administration Collection on Orange County, California, University of California, Irvine Libraries Special Collections and Archives; Lewinnek et al., *A People's Guide to Orange County*, 29–31, 53–54, 63–64.

116. González, *Labor and Community*, 48.

117. Works Progress Administration, "Chinese in Agriculture," *Orange County Historical Research Project #3105* (Santa Ana: WPA, 1936), 207, Box 4, Folder 8, Works Progress Administration Collection on Orange County, California, MS-R10, University of California, Irvine Libraries Special Collections and Archives.

118. González, *Labor and Community*, 46–48; Friis, *Orange County*, 104; Reccow, "Orange County Citrus Strike," 16; Esther R. Cramer, *La Habra: The Pass Through the Hills* (Fullerton: Sultana Press, 1969), 156–57; Carpenter, *Placentia*, 63, 87, 108; Armor, *History of Orange County*, 142, 162, 166; Jim Sleeper, "Two Tales of the Dragon: The Night They Burned Chinatown," *Orange County Illustrated*, June 1970, 30–33; Brigandi, *Orange County Chronicles*, 53–59; Haas, *Conquests and Historical Identities*, 76, 176–78. See also McWilliams, *Southern California*, 218–19; Garcia, *A World of Its Own*, 36–39; Sackman, *Orange Empire*, 126–31; Street, *Beast of the Field*, xv–xxv.

119. Williamson, "Labor in the California Citrus Industry," 3–4.

120. Williamson, "Labor in the California Citrus Industry," 4.

121. Williamson, "Labor in the California Citrus Industry," 6.

122. Santiago Orange Growers Association Minutes, Board of Directors Meetings, 1893–1900, Orange County Archives, Santa Ana, CA.

123. Williamson, "Labor in the California Citrus Industry," 6–8, 24–29; US Congress, *Violations of Free Speech and Rights of Labor*, Part 56, Exhibit 8962-B; Reccow, "Orange County Citrus Strike," 14–17.

124. Sackman, *Orange Empire*, 128–30. See also Teague, *Fifty Years a Rancher*, 141–44; Williams, "Labor in the California Citrus Industry," 31–52; McWilliams, *Factories in the Field*, 103–33; Camille Guerin-Gonzales, *Mexican Workers and American Dreams: Immigration, Repatriation, and California Farm Labor, 1900–1939* (New Brunswick: Rutgers University Press, 1994), 25, 45–47, 51–61; David G. Gutiérrez, *Walls and Mirrors: Mexican Americans, Mexican Immigrants, and the Politics of Ethnicity* (Berkeley: University of California Press, 1995),

46–51; Garcia, *A World of Its Own*, 50–61; Steven, *Beast of the Field*, 235–333, 407–526; Roediger and Esch, *The Production of Difference*, 193–203.

125. Molina, *How Race Is Made in America*, 6–11, 29–42. See also Mark Reisler, *By the Sweat of Their Brow: Mexican Immigrant Labor in the United States, 1900–1940* (Westport: Greenwood Press, 1976), 127–44; Natalia Molina, Daniel Martinez HoSang, and Ramón A. Gutiérrez eds., *Relational Formations of Race: Theory, Method, and Practice* (Oakland: University of California Press, 2019), 5–9.

126. Will J. French, G.H. Hecke, and Anna A. Saylor, *Mexicans in California: A Report of Governor C.C. Young's Mexican Fact-Finding Committee* (San Francisco: State Printing Office, 1930), 162.

127. French et al., *Mexicans in California*, 164.

128. French et al., *Mexicans in California*, 161–62.

129. French et al., *Mexicans in California*, 163.

130. Williamson, "Labor in the California Citrus Industry," 31.

131. Charles C. Chapman, "Citrus Talks-The Future of the Orange Industry," (1914), *Charles C. Chapman Citrus Speeches*, 7, https://digitalcommons.chapman. edu/chapman_citrus_speeches/7/?utm_source=digitalcommons.chapman. edu%2Fchapman_citrus_speeches%2F7&utm_medium=PDF&utm_campaign= PDFCoverPages.

132. Chapman, "The Future of the Orange Industry."

133. "Labor," *The California Citrograph*, June 1917; Reisler, *By the Sweat of Their Brow*, 28.

134. Combined, these pieces of legislation dramatically reduced the number of Asian and Southeastern European migrants through the imposition of an increased head tax, literacy test, and quota restrictions based on race and nationality. See Reisler, *By the Sweat of Their Brow*, 24–26; Mae Ngai, *Impossible Subjects: Illegal Aliens and the Making of Modern America* (Princeton: Princeton University Press, 2004), 18–19; Deborah Kang, *The INS on the Line: Making Immigration Law on the US-Mexico Border, 1917–1954* (New York: Oxford University Press, 2017), 16–18.

135. "Labor," *The California Citrograph*, June 1917; "War and Citrus," *The California Citrograph*, June 1917; "Mexican Laborers Admitted," *The California Citrograph*, July 1917; Dr. H.J. Webber, "War Time Economies for the Citrus Grower," *The California Citrograph*, February 1918; "Organization to Procure Labor," *The California Citrograph*, August 1918; "Immigration Regulations Suspended for Mexican Labor," *The California Citrograph*, September 1918; French et al., *Mexicans in California*, 18. See also Reisler, *By the Sweat of Their Brow*, 27–42; Lawrence A. Cardoso, *Mexican Emigration to the United States, 1897–1931* (Tucson: University of Arizona Press, 1980), 47–48; Guerin-Gonzales, *Mexican Workers and American Dreams*, 31–44; Kang, *The INS on the Line*, 20–35; Rachel St. John, *Line in the Sand: A History of the Western US-Mexico Border* (Princeton: Princeton University Press, 2011), 179–81.

136. Guerin-Gonzales, *Mexican Workers and American Dreams*, 44.

137. "Farm Wages," *Santa Ana Register*, July 26, 1918; R.S. Vaile, "Mexican Labor," *The California Citrograph*, March 1918; "The Well Housed Employee," *The California Citrograph*, September 1918; "How to House and Treat Citrus Ranch Employes [sic]," *The California Citrograph*, November 1919.

138. A.D. Shamel, "Housing of Employes [sic] of California's Citrus Ranches," *The California Citrograph*, October 1918; A.D. Shamel, "Housing of Employes [sic] of California's Citrus Ranches," *The California Citrograph*, February 1918. See also

Lewis G. Weathers, "History of the Citrus Research Center," (1982), Agriculture and Natural Resources Repository, University of California, accessed March 18, 2022, https://ucanr.edu/repository/view.cfm?article=72292%20&search=.

139. A.D. Shamel, "Housing of Employes [*sic*] of California's Citrus Ranches," *The California Citrograph*, October 1918.

140. Vaile, "Mexican Labor."

141. Vaile, "Mexican Labor."

142. "The Well Housed Employee," *The California Citrograph*, September 1918. Unsurprisingly, Governor C.C. Young's report found that twenty-three cents a day was the wage differential between Mexicans and whites, and Mexicans were paid up to five cents less per hour than Asians and Blacks. See French et al., *Mexicans in California*, 170.

143. "How to House and Treat Citrus Ranch Employes [*sic*]: Addresses Made Before the Lemon Men's Club," *The California Citrograph*, November 1919.

144. David E. Hayes-Bautista, Marco Antonio Firebaugh, Cynthia L. Chamberlin, and Christina Gamboa, "Reginaldo Francisco del Valle: UCLA's Forgotten Forefather," *Southern California Quarterly* 88, No. 1 (Spring 2006): 1–35; Kenneth C. Burt, "The Latino Democratic Trail Stretches Way Back," *Hispanic Link News Service*, June 22, 2011, http://kennethburt.com/blog/?p=1052.

145. "How to House and Treat Citrus Ranch Employes [*sic*]."

146. "Growth of Mexican Labor," *The California Citrograph*, December 1919.

147. Gilbert G. González, "Labor and Community: The Camps of Mexican Citrus Pickers in Southern California," *Western Historical Quarterly* 22, No. 3 (August 1991): 290–91.

148. French et al., *Mexicans in California*, 164–65.

149. This figure is based on the respondent's self-reported occupation for those identified as "Mexican" in enumeration districts assigned to Orange County by the 1930 US Census Bureau. Mexican respondents stating their occupation as "farmer," "farm hand," "laborer," "nurseryman," "packer," "picker," "pruner," "orchardist," "rancher," "ranch hand," "section hand," "sprayer," "teamster," and "truck driver" were included in this figure since each of these positions were associated with citrus and other agricultural products. Further, over 65 percent of Mexican respondents self-reported the industry of their occupation as one of the following: "cannery," "farming," "fertilizer," "fruit," "irrigation," "packing house," "ranching," "trucking," and "water," all of which were directly associated with citrus and agricultural work. Data and figures were tabulated by a team of researchers led by the author.

150. Culbertson, "Housing of Ranch Labor."

151. González, *Labor and Community*, 59. See also Mary Peters, "The Segregation of Mexican American Children in the Elementary Schools of California—Its Legal and Administrative Aspects," MA thesis (University of California at Los Angeles, 1948), 21.

152. Estimates of the number of ethnic Mexican barrios and colonias in Orange County during the 1930s range from thirty-one to fifty-three. See Vela, *Tracks to the Westminster Barrio*, 13; Albert V. Vela, "53 Mexican Barrios/Colonias of Orange County, 1900s–," March 9, 2017, unpublished list in possession of author; Bud Lembke, "Barrios Begin to Play Role in Politics: 31 in County," *The Los Angeles Times*, February 6, 1977; Brooke Larsen Garlock interview with Stephen Reyes, November 10, 1983, Pasadena Centennial Committee, Pasadena Public Library, Pasadena, CA; Gilbert G. González, "Mexican Communities

in Orange County," *Journal of Orange County Studies* 3/4 (Fall 1989/Spring 1990): 23; González, *Labor and Community*, 58–64; Santillán et al., *Mexican American Baseball in Orange County*, 10; "Barrios, Colonias & Campos: In Search of Orange County's Historic Mexican Neighborhoods," *Southern Empire 13* (blog), December 14, 2012, http://southernempire13.blogspot.com/2012/12/barrios-colonias-campos.html.

153. González, *Labor and Community*, 57–65; González, "Labor and Community," 292–93; Jessie Hayden, "The La Habra Experiment in Mexican Social Education," MA thesis (Claremont College, 1934); Cramer, *La Habra*, 262; Lewinnek et al., *A People's Guide to Orange County*, 72–73; Cruz Reynoso interview with Germaine La Berge, 2002–2004, Oral History Office, The Bancroft Library, University of California, Berkeley; Enrique "Kiki" Zuniga interview with David-James Gonzales, June 27, 2019, Yorba Linda, CA.

154. Prizer, "Early History of the Placentia Orange Growers Association"; "Placentia Mutual Orange Grower's Assn. Manager's Annual Report, 1924," Box 2, Folder 5, Placentia Orange Growers Association Records, LA-CA-02, University Archives and Special Collections, Pollack Library, California State University, Fullerton; González, *Labor and Community*, 61–62.

155. Stephen O'Neil, "The Role of Colonias in Orange County," unpublished paper, F868.06 022 1985 OC Pam, Special Collections and Archives, University of California, Irvine Libraries, Irvine, CA.

156. O'Neil, "The Role of Colonias in Orange County," 7.

157. Shamel, "Housing of Employes [sic] of California's Citrus Ranches," March 1918.

158. Shamel, "Housing of Employes [sic] of California's Citrus Ranches"; O'Neil, "The Role of Colonias in Orange County."

159. Chapman interview with Busby, October 16, 1975; Chapman interview with Busby, November 18, 1975.

160. Vela, *Tracks to the Westminster Barrio*, 13, 19; Armor, *History of Orange County*, 151–59.

161. Haas, *Conquests and Historical Identities*, 180–84; González, *Labor and Community*, 63. See also Garcia, *Santa Ana's Logan Barrio*.

162. Raymond Rast interview with Alex Maldonado, February 25, 2011, O.H. 4885.1, Center for Oral and Public History, California State University, Fullerton, Fullerton, CA. See also Alex Maldonado interview with Alex Tewes, January 26, 2012, transcript, Center for Oral and Public History, California State University, Fullerton, Fullerton, CA.

163. Chapman University, *A History of Key Structures in the Cypress Street Neighborhood* (Orange: Chapman University, 2007), 3; Chapman University, *Recollections of the Cypress Street Neighborhood* (Orange: Chapman University, 2006), 12–14.

164. Chapman University, *Recollections of the Cypress Street Neighborhood* (Orange, CA: Chapman University, 2006), 1–2; Douglas Westfall, "Killefer Grade School," *Somos Primos*, July 2017, http://somosprimos.com/sp2017/spjul17/spjul17.htm#ORANGE%20COUNTY,%20CA.

165. This figure is based on my analysis of enumeration districts in Orange County included in the 1930 Census. Moreover, the memories of Cypress St. barrio residents confirm the starkness of housing segregation and discrimination experienced by Mexicans in the city of Orange. See Angela Barrientos interview with Edna DeLeon, December 5, 2002, O.H. 3200, Center for Oral and Public History, California State University, Fullerton, Fullerton, CA. See also Shades of Orange—Cypress Street Barrio Oral History Project interviews with Leo

Castro, Paul Guzman, Lucy Cornejo Duran, Augapito Morales, Phillip Collin, 2005–2006, Orange Public Library, Orange, CA.

166. Michelle Tellez, *Border Women and the Community of Maclovio Rojas: Autonomy in the Spaces of Neoliberal Neglect* (Tucson: University of Arizona Press, 2021), 17.

167. Squatting was a common practice among early Anglo/European settlers in the Santa Ana Valley as well. See, Brigandi, *Orange County Chronicles*, 31–35.

168. Edward Castro interview, 51. See also, González, *Labor and Community*, 59–60.

169. Detailed descriptions of the colony, along with a hand drawn rendering were provided by longtime resident Edward Castro. See Castro interview, 52–55. Castro's descriptions and population estimates are supported by former principal of the La Jolla Mexican School, Chester Whitten. See, Chester Whitten interview by Gilbert González, August 20, 1987, Gilbert G. González Interviews, Special Collections and Archives, University of California, Irvine Libraries, Irvine, CA.

170. Chester Whitten, "An Experimental Study of the Comparison of 'Formal' and 'Progressive' Methods of Teaching Mexican Children," MA Thesis (University of Southern California, 1939), 6–7, 21.

171. Chester Whitten interview.

172. Eddie Castro interview, 5.

173. Eddie Castro interview, 3.

174. Eddie Castro interview, 4, 7.

175. Eddie Castro interview, 18.

176. González, *In Search of the Mexican Beverly Hills*, 4.

177. Carey McWilliams, "Spectrum of Segregation," *Survey Graphic* (January 1947), 24; McWilliams, *Southern California*, 219.

178. González, *In Search of the Mexican Beverly Hills*, 14; Téllez, *Border Women*, 17–18.

179. See supra note 152.

180. Carey, "From Hinterland to Metropolis," 151–53; O'Neil, "The Role of Colonias in Orange County," 3–7; González, *Labor and Community*, 64–65.

181. This figure was tabulated by a team of researchers led by the author and is based on the number of residents identified as "Mexican" in enumeration districts assigned to Orange County by the US Census Bureau in 1930.

182. Barker, *Citrus Powered the Economy*, 34–86; Albert V. Vela, "53 Mexican Barrios/Colonias of Orange County."

183. See supra note 68.

184. Armor, *History of Orange County*, 1560.

185. See Talbert, *The Historical Volume and Reference Works: Orange County*, Vols. 1–3.

186. Talbert, *Historical Volume and Reference Works*, Vol. 2, 414.

187. Interview with Stan Oftelie by author, August 24, 2016. See also Talbert, *The Historical Volume and Reference Works*, Vol. 2, 463; Armor, *History of Orange County*, 1541–38; LeRoy E. Lyon Jr. interview with Jacqueline S. Reinier, March 18 and 31, 1988, Oral History Program, Center for California Studies, California State University, Sacramento.

188. Chris Jepsen, "OC History: The Willard Smith Era," *County Connection*, May 2019.

189. "Willard Smith Appointed Orange County Supervisor," *The California Citrograph*, September 1925.

190. Jepsen, "The Willard Smith Era." See also Talbert, *Historical Volume and Reference Works*, Vol. 3, 559–60.

191. Jepsen, "The Willard Smith Era," 24–25.

192. Andrew Herod, "Social Engineering Through Spatial Engineering: Company Towns and the Geographical Imagination," in Dinius and Vergara eds., *Company Towns in the Americas*, 21.

193. Logan and Molotch, "City as a Growth Machine," 54.

194. Charles W. Mills, *The Racial Contract*, 25th Anniversary Edition (Ithaca: Cornell University Press, 2022), 11–19.

195. Giorgio Agamben, *Means Without End: Notes on Politics* (Minneapolis: University of Minnesota Press, 2000), 39.

196. Letter to Orange County Board of Supervisors from Orange County Farm Bureau, August 5, 1935, Orange County Planning Commission, Minutes, 220, 222–23, Orange County Archives, Santa Ana, CA. See also Carey, "From Hinterland to Metropolis," 117–18.

197. Carey, "From Hinterland to Metropolis," 103–5.

198. On the involvement and influence of the Farm Bureau on the development of the county building code and zoning ordinance see: Orange County Planning Commission, Minutes, May 15, 1930; June 5, 1930; September 4, 1930; May 7, 1931; May 21, 1931; June 4, 1931; January 7, 1932; March 3, 1932; August 5, 1932; September 1, 1932; October 6, 1932; November 3, 1932; May 23, 1935; June 20, 1935; June 27, 1935; August 22, 1935. The minutes of January 7, 1932, are most telling as representatives of the Farm Bureau appeared before the county planning commission and stated that they would support "the adoption of the Building Code under conditions which would permit certain designated ranch territory to be exempted from the operation of the regulations."

199. Trounstine, *Segregation by Design*, 23–40.

200. Hannah Arendt, *Eichmann in Jerusalem: A Report on the Banality of Evil*, Revised and Enlarged Edition (New York: Penguin Books, 1994), 287–88.

CHAPTER 2

1. Kathleen Frazee interview with Alfred V. Aguirre, June 15, 2001, transcript, Center for Oral and Public History, California State University, Fullerton, Fullerton, CA.

2. Figures tabulated by a team of researchers directed by the author using the 1930 Census.

3. On myth-consciousness and mythogenesis see Richard Slotkin, *Regeneration Through Violence: The Mythology of the American Frontier, 1600–1860* (Norman: University of Oklahoma Press, 1973), 4–9. On the influence of "settler memory" over US history, memory, and politics see Kevin Bruyneel, *Settler Memory: The Disavowal of Indigeneity and the Politics of Race in the United States* (Chapel Hill: University of North Carolina Press, 2021).

4. For examples of Orange County "pioneer" narratives see Armor, *History of Orange County*; Talbert, *Historical Volume and Reference Works: Orange County*, 3 Vols.; Friis, *Orange County*; Carpenter, *Placentia*; Quill Pen Club, *Rawhide and Orange Blossoms: Stories and Sketches of Early Orange County* (Santa Ana, CA: Pioneer Press, 1967); Merle Ramsey and Mabel Ramsey, *Pioneer Days of Laguna Beach* (Laguna Beach, CA: Hastie Printers, 1967); James Sleeper, *Orange County Almanac of Historical Oddities*, Third Edition, 1889–1986 (New York: OCUSA Press, 1986); Cramer, *A Hundred Years of Yesterdays*; Marge Bitetti, Guy Ball, and the Santa Ana Historical Preservation Society, *Early Santa Ana* (Charleston, SC: Arcadia Publishing, 2006); Phil Brigandi, *A Brief History of Orange, California: The Plaza City* (Charleston, SC: The History Press, 2011); Brigandi, *Orange County Chronicles*; Epting, *Orange County Pioneers*; Terry E. Stephenson, "The First Settlers," *Orange Countiana*, Vol. 10 (2014): 1–15.

5. On the whitewashing of Los Angeles' Mexican past see Deverell, *Whitewashed Adobe*, 6–10. On the Spanish Fantasy Past see McWilliams, *Southern California*, 70–83. On the Anglo Fantasy Past see Carpio, *Collisions at the Crossroads*, 22–25, 41–47. For examples of the Spanish Fantasy myth applied to Orange County by local historians see Homer Banks, "The Story of San Clemente: The Spanish Village," *El Heraldo de San Clemente*, 1930; Bessie M.H. Carrillo, "Old Days in San Juan Capistrano," *Orange County History Series*, Vol. 1 (1931); Alfonso Yorba, "Memories of Early California Haunt Ruined Chapel at Yorba," *Santa Ana Journal*, November 23, 1935; Alfonso Yorba, "'Santa Ana Abajo,' Old Adobe Pueblo at Orange, Now Entirely Vanished," *Santa Ana Journal*, May 15, 1936; W.W. Robinson, *The Old Spanish and Mexican Ranchos of Orange County* (Los Angeles, CA: Title Insurance and Trust Company, 1950); Don Meadows, "The March of Portolá," in Thomas B. Talbert ed., *Historical Volume and Reference Works: Orange County*, Vol. 1 (Whittier, CA: Historical Publishers, 1963), 33–44; Don Meadows, "The House of Bernardo Yorba, *Orange County History Series*, Vol. 4, No. 1 (1963); Mildred Yorba MacArthur, *Orange County under Spain, Mexico, and the United States* (Los Angeles: Dawson's Book Shop, 1968); Merle Ramsey and Mabel Ramsey, *This was Mission Country, Orange County, California* (Laguna Beach: Mission Printing Company, 1973); George Salzer, *Rancho Los Alamitos* (Ramona, CA: Acoma Books, 1975); Wayne Dell Gibson, *Tomas Yorba's Santa Ana Viejo, 1769–1847* (Santa Ana: Santa Ana College Foundation Press, 1976); Jim Sleeper, *Rancho Mission Viejo: "Where History is Still Happening"* (Santa Margarita, CA: Santa Margarita Company, 1985); Pamela Gibson, "Early California on Rios Street," *Orange Countiana*, Vol. 4 (1988): 15–20; Donald Rowland, "Jose Antonio Yorba," *Orange Countiana*, Vol. 8 (2012): 3–16; Miguel Kraszewski, "Juan Flores in San Juan Capistrano," *Orange Countiana*, Vol. 12 (2016): 21–30.

6. On self-indigenization see Stephen Pearson, "'The Last Bastion of Colonialism': Appalachian Settler Colonialism and Self-Indigenization," *American Indian Culture and Research Journal* 37, No. 2 (2013): 165–84.

7. According to the 1930 Census, 45.5 percent of Orange County's non-Hispanic white population was of German descent, 10.4 percent were Irish, 7.4 percent French, 7.1 percent Scottish, 6 percent Swedish, 4.8 percent Danish, 4.3 percent Norwegian, 3.4 percent Swiss, 2.7 percent Italian, 2.3 percent Russian, 2.1 percent Austrian, 1 percent Portuguese, 5.1 percent other.

8. My conceptualization of the white-brown color line builds on Kelly Lytle Hernández's term "Mexican Brown." Kelly Lytle Hernández, *Migra!: A History of the U.S. Border Patrol* (Berkeley: University of California Press, 2010), 10–13. On the creation of Mexicans as a racial group see Laura E. Gomez, *Manifest Destinies: The Making of the Mexican American Race* (New York: New York University Press, 2007), 1–6.

9. On the triracial hierarchy of Los Angeles agriculture see Yu Tokunaga, *Transborder Los Angeles: An Unknown Transpacific History of Japanese-Mexican Relations* (Oakland: University of California Press, 2022), 1–6, 52–53. On Los Angeles as a multiethnic-racial city see Sánchez, *Boyle Heights*, 5–8; Molina, *Fit to be Citizens*, 4–8; Anthony Macias, *Mexican American Mojo: Popular Music, Dance, and Urban Culture in Los Angeles* (Durham: Duke University Press, 2008), 1–6; Luis Alvarez, *The Power of the Zoot: Youth Culture and Resistance During World War II* (Berkeley: University of California Press, 2008), 4–8; Kurashige, *The Shifting Grounds of Race*, 3–5; García, Matt, *A World of Its Own: Race, Labor, and Citrus in the Making of Greater Los Angeles, 1900–1970* (Chapel Hill: University of North Carolina Press, 2002), 13–14.

10. González, *Labor and Community*, 54–55; Sánchez, *Becoming Mexican American*, 63–71; Romo, *East Los Angeles*, 35–50.

11. Sánchez, *Becoming Mexican American*, 18; Francisco Balderrama and Raymond Rodríguez, *Decade of Betrayal: Mexican Repatriation in the 1930s* (Albuquerque: University of New Mexico Press, 2006), 9; Gilbert G. González, *Culture of Empire: American Writers, Mexico, and Mexican Immigrants, 1880–1930* (Austin: University of Texas Press, 2004), 112–19; Douglas Monroy, *Rebirth: Mexican Los Angeles from the Great Migration to the Great Depression* (Berkeley: University of California Press, 1999), 93–94; Zaragosa Vargas, *Crucible of Struggle: A History of Mexican Americans From Colonial Times to the Present Era* (New York: Oxford University Press, 2011), 177.

12. Joe Venegas Interview by A. Dean Tatom, March 24, 1971, O.H. 515, transcript, Center for Oral and Public History, California State University, Fullerton, Fullerton, CA. See also Sánchez, *Becoming Mexican American*, 50–58; Balderrama and Rodríguez, *Decade of Betrayal*, 8–9; Monroy, *Rebirth*, 77–106; John McKiernan-González, *Fevered Measures: Public Health and Race at the Texas-Mexico Border, 1848–1942* (Durham: Duke University Press, 2012), 2–6, 9–15.

13. St. John, *Line in the Sand*, 184–86. See also Hernández, *Migra!*, 88–93; Julian Lim, *Porous Borders: Multiracial Migrations and the Law in the U.S.-Mexico Borderlands* (Chapel Hill: University of North Carolina Press, 2017), 50–51, 166; George T. Díaz, *Border Contraband: A History of Smuggling Across the Rio Grande* (Austin: University of Texas Press, 2015).

14. Reisler, *By the Sweat of their Brow*, 96–117; Balderrama and Rodríguez, *Decade of Betrayal*, 16–17; Gabriela F. Arredondo, *Mexican Chicago: Race, Identity, and Nation, 1916–1939* (Champaign: University of Illinois Press, 2008); Julie Weise, *Corazón de Dixie: Mexicanos in the US South Since 1910* (Chapel Hill: University of North Carolina Press, 2015).

15. Reisler, *By the Sweat of their Brow*, 30; Sánchez, *Becoming Mexican American*, 64–66.

16. Balderrama and Rodríguez, *Decade of Betrayal*, 9.

17. Reisler, *By the Sweat of their Brow*, 3–16; Gutiérrez, *Walls and Mirrors*, 39–68.

18. Figures tabulated by a team of researchers directed by the author using the 1930 Census.

19. Governor C.C. Young's Mexican Fact-Finding Committee, *Mexicans in California* (San Francisco: State of California, 1930), 181.

20. This figure was obtained by performing a digital word search on Newspapers.com for "Mexican" in the *Santa Ana Register* and *Anaheim Gazette* from January 1, 1900 to December 31, 1909 (1,483 mentions) and January 1, 1910 to December 31, 1919 (7050 mentions). Notably, over the same period, Los Angeles newspapers saw a much lower increase of approximately 60 percent (45,562 to 77,264 respectively).

21. "Says Mexicans Raise Per Cent," *Santa Ana Register*, January 18, 1912.

22. "Says Mexicans Raise Per Cent."

23. Robert O'Brien, *Survey on Mexicans and Crime in Southern California, 1926–1927* (Claremont: Lawson Roberts Publishing Company, 1928). See also Hayden, "The La Habra Experiment," 180–85.

24. "The 'Bad Mexican' in Orange County," *Santa Ana Register*, July 11, 1912.

25. "The 'Bad Mexican' in Orange County."

26. "Again, the Problem," *Santa Ana Register*, July 24, 1912. See also, "The 'Mexican Problem' Is a Menace to Health, Moral and Financial Welfare," *Santa Ana Register*, November 22, 1912.

27. McWilliams, *North from Mexico*, 207–17.

28. McWilliams, *North from Mexico*, 219.

29. Gilbert G. González, "The 'Mexican Problem': Empire, Public Policy, and the Education of Mexican Immigrants," *Aztlan: A Journal of Chicano Studies* 26, No. 2 (Fall 2001): 200; González, *Culture of Empire*, 7–11.

30. González, *Culture of Empire*, 22–34. See also Jessica M. Kim, *Imperial Metropolis: Los Angeles, Mexico, and the Borderlands of American Empire, 1865–1941* (Chapel Hill: University of North Carolina Press, 2019); Juliette Maiorana, "Birth of the Mexican Problem: Oil in Mexico, U.S. Social Sciences, and Transnational Labor, 1917–1920," *The Western Historical Quarterly* 53, No. 3 (Autumn 2022): 223–65.

31. González, *Culture of Empire*, 141; Juan Gonzalez, *Harvest of Empire: A History of Latinos in America*, Second Revised and Updated Edition (New York: Penguin, 2022), xii, xxvi–xxix.

32. By connecting the Mexican Problem narrative to the Anglo and Spanish fantasy narratives under the process of self-indigenization, I am not suggesting that Mexicans were indigenous to Orange County. Rather, I illustrate how these three narratives worked in concert to shape the development of the white settler psyche and response to Mexican migrants in the region. On Hispano/Chicano self-indigenization, see Roxanne Dunbar-Ortiz, *Not a Nation of Immigrants: Settler Colonialism, White Supremacy, and a History of Erasure and Exclusion* (Boston: Beacon Press, 2021), 110–20.

33. "Civics Club on The Mexican Problem," *Santa Ana Register*, May 5, 1913; "Saturday Mexican Day at Camp Meeting," *Santa Ana Register*, Santa Ana, CA, July 9, 1915; "Social Service Party," *Santa Ana Register*, April 17, 1917; "Our Future Citizens," *Santa Ana Register*, June 22, 1925; "Mexican Problems to be Discussed by Authorities at Lectures in Anaheim," *Santa Ana Register*, April 10, 1926.

34. "Social Events: For Americanization," *Santa Ana Register*, July 25, 1919.

35. "Americanization Problem is Mexican Problem," *Santa Ana Register*, July 25, 1919; Hayden, "The La Habra Experiment," 103–4. See also González, *Labor and Community*, 114–30.

36. See also Haas, *Conquests and Historical Identities*, 165–208; González, *Labor and Community*, 36–49.

37. "Ask Santa Ana School Board Segregate Mexicans," and "Schools for Mexicans," *Santa Ana Register*, November 18, 1916; "Our Mexican Problem, *Santa Ana Register*, June 3, 1925. See also Louis Reccow, "Orange County Citrus Strike," 51–52; González, *Labor and Community*, 58–65.

38. González, *Labor and Community*, 118.

39. Herod, "Social Engineering through Spatial Engineering," 21–22. See also, Andrew Herod, *Labor Geographies: Workers and the Landscapes of Capitalism* (New York: The Guilford Press, 2001), 5, 13–18, 33–37.

40. Vela, *Tracks to the Westminster Barrio*, 13; Vela, "53 Mexican Barrios/Colonias of Orange County, 1900s"; Lembke, "Barrios Begin to Play Role in Politics: 31 in County"; Stephen Reyes interview; González, "Mexican Communities in Orange County," 23; González, *Labor and Community*, 58–64; Santillán et al., *Mexican American Baseball in Orange County*, 10; "Barrios, Colonias & Campos," http://southernempire13.blogspot.com/2012/12/barrios-colonias-campos.html.

41. Trounstine, *Segregation by Design*, 3, 23–35; Herod, "Social Engineering through Spatial Engineering," 27–29. See also Michel Foucault, *Discipline and Punish: The Birth of the Prison* (New York: Pantheon Books, 1977).

42. George Lipsitz, *How Racism Takes Place* (Philadelphia: Temple University Press, 2011), 6.

43. Trounstine, *Segregation by Design*, 5–6.

44. Haas, *Conquests and Historical Identities*, 190–92; Gilbert G. González, *Chicano Education in the era of Segregation* (Denton: University of North Texas Press, 2013), 177. See also mention of Santa Ana's first Mexican schools in "A Good Museum," *Santa Ana Register*, October 25, 1913; "P.T. Association Meeting," *Santa Ana Register*, November 12, 1913; "Strong Against Having School of Mexicans at Lincoln," *Santa Ana Register*, August 8, 1918. School districts and municipalities throughout the Southwest likewise began segregating Mexican children during the early twentieth century. See David-James Gonzales, "Mexican Americans and the Long Fight against Segregation in the Southwest," in Michael C. LeMay ed., *The U.S.-Mexico Border: A Reference Handbook* (Santa Barbara: ABC-CLIO, 2022), 129–35; Rubén Donato and Jarrod Hanson, *The Other American Dilemma: Schools, Mexicans, and the Nature of Jim Crow, 1912–1953* (Albany: State University of New York Press, 2021).

45. This form of segregation was also practiced in the Westminster School District. See *Mendez et al* Court Transcripts, July 10, 1945, 461–62; Peters, "Segregation of Mexican American Children," 51. On the school-within-a-school model as a "foundational form of segregation" see García, *Strategies of Segregation*, 2–3.

46. "Ask Santa Ana School Board Segregate Mexicans," *Santa Ana Register*, November 18, 1916; "Strong Against Having School of Mexicans at Lincoln," *Santa Ana Register*, August 10, 1918; "Illiteracy Decreasing," *Santa Ana Register*, October 24, 1921; "Our Mexican Problem," *Santa Ana Register*, June 3, 1925.

47. "School for Mexicans," *Santa Ana Register*, November 18, 1916.

48. Treff, "The Education of Mexican Children in Orange County," 23–27; Peters, "Segregation of Mexican American Children," 30, 49; "Orange County's Hispanic Schools, *Orange County Register*, August 28, 1990; Hayden, "The La Habra Experiment," 144. See also González, *Labor and Community*, 100.

49. Peters, "Segregation of Mexican American Children," 49.

50. Peters, "Segregation of Mexican American Children," 50–51; Treff, "The Education of Mexican Children in Orange County," 24; California State Department of Education, *A Guide for Teachers of Beginning Non-English Speaking Children* (Sacramento: California State Printing Office, 1933), v; *Mendez et al* Court Transcripts, July 10, 1945, 461–62.

51. David Torres-Rouff, "Becoming Mexican: Segregated Schools and Social Scientists in Southern California, 1913–1946," *Southern California Quarterly* 94, No. 1 (Spring 2012): 93.

52. McWilliams, *North from Mexico*, 219.

53. García, *Strategies of Segregation*, 39–54; David G. García, Tara J. Yosso, and Frank P Barajas, "'A Few of the Brightest, Cleanest Mexican Children': School Segregation as a Form of Mundane Racism in Oxnard, California, 1900–1940," *Harvard Educational Review* 82, No. 1 (Spring 2012): 1–25.

54. Treff, "The Education of Mexican Children in Orange County," 15–21; Hayden, "The La Habra Experiment," 20–22, 30–43, 82–91; González, *Labor and Community*, 77–98; Haas, *Conquests and Historical Identities*, 138–64.

55. Gloria Valdez Lopez interview with Melissa Lee, May 31, 1982, audio recording, Center for Oral and Public History, California State University, Fullerton, Fullerton, CA, and Phyllis Ramirez Zepeda interview with Olivia Andrade and Lizette Ramirez, January 23, 2016, audio recording, Orange Public Library and History Center, Orange, CA. See also González, *Labor and Community*, 77–98;

Monroy, *Rebirth*, 7–66; Monica Perales, *Smeltertown: Making and Remembering A Southwest Border Community* (Chapel Hill: University of North Carolina Press, 2010), 57–93.

56. Haas, *Conquests and Historical Identities*, 185.
57. Bob Torres interview with Elizabeth Baez, July 27, 1982, O.H. 3857, audio recording, Center for Oral and Public History, California State University, Fullerton, Fullerton, CA. Citing precedent in other Southern California cities including Santa Ana and Anaheim, the Orange municipal swimming pool restricted Mexicans use of the facility to Mondays only. All other days and holidays were reserved for "white persons only." See "Ruling Given on Use of Plunge," *Orange Daily News*, August 15, 1936.
58. Louis Olivos Jr. and Gay Olivos interview with author, August 29, 2016.
59. *Mexicans in California*, 85–87.
60. *Mexicans in California*, 12.
61. Orange County Department of Social Welfare, "The Living Standards of Orange County Mexican Families," March 9, 1940, Orange County Archives, Santa Ana, CA.
62. "Living Standards of Orange County Mexican Families," 1. In conducting this survey, Orange County officials seemed to draw inspiration from a similar study conducted in Los Angeles, as referenced on the introductory page of the report, "Compare with a study of ninety-nine Los Angeles County Mexican families reported in Bulletin 639, U.S. Dept. of Labor."
63. "Living Standards of Orange County Mexican Families," 3.
64. "Living Standards of Orange County Mexican Families," 10.
65. "Living Standards of Orange County Mexican Families," 15.
66. "Living Standards of Orange County Mexican Families," 14. For additional estimates of Mexican family household income in Orange County, see Hayden, "The La Habra Experiment," 47–48; U.S. Congress, *Violations of Free Speech and Rights of Labor*, exhibit 8964; Reccow, "Orange County Citrus Strike," 18–19; González, *Labor and Community*, 30–35.
67. "Living Standards of Orange County Mexican Families." See also the attached letter of support from Edward Lee Russell, MD, Health Officer of Orange County, 2.
68. "Living Standards of Orange County Mexican Families," 15.
69. "Living Standards of Orange County Mexican Families," 15 and appendix 2, 1–17.
70. "Living Standards of Orange County Mexican Families," 15.
71. "Welfare Body Handles 1076 Aid Requests," *Santa Ana Register*, February 13, 1931.
72. See report on "Mexican Problem" in "Grand Jury Finds Business of County Is Run Satisfactorily," *Santa Ana Register*, December 3, 1915.
73. "Living Standards of Orange County Mexican Families," appendix 1, 5.
74. Letter to Mr. Joseph A. Beek, Secretary of the Senate, from Jack W. Snow, Director of the Department of Social Welfare, May 21, 1937, Willard Smith Papers, Box 1, Folder 4, Orange County Archives, Santa Ana, CA. See also Hayden, "The La Habra Experiment," 48–51.
75. A larger study conducted by University of California sociologist Paul Taylor reiterated the precarious nature of agricultural labor in California. Taylor's report found that severe underemployment, low wages, seasonal crop schedules, and migrant labor streams resulted in agricultural labors being twice as likely to depend on relief than farmers. See, U.S. Department of Agriculture Farm Security Administration Division of Information, "Statement of Paul S. Taylor before the Special Senate Committee to Investigate Unemployment and Relief," March 14, 1938, Orange County Board of Supervisors Records, Box 48, Folder 74, Orange County Archives, Santa Ana, CA.

76. Reccow, "Orange County Citrus Strike," 51.

77. Louis E. Plummer, *A History of the Fullerton Union High School and Fullerton Junior College, 1893–1943* (Fullerton: Fullerton College Press, 1949).

78. Robert L. Pritchard, "Orange County During the Depressed Thirties: A Study in Twentieth-Century California Local History," *Southern California Quarterly* 50, No. 2 (June 1968), 191; Reccow, "Orange County Citrus Strike," 6. See also "Two-thirds of Orange County's Agricultural Wealth from Citrus," *The California Citrograph*, August 1929; "Citrus Acreage in California Passes 300,000 Mark, Survey Discloses," *The California Citrograph*, May 1937; Bachus, "Who Took the Orange Out of Oranges County," 161.

79. Pritchard, "Orange County During the Depressed Thirties," 191; "Two-thirds of Orange County's Agricultural Wealth from Citrus," *The California Citrograph*, August 1929.

80. CA Department of Finance, "Historical Census Populations of California, 1850–2010," http://www.dof.ca.gov/Reports/Demographic_Reports/index.html#reports.

81. Pritchard, "Orange County During the Depressed Thirties," 192.

82. "M.O.D. Growers Get $914,320," *Orange Daily News*, Orange, CA, January 19, 1931.

83. "Citrus Growers of Anaheim Net Over Million Dollars," *Santa Ana Register*, January 20, 1931.

84. "Citrus Growers of Anaheim Net Over Million Dollars."

85. "Seek to Solve Work Problem in Santa Ana," *Santa Ana Register*, January 16, 1931.

86. "Seek to Solve Work Problem in Santa Ana."

87. "Chamber Asks Residents to Assist Needy," *Santa Ana Register*, January 26, 1931.

88. "Chamber Asks Residents to Assist Needy."

89. "Chamber Asks Residents to Assist Needy"; "Seek to Solve Work Problem in Santa Ana."

90. "Welfare Body Handles 1076 Aid Requests," *Santa Ana Register*, February 13, 1931.

91. "Name Committee on Unemployment," *Santa Ana Register*, January 25, 1931.

92. "Ask Public's Cooperation in Job Relief," *Santa Ana Register*, July 10, 1931.

93. "Place Responsibility Where Responsibility Belongs, *Santa Ana Register*, January 15, 1932.

94. "Mayors of Orange County Demand Board Aid Jobless," *Santa Ana Register*, March 6, 1932.

95. "Mayors of Orange County Demand Board Aid Jobless."

96. "Mayors of Orange County Demand Board Aid Jobless."

97. "300 Jobless Men from All Parts of County Storm Welfare Office," *Santa Ana Register*, March 7, 1932.

98. "300 Jobless Men from All Parts of County Storm Welfare Office."

99. "300 Jobless Men from All Parts of County Storm Welfare Office."

100. Orange County Board of Supervisors Minutes, Vol. 26, March 8, 1932, Orange County Archives, Santa Ana, CA.

101. "Orange County Welfare Department," Pamphlet, 1955, Orange County Archives, Santa Ana, CA.

102. "Orange County Welfare Department," Pamphlet.

103. OC Board of Supervisors Minutes, Vol. 26, March 8, 1932.

104. OC Board of Supervisors Minutes, Vol. 26, March 8, 1932. On the history of the "public charge" category as a basis for deportation see Eithne Luibhéid, *Entry*

Denied: Controlling Sexuality at the Border (Minneapolis: University of Minnesota Press, 2002), 2–10 and Ngai, *Impossible Subjects*, 59–60, 73–84.

105. OC Board of Supervisors Minutes, Vol. 26, August 2, 1932.

106. Pritchard, "Orange County During the Depressed Thirties," 194.

107. Sánchez, *Becoming Mexican American*, 210–11.

108. Pritchard, "Orange County During the Depressed Thirties," 195.

109. OC Board of Supervisors Minutes, Vol. 27, October 3, 1933.

110. OC Board of Supervisors Minutes, Vol. 27, October 3, 1933 and January 16, 1934. See also, OC Board of Supervisors Minutes, Vol. 28, January 30, 1934; May 3, 1934; June 1, 1934; July 1, 1934; and August 14, 1934.

111. Pritchard, "Orange County During the Depressed Thirties," 196. See also Epting, *The New Deal in Orange County California* (Charleston, SC: History Press, 2014).

112. OC Board of Supervisors Minutes, Vol. 30, November 26, 1935 to May 26, 1936.

113. "Seek to Solve Work Problem in Santa Ana," *Santa Ana Register*, January 16, 1931 and "Chamber Asks Residents to Assist Needy," *Santa Ana Register*, January 26, 1931.

114. Brigandi, *Orange County Chronicles*, 107.

115. On the development and use of coerced removal and voluntary departure as (self)deportation see Adam Goodman, *The Deportation Machine: America's Long History of Expelling Immigrants* (Princeton: Princeton University Press, 2020), 2–5, 30–39, 53–54, 108–9, 119–20.

116. "Immigration Office to Be Opened Here," *Santa Ana Register*, April 26, 1932. See also, "Immigration Officers to Come to S.A.," *Santa Ana Register*, May 9, 1932.

117. Balderrama and Rodríguez, *Decade of Betrayal*, 67–69.

118. Balderrama and Rodríguez, *Decade of Betrayal*, 73–74; Abraham Hoffman, *Unwanted Mexican Americans in the Great Depression: Repatriation Pressures, 1929–1939* (Tucson: University of Arizona Press, 1974), 39–45; Sánchez, *Becoming Mexican American*, 214–15; Erika Lee, *America for Americans: A History of Xenophobia in the United States* (New York: Basic Books, 2019), 167–72; Goodman, *The Deportation Machine*, 42–46.

119. Balderrama and Rodríguez, *Decade of Betrayal*, 81–82; Francisco E. Balderrama, *In Defense of La Raza: The Los Angeles Mexican Consulate and the Mexican Community, 1929 to 1936* (Tucson: University of Arizona Press, 1982), 15–32.

120. Rex Thomson interview with Christine Valenciana, August 4, 1976, transcript, Center for Oral and Public History, California State University, Fullerton, Fullerton, CA. See also, Balderrama and Rodríguez, *Decade of Betrayal*, 94.

121. Rex Thomson interview.

122. Rex Thomson interview.

123. John Anson Ford interview with Christine Valenciana, September 4, 1971, transcript, Center for Oral and Public History, California State University, Fullerton, Fullerton, CA.

124. John Anson Ford interview. See also, Sánchez, *Becoming Mexican American*, 223.

125. John Anson Ford interview.

126. Thomson interview.

127. Broadbent, "Distribution of Mexican Population in the U.S.," 71. See also, CA Department of Finance, "Historical Census Populations of California, 1850–2010," http://www.dof.ca.gov/Reports/Demographic_Reports/index.html#reports.

128. See Letter to Orange County Board of Supervisors from California Supervisors Association Acting President C.E. Grier, July 2, 1936; and also, Letter to California Governor Frank Merriam from OC Board of Supervisors representing

the "Boards of Supervisors, Sheriffs and Legal Advisors of the Ten Southern Counties of California," November 12, 1936, Orange County Board of Supervisors Records, Box 48, Folder 20, Orange County Archives, Santa Ana, CA. These letters illustrate the numerous communications sent between the Boards of Supervisors in Los Angeles, Orange, San Bernardino, and Riverside counties concerning issues of indigent migrant labor (i.e., Dust Bowl refugees) and migrant alien laborers (i.e., Mexican immigrants).

129. This point is further supported by the recollections of former "Mexican school" teacher Arletta Kelly. In her 1971 interview, Kelly remembered her time working in colonias near Fullerton, Placentia, and La Habra during the 1920s and 1930s. Kelly refers to another teacher, Ms. Mackey, who worked with the Los Angeles Health Department running "well-baby clinics" prior to moving to Orange County to do similar work. Kelly's recollections imply that county officials in Los Angeles and Orange maintained close communication and ran similar health, welfare, and education programs for Mexican communities. See Arletta Kelly interview with Fred Zuniga, May 20, 1971, transcript, Center for Oral and Public History, California State University, Fullerton, Fullerton, CA.

130. Sánchez, *Becoming Mexican American*, 215–16.

131. Sánchez, *Becoming Mexican American*, 215–16; Balderrama and Rodríguez, *Decade of Betrayal*, 138, 148–49; Gilbert G. González, *Mexican Consuls and Labor Organizing: Imperial Politics in the American Southwest* (Austin: University of Texas Press, 1999), 31–36.

132. "Mexicans Will Welcome New Consul Sunday," *Santa Ana Register*, July 12, 1931 and "Officials to Honor Mexican Consul Sunday," *Santa Ana Register*, August 31, 1935.

133. Reccow, "Orange County Citrus Strike," 63; "Cites Mexican Relief Status," *Santa Ana Register*, March 15, 1939.

134. Ray Easton interview with Louis Reccow, November 10, 1970. See, Reccow, "Orange County Citrus Strike," 77.

135. Lucas Lucio interview with Louis Reccow, August 17, 1970. See, Reccow, "Orange County Citrus Strike," 66. See also "Mexicans Deported as Charity Burden Grows," *Fullerton News Tribune*, March 7, 1933. In this article the *Tribune* noted "nine car loads of Mexicans, including 427 adults and children—mostly children—were deported from Orange county today."

136. Lucas Lucio interview with Francisco Balderrama, March 16 and 23, 1976. See Balderrama and Rodríguez, *Decade of Betrayal*, 130.

137. Balderrama and Rodríguez, *Decade of Betrayal*, 142–43.

138. On the trauma and erasure of repatriation's impact on ethnic Mexicans see Laura D. Gutiérrez, "'Trains of Misery': Repatriate Voices and Responses in Northern Mexico During the Great Depression," *Journal of American Ethnic History* 39, No. 4, (Summer 2020): 13–26; Marla A. Ramírez, "Gendered Banishment: Rewriting Mexican Repatriation Through a Transgenerational Oral History Methodology," *Latino Studies* 20 (2022): 306–33.

139. Alfred Munoz interview with unknown, 1982, audio recording, Center for Oral and Public History, California State University, Fullerton, Fullerton, CA.

140. Alfred Munoz interview.

141. Both Pete Moreno and Bob Torres, longtime residents of El Modena also recalled, "train loads" of Mexicans leaving Orange County during the depression years. Bob Torres interview with Elizabeth Baez, July 27, 1982; and Pete Moreno interview with Lucy McDonald, June 30, 1982 and July 7, 1982, audio

recording, Center for Oral and Public History, California State University, Fullerton, Fullerton, CA. Likewise, Alex Maldonado, who lived in Santa Ana's Artesia barrio, remembered the deportation sweeps and forced repatriations that occurred throughout the county. Although he was just a child of six or seven years old, Maldonado recalled coming home one day and seeing his best friend's family packing up their belongings. He later learned the family, whom he never saw again, was repatriated. Maldonado interview with Tewes. See also, O'Neil, "The Role of Colonias in Orange County"; and James Maurice Jensen, "The Mexican-American in an Orange County Community," MA thesis (Claremont College, 1947).

142. Roch Bradshaw, "Fame for Immigrant Boy: Started Bastanchury Ranch," *Santa Ana Journal,* April 23, 1936; and John B. Bowen, "Bastanchury Ranch Company, Fullerton, CA: From Largest Citrus Ranch in the World to Bankruptcy," *The Citrus Peel*, Vol. 22, No. 1 (January 2002), 1.

143. "Those Who Have Achieved in the Citrus Industry," *The California Citrograph*, July 1923, 311, 320–23.

144. "Those Who Have Achieved in the Citrus Industry." See also Gustavo Arellano, "The Lost Mexicans of Bastanchury Ranch," *OC Weekly*, April 11, 2013.

145. Plummer, *A History of the Fullerton Union High School*, 86.

146. Plummer, *A History of the Fullerton Union High School*, 82–83. See also Hayden, "The La Habra Experiment," 94, 160–62; "Mexican Camp to Get School," *Fullerton News Tribune*, April 12, 1929; "Miss Mackey Leads Course, *Fullerton News Tribune*, December 31, 1929; "Teachers Tell Mexican Work Done Here," *Fullerton News Tribune*, August 30, 1927.

147. Plummer, *A History of the Fullerton Union High School*, 85.

148. Plummer, *A History of the Fullerton Union High School*, 86.

149. Plummer, *A History of the Fullerton Union High School*, 86.

150. "Colorful Era of Old Ranch School in Fullerton Recalled by Instructor," *Fullerton News Tribune*, June 1, 1955.

151. "Colorful Era of Old Ranch School in Fullerton Recalled by Instructor"; and Arletta Kelly interview with B.E. Schmidt, May 22, 1968, transcript, Center for Oral and Public History, California State University, Fullerton, Fullerton, CA.

152. Plummer, *A History of the Fullerton Union High School*, 86.

153. Plummer, *A History of the Fullerton Union High School*, 86.

154. Plummer, *A History of the Fullerton Union High School*, 84.

155. Arletta Kelly interview, May 22, 1968.

156. Arletta Kelly interview; Plummer, *A History of the Fullerton Union High School and Fullerton Junior College, 1893–1943*, 84.

157. "Two Million in Liabilities Are Revealed," *Fullerton News Tribune*, October 3, 1931. See also, "Bank Awarded Control of Bastanchury Ranch," *Fullerton News Tribune*, December 17, 1932.

158. "Company Formed to Run Portion of Citrus Ranch," *Fullerton News Tribune*, October 24, 1933.

159. "Those Who Have Achieved in the Citrus Industry," *The California Citrograph*, July 1923, 320; and Bowen, "Bastanchury Ranch Company," 1.

160. Bowen, "Bastanchury Ranch Company," 3.

161. Plummer, *A History of the Fullerton Union High School*, 88.

162. "Mexicans Deported as Charity Burden Grows," *Fullerton News Tribune*, March 1933.

163. "96 Percent of Mexicans Held Here Aliens," *Santa Ana Register*, July 17, 1936.

164. Ordinance No. 298 specified that aliens applying for county relief within five years of entry to the US should be reported to the Immigration Service for investigation on suspicion that they qualified for deportation as a "public charge." Orange County Board of Supervisors Minutes, Vol. 26, March 8, 1932, Orange County Archives, Santa Ana, CA. See also Luibhéid, *Entry Denied*, 2–10.

165. Ramírez, "Gendered Banishment," 309–10.

166. "Company Formed to Run Portion of Citrus Ranch," *Fullerton News Tribune*, October 24, 1933.

167. Plummer, *A History of the Fullerton Union High School*, 88.

168. "Survey Reveals Indigent Aliens Cost County $250,000 Yearly," *Santa Ana Register*, March 2, 1939; "Cites Mexican Relief Status," *Santa Ana Register*, March 15, 1939.

169. Reccow, "Orange County Citrus Strike," 66; González, *Labor and Community*, 74, 133.

170. Reccow, "Orange County Citrus Strike," 66; "500 Enthusiastic Mexicans Hear of Cardenas Program," *Santa Ana Register*, January 14, 1939; and "Cardenas Reveals Plans to Return Mexicans to Mexico," *Santa Ana Register*, July 11, 1939. See also, Sánchez, *Becoming Mexican American*, 121–24; Balderrama and Rodríguez, *Decade of Betrayal*, 149–51; and Gutiérrez, *Walls and Mirrors*, 72–74.

171. "Illegal Entry Hearings to Be Held Soon," *Santa Ana Register*, December 2, 1932.

172. OC Board of Supervisors Minutes, Vol. 30, November 26, 1935.

173. OC Board of Supervisors Minutes, Vol. 30, November 26, 1935; "Federal Officers Book 9 at Jail," *Santa Ana Register*, May 16, 1934; and "9 Held as U.S. Officers Act," *Santa Ana Register*, March 13, 1937.

174. "Immigration Chief Starts Probe for WPA," *Santa Ana Register*, July 9, 1936; and "Majority Foreign Born WPA Workers in U.S. Illegally," *Santa Ana Register*, January 12, 1937.

175. "Survey Reveals Indigent Aliens Cost County $250,000 Yearly, *Santa Ana Register*, March 2, 1939.

176. Plummer, *A History of the Fullerton Union High School*, 88.

177. This figure was provided by Lucas Lucio, head of the Mexican Honorary Commission and representative of the Mexican Consulate in the region, to the Board of Supervisors in 1939. 18,000 was the estimate of how many Mexicans remained in Orange County during the off-season, while 25,000 was an estimate of those in the county during the Valencia harvest from April to November. See, "Cites Mexican Relief Status," *Santa Ana Register*, March 15, 1939.

178. "Survey Reveals Indigent Aliens Cost County $250,000 Yearly," *Santa Ana Register*, March 2, 1939; and Reccow, "Orange County Citrus Strike," 9–10.

179. OC Board of Supervisors Minutes, Vol. 27, October 3, 1933.

180. Reccow, "Orange County Citrus Strike," 7. See also Richard Lowitt, *The New Deal and the American West* (Norman: University of Oklahoma Press, 1993), 17–18, 23; and Devra Weber, *Dark Sweat, White Gold: California Farm Workers, Cotton, and the New Deal* (Berkeley: University of California Press, 1994), 126–32.

181. CA Department of Finance, "Historical Census Populations of California, 1850–2010."

182. Benedict Anderson, *Imagined Communities: Reflections on the Origin and Spread of Nationalism* (New York: Verso, 2006).

183. On the consolidation of white identity within the New Deal state see: Lizabeth Cohen, *Making a New Deal: Industrial Workers in Chicago, 1919–1939* (New York: Cambridge University Press, 1991); and Ira Katznelson, *When*

Affirmative Action Was White, An Untold History of Racial Inequality in Twentieth-Century America (New York: W.W. Norton, 2005).

184. Like George Sánchez, I locate the formation of Mexican American identity, and its attendant political action, as emerging out of a struggle forged during the late 1920s and 1930s. Sánchez, *Becoming Mexican American*, 12. My interpretation of the merging and/or fusion of cultural forms, identities, and political action is also based on Vicki Ruiz's notion of "cultural coalescence." See also, Vicki L. Ruiz, *From Out of the Shadows: Mexican Women in Twentieth-Century America* (New York: Oxford University Press, 1998), xvi.

185. Bob Torres interview with Elizabeth Baez, July 27, 1982.

186. "Mexican Groups Form Organization," *Orange Daily News*, Orange, CA, March 21, 1939.

CHAPTER 3

1. "Atentamente a Toda la Gente de Habla Espanola de Santa Ana, California," *El Anunciador Mexicano*, November 2, 1934. See also "Lugares Donde Circula el Anunciador Mexicano," *El Anunciador Mexicano*, November 2, 1934.

2. Out of 11,349 votes cast throughout 72 precincts in Santa Ana, 5,818 went for Mitchell, while 5,531 went to his opponent. See "Victorious Candidates in Tuesday's Election," *Santa Ana Register*, November 7, 1934.

3. On translocalism see Clemens Greiner and Patrick Sakdapolrak, "Translocality: Concepts, Applications and Emerging Research Perspectives," *Geography Compass*, 7/5 (2013): 373–84.

4. Hall, "The Long Civil Rights Movement and the Political Uses of the Past," 1233–63.

5. H. Bulmaro Chavez, "Historia Breve de la Sociedad Progresista Mexicana," May 28, 1966, Placentia, CA in *Historia de la Sociedad Progresista Mexicana* (Los Angeles: Cinco Decadas Press, 1996), 179; Jose Amaro Hernandez, *Mutual Aid for Survival: The Case of the Mexican American* (Malabar, FL: Robert E. Krieger Publishing, 1983), 99.

6. Chavez, "Historia Breve de la Sociedad Progresista Mexicana."

7. Jose R. Marquette Jr. "Datos Historicos," June 25, 1929, and Chavez, "Historia Breve," in *Historia de la Sociedad Progresista Mexicana*, II–IV and 179. See also Hernandez, *Mutual Aid for Survival*, 100.

8. Marquette Jr. "Datos Historicos"; Hernandez, *Mutual Aid for Survival*, 100.

9. "Datos Historicos," June 25, 1929.

10. Hernandez, *Mutual Aid for Survival*, 100.

11. Celso De Casas, "Informe de socios al terminar el mes de Diciembre de 1987," January 10, 1988. See *Historia de la Sociedad Progresista Mexicana*, 366.

12. *Historia de la Sociedad Progresista Mexicana*, 45.

13. Chavez, "Historia Breve de la Sociedad Progresista Mexicana."

14. Omar Valerio-Jiménez, *Remembering Conquest: Mexican Americans, Memory, and Citizenship* (Chapel Hill: University of North Carolina Press, 2024), 135.

15. *Historia de la Sociedad Progresista Mexicana*, 18.

16. *Historia de la Sociedad Progresista Mexicana*, 19–63.

17. Chavez, "Historia Breve de la Sociedad Progresista Mexicana."

18. Lisa Garcia Bedolla, *Fluid Borders: Latino Power, Identity, and Politics in Los Angeles* (Berkeley: University of California Press, 2005), 9–12.

19. Bedolla, *Fluid Borders*, 6–9.

20. Following Chicano historian Ignacio M. Garcia, I use "political ethos" to indicate "the manner in which a community rationalizes and justifies its political participation in society." Ignacio M. Garcia, *Chicanismo: The Forging of a Militant Ethos among Mexican Americans* (Tucson: University of Arizona Press, 1997), 8–9.

21. Chavez, "Historia Breve de la Sociedad Progresista Mexicana."

22. Camacho, *Migrant Imaginaries: Latino Cultural Politics in the U.S.-Mexico Borderlands* (New York: New York University Press, 2008), 5.

23. Mills, *The Racial Contract*, 9–19.

24. Camacho, *Migrant Imaginaries*, 9.

25. González, *Chicano Education in the Era of Segregation*, 182; Haas, *Conquests and Historical Identities*, 191.

26. "¿Sabes Leer?," *El Anunciador Mexicano*, November 2, 1934.

27. Hernandez, *Mutual Aid for Survival*, 102.

28. Hernandez, *Mutual Aid for Survival*, 112.

29. "Mexican Benefit Fund Turned Over," *Santa Ana Register*, January 6, 1932.

30. "Mexican Organization in Santa Ana to Sponsor Big Independence Celebration," *Santa Ana Register*, August 24, 1931; "Cinco de Mayo Celebrated at County Gatherings," *Santa Ana Journal*, May 6, 1935; "Permit Granted to Mexican Honorary Commission" in "Local Briefs," *Santa Ana Register*, June 9, 1936; "Mexican Honorary Commission granted permission to conduct a benefit carnival," in "Local Briefs," *Santa Ana Register*, June 4, 1940.

31. "Cites Mexican Relief Status," *Santa Ana Register*, March 15, 1939.

32. "Cites Mexican Relief Status." Indeed, financial holdings and contributions of this magnitude more than offset the claim that Mexican "indigent aliens" cost the county as much as $250,000 annually. See, "Survey Reveals Indigent Aliens Cost County $250,000 Yearly," *Santa Ana Register*, March 2, 1939.

33. Orange County Department of Social Welfare, "The Living Standards of Orange County Mexican Families," March 9, 1940, Orange County Archives, Santa Ana, CA.

34. "Mexican Workers Protest Paying Contractor Bonus," *Santa Ana Register*, May 3, 1935; "Crop Labor," *Santa Ana Journal*, May 11, 1935; "Says Contract Labor System Causes Trouble," *Santa Ana Register*, May 11, 1935; "Mexican Vice-Consul Here on Strike Matter," *Santa Ana Register*, October 31, 1935.

35. "Orange County Citrus Strike Starts and Growers Seek New Workers Guards Sent into Groves," *Los Angeles Times*, June 12, 1936; "Hill, Lucio Wash Hands of Violence," *Santa Ana Register*, June 26, 1936; "Agitators in Citrus Strike Are Arrested," *Santa Ana Register*, June 27, 1936; "Arrest Seven Agitators in Strike Fight," *Santa Ana Register*, June 29, 1936; "Hundreds Jailed as Citrus Rioters Attack Workers," *Los Angeles Times*, July 7, 1936; "Trial of 13 Mexicans Put Over 2 Weeks," *Santa Ana Register*, July 15, 1936; "Citrus Strike Hearings Will Cost $200,000," *Santa Ana Register*, July 22, 1936; "Judge Frees 115 Mexicans," *Santa Ana Register*, July 28, 1936.

36. "Armed Men to Protect Every Crew," *Santa Ana Register*, July 2, 1936; and "Tear Bombs Used to End Conference," *Santa Ana Register*, July 8, 1936.

37. "'Shoot to Kill,' Says Sheriff," *Santa Ana Register*, July 7, 1936.

38. Orange County Board of Supervisors Minutes, Vol. 30, July 7, 1936, Orange County Archives, Santa Ana, CA. For more on the Orange County Citrus Strike see: Reccow, "Orange County Citrus Strike"; Clara Huber Engle, "The Orange County Citrus Strike, 1936: Historical Analysis and Social Conflict," MA thesis

(California State University, Fullerton, 1975); González, *Labor and Community*, 135–60; Haas, *Conquests and Historical Identities*, 206–8; Castro interview, 69–72; Gustavo Arellano, "The Citrus War of 1936 Changed Orange County Forever and Cemented Our Mistrust of Mexicans," *OC Weekly*, June 8, 2006.

39. Friis, *Orange County*, 145.

40. "Residents of County Dig Out, As Death's Flood Toll Reaches 58," *Santa Ana Register*, March 5, 1938; "Deluge revives memories," *The Orange County Register*, March 20, 1982. See also "O.C.'s Great Flood—of 1938," *The Orange County Register*, March 3, 1998; and "12,000,000 Flood Loss Seen," *Santa Ana Register*, March 8, 1938.

41. "Comb Ruins at Atwood for Bodies," *Santa Ana Register*, March 4, 1938; "Search Ruins for Bodies of Flood Victims; Many Missing in Atwood Area," *Santa Ana Register*, March 4, 1938; "Where Death Rode the Raging Tide," *Santa Ana Register*, March 4, 1938; "And Sadness Is Their Lot," *Santa Ana Register*, March 4, 1938; "Flood Victims," *Santa Ana Register*, March 4, 1938.

42. Ancestry.com, *U.S., Find a Grave* ® *Index*, 1600s-Current [database on-line] (Lehi, UT: Ancestry.com Operations, 2012), accessed March 29, 2023, https://www.fin dagrave.com/memorial/179762907/maria-nicolasa-retana.

43. "Orange County Counts Its Dead," *Santa Ana Register*, March 5, 1938; Castro interview 21.

44. "Fullerton Is Scene of Mass Rites," *Santa Ana Register*, March 7, 1938. See also Gustavo Arellano, "The Santa Ana River Flood of 1938 Remains Orange County's Worst Natural Disaster," *OC Weekly*, September 15, 2005.

45. "Rainstorms and Floods Bring Death, Destruction to County," *Santa Ana Register*, February 15, 1937; "County's Flood Loss $1,000,000," *Santa Ana Journal*, February 15, 1937; "Map of Flood Control Plan for County," *Santa Ana Register*, September 4, 1935; "Prominent Citizens Oppose Dam Bonds," *Orange Daily News*, June 27, 1929.

46. Castro interview, 3, 8, 11.

47. "Mexicans Plan to Aid Flood Victims Here," *Santa Ana Register*, March 4, 1938; *Historia de la Sociedad Progresista Mexicana*, 16; Castro interview, 15, 17–23; Interview with Leonel Magana by A. Dean Tatom, May 24, 1971, O.H. 661, Center for Oral and Public History, California State University, Fullerton, Fullerton, CA, 7–11.

48. Ortiz, *An African American and Latinx History of the United States*, 5–6.

49. Ortiz, *An African American and Latinx History of the United States*, 120–21.

50. Chavez, "Historia Breve de la Sociedad Progresista Mexicana."

51. Ana Aparicio, *Dominican Americans and the Politics of Empowerment* (Gainesville: University Press of Florida, 2006), 3 and 113. See also Valerio-Jiménez, *Remembering Conquest*, 134–37.

52. "Mexican Groups Form Organization," *Orange Daily News*, March 21, 1939.

53. "Mexican Groups Form Organization."

54. *Historia de la Sociedad Progresista Mexicana*, 141, 262; Phyllis Ramirez Zepeda interview by Olivia Andrade and Lizeth Ramirez, January 23, 2016, audio recording, Latina American Oral History Project, Orange Public Library, Orange, CA.

55. Sánchez, *Becoming Mexican American*, 255. See also Carlos Muñoz Jr., *Youth, Identity, Power: The Chicano Movement* (New York: Verso, 1989), 43. In the first edition of *Forward*, a newspaper published by MAM just prior to its incorporation in December of 1945, President and Placentia resident Gualberto Valadez cited

an article published by *La Opinion,* wherein MAM was recognized as "the first organization of its kind that has arisen from within the great segment of Mexican-American people living in the Southwest." See, "The President Speaks," *Forward,* Vol. 1, No. 1, October 28, 1945, Box 2, Folder 1, Supreme Council of the Mexican-American Movement Collection, 1942–1945, Oviatt Library Special Collections and Archives, California State University, Northridge.

56. On the origins of the Mexican Youth Conference/MAM and its connection to the YMCA see A.B. Collins, "In Service with Youth," *The Mexican Voice,* Spring 1941; Muñoz Jr., *Youth, Identity, Power,* 29–44.

57. Haas, *Conquests and Historical Identities,* 1–2, 89–93.

58. Squire ed., *The Contested Politics of Mobility,* 3–6.

59. Sánchez, *Becoming Mexican American,* 255–56.

60. Supreme Council of the Mexican American Movement, *Mexican American Movement Handbook* (December 1945), 3.

61. *MAM Handbook,* 3.

62. *MAM Handbook,* 3.

63. Muñoz Jr., *Youth, Identity, Power,* 31; Sánchez, *Becoming Mexican American,* 256.

64. Manuel De La Raza, "Nosotros," *Mexican Voice,* August 1938, YMCA Mexican Voice Collection, Wardman Library Special Collections and Archives, Whittier College, Whittier, CA.

65. Manuel Ceja, "Are We Proud of Being Mexicans?," *Mexican Voice,* August 1938.

66. José Vasconcelos, *La raza cósmica* (Madrid: Agencia Mundial de Librería, 1925). On the controversy and debate over Vasconelos and his writings see Marilyn Grace Miller, *Rise and Fall of the Cosmic Race: The Cult of Mestizaje in Latin America* (Austin: University of Texas Press, 2004); Illan Stavans, *José Vasconcelos: The Prophet of Race* (New Brunswick: Rutgers University Press, 2011); María L. Amado, "The 'New Mestiza,' the Old Mestizos: Contrasting Discourses on Mestizaje," *Sociological Inquiry* 82, No. 3 (2012): 446–59; Agustín Palacios, "Multicultural Vasconcelos: The Optimistic, and at Times Willful, Misreading of *La Raza Cosmica,*" *Latino Studies* 15 (2017): 416–38.

67. Sánchez, *Becoming Mexican American,* 13.

68. Virginia Vargas interview by George Maisch, April 27, 1971, O.H. 588, Center for Oral and Public History, California State University, Fullerton, Fullerton, CA. See also Teresa Haught interview by Luis F. Fernandez, January 22, 2011, audio recording, Center for Oral and Public History, California State University, Fullerton, Fullerton, CA.

69. Lucy Cornejo Duran interview by Chapman University, 2006, video recording, Shades of Orange Oral History Project, Orang Public Library, Orange, CA.

70. Muñoz Jr., *Youth, Identity, Power,* 33; Sánchez, *Becoming Mexican American,* 260. See also Manuel de la Raza, "Nosotros," *The Mexican Voice,* July 1939.

71. Manuel de la Raza, "Nosotros," *The Mexican Voice,* September 1938.

72. Historian Mae Ngai defines alien citizens as "persons who are American citizens by virtue of their birth in the United States but who are presumed to be foreign by the mainstream American culture and, at times, by the state." Ngai, *Impossible Subjects,* 2.

73. Stephen Reyes, "A Letter," *Mexican Voice,* August 1938.

74. Reyes, "A Letter."

75. Reyes, "A Letter."

76. Reyes, "A Letter."

77. *Mexican Voice*, August 1938, 5.

78. "Executive Committee Plan," unknown date, Box 1, Folder 27, Supreme Council of the Mexican-American Movement Collection, 1942–1945, Oviatt Library Special Collections and Archives, California State University, Northridge.

79. Anthony Quiroz ed., *Leaders of the Mexican American Generation: Biographical Essays* (Boulder: University of Colorado Press, 2015), 2–5.

80. *MAM Handbook*, 17, 21.

81. *MAM Handbook*, 2.

82. *MAM Handbook*, 3; "Historia Breve de la Sociedad Progresista Mexicana," May 28, 1966.

83. *MAM Handbook*, 5.

84. Stephen Reyes, "Pasadena Settlement Loan Fund," *Mexican Voice*, November–December 1939.

85. Sánchez, *Becoming Mexican American*, 12–13, 228–29, 249. In addition to Mexican Americans, the Depression had a tremendous impact on early twentieth century youth activism more generally. See Britt Haas, *Fighting Authoritarianism: American Youth Activism in the 1930s* (New York: Fordham University Press, Empire State Editions, 2018), 1–3.

86. Studies of ethnic Mexican organizations in Arizona, Texas, and New Mexico detail this shift occurring somewhat earlier in those states due to the existence of a larger and more established Mexican American middle-class and/or the prevalence of ethnic Mexican participation in labor unions. See Gutiérrez, *Walls and Mirrors*; Vargas, *Labor Rights Are Civil Rights: Mexican American Workers in the Twentieth Century America* (Princeton: Princeton University Press, 2005), and Orozco, *No Mexicans Women or Dogs Allowed*.

87. Sánchez, *Becoming Mexican American*, 255–56.

88. Stephen Reyes' biographical information is taken from his 1983 interview with Brooke Larsen Garlock for the Pasadena Centennial Committee, vital and Census records obtained through *Family Search* and *Ancestry*, and newspaper clippings and other materials provided by granddaughter Stephanie Reyes-Tuccio.

89. Stephen Reyes interview.

90. Stephen Reyes interview; "El Modena Has New School Ready for Use," *Orange Daily News,* April 4, 1923; Christopher Arriola, "Knocking on the Schoolhouse Door," Mendez v. Westminster, equal Protection, Public Education, and Mexican 14.

91. Treff, "The Education of Mexican Children in Orange County," 23.

92. On the history of school segregation in California see Charles Wollenberg, *All Deliberate Speed: Segregation and Exclusion in California Schools, 1855–1975* (Berkeley: University of California Press, 1976); Ruben Donato, *The Other Struggle for Equal Schools: Mexican Americans During the Civil Rights Era* (Albany: State University of New York Press, 1997), 13–15. See also McWilliams, *Southern California*, 219; McWilliams, "Spectrum of Segregation"; McWilliams, *North from Mexico*, 217–21.

93. González, *Chicano Education in the Era of Segregation*.

94. Stephen Reyes interview.

95. Stephen Reyes interview.

96. "Past Conference Prexys," *The Mexican Voice*, March 1940.

97. Stephen Reyes interview.

98. Stephen Reyes interview.

99. Stephen Reyes, "We Can Do These," *The Mexican Voice*, March 1940.

100. Stephen Reyes interview; Elizabeth Lochridge, "Pasadena Settlement Association," *Pasadena Junior League News* 21, No. 6 (March 1948): 11–13; "History of the Pasadena Settlement Ass'n," *Pasadena Settlement Association Monthly Newsletter*, unknown date (c. 1934).

101. Stephen Reyes interview; Paul Coronel, "As We Move . . . ," *The Mexican Voice*, Summer 1944; "The President Speaks," *Forward*, Vol. 1, No. 1, October 28, 1945; Muñoz, *Youth, Identity, Power*, 37–38.

102. *MAM Handbook*, 2.

103. Stephen Reyes interview; Manuel De La Raza, "Nosotros," *The Mexican Voice*, Summer 1943.

104. Felix Gutierrez, "For Your Approval and Recommendation," c. 1945, Box 1, Folder 1, Supreme Council of the Mexican-American Movement Collection, 1942–1945, Oviatt Library Special Collections and Archives, California State University, Northridge; *MAM Handbook*, 6; "President Speaks," *Forward*, Vol. 1, No. 1 (October 28, 1945).

105. Gutierrez, "For Your Approval and Recommendation"; *MAM Handbook*, 9.

106. Gutierrez, "For Your Approval and Recommendation"; Felix Gutierrez, "'Mr. Reyes' there when Hispanics needed him," *Star-News*, July 5, 1983.

107. Gutierrez, "For Your Approval and Recommendation."

108. Gutierrez, "'Mr. Reyes' there when Hispanics needed him."

109. 1920 US Census, Yavapai, Arizona, Clarkdale precinct, ED 102, Sheet 10B, database with images s.v. "Luis Sandovar" in household of "Jose Sandovar," *FamilySearch.org*; "California, World War II Draft Registration Cards, 1940–1945," database with images s.v. "Luis Sandoval," *FamilySearch.org*; "Arizona, County Marriage Records, 1865–1972," database with images s.v. "Luis Sandoval" and "Charlotte Negrette," *Ancestry.com*.

110. Gualberto Valadez, "Progressive Club Work in Placentia," *The Mexican Voice*, June 1940. See also "Arizona Holds First Conference," *The Mexican Voice*, November–December 1939; Rebecca Munoz, "The Mexican Youth Movement in Mesa, Ariz.," *The Mexican Voice*, c. Spring 1941; "Regional Conferences," *The Mexican Voice*, c. Spring 1942.

111. Valadez, "Progressive Club Work in Placentia"; Margie de la Torre Aguirre, *LULAC Project: Patriots with Civil Rights, Early History of the League of United Latin American Citizens in California (1929–1957) and Gonzalo Mendez et al. vs. Westminster School District of Orange County et al.* (Abrazo Productions, 2009), 87.

112. Felix Gutierrez, "Placentia Council in Movement Work," *Forward*, Vol. 1, No. 1, October 28, 1945. See also Paul Coronel, "As We Move," *The Mexican Voice*, c. Summer 1944; "Local M.A.M. Councils," *The Mexican Voice*, c. Summer 1944.

113. "Articles of Incorporation," December 19, 1945; and "Minutes of First Meeting of Board of Directors of the Supreme Council of the Mexican American Movement," Box 1, Folder 1, Supreme Council of the Mexican-American Movement Collection, 1942–1945, Oviatt Library Special Collections and Archives, California State University, Northridge. See also, *MAM Handbook*, 5–6.

114. Arizona State University Registrar Services, email message to author, June 13, 2023.

115. "California Great Register of Voters, 1900–1968," database with images s.v. "Luis Sandoval," *Ancestry.com*.

116. Jensen, "The Mexican-American in an Orange County Community," 93.

117. Tabitha R. Frost interview with Celia Salas, December 3, 2002, O.H. 3202, Center for Oral and Public History, California State University, Fullerton, Fullerton, CA.

118. Celia Salas interview.
119. Celia Salas interview; Virginia Vargas interview; Harvey Reyes interview with Robert Villalobos, October 12, 2006, O.H. 3808, Center for Oral and Public History, California State University, Fullerton, Fullerton, CA. See also Ruling Given on Use of Plunge," *Orange Daily News*, August 15, 1936.
120. Celia Salas interview; Virginia Vargas interview.
121. Virginia Vargas interview; Celia Salas interview; Jensen, "The Mexican-American in an Orange County Community," 93.
122. "Se Banan en Anaheim," *Forward*, Vol. 1, No. 1, October 28, 1945. Note, this article is a reprint of an article by the same title in *Accion* which the author could not locate. See also, Jensen, "The Mexican-American in an Orange County Community," 93–97.
123. "Se Banan en Anaheim."
124. "Se Banan en Anaheim."
125. Celia Salas interview.
126. On the impact of World War II and the Cold War on civil rights efforts see: Mary L. Dudziak, *Cold War Civil Rights: Race and the Image of American Democracy* (Princeton: Princeton University Press, 2000); Thomas Borstelmann, *The Cold War and the Color Line: American race Relations in the Global Arena* (Cambridge, MA: Harvard University Press, 2001); Carol Anderson, *Eyes off the Prize: The United Nations and the African American Struggle for Human Rights, 1944–1955* (Cambridge: Cambridge University Press, 2003); Thomas A. Guglielmo, "Fighting for Caucasian Rights: Mexicans, Mexican Americans, and the Transnational Struggle for Civil Rights in World War II Texas," *Journal of American History* 92, No. 4 (March 2006): 1212–37; Richard Griswold del Castillo ed., *World War II and Mexican American Civil Rights* (Austin: University of Texas Press, 2008); Neil Foley, *Quest for Equality: The Failed Promise of Black-Brown Solidarity* (Cambridge, MA: Harvard University Press, 2010); Shana Bernstein, *Bridges of Reform: Interracial Civil Rights Activism in Twentieth-Century Los Angeles* (New York: Oxford University Press, 2011).
127. "Club News," *The Mexican Voice*, Spring 1939.
128. "Letters to the Editor," *The Mexican Voice*, January–February 1939; Manuel Ceja, "Sports," *The Mexican Voice*, January–February 1939; "Mexican Youth Rally," *The Mexican Voice*, Spring 1939; "Did You Know," *The Mexican Voice*, January 1940; "Institute at Anaheim," *The Mexican Voice*, February 1940; Felix Gutierrez, "Fullerton Regional Conference," *The Mexican Voice*, February 1940; "Conference Rally at Santa Ana," *The Mexican Voice*, March 1940; "El Dorado Club," *The Mexican Voice*, June 1940; Gualberto Valadez, "Progressive Club Work in Placentia," *The Mexican Voice*, June 1940; "Youth Conferences," *The Mexican Voice*, c. Winter 1941; "Regional Conferences," *The Mexican Voice*, c. Spring 1942.
129. Jensen, "The Mexican-American in an Orange County Community," 27–35; Kathy Landis interview with Melbourne A. Gauer, March 16, 1974, Center for Oral and Public History, California State University, Fullerton, Fullerton CA. The more likely reason that Anaheim Unified was not included as a defendant in *Mendez et al.* is discussed in the pretrial hearing on June 26, 1945. In determining the "procedure" of the case, McCormick decided the case could be expedited by selecting a few districts that were representative of the type of segregation existing throughout the county. See *Mendez et al.* Reporter's Transcript of Proceedings, June 26, 1945, 84–118.

130. Melbourne Gauer interview; "Purchase Site for Mexican School," *Anaheim Bulletin*, December 14, 1925; "Contract Let for Mexican School," *Anaheim Gazette*, July 29, 1926; "School Opens for Mexicans, *Anaheim Bulletin*, October 11, 1926; "La Palma School Students Enroll," *Anaheim Bulletin*, October 13, 1926. On the connection between residential and school segregation in Anaheim see Rudy Becerra Solorio, "Evolution of a Chicano Barrio in German Town," unpublished paper, March 8, 1982, Mexican American Folder, Anaheim Muzeo, Anaheim, CA.

131. Jensen, "The Mexican-American in an Orange County Community," 54–58; Treff, "The Education of Mexican Children in Orange County," 23–27; "Gloria Valdez Lopez," in Alice Lopez-Perez and Cynthia Pryor Coad eds., *La Colonia Independencia: A Collection of the History and Memories of the Hispanic Community, La Colonia Independencia, West Anaheim, California* (2009), Mexican American Folder, Anaheim Muzeo, Anaheim CA; Virginia Vargas interview; Celia Salas interview.

132. Melbourne Gauer interview.

133. Jensen, "The Mexican-American in an Orange County Community," 54–58, 64–70, 105; Celia Salas interview; Robert Villalobos interview; Leo Castro interview; Stephen Reyes interview.

134. "Se Banan en Anaheim," *Forward*, Vol. 1, No. 1, October 28, 1945.

135. Letter from Gualberto Valadez, unknown date, Box 1, Folder 11, Supreme Council of the Mexican-American Movement Collection, 1942–1945, Oviatt Library Special Collections and Archives, California State University, Northridge.

136. Letter from Gualberto Valadez.

137. "Teacher's Second Meeting," *The Mexican Voice*, June 1940; "Youth Conferences," *The Mexican Voice*, c. Winter 1941; "Teachers' Association Formed," *The Mexican Voice*, c. Winter 1941; "Regional Conferences," *The Mexican Voice*, c. Spring 1942; Paul Coronel, "As We Move," *The Mexican Voice*, c. Summer 1944; "Mexican-American Group Meet at Fullerton Sunday," *Anaheim Gazette*, May 18, 1944; "Conferences," *The Mexican Voice*, c. Summer 1944; "The President Speaks," *Forward*, Vol. 1, No. 1, October 28, 1945; Gutierrez, "Placentia Council in Movement Work"; "Prominent Group Holds Congress," *Forward*, October 28, 1945.

138. Article III, No. 4, "Articles of Incorporation of the Supreme Council of the Mexican-American Movement," *MAM Handbook*, 6.

139. Jensen, "The Mexican-American in an Orange County Community," 96–97.

140. On ethnic-racial cultural brokers see Eiichiro Azuma, "Negotiating the Boundaries of Race and Citizenship: Nisei Cultural Brokers in Occupied Japan," paper delivered to the American Studies Association, October 14, 2006, Oakland, CA; Hilary Jenks, "Seasoned Long Enough in Concentration: Suburbanization and Transnational Citizenship in Southern California's South Bay," *Journal of Urban History* 40, No. 1 (2014): 6–30.

141. "Luis Sandoval to El Paso Store," *Anaheim Gazette*, April 6, 1950.

142. "Luis Sandoval to El Paso Store." See also "Mexican-American Group Meet at Fullerton Sunday," *Anaheim Gazette*, May 18, 1944; "Camp Osceola Opens June 11," *Anaheim Gazette*, May 31, 1945; "M.A.M Works for Betterment of Its People-Nation," *Anaheim Gazette*, April 18, 1946; "M.A.M. Chairmen Present Reports, Receive Charter," *Anaheim Gazette*, March 21, 1946: "Bill Koontz Heads Local Hi-Y Council," *Anaheim Gazette*, May 16, 1946; "New Location Plans Approved by YMCA Board," *Anaheim Gazette*, May 23, 1946; "Two Teen-Age Canteen Groups Elect Officers," *Anaheim Gazette*, October 9, 1947; "Slate Annual Gray-Y

Pow Wow," *Anaheim Gazette*, October 16, 1947; "YMCA Holds Annual Dinner Meeting," *Anaheim Gazette*, February 1, 1952; "Anaheimer Write to Distinguish Name from that of Accused 'Pusher,'" *Anaheim Gazette*, April 9, 1953; "Jaycees Hear Talk by Bank Manager Jordan," *Anaheim Gazette*, October 29, 1953; "100 Youths Back from 'Y' Camp," *Anaheim Gazette*, July 28, 1955; "These Public Spirited Organization and Citizens Believe in the Elementary School Bond Program and Heartily Endorse Its Acceptance," *Anaheim Gazette*, January 26, 1956; "New Service Club for Men Being Formed in Anaheim," *Anaheim Gazette*, June 7, 1956.

143. Gualberto Valadez interview with Isabel Hlavac, August 16, 1995, transcript, Placentia Historical Committee Oral History Project, Center for Oral and Public History, California State University, Fullerton, Fullerton CA. See also, Gualberto Valadez interview with Gilbert G. González, 1987, Special Collections and Archives, University of California, Irvine Libraries, Irvine, CA. On the development of the Latina/o community in San Francisco see, Tomás F. Summers Sandoval Jr., *Latinos at the Golden Gate: Creating Community and Identity in San Francisco* (Chapel Hill, NC: University of North Carolina Press, 2013).

144. Valadez interview with González.

145. Valadez interview with González; Jose Alamillo interview with Gualberto Valadez, July 21, 2005; "Mexican 'Y' Club," *The Mexican Voice*, July 1939.

146. Stephen Reyes interview.

147. Valadez interview with González; Valadez interview with Hlavac; Gilbert G. González interview with Chester Whitten, August 20, 1987, Special Collections and Archives, University of California, Irvine Libraries, Irvine, CA; Alamillo interview with Valadez.

148. Treff, "The Education of Mexican Children in Orange County," 23.

149. Valadez interview with González; J.L. Meriam, "Learning English Incidentally: A Study of Bilingual Children," Bulletin 1937, No. 15, Department of the Interior, Washington, D.C., 27–30.

150. Valadez interview with González.

151. Valadez interview with González.

152. Chester Whitten interview.

153. Valadez interview with Hlavac.

154. Valadez interview with Hlavac.

155. Valadez interview with Hlavac. See also, Santillan et al., *Mexican American Baseball in Orange County*.

156. "Seventh Conference," *The Mexican Voice*, Vol. 3, No. 4, May 1940.

157. "Mexican Youth Rally," *The Mexican Voice*, Vol. 2, No. 2, Spring 1939.

158. In the end, the team from Orange bested Santa Ana, securing their third Mexican Youth Conference basketball tournament championship in six years. Manuel Ceja, "Mexican Youth Conference Basketball Tournament," *The Mexican Voice*, Vol. 2, No. 2, Spring 1939.

159. "Did You Know," *The Mexican Voice*, January 1940; "Fullerton Regional Conference," *The Mexican Voice*, February 1940; Ina Gerritt, "El Dorado Club," *The Mexican Voice*, June 1940; Valadez interview with González.

160. "Institute at Anaheim," *Mexican American Voice*, February 1940; "Youth Conferences," *The Mexican Voice*, Winter 1941; "Regional Conferences," *The Mexican Voice*, Spring 1942.

161. Valadez interview with Hlavac.

162. Tillie Arias, "What the Regional Conference Meant to Me," *The Mexican Voice*, February 1940.

163. Arias, "What the Regional Conference Meant to Me."

164. See: "Executive Committee Plan," and "The President Speaks," *Forward*, Vol. 1, No. 1, October 28, 1945. See also, "Local People Assist in Organizing M.A.M. Council," *Placentia Courier*, January 18, 1946.

165. *MAM Handbook*, 5.

166. *MAM Handbook*, 6.

167. See "The President Speaks" and "On the Map," *Forward*, Vol. 1, No. 1, October 28, 1945. Placentia's influence in MAM's early development is also evident in the financial contributions of local businesses purchasing ads in *Forward*. In the publication's first issue, Placentia business owners were responsible for twelve of fourteen paid advertisements.

168. *MAM Handbook*, 6.

169. "Placentia Council in Movement Work," *Forward*, Vol. 1, No. 1, October 28, 1945.

170. "Placentia Council in Movement Work."

171. "On the Map," *Forward*, Vol. 1, No. 1, October 28, 1945.

172. Valadez interview with González.

173. Valadez interview with González.

174. Valadez interview with González.

175. Valadez interview with González. Indeed, the involvement of Anglo/white educators and YMCA officials, either as advisors or guest speakers, was a central component of MAM's philosophy and strategy from the outset, beginning with the annual Mexican Youth Conference held in San Pedro from 1934 to 1942.

176. Valadez interview with González.

177. "Civic Unity Group Convenes," *Forward*, Vol. 1, No. 5, May 8, 1947.

178. "Civic Unity Group Convenes."

179. See Letter from Manuel Ruiz Jr., of the Coordinating Council for Latin American Youth to Gualberto Valadez, October 20, 1945; Letter from Curtis Whaley of the California Youth Authority to Gualberto Valadez, March 21, 1946; and Letter from Jane W. Pijoan of the Institute of Ethnic Affairs to Gualberto Valadez, Box 1, Folder 11, Supreme Council of the Mexican-American Movement Collection, 1942–1945, Oviatt Library Special Collections and Archives, California State University, Northridge.

180. "Where Is the Mexican Youth conference Aiming?," *The Mexican Voice*, Vol. 2 No. 6, February 1940. See also "Jaunts," *Mexican Voice*, Spring 1939; and "Casas in Mexico," *Forward*, Vol. 1, No. 5, May 8, 1947.

181. "Social Conditions of the Mexican People in General," *Mexican Voice*, January–February 1939; and "What They Say About," *Forward*, Vol. 1, No. 1, October 28, 1945.

182. Valadez interview with González.

183. Muñoz Jr., *Youth, Identity, Power*, 42–43, 58, 66–68, 75–85, 134–42. See also Mario T. García and Sal Castro, *Blowout! Sal Castro and the Chicano Struggle for Educational Justice* (Chapel Hill: University of North Carolina Press, 2011), 106; Mario T. García, *The Chicano Generation: Testimonios of the Movement* (Oakland: University of California Press, 2015), 126–27.

184. Letter to Placentia-Yorba Linda Unified School District from the Septuagenarian Tigers of Placentia-Yorba Linda, October 2005, Valadez interview with Hlavac, transcript. See also, "Ex-Students Seek to Honor Teacher," *Orange County Register*, October 27, 2005.

185. "Valadez Middle School Honors Namesake in Dedication Ceremony," *OC Register*, December 12, 2008. See also https://valadez-pylusd-ca.schoolloop.com/historyofschool.

186. This approach exemplifies Tara J. Yosso's theory of community cultural wealth. Employing their ethnic Mexican culture (i.e., bilingualism, binationalism, and biculturalism) and working-class subjectivity as aspirational, linguistic, familial, social, navigational, and resistant capital, members of *La Progresista* and MAM mobilized to improve their socioeconomic circumstances. See Tara J. Yosso, "Whose Culture Has Capital? A Critical Race Theory Discussion of Community Cultural Wealth," *Race Ethnicity and Education* 8, No. 1 (2005): 69–91.

CHAPTER 4

1. Herman Gallegos, Eric Kutner, and Gilbert Padilla interview with Hector Tarango, transcript, November 15, 2005, Community Service Organization, History Project Records, M1669, Department of Special Collections and University Archives, Stanford University Libraries, Stanford, CA (hereafter referred to as "CSO Project Tarango Interview").
2. This comment was made by Robert L. Carter, who as NAACP attorney alongside Thurgood Marshall presented oral arguments in *Brown v. Board of Education*. Vernon M. Billy, "The Echo of Mendez v. Westminster 70 Years Later," *California School Boards Association*, July 28, 2018, https://medium.com/@CSBA/the-echo-of-mendez-v-westminster-70-years-later-b24d11438fe4#.er2icu3cc.
3. For more on the background and significance of *Mendez et al. v. Westminster School Board et al.* see: Lester H. Phillips, "Segregation in Education: A California Case Study," *Phylon* 10, No. 4 (1949): 407–13; Charles Wollenberg, "Mendez v. Westminster: Race, Nationality and Segregation in California Schools," *The California Historical Quarterly* 53, No. 4 (Winter 1974): 317–32; Charles Wollenberg, *All Deliberate Speed: Segregation and Exclusion in California Schools, 1855–1975* (Berkeley: University of California Press, 1976), 108–35; Gilbert G. González, "Segregation of Mexican Children in a Southern California City: The Legacy of Expansionism and the American Southwest," *The Western Historical Quarterly* 16, No. 1 (January 1985): 55–76; Christopher Arriola, "Knocking on the Schoolhouse Door: Mendez v. Westminster, Equal Protection, Public Education, and Mexican Americans in the 1940's," *Berkeley La Raza Law Journal* 8, No. 2 (1995): 166–207; Vicki L. Ruiz, "South by Southwest: Mexican Americans and Segregated Schooling, 1900–1950," OAH Magazine of History 15, No. 2 (Winter 2001): 23–27; Steven Wilson, "Brown over 'Other White: Mexican Americans' Legal Arguments and Litigation Strategy in School Desegregation Lawsuits," *Law and History Review* 21, No. 1 (Spring 2003): 145–94; Toni Robinson and Greg Robinson, "*Mendez v. Westminster*: Asian-Latino Coalition Triumphant?," *Asian Law Journal* 10, No. 161 (2003): 161–83; Phillipa Strum, *Mendez v. Westminster: School Desegregation and Mexican-American Rights* (Lawrence: University Press of Kansas, 2010); Amanda Marie Liang, "Inland Empire Schools and Mendez v. Westminster, MA thesis (University of California, Riverside, 2012); Norma E. Cantú and Valerie M. Mendoza guest editors, Special Issue: Latinx Civil Rights and Beyond, *American Studies* 56, No. 2 (2017): 9–62; David-James Gonzales, "Mendez v. Westminster, 1945–1947," in Lilia Fernandez ed., *50 Events that Shaped Latino History: An Encyclopedia of the American Mosaic*, 2 vol. (Goleta: Greenwood, 2018), 417–34; Jennifer McCormick, "*Mendez v. Westminster*: Domestic Forces Underlying the Fight for School Desegregation," *Journal of American Ethnic History* 39, No. 1 (2019): 5–34; Jose Luis Castro Padilla, "Before *Brown v. Board of Education*: Paul J. McCormick, the *Mendez v. Westminster* Decision, and Its Religious-Social Context," *U.S. Catholic Historian* 41, No. 4 (Fall 2023): 79–98.

4. *Mendez et al* was the first class-action school desegregation case won at the federal level. Several successful desegregation efforts predated *Mendez et al.* at the local and county level. See Donato and Hanson, *The Other American Dilemma*, 15–71; Laura K. Muñoz, *"Romo v. Laird*: Mexican American Segregation and the Politics of Belonging in Arizona," *Western Legal History: The Journal of the Ninth Judicial Circuit Historical Society* 26 (2013): 97–132; Robert Alvarez Jr., "The Lemon Grove Incident: The Nation's First Successful Desegregation Court Case," *The Journal of San Diego History* 32, No. 2 (Spring 1986), n.p.; Guadalupe San Miguel Jr., *Let All of Them Take Heed: Mexican Americans and the Campaign for Educational Equality in Texas, 1910–1981* (Austin: University of Texas Press, 1987); Valencia, *Chicano Students and the Courts*, 22–42; Jesús Jesse Esparza, *Raza Schools: The Fight for Latino Educational Autonomy in a West Texas Borderlands Town* (Norman: University of Oklahoma Press, 2023).

5. For exceptions to the Mendez dominant narrative see Christopher Arriola, "Knocking on the Schoolhouse Door: Mendez v. Westminster, Equal Protection, Public Education, and Mexican Americans in the 1940's," *La Raza Law Journal* 8, No. 2 (1995): 166–207; Aguirre, *LULAC Project: Patriots with Civil Rights*, 15–100; Nadine Bermudez, "Reinscribing History: *Mendez et al. v. Westminster et al.* from the Standpoint of Mexican Origin Women," *American Studies* 56, No. 2 (2017): 9–29; Gonzales, "Mendez v. Westminster, 1945–1947," 421–33.

6. Earlier examples of the spatial turn in Chicano/a scholarship include Lisbeth Haas, *Conquests and Historical Identities in California, 1769–1936* (Berkeley: University of California Press, 1996), 4–6. García, *A World of Its Own*, 4–9; and Eric Avila, *Popular Culture in the Age of White Flight: Fear and Fantasy in Suburban Los Angeles* (Berkeley: University of California Press, 2006), xiv–xv.

7. For additional examples of civil rights beyond the black-white binary see Bernstein, *Bridges of Reform*; Brilliant, *The Color of America Has Changed*; Neil Foley, *Quest for Equality: The Failed Promise of Black-Brown Solidarity* (Cambridge, MA: Harvard University Press, 2010); Daniel Martinez HoSang, *Racial Propositions: Ballot Initiatives and the Making of Postwar California* (Berkeley: University of California Press, 2010); Kurashige, *The Shifting Grounds of Race*; Guadalupe San Miguel Jr., *Chicana/o Struggles for Education: Activism in the Community* (College Station: Texas A&M University Press, 2013); Sonia Song-Ha Lee, *Building a Latino Civil Rights Movement: Puerto Ricans, African Americans, and the Pursuit of Racial Justice in New York City* (Chapel Hill: University of North Carolina Press, 2014); Darrel Wanzer-Serrano, *The New York Young Lords and the Struggle for Liberation* (Philadelphia: Temple University Press, 2015); Max Krochmal, *Blue Texas: The Making of a Multiracial Democratic Coalition in the Civil Rights Era* (Chapel Hill: University of North Carolina Press, 2016); Ortiz, *An African American and Latinx History of the United States*; Abigail Rosas, *South Central Is Home: Race and the Power of Community Investment in Los Angeles* (Stanford: Stanford University Press, 2019); Eduardo Contreras, *Latinos and the Liberal City: Politics and Protest in San Francisco* (Philadelphia: University of Pennsylvania Press, 2019); Johanna Fernández, *The Young Lords: A Radical History* (Chapel Hill: University of North Carolina Press, 2020); Sánchez, *Boyle Heights*; Felipe Hinojosa, *Apostles of Change: Latino Radical Politics, Church Occupations, and the Fight to Save the Barrio* (Austin: University of Texas Press, 2021); Danielle R. Olden, *Racial Uncertainties: Mexican Americans, School Desegregation, and the Making of Race in Post-Civil Rights America* (Oakland: University of California Press, 2022).

8. CSO Project Tarango Interview; Gilbert González interview with Hector Tarango, April 15, 1989, Gilbert G. González Interviews, University of California, Irvine Special Collections. On the socioeconomic conditions of the Clifton-Morenci mining district see: Ted Cogut and Bill Conger, *History of Arizona's Clifton-Morenci Mining District: A Personal Approach, Vol. 1* (Thatcher, AZ: Minning History, 1999); James Patton, *History of Clifton* (NP: Greenlee County Chamber of Commerce, 1977); Phil Mellinger, "'The Men Have Become Organizers': Labor Conflict and Unionization in the Mexican Mining Communities of Arizona, 1900–1915," *Western Historical Quarterly* 23 (Fall 1992): 323–47.

9. CSO Project Tarango Interview.

10. Sánchez, *Becoming Mexican American*, 76–77; Sánchez, *Boyle Heights*, 39–66; Japanese American National Museum, *Los Angeles's Boyle Heights* (Charleston, SC: Arcadia Publishing, 2005), 27, 33–38. For examples of the intense anti-Mexican sentiment existent throughout the Clifton-Morenci region during the early twentieth century see Rodolfo Acuña, *Corridors of Migration: The Odyssey of Mexican Laborers, 1600–1933* (Tucson: University of Arizona Press, 2008), 119–41; Linda Gordon, *The Great Arizona Orphan Abduction* (Cambridge, MA: Harvard University Press, 1999).

11. Bureau of the Census, *Fourteenth Census of the United States, 1930*, Los Angeles, CA, accessed December 12, 2012, https://familysearch.org/pal:/MM9.1.1/ MCRJ-YRR.

12. Sánchez, *Becoming Mexican American*, 38, 216–21; Anthony Macias, *Mexican American Mojo: Popular Music, Dance, and Urban Culture in Los Angeles, 1935–1968* (Durham: Duke University Press, 2008), 18.

13. Macias, *Mexican American Mojo*, 18–20.

14. Sánchez, *Becoming Mexican American*; Sánchez, *Boyle Heights*; Molina, *Fit to Be Citizens*; Douglas Monroy, *Rebirth: Mexican Los Angeles from the Great Migration to the Great Depression* (Berkeley: University of California Press, 1999).

15. CSO Project Tarango interview.

16. CSO Project Tarango interview.

17. Brigandi, *A Brief History of Orange, California*, 54–56; Orange Public Library, "Historic Orange Preservation Online," accessed December 12, 2012, http:// www.cityoforange.org/localhistory/default.htm; Bureau of the Census, *Sixteenth Census of the United States, 1940*, Orange, CA, accessed December 5, 2012, https:// familysearch.org/pal:/MM9.1.1/K94D-86J.

18. CSO Project Tarango Interview. See Ward Leis, "The Status of Education for Mexican Children in Four Border States," MA thesis (University of Southern California, 1931), 26; González, *Chicano Education in the Era of Segregation*, 143; McWilliams, *Southern California*, 205–26; Garcia, *A World of Its Own*, 47–78.

19. Ruben Donato, *The Other Struggle for Equal Schools: Mexican Americans During the Civil Rights Era* (Albany: Statue University of New York Press, 1997), 13.

20. Arriola, "Knocking on the Schoolhouse Door," 173–76; Strum, *Mendez v. Westminster*, 45–46.

21. Arriola, "Knocking on the Schoolhouse Door," 172.

22. Christopher Arriola interview with Dan Gomez, July 26, 1991, transcript, Mendez v. Westminster: research materials, M0938, Department of Special Collections, Stanford University Libraries, Stanford, CA.

23. Melissa Lee interview with Rudy Hernandez, August 2, 1982, audio recording, Center for Oral and Public History, California State University, Fullerton, Fullerton, CA.

24. Arriola, "Knocking on the Schoolhouse Door," 173.
25. *Mendez et al.* Reporter's Transcript of Proceedings, July 6, 1945, 262; *Mendez et al.* Reporter's Transcript of Proceedings, July 9, 1945, 439.
26. McWilliams, *North from Mexico*, 249–51.
27. Osman R. Hull and Willard S. Ford, "Santa Ana School Housing Survey" (University of Southern California Studies, 2nd series, No. 6, 1928); cited from González, "Segregation of Mexican Children in a Southern California City," 65. See also, Osman Ransom Hull et al., *Survey of the Los Angeles City Schools* (Los Angeles: Wolfer Print, 1934); and Osman Ransom Hull, et al, *Forward in the Fundamentals of Education* (Inglewood, CA, 1941).
28. González, *Chicano Education in the Era of Segregation*; Robert Alvarez Jr., "The Lemon Grove Incident," *The Journal of San Diego History* 32, No. 2 (Spring 1986), https://sandiegohistory.org/journal/1986/april/lemongrove/; Wollenberg, *All Deliberate Speed*; and Strum, *Mendez v. Westminster*.
29. González, *Chicano Education in the Era of Segregation*, 137–38; Donato, *The Other Struggle for Equal Schools*, 19–33. See also C.J. Marks interview with González.
30. *Mendez et al.* Reporter's Transcript of Proceedings, July 5, 1945, 34.
31. Christopher Arriola with Annie Quintana, July 26, 1991, transcript, Mendez v. Westminster: research materials, M0938, Department of Special Collections, Stanford University Libraries, Stanford, CA.
32. Gomez interview, July 26, 1991.
33. Cindy Peronto interview with Clarence Peralta, May 26, 1982, audio recording, Center for Oral and Public History, California State University, Fullerton, Fullerton, CA.
34. González, *Chicano Education in the Era of Segregation*, 95, 146–47: Hass, *Conquests and Historical Identities in California*, 189–96; *Mendez et al.* Reporter's Transcript of Proceedings, July 6, 1945, 283–84.
35. González, *Chicano Education in the Era of Segregation*, 138–39.
36. González, *Chicano Education in the Era of Segregation*, 47–49; Molina, *Fit to Be Citizens*, 78, 115; Perales, *Smeltertown*, 185–208; Dorothy Roberts, "Who May Give Birth to Citizens? Reproduction, Eugenics, and Immigration," in Juan F. Perea ed., *Immigrants Out! The New Nativism and Anti-Immigrant Impulse in the U.S.* (New York: New York University Press, 1997), 205–19; Ruiz, *From Out of the Shadows*, 33–50, 72–98.
37. Karen J. Leong, "'A Distinct and Antagonistic Race': Constructions of Chinese Manhood in the Exclusionist Debates, 1869–78," in Donna R. Gabaccia and Vicki Ruiz eds., *American Dreaming, Global Realities: Rethinking U.S. Immigration History* (Urbana: University of Illinois Press, 2006); Peggy Pascoe, *What Comes Naturally: Miscegenation Law and the Making of Race in America* (New York: Oxford University Press, 2009), 11–14, 106–8; Dara Orenstein, "Void for Vagueness," *Pacific Historical Review* 74, No. 3 (August 2005): 367–408.
38. See tables I and II in Treff, "The Education of Mexican Children in Orange County," 26, 28.
39. Tarango interview with González, April 15, 1989.
40. CSO Project Tarango interview. Although not the primary motivating factor, the wartime context resonated with many ethnic Mexicans involved in the struggle to desegregate Orange County schools. See, Nadine Bermudez, "*Mendez et al. v. Westminster et al.*: Mexican American Female Activism in the Age of *De Jure* Segregation," PhD diss. (University of California, Los Angeles, 2015), 155–58.

41. There's some ambiguity surrounding the name of this initial organization founded by Hector Tarango, Cruz Barrios, Manuel Veiga Jr., and Isadore Gonzales. In both his 1989 and 2005 interviews, Tarango was uncertain when he referred to this organization as "The Orange County Voters League." In an unpublished memoir, Fred Ross referred to the organization as "The Latin American Voters League," which is also referred to as such in a March 1, 2003 letter to Tarango from the Chair of the California LULAC Heritage Committee. However, official minutes from a September 19, 1944 meeting of the Westminster Elementary School Board, recorded the name of this group as "The Latin American Voters Council," while Gonzalo Mendez referred to the group in his court testimony as the "Latin American League of Voters." Finally, this the same organization Philippa Strum and Gilbert González refer to as the "Latin American Organization" and the "Mexican American Voters League in Orange County." Hereafter, I refer to the organiza-tion as the Latin American Voters League or LAVL. See Westminster Elementary School Board of Trustees, Minutes, September 19, 1944 (Westminster School District Office, Westminster, CA); CSO Project Tarango interview; González inter-view with Tarango; Letter to Hector Tarango from Margie Aguirre, March 1, 2003, CSO Project UC San Diego; Court Testimony of Gonzalo Mendez, Mendez et. al. v. Westminster et al. Archive, Frank Mt. Pleasant Library of Special Collections and Archives, Chapman University, CA, Box 4, Folder 1; Strum, *Mendez v. Westminster*, 131; González, *Labor and Community*, 172–73; Aguirre, *LULAC Project*, 24, 28–30, 37.

42. The names of these organizations were the Latin American Voters League (also referred to as the "Latin American Organization"), the "El Modena Unity League," and Santa Ana LULAC Council 147. See Margie Aguirre, "Letter to Tarango" and Strum, *Mendez v. Westminster*, 131; Santa Ana LULAC Council Minutes, May 8, 1946, Personal Collection of Hector Tarango; Fred Ross, Unpublished Autobiography, 14–15.

43. Chicano (a/x/e) historians have detailed the widespread labor activism of Mexican mutual-aid societies in the United States and Mexico beginning at the turn of the twentieth century. This included the occurrence of over 160 "major strikes" in California between the years 1933–1937 that were primarily organized through the leadership of Mexican mutualistas. During this period, several similar actions by ethnic Mexicans occurred throughout the Southwest. See Gutiérrez, *Walls and Mirrors*, 99–105; Vargas, *Labor Rights Are Civil Rights*; Juan Gómez-Quinoñes, *Chicano Politics Reality and Promise, 1940–1990* (Albuquerque: University of New Mexico Press, 1990), 63–80.

44. Carlos K. Blanton, "The Citizenship Sacrifice: Mexican Americans, the Saunders-Leonard Report, and the Politics of Immigration, 1951–52," *Western Historical Quarterly* 40, No. 3 (Autumn 2009): 299–320; Carlos K. Blanton, "George I. Sánchez, Ideology, and Whiteness in the Making of the Mexican American Civil Rights Movement, 1930–1960," *The Journal of Southern History* 72, No. 3 (August 2006): 569–604; Thomas A. Guglielmo, "Fighting for Caucasian Rights: Mexicans, Mexican Americans, and the Transnational Struggle for Civil Rights in World War II Texas," *The Journal of American History* 92, No. 4 (March 2006): 1212–37.

45. Haas, *Conquests and Historical Identities*, 191; González, *Chicano Education*, 141.

46. Haas, *Conquests and Historical Identities*, 191.

47. Haas, *Conquests and Historical Identities*, 192.

48. *Mendez et al.* Reporter's Transcript of Proceedings, July 5, 1945, 27, 58, 65–67, 155–57; *Mendez et al.* Reporter's Transcript of Proceedings, July 6, 1945, 209–10,

239–40, 250–54; *Mendez et al.* Reporter's Transcript of Proceedings, July 9, 1945, 442–43; *Mendez et al.* Reporter's Transcript of Proceedings, July 11, 1945, 612–13.

49. Christopher Arriola interview with Bob Torres, August 16, 1991, transcript, Mendez v. Westminster: research materials, M0938, Department of Special Collections and Archives, Stanford University, Stanford, CA.

50. Arriola interview with Gomez, July 26, 1991.

51. Arriola interview with Quintana, July 26, 1991; *Mendez et al.* Reporter's Transcript of Proceedings, July 5, 1945, 41–45; Christopher Arriola interview with Oscar Valencia, August 23, 1991, Mendez v. Westminster: research materials, M0938, Department of Special Collections, Stanford University Libraries, Stanford, CA.

52. Bermudez, "*Mendez et al. v. Westminster et al.*: Mexican American Female Activism," 181.

53. On everyday forms of resistance see: James C. Scott, *Weapons of the Weak: Everyday Forms of Peasant Resistance* (New Haven, CT: Yale University Press, 1985); and Robin D.G. Kelley, *Race Rebels: Culture, Politics, and the Black Working Class* (New York: The Free Press, 1994).

54. Arriola interview with Gomez, July 26, 1991; Virginia Guzman interview with Ray Rast, July 31, 2011, audio recording, Center for Oral and Public History, California State University, Fullerton, Fullerton, CA.

55. Lizeth Ramirez interview with Carol Torres, May 1, 2010, Shades of Orange Oral History Project, Orange Public Library Local History Room, Orange, CA.

56. CSO Project Tarango Interview; González interview with Tarango, April 15, 1989; Fred Ross, "Community Organization in Mexican American Colonies: A Progress Report," 39–40, Box 20, Folder 19, Fred Ross Papers, M0812, Department of Special Collections and University Archives, Stanford University, Stanford, CA.

57. Bermudez, "*Mendez et al. v. Westminster et al.*: Mexican American Female Activism," 181–89.

58. *Mendez et al.* Petition, March 2, 1945.

59. *Mendez et al.* Reporter's Transcript of Proceedings, July 5, 1945, 44.

60. Trounstine, *Segregation by Design*, 3; *Mendez et al.* Reporter's Transcript of Proceedings, June 26, 1945, 95–97.

61. *Mendez et al.* Reporter's Transcript of Proceedings, June 26, 1945, 97.

62. *Mendez et al.* Reporter's Transcript of Proceedings, July 5, 1945, 150–52.

63. *Mendez et al.* Reporter's Transcript of Proceedings, July 5, 1945, 154–57.

64. Chris Arriola points out that in 1943 the Latin American Organization was formed in Santa Ana, "as a civil rights group designed to combat school segregation." Tarango was a known organizer throughout the communities of Santa Ana, El Modena, and Westminster, as confirmed by Phillipa Strum and Gilbert González. See Arriola, "Knocking on the Schoolhouse Door," 185; Strum, *Mendez v. Westminster*, 36–37, 131; González, *Labor and Community*, 172–77; González, *Chicano Education in the Era of Segregation*, 190–94; González interview with Tarango.

65. LAVL member and later LULAC organizer Alex Maldonado confirmed that *Mendez et al.* co-plaintiffs Frank Palomino, William Guzman, Gonzalo Mendez, and Lorenzo Ramirez were members of the LAVL. He also recalled a "falling out" between the men sometime after the case was filed in March 1945 and McCormick's decision in May 1946. Ray Rast interview with Alex Maldonado, OH 4885.2, May 27, 2011, Center for Oral and Public History, California State University, Fullerton, Fullerton, CA; Virginia Guzman interview.

66. Santa Ana Board of Education, Minutes, October 25, 1943; and CSO Project Tarango interview. See also, González, *Chicano Education in the Era of Segregation*, 190–91.

67. Santa Ana Board of Education, Minutes, October 29, 1944; González, *Chicano Education in the Era of Segregation*, 191–92.

68. The exact date of when the Mendez family moved to the Munemitsu farm is uncertain. In oral history interviews conducted decades later, Felicitas Mendez had trouble recalling the year the family leased the farm, estimating that it occurred in 1942 or 1943, even though the date of first the lease is December 20, 1944. In his court testimony, Gonzalo Mendez stated that Westminster Superintendent Richard Harris visited him on the farm in 1943 after he and Felicitas refused to enroll their children in the Hoover Mexican school. However, Gonzalo's niece Alice Vidaurri recalled in her interview with Albert Vela that the family moved to the Munemitsu farm with the Mendezes and attempted to enroll at Westminster Main in 1944. Finally, Janice Munemitsu states in her memoir *The Kindness of Color* that the Mendezes "settled into living on the Westminster farm throughout the summer of 1944." Janice also states, "No one knows who oversaw the farm from May 1942," when the family was interned, to June 7, 1944, which is when Sylvia Mendez remembers celebrating her eighth birthday on the property. Janice believes it is likely that there may have been an informal agreement between the families prior to December 1944 and places the Mendezes on the farm that summer. Janice Munemitsu, *The Kindness of Color: The Story of Two Families and Mendez, et al. v. Westminster, the 1947 Desegregation of California Public Schools* (Self-published, 2021), 63–66, 81, 95. See also Felicitas Mendez interview with Zuniga; Felicitas Mendez interview with González; Strum, *Mendez v. Westminster*, 36; Seiko Munemitsu and Gonzalo Mendez lease agreements, Mendez v. Westminster Box 2, Folder 6–7, 2009-041-r, Frank Mt. Pleasant Library of Special Collections and Archives, Leatherby Libraries, Chapman University, Orange, CA; *Mendez et al.* Reporter's Transcript of Proceedings, July 9, 1945, 445–46; Vela, *Tracks to the Westminster Barrio*, 146–49.

69. On the California Alien Land Laws and their impact on Japanese families in California see Carey McWilliams, *Prejudice: Japanese Americans Symbol of Racial Intolerance* (Boston: Little, Brown, 1944), 23–25, 45–51, 60–66; Robert Higgs, "Landless by Law: Japanese Immigrants in California Agriculture to 1942," *The Journal of Economic History* 38, No. 1 (March 1978): 205–25; Yuji Ichioka, "Japanese Immigrant Response to the 1920 California Alien Land Law," *Agricultural History* 58, No. 2 (April 1984): 157–78; Eiichiro Azuma, "Japanese Immigrant Farmers and California Alien Land Laws," *California History* 73, No. 1 (Spring 1994): 14–29; Tokunaga, *Transborder Los Angeles*, 18–26, 59–65.

70. Munemitsu, *The Kindness of Color*, 53, 63. See also Strum, *Mendez v. Westminster*, 159–61; Annie Tang, "The Munemitsu Legacy," *Pacific* Citizen, December 18, 2020, https://www.pacificcitizen.org/the-munemitsu-legacy/.

71. On the multiple and often intersecting "axes of discrimination" faced by minority groups and activists in twentieth century California see, Brilliant, *The Color of America Has Changed*, 9.

72. *Mendez, et al v. Westminster School District of Orange County, et al*, 64 F.Supp. 544 (S.D. Cal. 1946). See also Felicitas Mendez interview with Zúñiga; Felicitas Mendez interview with González; Alfredo H. Zúñiga interview with Soledad Vidaurri and Felicitas Mendez, December 21, 1974, Box 2, A047; Strum, *Mendez v. Westminster*, 37; Vela, *Tracks to the Westminster Barrio*, 199–206.

73. *Mendez et al.* Reporter's Transcript of Proceedings, July 10, 1945, 461–62. See also Strum, *Mendez v. Westminster*, 35; Munemitsu, *The Kindness of Color*, 98.

74. Vela, *Tracks to the Westminster Barrio*, 154–55, 197.

75. This is the same organization referred to as the Association of Parents of Mexican American Children by Felicitas Mendez and Soledad Vidaurri in oral history interviews. See Zúñiga interview with Soledad Vidaurri and Felicitas Mendez and Zúñiga interview with Felicitas Mendez.

76. *Mendez, et al v. Westminster School District of Orange County, et al*, 64 F.Supp. 544 (S.D. Cal. 1946).

77. According to Gonzalo Mendez's court testimony the Westminster Father's Association and LAVL were working together prior to September 1944. *Mendez et al.* Reporter's Transcript of Proceedings, July 9, 1945, 447–49. Felicitas Mendez also confirmed that she and Gonzalo "belonged to" and worked with "the LULACs" during the buildup to *Mendez et al.* By "LULACs" she meant the founders of Santa Ana LULAC Council 147, which were the same men that established the LAVL. See Zúñiga interview with Felicitas Mendez. See also Sylvia Mendez, "Gonzalo Mendez: First Chicano to Challenge Segregation," *El Quetzal*, January 4, 1977; Aguirre, *LULAC Project*, 75–84, 253–57.

78. Westminster Elementary School Board of Trustees, Minutes, September 19, 1944; Court Testimony of Gonzalo Mendez, Mendez et. al. v. Westminster et. al. Archive, Frank Mt. Pleasant Library of Special Collections and Archives, Chapman University, CA, Box 4, Folder 1.

79. Petition to Westminster Unified School District, September 8, 1944, Mendez et. al. v. Westminster et. al. Archive, Frank Mt. Pleasant Library of Special Collections and Archives, Chapman University, CA, Box 3, Folder 1.

80. Westminster Elementary School Board of Trustees, Minutes, September 19, 1944.

81. Santa Ana Board of Education, Minutes, October 25, 1943.

82. According to William Guzman's court testimony, he and Virginia had hired attorney Charles Martin and appeared before the Santa Ana School Board on September 14, 1944. According to trial transcripts, Martin was the first attorney to represent Mexican families in the lead up to the case. *Mendez et al.* Reporter's Transcript of Proceedings, July 6, 1945, 169–70.

83. *Mendez et al.* Reporter's Transcript of Proceedings, July 6, 1945, 170–74, 204–6.

84. Santa Ana Board of Education, Minutes, October 23, 1944. See also Strum, *Mendez v. Westminster*, 129–31 and Arriola, "Knocking on the Schoolhouse Door," 183.

85. Valerie M. Mendoza, "Beverly Guzman Gallegos's *Testimonio*," *American Studies* 56, No. 2 (2017): 58–59.

86. Bermudez, "*Mendez et al. v. Westminster et al.*: Mexican American Female Activism," 224. See also Virginia Guzman interview.

87. On the Bracero Program in Orange County, see Lisbeth Haas, "The Bracero in Orange County: A Workforce for Economic Transition," *Working Papers in U.S.-Mexican Studies*, Vol. 29, University of California, San Diego (1981). On the Bracero Program more generally see: Ernesto Galarza, *Merchants of Labor: The Mexican Bracero Story* (San Jose, CA: McNally and Loftin, 1964); Deborah Cohen, *Braceros: Migrant Citizens and Transnational Subjects in the Postwar United States and Mexico* (Chapel Hill: University of North Carolina Press, 2011); Ana Elizabeth Rosas, *Abrazando el Espiritu: Bracero Families Confront the US-Mexico Border* (Berkeley: University of California Press, 2014); and Mireya Loza, *Defiant Braceros: How Migrant Workers Fought for Racial, Sexual, and Political Freedom* (Chapel Hill: University of North

Carolina Press, 2016); Maria L. Quintana, *Contracting Freedom: Race, Empire, and U.S. Guestworker Programs* (Philadelphia: University of Pennsylvania Press, 2022).

88. Information regarding Marcus' relationship with Lorenzo Ramirez was acquired through correspondence and conversations between the author and the Ramirez family. For more on Marcus' central role in litigating civil rights victories on behalf of Mexican American communities in Southern California see Genevieve Carpio, "Unexpected Allies: David C. Marcus and His Impact on the Advancement of Civil Rights in the Mexican-American Legal Landscape of Southern California," in Sánchez ed., *Beyond Alliances*, 1–32. See also, Brilliant, *The Color of America Has Changed*, 45–71; Arriola, "Knocking on the Schoolhouse Door," 182–85; Bernstein, *Bridges of Reform*, 188–92; Strum, *Mendez v. Westminster*, 35–53, 129–31.

89. Josefina Ramirez de Soto interview with Maria Quintero, June 24, 2010, transcript, Center for Oral and Public History, California State University, Fullerton, Fullerton, CA.

90. *Mendez et al.* Reporter's Transcript of Proceedings, July 6, 1945, 273–85.

91. Arriola interview with Gomez. See also, Olivia Andrade and Lizette Ramirez interview with Phyllis Ramirez Zepeda, January 23, 2016; "Lider de Lideres," *El Politico*, November 3, 1967.

92. The exact date when Marcus was acquired by the plaintiff families is uncertain. Court documents and minutes from the Westminster, Santa Ana, and El Modena school board meetings indicate that the securing of Marcus' services happened sometime between November of 1944 and January of 1945. There has also been considerable debate among the plaintiff families as to who was responsible for finding, selecting, and paying Marcus, after other attorneys like Charles Martin had provided counsel to families like the Guzman's prior to filing the lawsuit in March of 1945. Although the Mendez family has maintained that they alone secured and paid for Marcus' services, the people in the region who had the most experience working with Marcus prior to *Mendez, et al.* were Lucas Lucio, Alex Bernal, and Lorenzo Ramirez. On Marcus' successful defense of Fullerton resident Alex Bernal in the 1943 housing desegregation case *Doss v. Bernal* see Carpio, "Unexpected Allies," 11–16, 20–23; and Robert Chao Romero and Luis Fernando Fernandez, "*Doss v. Bernal*: Ending Mexican Apartheid in Orange County," *CSRC Research Report*, No. 14 (February 2012); Teresa Haught interview. Further, in oral history interviews, Tarango, the et al. families, Alex Maldonado, Hector Godinez, and other community members maintained that the LAVL (and later LULAC) was involved in the decision to locate, hire, and pay for Marcus' services. See Tarango interviews with CSO Project, Gilbert González, and Margie Aguirre; Aguirre, *LULAC Project*, 27, 36–38, 45, 48, 54, 57–58, 65, 75, 81, 83, 95–97; Alex Maldonado interview. Moreover, the *LULAC News* confirmed that "the Santa Ana Council was mainly responsible for the prosecution of the case [*Mendez et al.* appeal] and had borne most of the expense, without practically any help from other Councils of the League." See *LULAC News*, July 1947, 20–21.

93. Westminster School Board of Trustees, Minutes, January 10, 1945.

94. Westminster School Board of Trustees, Minutes, January 10, 1945. Interestingly, in the very same meeting, the Westminster board approved the admission of "children of Japanese descent" at Westminster Main, even though at the time California law allowed for their segregation. See Alvarez, "Lemmon Grove Incident"; Foley, *Quest for Equality*, 110, 197; Bernstein, *Bridges of Reform*, 188.

95. Westminster School Board of Trustees, Minutes, January 16, 1945. See also court testimony of Gonzalo Mendez, *Mendez, et al v. Westminster School District of Orange County, et al*, 64 F.Supp. 544 (S.D. Cal. 1946).

96. Westminster School Board of Trustees, Minutes, January 16, 1945.

97. Westminster School Board of Trustees, Minutes, March 12, 1945; Santa Ana Board of Education, Minutes, March 12, 1945.

98. *Mendez, et al v. Westminster School District of Orange County, et al*, Petition, March 2, 1945. "Segregation Is Charged Against County Schools," *Santa Ana Register*, March 3, 1945.

99. Treff, "The Education of Mexican Children in Orange County," 23–28.

100. *Mendez et al.* Reporter's Transcript of Proceedings, June 26, 1945, 41–42, 84–86.

101. *Mendez et al* was the first class-action school desegregation case won at the federal level. Several successful desegregation efforts predated *Mendez et al.* at the local and county level. See Donato and Hanson, *The Other American Dilemma*, 15–71; Laura K. Muñoz, "*Romo v. Laird*: Mexican American Segregation and the Politics of Belonging in Arizona," *Western Legal History: The Journal of the Ninth Judicial Circuit Historical Society* 26 (2013): 97–132; Robert Alvarez Jr., "The Lemon Grove Incident: The Nation's First Successful Desegregation Court Case," *The Journal of San Diego History* 32, No. 2 (Spring 1986), n.p.; Guadalupe San Miguel Jr., *Let All of Them Take Heed: Mexican Americans and the Campaign for Educational Equality in Texas, 1910–1981* (Austin: University of Texas Press, 1987); Valencia, *Chicano Students and the Courts*; Jesús Jesse Esparza, *Raza Schools: The Fight for Latino Educational Autonomy in a West Texas Borderlands Town* (Norman: University of Oklahoma Press, 2023).

102. *Mendez et al.* Reporter's Transcript of Proceedings, June 26, 1945, 44–50, 103–6; *Mendez, et al. v. Westminster School District of Orange County, et al*, Conclusions of the Court, February 18, 1946, 4.

103. *In re Ricardo Rodriguez* was a naturalization case that determined Mexicans were eligible for US citizenship through the annexation of Texas and the Treaty of Guadalupe Hidalgo. The decision conferred a form of "legal whiteness" to Mexicans and was one of fifty-two "racial prerequisite cases" decided by the courts between 1878 and 1944. *In re Rodriguez* 81 F.337 (W.D. Tex. 1897); Arnoldo De León, *In Re Ricardo Rodriguez: An Attempt at Chicano Disenfranchisement* (San Antonio, TX: Caravel Press, 1979); Ian Haney Lopez, *White by Law: The Legal Construction of Race* (New York: New York University Press, 2006), 43–44, 163–67.

104. *Mendez et al.* Reporter's Transcript of Proceedings, June 26, 1945, 84–85, 107–15.

105. *Mendez, et al. v. Westminster School District of Orange County, et al*, Petition, March 2, 1945.

106. *Mendez et al.* Reporter's Transcript of Proceedings, June 26, 1945, 4–6; *Mendez, et al.* Conclusions of the Court, February 18, 1946, 6–7.

107. In oral histories and public statements, members of the Mendez family, including Felicitas and Sylvia, have claimed that the Mendez children testified during the case. However, neither Sylvia, Geronimo, nor Gonzalo Jr.'s names are listed among the plaintiff witnesses in court transcripts. The Mendez children's names did appear, along with the other plaintiff children (Billy Guzman, Arthur and Sally Palomino, Ignacio, Silverio, and Jose Ramirez, and Clara, Roberto, Francisco, Syria, Daniel, and Evelina Estrada) on the initial petition filed by attorney David Marcus on March 2, 1945. Carol Torres and Robert Perez were the only two minors to testify on the stand during the trial from July 5–11, 1945.

108. *Mendez et al.* Reporter's Transcript of Proceedings, July 6, 1945, 85–88.

109. *Mendez et al.* Reporter's Transcript of Proceedings, July 5, 1945, 119–23.

110. *Mendez et al.* Reporter's Transcript of Proceedings, July 6, 1945, 395–96.

111. *Mendez, et al. v. Westminster School District of Orange County, et al,* Brief of National Lawyers Guild, and American Civil Liberties Union, Amici Curiae, October 1, 1945, 1.

112. On Beal's scholarly background and the influence of his research in post-revolutionary Mexico on school desegregation in Southern California, see Ruben Flores, *Backroads Pragmatists: Mexico's Melting Pot and Civil Rights in the United States* (Philadelphia, University of Pennsylvania Press, 2014), 209–25.

113. *Mendez et al.* Reporter's Transcript of Proceedings, July 11, 1945, 668.

114. *Mendez et al.* Reporter's Transcript of Proceedings, July 11, 1945, 670–71.

115. Flores, *Backroads Pragmatists,* 220–23.

116. *Mendez et al.* Reporter's Transcript of Proceedings, July 11, 1945, 672.

117. *Mendez et al.* Reporter's Transcript of Proceedings, July 11, 1945, 676–77.

118. *Mendez et al.* Reporter's Transcript of Proceedings, July 11, 1945, 676–77.

119. *Mendez et al.* Reporter's Transcript of Proceedings, July 11, 1945, 686–87.

120. Flores, *Backroads Pragmatists,* 225–31.

121. *Mendez et al.* Reporter's Transcript of Proceedings, July 11, 1945, 688–89.

122. *Mendez et al.* Reporter's Transcript of Proceedings, July 11, 1945, 697–700.

123. *Mendez et al.* Reporter's Transcript of Proceedings, July 11, 1945, 700–702.

124. *Mendez et al.* Reporter's Transcript of Proceedings, July 11, 1945, 707; *Mendez et al.* Reporter's Transcript of Proceedings, June 26, 1945, 106–7.

125. *Mendez, et al.* Conclusions of the Court, February 18, 1946, 5–8.

126. *Mendez, et al.* Conclusions of the Court, February 18, 1946, 8–9.

127. *Mendez, et al.* Conclusions of the Court, February 18, 1946, 11.

128. *Mendez, et al.* Conclusions of the Court, February 18, 1946, 18–19.

129. *Mendez, et al.* Conclusions of the Court, February 18, 1946, 12.

130. *Mendez, et al.* Notice of Motion to Dismiss Petition, April 4, 1945; *Mendez, et al.* Answer of El Modeno School District, et al., May 5, 1945; *Mendez, et al.* Defendants Reply Brief, October 17, 1945.

131. *Mendez, et al.* Conclusions of the Court, February 18, 1946, 12–19. See also *Mendez, et al.* Findings of Fact and Conclusions of Law, March 21, 1946, 9–14.

132. *Mendez, et al.* Notice of Appeal, March 29, 1946.

133. Strum, *Mendez v. Westminster,* 128–29.

134. Westminster School Board of Trustees, Minutes, March 29, 1946; Joel Ogle, Letter to Richard Harris, District Superintendent of Westminster Schools, April 23, 1946, Westminster Unified School District; Strum, *Mendez v. Westminster,* 121–31.

135. Carey McWilliams, "Is Your Name Gonzales?," *The Nation,* April 8, 1947; "School Bias Draws Blast from Justices," *Pittsburgh Courier,* April 26, 1947. See also, "Ruling Gives Mexican Children Equal Rights," *Los Angeles Times,* February 19, 1946; Ignacio Lopez, "El Caso De Segregacion En Orange County Toma Proporciones Nacionales," *El Espectador,* November 15, 1956; "Minorities Jim Crow Attacked," *The Weekly Review,* December 7, 1947; "Separate School Law Violates Constitution," *Afro-American,* December 14, 1946.

136. Aguirre, "*Mendez v. Westminster School District*: How It Affected Brown v. Board of Education," 326. See also Bernstein, *Bridges of Reform,* 189–90; Strum, *Mendez v. Westminster,* 133–40; Foley, *Quest for Equality,* 102–8.

137. *Westminster School District of Orange County, et al., v. Gonzalo Mendez, et al.,* United States Court of Appeals for the Ninth Circuit Court of Appeals, Brief

for the National Association for the Advancement of Colored People as Amicus Curiae, October 2, 1946, 5–6.

138. Westminster School District of Orange County, et al., NAACP Amicus brief, 8–9.

139. Westminster School District of Orange County, et al., NAACP Amicus brief, 10–12. Examples of the studies cited by the NAACP in their amicus brief include Alain Locke, "The Dilemma of Segregation," *Journal of the Negro Education* 4, No. 3 (July 1935): 406–11; David T. Blose and Ambrose Caliver, "Statistics of the Education of Negroes: A Decade of Progress," Part I, Circular No. 215, US Office of Education, Department of Interior, 1943; Richard Sterner, *The Negro's Share: A Study of Income, Consumption, Housing and Public Assistance* (New York, Harper & Brothers, 1943); Gunnar Myrdal, *An American Dilemma: The Negro Problem and American Democracy* (New York, Harper & Brothers, 1944).

140. Foley, *Quest for Equality*, 108–10; Blanton, *George I. Sánchez*, 166–70.

141. CSO Project Tarango Interview; Tarango interview with González; Alex Maldonado interview; Santa Ana LULAC Council 147, Minutes, May 8, 1946, Personal Collection of Hector Tarango; "Santa Ana LULAC Council," *LULAC News*, June 1946; Amy Waters Yarsinske, *All for One & One for All: A Celebration of 75 Years of the League of United Latin American Citizens (LULAC)* (Virginia Beach, VA: Donning Company Publishers, 2004), 56–58; Aguirre, *LULAC Project*, 37–40, 118, 123–24; Strum, *Mendez v. Westminster*, 131.

142. John O. Gonzales, "Calling All LULACS," *LULAC News*, December 1946. See also Aguirre, *LULAC Project: Patriots with Civil Rights*, 125–28.

143. CSO Project Tarango Interview; Alex Maldonado interview; Aguirre, *LULAC Project: Patriots with Civil Rights*, 129, 133; Strum, *Mendez v. Westminster*, 131–32.

144. "Community Organization in Mexican American Colonies, 1946–1947, Box 20, Folder 19; and Box 22, Folder 17, "San Bernardino. Ruth and Ignacio," Fred Ross Papers, M0812, Department of Special Collections, Stanford University Libraries, Stanford, CA. See also Gabriel Thompson, *America's Social Arsonist: Fred Ross and Grassroots Organizing in the Twentieth Century* (Berkeley: University of California Press, 2016), 63–82.

145. Fred Ross, "Book Santa Ana," 5–8, Box 20, Folder 12, Fred Ross Papers, M0812, Department of Special Collections, Stanford University Libraries, Stanford, CA.

146. CSO Project Tarango Interview; Fred Ross, Letter to Hector Tarango, October 20, 1946, Personal Collection of Hector Tarango; Ross, "Book Santa Ana," 9.

147. CSO Project Tarango Interview; Ross, "Book Santa Ana," 7.

148. CSO Project Tarango Interview; Ross, "Book Santa Ana," 9–12. The emerging rift between Tarango and Manuel Veiga Jr. appears to have been rooted in Veiga's dislike of Fred Ross and his desire to maintain his professional and religious associations while serving as the first president of LULAC Council 147. See Ross, "Book Santa Ana"; CSO Project Tarango interview; Alex Maldonado interview. Divisions within Mexican American civil rights organizations were quite common during this era. See Gutiérrez, *Walls and Mirrors*, chapters 4 and 5; Blanton, "The Citizenship Sacrifice," 299–305.

149. Ross, "Book Santa Ana," 9. Indeed, Alex Maldonado recalled that the El Modena Unity League was essentially an "extension" of Santa Ana LULAC Council 147. Likewise, Isadore Gonzalez referred to the El Modena Unity League as a "suborganization" of Santa Ana LULAC. See Alex Maldonado interview and González, "Odds and Ends," *LULAC News*, February 1947.

150. Ross, "Book Santa Ana," 15–16. Hector Tarango, "Vote Yes on Proposition No. 11 and Smash Discrimination," Letter to Mexican American Voters in Orange County, Circa October 1946, Personal Collection of Hector Tarango; Fred Ross letter to Hector Tarango, October 20, 1946, Personal Collection of Hector Tarango.
151. Strum, *Mendez v. Westminster*, 128.
152. Santa Ana Board of Education, Minutes, September 12, 1946.
153. Santa Ana Board of Education, Minutes, November 14, 1946.
154. Ross, "Book Santa Ana," 13.
155. Ross, "Book Santa Ana," 29–32; Strum, *Mendez v. Westminster*, 129–30.
156. Ross, "Book Santa Ana," 29–40.
157. El Modena Elementary School District, Minutes, October 9, 1946. See also Ross, "Book Santa Ana," 42.
158. Ross, "Book Santa Ana," 40.
159. Ross, "Book Santa Ana," 35–40. According to the El Modeno board's own admission, between "25 or 30 Latin America children" were enrolled at Roosevelt by the October 9 meeting. These admissions, however, were based on a system of favoritism to children with lighter skin whose parents usually claimed Spanish ancestry, rather than efforts to abide by McCormick's ruling. See El Modena Elementary School District, Minutes, October 9, 1946.
160. Ross, "Book Santa Ana," 49.
161. "El Modena School Officials Announce New Class Setup," *Orange Daily News*, October 12, 1946.
162. El Modena Elementary School District, Minutes, October 9, 1946.
163. Ross, "Book Santa Ana," 49.
164. Alex Maldonado interview; Ross, "Book Santa Ana," 40, 52.
165. "County School Board Election Set Tomorrow," *Santa Ana Register*, May 15, 1947; Alex Maldonado interview.
166. Alex Maldonado interview.
167. Alex Maldonado interview.
168. Yarsinske, *All for One & One for All*, 32. See also David-James Gonzales interview with Hector Godinez Jr., December 17, 2022, audio recording, Newport Beach, CA.
169. CSO Project Tarango interview; Ross, "Book Santa Ana," 43–48; Alex Maldonado interview. See also Associated Farmers of Orange County, Inc., Letter to Isadore Gonzales, May 5, 1947, Personal Collection of Hector Tarango.
170. Yarsinske, *All for One & One for All*, 30, 32.
171. "Rancher Polls More Than 2-1 Vote," *Orange Daily News*, May 17, 1947; "Villa Park School Bonds Are Carried," *Orange Daily News*, May 17, 1947; "Orange School Election Brings Out Heaviest Vote on Record," *Santa Ana Register*, May 17, 1947.
172. Arriola, "*Mendez v. Westminster*," 200.
173. Alex Maldonado interview; Arriola, "*Mendez v. Westminster*," 201–3.
174. CSO Project Tarango interview; González interview with Tarango; Alex Maldonado interview.
175. Arriola, "Knocking on the Schoolhouse Door," 200.
176. *Westminster School Dist. of Orange County et al. v. Mendez et al.*, United States Court of Appeals for the Ninth Circuit, 161 F.2d 774; 1947 U.S. App.
177. As detailed by historian Mark Brilliant, Governor Warren was pressured by Los Angeles-based attorney and activist, Manuel Ruiz Jr., to repeal the state's

segregationist school codes in 1943. Warren later admitted to Ruiz that he felt section 8003 should be repealed though he refused to pressure the legislature to do so before the Ninth Circuit's ruling. Brilliant, *The Color of America Has Changed*, 82–84.

178. *Brown v. board of Education of Topeka*, 347 U.S. 483 (1954).

179. Alex Maldonado interview. Moreover, the ongoing struggle to desegregate Orange County schools was discussed by Manuel Veiga Jr. and Alex Maldonado, delegates of Santa Ana LULAC Council 147, at LULAC's national convention in Austin, Texas, June 11–13. *LULAC News*, August 1948, 12–13.

180. Treff, "The Education of Mexican Children in Orange County," 14.

181. 1930 US Census, Orange, CA, Placentia City, ED 35, Sheets 12A-12B, database with images s.v. "Alfred Aguirre" in household of "Joe Aguirre," *FamilySearch.org*; "California, World War II Draft Registration Cards, 1940–1945," database with images s.v. "Alfred Aguirre," *FamilySearch.org*.

182. Isabel Hlavac interview with Alfred Vargas Aguirre, August 18, 1995; Joseph V. Aguirre, "The Veterans and Citizens of Placentia: The Story of Placentia Latinos Who Organized After World War II to End School Segregation," unpublished manuscript, PYLUSD Desegregation folder, Local History Collection, Placentia Library, Placentia, CA; Aguirre, *LULAC Project*, 88–89. See also John Westcott, "Fighting for Equality in Placentia," *Orange County Register*, July 8, 2000.

183. Gilbert González interview with Alfred V. Aguirre, September 17–22, 1987, Gilbert G. González Interviews, University of California, Irvine Special Collections.

184. Aguirre, "The Veterans and Citizens of Placentia."

185. Aguirre, "The Veterans and Citizens of Placentia"; Aguirre, *LULAC Project*, 88.

186. Isabel Hlavac interview with Alfred V. Aguirre, August 18, 1995, transcript, Placentia Historical Commission Oral History Project, Center for Oral and Public History, California State University, Fullerton, Fullerton, CA; Gardner interview with Castro; Hlavac interview with Valadez.

187. Aguirre interview with Hlavac.

188. Kathleen Frazee interview with Rosalio Gonzalez and Alfred Aguirre, May 13, 2004, transcript, Center for Oral and Public History, California State University, Fullerton, Fullerton, CA; Eleanor Flores interview with Edmund M. Ponce, March 23, 1972, transcript, Center for Oral and Public History, California State University, Fullerton, Fullerton, CA. See also "Placita Santa Fe" in Vela, "53 Mexican Barrios/Colonias of Orange County." Census records also support the existence of a Mexican barrio in South Placentia. See 1930 US Census, Orange, CA, Placentia City, ED 35, Sheets 10B to 16B.

189. On the "white spatial imaginary," see Lipsitz, *How Racism Takes Place*, 13–14. The formation of urban barrios in Orange County was different from the process of "barrioization" in other parts of Southern California where existing Mexican neighborhoods where marginalized through the processes of displacement, outmigration, concentration, and redevelopment. On barrioization see Albert Camarillo, *Chicanos in a Changing Society: From Mexican Pueblos to American Barrios in Santa Barbara and Southern California, 1848–1930* (Cambridge, MA: Harvard University Press, 1979), 53–78. See also Haas, *Conquests and Historical Identities*, 166–89.

190. González interview with Valadez. Note, Valadez credited activists in El Modena (i.e., Hector Tarango and local Unity League leadership) as providing the momentum and tactics employed by the VCP.

191. Aguirre, "The Veterans and Citizens of Placentia."

192. Aguirre interview with Hlavac.

193. Aguirre interview with Hlavac; Alex Maldonado interview.

194. Aguirre interview with Hlavac. Alfred Aguirre recalled Warren Bradford as the "number one" proponent of segregation in the Placentia Unified School District. The district was so intent on segregation that it expanded the La Jolla School to include grades nine and ten, which was truly exceptional for Mexican schools in Orange County. See Kathleen Frazee interview with Alfred V. Aguirre, June 15, 2001, transcript, Center for Oral and Public History, California State University, Fullerton, Fullerton, CA.

195. Aguirre interview with Hlavac.

196. Aguirre interview with Hlavac.

197. Kathleen Frazee interview with Alfred V. Aguirre, June 21, 2001, transcript, Center for Oral and Public History, California State University, Fullerton, Fullerton, CA; González interview with Aguirre.

198. Aguirre interview with Frazee.

199. Aguirre, "The Veterans and Citizens of Placentia."

200. Aguirre interview with Frazee, June 21, 2001.

201. Aguirre, "The Veterans and Citizens of Placentia"; "Budget for School Set at Maximum," *Placentia Courier*, July 9, 1948; "Faculty for Schools Next Year Named: Board to Abandon Chapman Hill as Economy Measure," *Placentia Courier*, May 13, 1949.

202. "Is Candidate," *Placentia Courier*, May 13, 1949; "Record Voting for Election," *Placentia Courier*, May 27, 1949.

203. Natalie Navar interview with Frederick Aguirre, November 1, 2014, transcript, Center for Oral and Public History, California State University, Fullerton, Fullerton, CA. See also Frederick P. Aguirre, "About the Hispanic Bar Association of Orange County," Hispanic Bar Association Orange County, April 22, 2008, https://www.ochba.org/about.

204. "Segregation in Schools as a Violation of the XIVTH Amendment (Mendez v. Westminster School District, S.D. Cal. 1946)," *Columbia Law Review* 47, No. 2 (March 1947): 325–27; "Segregation in Public Schools: A Violation of 'Equal Protection of the Laws,'" *Yale Law Journal* 56, No. 6 (June 1947): 1059–67; "Constitutional Law-Equal Protection of the Laws-Schools-Requirement That Children of Mexican or Latin Descent Attend Separate Schools Held Invalid," *Minnesota Law Review* 30 (1945–1946): 646–47; "Segregation of Races in Public Schools and Its Relation to the Fourteenth Amendment," *Illinois Law Review* 42 (1947–1948): 545–49; Lester H. Phillips, "Segregation in Education: A California Case Study," *Phylon* 10, No. 4 (1949): 407–13; Wollenberg, *All Deliberate Speed*, 133–35, 179; San Miguel Jr., *"Let All of Them Take Heed,"* 118–19; Arriola, "Knocking on the Schoolhouse Door," 199–200, 207; Aguirre, *"Mendez v. Westminster School District:* How It Affected *Brown,"* 321–32; Powers and Patton, "Between Mendez and Brown: Gonzales v. Sheely (1951)," 127–71; Richard Delgado, Juan F. Perea, and Jean Stefancic eds., *Latinos and the Law: Cases and Materials* (St. Paul: Thomson/West, 2008), 42–45; Valencia, *Chicano Students and the Courts*, 22–42; Brilliant, *The Color of America Has Changed*, 58–88; Gonzales, "Mendez v. Westminster 1945–1947," 421–33; Gonzales, "Mexican Americans and the Long Fight Against Segregation in the Southwest," 129–35.

205. Valencia, *Chicano Students and the Courts*, 37–39. See also *James v. Marinship, et al.*, 25 Cal.2d 721 (1944).

206. "Segregation in Schools as a Violation of the XIVTH Amendment," 326–27.
207. First quote taken from Sandra Robbie interview with Robert L. Carter in Sandra Robbie, *Mendez vs. Westminster [Video recording]: For All the Children/Para Todos los Ninos. Huntington Beach, CA: KOCE-TV Foundation, 2002.* See also Strum, *Mendez v. Westminster*, 135; Foley, *Quest for Equality*, 108. Second quote from Brilliant, *The Color of America Has Changed*, 82, 59–60, 80–81.

CONCLUSION

1. Bud Lembke, "Barrios Begin to Play Role in Politics," *Los Angeles Times*, February 6, 1977.
2. Lembke, "Barrios Begin to Play Role in Politics," Aguirre, *LULAC Project*, 87–88, 91–92.
3. McGirr, *Suburban Warriors*, 4–9; Dochuk, *From Bible Belt to Sun Belt*, xv–xxi. For a recent historiographical assessment of the literature on the new Right see "Conservatism: A Round Table," *Journal of American History* 98, No. 3 (December 2011): 723–73.
4. "Santa Ana Council No. 147," *LULAC News*, January 1948; "Founding History," *LULAC News*, February 1955; Aguirre, *LULAC Project*, 55–56.
5. Alex Maldonado interview; *LULAC News*, July 1946, 13, 15; Gonzales, "Calling All LULACS," *LULAC News*, December 1946; Gonzales, "Odds and Ends Down California Way," *LULAC News*, February 1947; "Council no. 147, Santa Ana," *LULAC News*, August 1947; *LULAC News*, November 1947, 7, 9, 13–14, 17, 19–21.
6. Gonzales, "Calling all LULACS," *LULAC News*, December 1946.
7. "LULAC Council is installed in Bakersfield," *LULAC News*, April 1950; "In Our Mailbox," *LULAC News*, June 1955; Ramon Garces, "Lulacs in California," *LULAC News*, August 1955; "California," *LULAC News*, April 1956; *LULAC News*, July 1958, 13; "LULACS Name New Term Leaders," *Wilmington Daily Press Journal*, July 29, 1959; "LULAC Hosts Convention," *Progress-Bulletin*, May 1, 1960; "Santa Anan Heads U.S. Latin Group," *Independent*, July 4, 1960.
8. *LULAC News*, April 1950, 13; "Hector Godinez New Regional Governor of California," *LULAC News*, June 1957; *LULAC News*, May 1961; "Santa Ana Postmaster Godinez," *LULAC News*, June 1964; Aguirre, *LULAC Project*, 70, 86–92.
9. Alex Maldonado interview; Alfred Aguirre interview by Hlavac; Frederick Aguirre interview; Enrique Zuniga interview; Aguirre, *LULAC Project*, 13; Hector Godinez Jr. interview by David-James Gonzales, December 17, 2022, audio recording, Newport Beach, CA.
10. Joe O'Campo interview.
11. "Council No. 147, Santa Ana," *LULAC News*, August 1947; *LULAC News*, July 1950, 13; "Activities of the JR. LULAC Councils," *LULAC News*, March 1955; *LULAC News*, March 1958, 8; LULACS Cover 1100 Homes in Heart Drive," *Anaheim Bulletin*, February 28, 1959; " 'Little Lulacs' Made Official at Banquet," *Anaheim Bulletin*, April 29, 1959; "Placentia Youth Heads Jr. LULAC," *Santa Ana Register*, July 22, 1965; "Fullerton Council Members Come Away with Several State Offices" and "Fullerton Council Receive Top National Honors," *LULAC News*, July 1966; Aguirre, *LULAC Project*, 93–96, 194, 198–201, 225.

　　　On the role of Mexican American women within LULAC see Cynthia E. Orozco, "Ladies LULAC," *Handbook of Texas* (Austin: Texas State Historical Association, 1995); Orozco, *No Mexicans, Women, or Dogs Allowed*, 196–219; Cynthia E. Orozco, *Agent of Change: Adela Sloss-Vento* (Austin: University of

Texas Press, 2020); "The Women of LULAC," *League of United Latin American Citizens*, accessed March 1, 2024, https://lulac.org/about/history/women/. On the role of Chicanas/Latinas in movement history see Vicki L. Ruiz, *Cannery Women, Cannery Lives: Mexican Women, Unionization, and the California Food Processing Industry, 1930–1950* (Albuquerque: University of New Mexico Press, 1987); Maria Linda Apodaca, "They Kept the Home Fires Burning: Mexican-American Women and Social Change," PhD diss. (University of California, Irvine, 1994); Margaret Rose, "Gender and Civic Activism in Mexican American Barrios in California: The Community Service Organization, 1947–1962," in Joanne Meyerowitz ed., *Not June Cleaver: Women and Gender in Postwar America, 1945–1960*, (Philadelphia: Temple University Press, 1994); Ruiz, *From Out of the Shadows*; Maylei Blackwell, *Chicana Power!: Contested Histories of Feminism in the Chicano Movement* (Austin: University of Texas Press, 2011); Enriqueta L. Vasquez, *The Women of La Raza: An Epic History of Chicana/Mexican American Peoples* (USA: El Grito del Norte, 2016); Dionne Espinoza, María Eugenia Cotera, and Maylei Blackwell eds. *Chicana Movidas: New Narratives of Activism and Feminism in the Movement Era* (Austin: University of Texas Press, 2018).

12. "1957 Convention to California," *LULAC News*, June 1956; "28th National Convention of the League of United Latin American Citizens Convened at Disneyland Hotel Anaheim, California," *LULAC News*, June 1957, 2; "LULAC Convention Set for Buena Park," *Santa Ana Register*, February 2, 1958; "Anaheim Lulacs to Host Annual Confab April 19," *Anaheim Bulletin*, April 15, 1959; "Anaheim LULACS Are Hosts Unit to Annual Regional Convention Here," *Anaheim Bulletin*, May 2, 1959; "LULAC Maps Convention Plans," *Santa Ana Register*, April 30, 1962; "LULAC Convention Set Here July 4," *Anaheim Bulletin*, June 28, 1963; "Stanton LULAC to Host '69 Convention," *Anaheim Bulletin*, July 7, 1967. See also 1957 convention program in Aguirre, *LULAC Project*, 216–21.

13. "III. Reports of Regional Governors," *LULAC News*, April 1956; Goodwin K. Knight to California LULAC, January 30, 1958, copy of letter provided to author courtesy of Hector Godinez Jr. See also Aguirre, *LULAC Project*, 222.

14. Alex Maldonado interview.

15. Ten years after McCormick's decision, Danny Olivas confirmed to the LULAC News that "Elimination of All segregation in the Orange County Schools" was complete. "III. Reports of Regional Governors," *LULAC News*, April 1956.

16. "Santa Ana to Hold Election April 12," *Latin American*, April 7, 1949; "What Price Unity!," *Latin American*, April 28, 1949; "Keynote Talk," *Santa Ana Register*, April 22, 1958; "LULAC's Elect Governor," *Santa Ana Register*, April 26, 1959; "Gil Klima Our Choice for Marshal," *Santa Ana Register*, May 29, 1960; "Cranston Slates County Conclave," *Santa Ana Register*, July 12, 1962.

17. "Stanton's Incorporation Authorized by Residents," *Anaheim Bulletin*, May 16, 1956; "Placentia Vote Recalls 3 on Board," *Santa Ana Register*, March 12, 1958; "Breting, Aguirre, Victorious in Placentia Vote," *Santa Ana Register*, April 9, 1958; "Placentia Elects Gomez, Winney," *Anaheim Bulletin*, April 11, 1962; "New City Clerk," *Santa Ana Register*, July 29, 1969; John Yench, "Jess Perez New Mayor of Orange," *Anaheim Bulletin*, April 19, 1972; "Adios Zavala," *El Quetzal*, April 1977; Alfred Aguirre interview by Hlavac; Frederick Aguirre interview; Jess Perez interview by Jane Mueller, June 15, 1977, transcript, Center for Oral and Public History, California State University, Fullerton, Fullerton, CA; "Placentia Vet Fought to End Segregation," *Orange County Register*, February 2, 2006; Heather Mcrea, "400 Attend Funeral Services for Alfred Aguirre," *Orange County Register*, January 15, 2008; "Stanton: The City that Was Born Twice," *Orange County Register*, May 20, 2010.

18. "Political Front in County," *Santa Ana Register*, October 7, 1960; Frank Martinez, "Political Activity Among Latin-Americans Charged to Union," *Santa Ana Register*, October 12, 1960; "Demo Women Slate O'Campo," *Santa Ana Register*, April 3, 1963. On Latinos and the development of multiethnic political coalitions in California see Kenneth C. Burt, *The Search for a Civic Voice* (Claremont: Regina Books, 2007); Bernstein, *Bridges of Reform*; Brilliant, *The Color of America Has Changed*; Sánchez, *Beyond Alliances*; Sánchez, *Boyle Heights*.

19. Bob Torres interview by Baez.

20. "From Texas Thorns to Orange Council," *Santa Ana Register*, April 14, 1968.

21. "Jess Perez New Mayor of Orange," *Anaheim Bulletin*, April 19, 1972.

22. "Cites Mexican Relief Status," *Santa Ana Register*, March 15, 1939; "Mexican-Americans Spur County Political Machine," *Santa Ana Register*, October 31, 1963. Santa Ana was one of the few cities in the county that realized a dramatic increase in the Latino population as white residents moved to the suburbs during the postwar decades. By 1980, 44.5 percent of Santa Ana's residents were Latino. See Erualdo R. González, *Latino City: Urban Planning, Politics, and the Grassroots* (New York: Routledge, 2017), 22.

23. "Political Front in County," *Santa Ana Register*, October 7, 1960; "Sen. Chavez Urges Heavy Vote Turnout," *Santa Ana Register*, October 10, 1960; "Political Activity Among Latin-Americans Charged to Union," *Santa Ana Register*, October 12, 1960; "Viva Kennedy Clubs Slate Dinner, Dance," *Anaheim Bulletin*, October 26, 1960.

24. "Political Front in County," *Santa Ana Register*, October 7, 1960.

25. Joe O'Campo interview by Natalie Navar, June 15, 2015, Center for Oral and Public History, California State University, Fullerton, Fullerton, CA.

26. Kenneth C. Burt, *The Search for a Civic Voice: California Latino Politics* (Claremont: Regina Books, 2007), 194. See also Ignacio M. García, *Viva Kennedy: Mexican Americans in Search of Camelot* (College Station: Texas A&M University Press, 2000), 5–8; Benjamin Francis-Fallon, *The Rise of the Latino Vote: A History* (Cambridge: Harvard University Press, 2020), 55–56, 83.

27. "Sen. Chavez Urges Heavy Vote Turnout," *Santa Ana Register*, October 10, 1960; Telegram from J. Carlos McCormick to Hector Godinez, June 29, 1961; Telegram from John F. Kennedy to Hector Godinez, June 29, 1951; Burt, *Search for a Civic Voice*, 197.

28. "Hector Godinez Recommended for Postmaster, Petitions Begin to Circulate in 'Disguised' Protest," *The Latin Citizen*, February 23, 1961; James B. Utt to Mr. Rod Gonzales, April 21, 1959, letter provided to author by Hector Godinez Jr.; "Godinez Sworn in as S.A. Postmaster in Midst of Charges Raised by James," *Santa Ana Register*, April 1, 1961; "Godinez Appointed to S.A. Postmaster's Job," *Los Angeles Times*, April 6, 1961; "Santa Ana Postmaster Grateful for Backing," *Santa Ana Register*, April 5, 1961.

29. "Postmasters Confirmed," *Santa Ana Register*, July 13, 1962; "Local Postal Receipt Tally: 2.8 Million," *Santa Ana Independent*, December 28, 1961; "Postal Award," *Santa Ana Register*, December 2, 1965; "Presidential Citation," *Santa Ana Register*, January 27, 1965; "Godinez Candidate for Postmaster General," *LULAC News*, Vol. 34, No. 4, Santa Ana, October 1971; "Hector Godinez; First Latino Postmaster," *Los Angeles Times*, May 17, 1999; Amalia Gonzales interview by Hector Godinez, October 24, 1974, transcript, Center for Oral and Public History, California State University, Fullerton, Fullerton, CA.

30. Joe O'Campo interview; "Coronation Ceremonies," *Santa Ana Register*, May 8, 1961; "Brown Due Here for Campaign Tour," *Anaheim Bulletin*, October 11, 1962; "New County Judge Named," *Santa Ana Register*, December 22, 1966; "New Judge to Be Sworn In, Seated in Anaheim," *Anaheim Bulletin*, December 26, 1966.

31. "Mexican-Americans Spur County Political Machine," *Santa Ana Register*, October 21, 1963. On Hispanics/Latinos and the Republican Party see Richard Santillan and Federico A. Subervi-Vélez, "Latino Participation in Republican Party Politics in California," in Bryan O. Jackson and Michael B. Preston, eds., *Racial and Ethnic Politics in California* (Berkeley: IGS Press, 1991), 285–319; Linda Chavez, *An Unlikely Conservative* (New York: Basic Books, 2002); Henry M. Ramirez, *A Chicano in the White House: The Nixon No One Knew* (Self-published, 2013); Gene Kopelson, "'Ya Basta?!' Ronald Reagan's 1966 Success with Mexican American Voters," *California History* 91, November 4 (Winter 2014): 31–42; Geraldo Cadava, *The Hispanic Republican: The Shaping of an American Political Identity, From Nixon to Trump* (New York: Ecco, 2020).

32. "Mexican-Americans Spur County Political Machine," *Santa Ana Register*, October 21, 1963.

33. Lino Tinajero, "How the Movement of 'Mexican-American for Nixon' Was Born," *Despertar*, October 31, 1962. See also political ads thanking Mexican American voters for helping to re-elect Orange County Sheriff James A. Musick and Republican Congressman James B. Utt in the June 6, 1958 edition of *Noticias*, a local Spanish-language weekly. For more on the Luis and Phoebe Olivos family and their role as cultural brokers in Orange County see David-James Gonzales, "El Cine Yost and the Power of Place for Mexican Migrants in Orange County, California, 1930–1990," *Journal of American Ethnic History* 39, No. 4 (Summer 2020): 42–59.

34. "Editorial," *Despertar*, October 31, 1962.

35. Lino Tinajero, "Thoughts to Dwell on Concerning Mr. Richard M. Nixon's Campaign," *Despertar*, October 31, 1962.

36. "Verdad: El Record de Mr. Brown," *Despertar*, October 31, 1962; "Problemas Y la Actitud de Richard Nixon Ante ellos," *Despertar*, October 31, 1962.

37. "Mexican-Americans Spur County Political Machine," *Santa Ana Register*, October 21, 1963.

38. "No Vote por Brown," *Despertar*, October 31, 1962.

39. Miriam Pawel, *The Browns of California: The Family Dynasty that Transformed a State and Shaped a Nation* (New York: Bloomsbury, 2018), 169; Burt, *Search for a Civic Voice*, 205–8; Kenneth C. Burt, "Pat Brown and the Emergence of Latinos in California Politics," *Edmund G. "Pat" Brown Institute for Public Affairs* (2014), http://files.ctctcdn.com/17fd796f001/a05cee9a-a2d7-4a72-b9cb-d716d54bb782.pdf. On the success of Mexican Americans in receiving patronage appointments and elected office nationally see San Miguel Jr., *In the Midst of Radicalism*, 6–16, 70–75.

40. Charles Sutton, "Mexican-Americans Move Up Social Ladder," *Press-Telegram*, January 6, 1964.

41. "Hispanic Postmasters: Rising Through the Ranks Over 40 Years of Service," *Hispanic Community Magazine*, Vol. 4, No. 3 (July/August 1988); Hector Godinez Jr. interview; Alfonso Olivos interview with David-James Gonzales, December 20, 2021, audio recording, Santa Ana, CA.

42. Sutton, "Mexican-Americans Move Up Social Ladder."

43. On the politics of status see García, *The Making of a Mexican American Mayor*, x–xi, 5–6; Everett Ladd Jr., *Political Leadership in the South* (Ithaca: Cornell University Press, 1966), 156.

44. Jill Lepore, *These Truths: A History of the United States* (New York: W.W. Norton, 2018), xv. Among these founding principles, perhaps none have been so thoroughly debated as the equality ideal. See Jack N. Rakove ed., "Introduction," in *The Annotated U.S. Constitution and Declaration of Independence* (Cambridge, MA: The Belknap Press of Harvard University Press, 2009), 4–7, 22–23, 69–72.

45. Nikole Hannah Jones, et al., *The 1619 Project: A New Origin Story* (New York: One World, 2021), 11.

BIBLIOGRAPHY

Primary Sources

Manuscript Collections
Anaheim Heritage Center Archives and Reading Room
Barrios Collection
Ku Klux Klan Collection
Mexican American Collection

California State University, Fullerton, Pollack Library,
Special Collections and Archives
A.S. Bradford Collection
Anaheim Citrus Fruit Association
Citrus Association Records
Citrus Books and Pamphlets Collection
Citrus Industry Magazine Collection
Ed Salter Collection
Foothill Groves Inc. Records
Local History Subject Files
Placentia Mutual Orange Growers Records
Placentia Orange Growers Association Records
Sunkist Growers Incorporated Records
Valencia Orange Association Committee
Yorba Linda Citrus Association Records

California State University, Fullerton, Lawrence de Graaf Center for
Oral and Public History
Anaheim Community History Project
California LULAC Project
California School Desegregation Project
Citrus Industry Project
Fullerton Community History Project
Iowa Migrants and Conservatism in Southern CA Project
Irvine El Toro Community History Project
La Habra Community History Project
Mexican American Project
Mexican American Veterans Project
Orange City Collection

Orange County Mexican Colonias Project
Orange County Project
Personal and Family History Collection
Placentia Historical Society Project
Placentia Packing Houses Project
Santa Ana Community History Project
Villa Park Orchard Association Project
Yorba Linda Project

California State University, Northridge, Special Collections and Archives
Supreme Council of the Mexican American Movement Collection, 1942–1955

Chapman University, Special Collections and Archives
Charles C. Chapman Citrus Speeches
Mendez v. Westminster Archive, 1920–2008

Fullerton Public Library, Local History Room
Alex Bernal Collection
Bastanchury Ranch Collection
Photograph Collection

Hector Godinez Family Collection
National Archives and Records Administration, Riverside, CA
Fourteenth Census of the United States
Fifteenth Census of the United States
Mendez et al. v. Westminster et al. Court Records
Sixteenth Census of the United States

Orange County Archives
Digital Photograph Collection
Directories
Orange County Board of Supervisors Minutes
Orange County Board of Supervisors Records
Orange County Map Collection
Orange County Planning Commission Minutes
McFadden
Sanborn Fire Insurance Maps
Santa Ana Journal
Santiago Packing House Records
Tom Pulley Crate Label Collection
Willard Smith Papers

Orange County Historical Society Archives
Alice Grimshaw Collection
George Amerige Collection
James Sleeper Collection
Santiago Fruit Growers Association Annual Records
Tom Pulley Collection
Virginia Carpenter Collection

Orange Public Library, Local History Room
Orange Daily News
Lorenzo Ramirez Collection
Shades of Orange Oral History Collection
Shades of Orange Photograph Collection

Lorenzo Ramirez Family Collection
Placentia Public Library, Local History Room
Oral History Collection
Photograph Collection
Placentia Courier
Subject Files

Santa Ana Public Library, Local History Room
Rare Books Collection

Santa Ana Unified School District Public Information Office
Santa Ana Board of Education Minutes

Stanford University, Cecil H. Green Library, Special Collections
Community Service Organization History Project Records
Fred Ross Papers
Mendez v. Westminster: Research Materials, 1879–1995

University of California, Irvine, Special Collections and Archives
California Newspaper Collection, 1848–1994
Don Meadows Papers
Gilbert G. González Interviews
Irvine Valencia Growers Packing House Records
Jim Sleeper Papers
Orange County Newspaper and Magazine Clippings Collection
Samuel Armor Papers
Willis H. Warner Papers
Works Progress Administration Collection on Orange County, CA

University of California, Los Angeles, Special Collections
Mexican American Voice

University of Southern California, Special Collections
Rare Books Collection

Westminster Unified School District Public Information Office
Westminster Elementary School Board of Trustees Minutes

Whittier College, Wardman Library, Special Collections and Archives
YMCA Mexican Voice

Government Documents

1920 US Census, Federal Manuscript, Orange County, California.

1930 US Census, Federal Manuscript, Orange County, California.

1940 US Census, Federal Manuscript, Orange County, California.

1950 US Census, Federal Manuscript, Orange County, California.

Arizona County Marriage Records, 1865–1972.

California Department of Finance. "1850–2020 Historical US Census Populations of Counties and Incorporated Cities/Towns in California." August 13, 2021.

California Great Register of Voters, 1900–1968.

California World War II Draft Registration Cards, 1940–1945.

United States Congress, Senate Committee on Education and Labor. *Violations of Free Speech and Rights of Labor*. Hearings Before a Subcommittee of the Committee on Education and Labor, Part 56. Washington, DC: Government Printing Office, 1940.

United States Congress, Senate Committee on Education and Labor. *Violations of Free Speech and Rights of Labor*. Report of the Committee on Education and Labor, Part I, Washington, DC: Government Printing Office, 1942.

United States Congress, Senate Committee on Education and Labor. *Violations of Free Speech and Rights of Labor*. Report of the Committee on Education and Labor, Part IV, Washington, DC: Government Printing Office, 1942.

United States Department of Agriculture. "Florida Citrus Fruit: Acreage, Production, Utilization, Prices and Tree Numbers," accessed February 8, 2022, https://www.nass.usda.gov/Statistics_by_State/Florida/Publications/Historical_Summaries/citrus/cs/acreage,%20production%20%20utilization-1948.pdf.

Newspapers and Periodicals

Accion

Afro-American

Anaheim Bulletin

Anaheim Gazette

California Citrograph

Despertar

El Anunciador Mexicano

El Espectador

El Hispano

El Nuevo Mundo

El Politico

El Quetzal

Forward

Fullerton News Tribune

Fullerton Observer

Hispanic Community Magazine

La Opinion

La Prensa

Latin American

Latin Citizen

Los Angeles Herald
Los Angeles Times
LULAC News
Mexican Voice
Noticias
OC Weekly
Orange Coast Magazine
Orange County Illustrated
Orange County News
Orange County Register
Orange Daily News
Pittsburg Courier
Placentia Courier
Press-Telegram
Progress-Bulletin
Santa Ana Independent
Santa Ana Journal
Santa Ana Register
The American Magazine
The Nation
The Weekly Review
Time Magazine
Tustin News
Wilmington Daily Press Journal

Oral History Interviews

Aguirre, Alfred V. Interview by Gilbert González, September 17, 1987, audio recording, Gilbert G. González Interviews, MS.R.144, University of California, Irvine Special Collections, Irvine, CA.

Aguirre, Alfred V. Interview by Isabel Hlavac, August 18, 1995, transcript, Center for Oral and Public History, California State University, Fullerton, Fullerton, CA.

Aguirre, Alfred V. Interview by Kathleen Frazee, June 15 and 21, 2001, transcript, Center for Oral and Public History, California State University, Fullerton, Fullerton, CA.

Aguirre, Frederick. Interview by Natalie Navar, November 1, 2014, transcript, Center for Oral and Public History, California State University, Fullerton, Fullerton, CA.

Barrera, Fred. Interview by Chapman University, 2006, video recording, Shades of Orange Oral History Project, Orange Public Library, Orange, CA.

Bowen, Helen. Interview by Kay Heil, October 28, 1973, transcript, Center for Oral and Public History, California State University, Fullerton, Fullerton, CA.

Bradford, A.S. "Bud." Interview by Lynda Baker and Kathleen Frazee, February 3, 2000, transcript, Center for Oral and Public History, California State University, Fullerton, Fullerton, CA.

Bryant (Bernal), Irene Louise. Interview by Luis F. Fernandez, January 22, 2011, audio recording, Center for Oral and Public History, California State University, Fullerton, Fullerton, CA.

Castro, Edward. Interview by Jeanette Gardner, January 14, 2009, transcript, Center for Oral and Public History, California State University, Fullerton, Fullerton, CA.

Castro, Leo. Interview by Chapman University, 2006, video recording, Shades of Orange Oral History Project, Orange Public Library, Orange, CA.

Castro, Leo. Interview by David-James Gonzales, July 30, 2016, audio recording, Orange, CA.

Chapman, C. Stanley. Interview by Arlene R. Sayre, February 14 and March 29, 1968, transcript, Center for Oral and Public History, California State University, Fullerton, Fullerton, CA.

Chapman, C. Stanley. Interview by Nita June Busby, October 16 and November 18, 1975, transcript, Center for Oral and Public History, California State University, Fullerton, Fullerton, CA.

Chapman, C. Stanley. Interview by C. Stanley Chapman Jr., January 6, 1979, transcript, Center for Oral and Public History, California State University, Fullerton, Fullerton, CA.

Christiansen, Jeanne. Interview by Kathleen Frazee, April 14, 2004, transcript, Center for Oral and Public History, California State University, Fullerton, Fullerton, CA.

Collin, Phillip. Interview by Chapman University, 2006, video recording, Shades of Orange Oral History Project, Orange Public Library, Orange, CA.

Duran, Burt. Interview by Ronald Banderes, May 10, 1971, transcript, Center for Oral and Public History, California State University at Fullerton, Fullerton, CA.

Duran, Lucy Cornejo. Interview by Chapman University, 2006, video recording, Shades of Orange Oral History Project, Orange Public Library, Orange, CA.

Figueroa, Raymond M. Interview by Chapman University, 2006, video recording, Shades of Orange Oral History Project, Orange Public Library, Orange, CA.

Ford, John Anson. Interview by Christine Valenciana, September 4, 1971, transcript, Center for Oral and Public History, California State University, Fullerton, Fullerton, CA.

Garcia, Gilbert. Interview by Chapman University, 2006, video recording, Shades of Orange Oral History Project, Orange Public Library, Orange, CA.

Gauer, Melbourne. Interview by Kathy Landis, March 16, 1974, transcript, Center for Oral and Public History, California State University, Fullerton, Fullerton, CA.

Godinez, Hector. Interview by Amalia Gonzales, October 24, 1974, transcript, Center for Oral and Public History, California State University, Fullerton, Fullerton, CA.

Godinez, Hector, Jr. Interview by David-James Gonzales, December 17, 2022, audio recording, Newport Beach, CA.

Gomez, Daniel. Interview by Christopher Arriola, July 26, 1991, transcript, Mendez v. Westminster: research materials, M0938, Department of Special Collections, Stanford University Libraries, Stanford, CA.

Gonzalez, Rosalio and Alfred Aguirre. Interview by Kathleen Frazee, May 13, 2004, transcript, Center for Oral and Public History, California State University, Fullerton, Fullerton, CA.

Guzman, Paul. Interview by Chapman University, 2006, video recording, Shades of Orange Oral History Project, Orange Public Library, Orange, CA.

Guzman, Virginia. Interview by Ray Rast, July 31, 2011, audio recording, Center for Oral and Public History, California State University, Fullerton, Fullerton, CA.

Haught, Teresa. Interview by Luis F. Fernandez, January 22, 2011, audio recording, Center for Oral and Public History, California State University, Fullerton, Fullerton, CA.

Hernandez, Rudy. Interview by Melissa Lee, August 2, 1982, audio recording, Center for Oral and Public History, California State University, Fullerton, Fullerton, CA.

Kelly, Arletta. Interview by B.E. Schmidt, May 22, 1968, transcript, Center for Oral and Public History, California State University, Fullerton, Fullerton, CA.

Kelly, Arletta. Interview by Fred Zuniga, May 20, 1971, transcript, Center for Oral and Public History, California State University, Fullerton, Fullerton, CA.

Koral, Joseph P. Interview by Suzanne Wood, February 24, 1984, transcript, Center for Oral and Public History, California State University, Fullerton, Fullerton, CA.

Lopez, Gloria Valdez. Interview by Melissa Lee, May 31, 1982, audio recording, Center for Oral and Public History, California State University, Fullerton, Fullerton, CA.

Lyon, LeRoy E., Jr. Interview by Jacqueline S. Reinier, March 18 and 31, 1988, transcript, Center for Oral and Public History, California State University, Fullerton, Fullerton, CA.

Maldonado, Alex. Interview by Ray Rast, May 27, 2011, audio recording, Center for Oral and Public History, California State University, Fullerton, Fullerton, CA.

Maldonado, Alex. Interview by Alex Tewes, January 26, 2012, transcript, Center for Oral and Public History, California State University, Fullerton, Fullerton, CA.

Marks, C.J. Interview by Gilbert G. González, November 12, 1986, UCI Libraries Special Collections and Archives, Irvine, CA.

Mendez, Felicitas. Interview by Alfredo H. Zúñiga, September 10, 1975, UCI Libraries Special Collections and Archives, Irvine, CA.

Mendez, Felicitas. Interview by Gilbert G. González, 1987, audio recording, Gilbert G. González Interviews, MS.R.144, University of California, Irvine Special Collections, Irvine, CA.

de Montoya, Jessie Corona. Interviewed by Esther Katz, October 27, 1975, transcript, Center for Oral and Public History, California State University, Fullerton, Fullerton, CA.

Morales, Augapito. Interview by Chapman University, 2006, video recording, Shades of Orange Oral History Project, Orange Public Library, Orange, CA.

Moreno, Pete. Interview by Lucy McDonald, June 30, 1982 and July 7, 1982, audio recording, Center for Oral and Public History, California State University, Fullerton, Fullerton, CA.

Munoz, Alfred. Interview by unknown, 1982, audio recording, Center for Oral and Public History, California State University, Fullerton, Fullerton, CA.

Negrete, Art. Interview by Ronald Banderes, May 12, 1971, transcript, Center for Oral and Public History, California State University, Fullerton, Fullerton, CA.

O'Campo, Joe. Interview by Natalie Navar, June 15, 2015, transcript, Center for Oral and Public History, California State University, Fullerton, Fullerton, CA.

Oftelie, Stan. Interview by David-James Gonzales, August 24, 2016, audio recording, Santa Ana, CA.

Olivos, Alfonso. Interview by David-James Gonzales, December 21, 2021, audio recording, Santa Ana, CA.

Olivos, Louis, Jr. and Gay Olivos. Interview by David-James Gonzales, August 29, 2016, audio recording, Santa Ana, CA.

Peralta, Clarence. Interview by Cindy Peronto, May 26, 1982, audio recording, Center for Oral and Public History, California State University, Fullerton, Fullerton, CA.

Perez, Jess. Interview by Jane Mueller, June 15, 1977, transcript, Center for Oral and Public History, California State University, Fullerton, Fullerton, CA.

Poblano, Esther. Interview by Chapman University, 2006, video recording, Shades of Orange Oral History Project, Orange Public Library, Orange, CA.

Ponce, Edmund M. Interview with Eleanor Flores, March 23, 1972, transcript, Center for Oral and Public History, California State University, Fullerton, Fullerton CA.

Ramirez de Soto, Josefina. Interview by Maria Quintero, June 24, 2010, transcript, Center for Oral and Public History, California State University, Fullerton, Fullerton, CA.

Reyes, Stephen. Interview by Brooke Larsen Garlock, November 10, 1983, transcript, Pasadena Centennial Committee, Pasadena Public Library, Pasadena, CA.

Reynoso, Cruz. Interview by Germaine La Berge, 2002–2004, Oral History Office, The Bancroft Library, University of California, Berkeley, Berkeley, CA.

Salas, Celia. Interview by Tabitha R. Frost, December 3, 2002, transcript, Center for Oral and Public History, California State University, Fullerton, Fullerton, CA.

Tarango, Hector Interview by Gilbert González, April 15, 1989, audio recording, Gilbert G. González Interviews, MS.R.144, University of California, Irvine Special Collections, Irvine, CA.

Tarango, Hector. Interview by Herman Gallegos, Eric Kutner, and Gilbert Padilla, transcript, November 15, 2005, Community Service Organization, History Project Records, M1669, Department of Special Collections and University Archives, Stanford University Libraries, Stanford, CA.

Thomson, Rex. Interview by Christine Valenciana, August 4, 1976, transcript, Center for Oral and Public History, California State University, Fullerton, Fullerton, CA.

Torres, Bob. Interview by Elizabeth Baez, July 27, 1982, audio recording, Center for Oral and Public History, California State University, Fullerton, Fullerton, CA.

Torres, Bob. Interview by Christopher Arriola, August 16, 1991, transcript, Mendez v. Westminster: research materials, M0938, Department of Special Collections, Stanford University Libraries, Stanford, CA.

Torres, Bob, Jr. Interview by David-James Gonzales, June 27, 2019, Orange, CA.

Valadez, Gualberto. Interview by Gilbert González, 1987, recording, Gilbert G. González Interviews, MS.R.144, Special Collections and Archives, University of California, Irvine Libraries.

Valadez, Gualberto. Interview by Isabel Hlavac, August 16, 1995, transcript, Placentia Historical Committee Oral History Project, Center for Oral and Public History, California State University, Fullerton, Fullerton, CA.

Valadez, Gualberto. Interview by Jose Alamillo, July 21, 2005, audio recording, Yorba Linda, CA.

Valencia, Oscar. Interview by Christopher Arriola, August 23, 1991, transcript, Mendez v. Westminster: research materials, M0938, Department of Special Collections, Stanford University Libraries, Stanford, CA.

Vargas, Virginia. Interview by George Maisch, April 27, 1971, transcript, Center for Oral and Public History, California State University at Fullerton, Fullerton, CA.

Vasquez, Choi. Interview by Ronald Banderes, May 17, 1970, transcript, Center for Oral and Public History, California State University at Fullerton, Fullerton, CA.

Venegas, Joe. Interview by A. Dean Tatom, March 24, 1971, transcript, Center for Oral and Public History, California State University, Fullerton, Fullerton, CA.

Villalobos, Robert. Interview by Harvey Reyes, October 12, 2006, audio recording, Center for Oral and Public History, California State University, Fullerton, Fullerton, CA.

Whitten, Chester. Interview by Gilbert González, August 20, 1987, Gilbert G. González Interviews, MS.R.144, Special Collections and Archives, University of California, Irvine Libraries, Irvine, CA.

Zepeda, Phyllis Ramirez. Interview by Olivia Andrade and Lizette Ramirez, January 23, 2016, audio recording, Orange Public Library and History Center, Orange, CA.

Zuniga, Enrique. "Kiki." Interview by David-James Gonzales, June 27, 2019, audio recording, Yorba Linda, CA.

Published Primary Sources

Armor, Samuel. *History of Orange County California: With Biographical Sketches of The Leading Men and Women of the County Who Have Been identified with Its Growth and Development from the Early Days to the Present.* Los Angeles, CA: Historic Record Company, 1921.

Brook, Harry Ellington. *The Land of Sunshine: Southern California: An Authentic Description of its Natural Features, Resources and Prospects.* Los Angles: World's Fair Association and Bureau of Information, 1893.

California State Department of Education. *A Guide for Teachers of Beginning Non-English Speaking Children.* Sacramento: California State Printing Office, 1933.

Carpenter, Virginia L. *Placentia, A Pleasant Place.* Santa Ana: Pioneer Press, 1977.

Commons, John R. *Race and Immigrants in America.* New York: The Macmillan Company, 1907.

"Constitutional Law-Equal Protection of the Laws-Schools-Requirement That Children of Mexican or Latin Descent Attend Separate Schools Held Invalid." *Minnesota Law Review* 30 (1945–1946): 646–47.

Cook, A.J. *California Citrus Culture.* Sacramento: California State Printing Office, 1913.

Cumberland, W.W. *Cooperative Marketing: Its Advantages as Exemplified in the California Fruit Growers Exchange.* Trenton, NJ: Princeton University Press, 1917.

Fogleberg, Nephtune and A.W. McKay. *The Citrus Industry and the California Fruit Growers Exchange.* Washington, DC: Farm Security Administration, 1940.

French, Will J., G.H. Hecke, and Anna A. Saylor. *Mexicans in California: A Report of Governor C.C. Young's Mexican Fact-Finding Committee.* San Francisco: State Printing Office, 1930.

Governor C.C. Young's Mexican Fact-Finding Committee. *Mexicans in California.* San Francisco, CA: State of California, 1930.

MacCurdy, Rahno Mabel. *The History of the California Fruit Growers Exchange.* Los Angeles: [G. Rice & Sons], 1925.

Nordhoff', Charles. *California for Health, Pleasure and Residence: A Book for Travelers and Settlers.* New York: Harper & Brothers Publishers, 1873.

Plummer, Louis E. *A History of the Fullerton Union High School and Fullerton Junior College, 1893–1943.* Fullerton: Fullerton Junior College Press, 1949.

Powel, G. Harold. *Cooperation in Agriculture.* New York: The Macmillan Company, 1921.

"Segregation in Public Schools: A Violation of 'Equal Protection of the Laws,'" *Yale Law Journal* 56, No. 6 (June 1947): 1059–67.

"Segregation of Races in Public Schools and Its Relation to the Fourteenth Amendment." *Illinois Law Review* 42 (1947–1948): 545–46.

"Segregation in Schools as a Violation of the XIVTH Amendment (Mendez v. Westminster School District, S.D. Cal. 1946)." *Columbia Law Review* 47, No. 2 (March 1947): 325–27.

Sociedad Progresista Mexicana. *Historia de la Sociedad Progresista Mexicana.* Los Angeles: Cinco Decadas Press, 1996.

Sunkist Growers. *The Story of California Oranges and Lemons*. Los Angeles: California Fruit Growers Exchange, 1932.

Sunkist Growers. *Heritage of Gold: The First 100 Years of Sunkist Growers, Inc. 1893–1993*. Los Angeles: Sunkist Growers, 1994.

Talbert, Thomas B. ed. *The Historical Volume and Reference Works: Orange County*. Vols. 1–3. Whittier, CA: Historical Publishers, 1963.

Teague, Charles C. *Fifty Years a Rancher*. Los Angeles: The Ward Ritchie Press, 1944.

Weathers, Lewis G. "History of the Citrus Research Center," (1982), Agriculture and Natural Resources Repository, University of California, https://ucanr.edu/rep ository/view.cfm?article=72292%20&search=. Accessed March 18, 2022.

Published Secondary Sources

Agamben, Giorgio. *Means Without End: Notes on Politics*. Minneapolis: University of Minnesota Press, 2000.

Aguirre, Frederick P. "*Mendez v. Westminster School District*: How It Affected Brown v. Board of Education." *Journal of Hispanic Higher Education* 4, No. 4 (October 2005): 321–32.

Akins, Damon B. and William J. Bauer Jr., *We Are the Land: A History of Native California*. Oakland: University of California Press, 2021.

Alamillo, José. *Making Lemonade out of Lemons: Mexican American Labor and Leisure in a California Town, 1880–1960*. Champaign: University of Illinois Press, 2006.

Almaguer, Tomás. *Racial Fault Lines: The Historical Origins of White Supremacy in California*. Berkeley: University of California Press, 1994.

Alvarez, Luis. *The Power of the Zoot: Youth Culture and Resistance During WWII*. Berkeley: University of California Press, 2008.

Alvarez, Robert R., Jr. "The Lemon Grove Incident: The Nation's First Successful Desegregation Court Case." *The Journal of San Diego History* 32, No. 2 (Spring 1986), https://sandiegohistory.org/journal/1986/april/lemongrove/ .

Amado, María L. "The 'New Mestiza,' the Old Mestizos: Contrasting Discourses on Mestizaje." *Sociological Inquiry* 82, No. 3 (2012): 446–59.

Anaheim Colony Historic District. "How Anaheim Got Its Name," http://www.anahei mcolony.com/EarlyAnaheim/name.htm.

Anderson, Benedict. *Imagined Communities: Reflections on the Origin and Spread of Nationalism*. New York: Verso, 2006.

Anderson, Carol. *Eyes off the Prize: The United Nations and the African American Struggle for Human Rights, 1944–1955*. Cambridge: Cambridge University Press, 2003.

Aparicio, Ana. *Dominican Americans and the Politics of Empowerment*. Gainesville: University Press of Florida, 2006.

Arendt, Hannah. *Eichmann in Jerusalem: A Report on the Banality of Evil*. Revised and Enlarged Edition. New York: Penguin Books, 1994.

Arellano, Gustavo. "The Citrus War of 1936 Changed Orange County Forever and Cemented Our Mistrust of Mexicans." *OC Weekly*, June 8, 2006.

Arellano, Gustavo. "The Lost Mexicans of Bastanchury Ranch." *OC Weekly*, April 11, 2013.

Arellano, Gustavo. *Orange County: A Personal History*. New York: Scribner, 2008.

Arnesen, Eric. "Reconsidering the 'Long Civil Rights Movement'." *Historically Speaking* 10, No. 2 (2009): 31–34.

Arredondo, Gabriela F. *Mexican Chicago: Race, Identity, and Nation, 1916–1939.* Champaign: University of Illinois Press, 2008.

Arriola, Christopher J. "Knocking on the Schoolhouse Door: Mendez v. Westminster, Equal Protection, Public Education, and Mexican Americans in the 1940's." *Berkeley La Raza Law Journal* 8, No. 2 (1995): 166–207.

Arriola, Christopher J. *Mendez v. Westminster (1946): A Research Pathfinder to Chicano Legal History: With an Emphasis on Equal Protection and Orange County, California.* San Jose, CA: Office of the District Attorney, County of Santa Clara, 2000.

Avila, Eric. *Popular Culture in the Age of White Flight: Fear and Fantasy in Suburban Los Angeles.* Berkeley: University of California Press, 2004.

Azuma, Eiichiro. "Japanese Immigrant Farmers and California Alien Land Laws." *California History* 73, No. 1 (Spring 1994): 14–29.

Azuma, Eiichiro. "Negotiating the Boundaries of Race and Citizenship: Nisei Cultural Brokers in Occupied Japan." Paper delivered to the American Studies Association, October 14, 2006, Oakland, CA.

Bachus, Edward J. "Who Took the Oranges out of Orange County?: The Southern California Citrus Industry in Transition." *Southern California Quarterly* 63, No. 2 (Summer 1981): 157–73.

Balderrama, Francisco E. *In Defense of La Raza: The Los Angeles Mexican Consulate and the Mexican Community, 1929 to 1936.* Tucson: University of Arizona Press, 1982.

Balderrama, Francisco and Raymond Rodríguez. *Decade of Betrayal: Mexican Repatriation in the 1930s.* Albuquerque: University of New Mexico Press, 2006.

Barker, Richard H. "The Building Boom of 1925–26 Caused a Relinquishment of Citrus Acreage." *Citrograph Magazine* (May/June 2013), 60–62.

Barker, Richard H. *Citrus Powered the Economy of Orange County for over a Half Century Induced by "a Romance": An Illustrated History.* Balboa, CA: Citrus Roots, Preserving Citrus Heritage Foundation, 2009.

Barker, Richard H. "Citrus Roots: California Citrus Spurred Colonization." *Citrograph Magazine* (March/April 2013), 60–64.

Barker, Richard H. "Citrus Roots: How Important Was California's Citrus Industry?" *Citrograph Magazine* (Winter 2014), 76–78.

Batman, Richard Dale. "Orange County, California: A Comprehensive History—Part I: Anaheim Was an Oasis in a Wilderness.'" *Journal of the West* 4, No. 1 (January 1965): 1–20.

Batman, Richard Dale. "Orange County, California: A Comprehensive History—Part I: 'Gospel Swamp . . . The Land of Hog and Hominy.'" *Journal of the West* 4, No. 2 (April 1965), 231–56.

Bedolla, Lisa Garcia. *Fluid Borders: Latino Power, Identity, and Politics in Los Angeles.* Berkeley: University of California Press, 2005.

Benton-Cohen, Katherine. *Inventing the Immigration Problem: The Dillingham Commission and Its Legacy.* Cambridge, MA: Harvard University Press, 2018.

Bermudez, Nadine. "Reinscribing History: *Mendez et al. v. Westminster et al.* from the Standpoint of Mexican Origin Women." *American Studies* 56, No. 2 (2017): 9–29.

Bernstein, Shana. *Bridges of Reform: Interracial Civil Rights Activism in Twentieth-Century Los Angeles.* New York: Oxford University Press, 2010.

Bitetti, Marge, Guy Ball, and the Santa Ana Historical Preservation Society. *Early Santa Ana.* Charleston, SC: Arcadia Publishing, 2006.

Blackwell, Maylei. *Chicana Power!: Contested Histories of Feminism in the Chicano Movement.* Austin: University of Texas Press, 2011.

Blanton, Carlos. "The Citizenship Sacrifice: Mexican Americans, the Saunders-Leonard Report, and the Politics of Immigration, 1951–52." *The Western Historical Quarterly* 40, No. 3 (Autumn 2009): 299–320.

Blanton, Carlos. *George I. Sánchez: The Long Fight for Mexican American Integration*. New Haven: Yale University Press, 2014.

Blanton, Carlos. *A Promising Problem: The New Chicana/o History*. Austin, TX: University of Texas Press, 2016.

Borstelmann, Thomas. *The Cold War and the Color Line: American Race Relations in the Global Arena*. Cambridge, MA: Harvard University Press, 2001.

Boulé, David. *The Orange and the Dream of California*. Santa Monica: Angel City Press, 2013.

Boustan, Leah Platt. *Competition in the Promised Land: Black Migrants in Northern Cities and Labor Markets*. Princeton: Princeton University Press, 2017.

Brigandi, Phil. *A Brief History of Orange California: The Plaza City*. Charleston, SC: The History Press, 2011.

Brigandi, Phil. *Orange County Chronicles*. Charleston, SC: The History Press, 2013.

Brigandi, Phil. *Orange County Place Names A to Z*. San Diego, CA: Sunbelt Publications, 2006.

Brilliant, Mark. *The Color of America Has Changed: How Racial Diversity Shaped Civil Rights Reform in California 1941–1978*. New York: Oxford University Press, 2010.

Bruyneel, Kevin. *Settler Memory: The Disavowal of Indigeneity and the Politics of Race in the United States*. Chapel Hill: University of North Carolina Press, 2021.

Burt, Kenneth C. "The Latino Democratic Trail Stretches Way Back." *Hispanic Link News Service*, June 22, 2011, http://kennethburt.com/blog/?p=1052.

Burt, Kenneth C. "Pat Brown and the Emergence of Latinos in California Politics." *Edmund G. "Pat" Brown Institute for Public Affairs* (2014), http://files.ctctcdn.com/17fd796f001/a05cee9a-a2d7-4a72-b9cb-d716d54bb782.pdf.

Burt, Kenneth C. *The Search for a Civic Voice: California Latino Politics*. Claremont, CA: Regina Books, 2007.

Cadava, Geraldo. *The Hispanic Republican: The Shaping of an American Political Identity, From Nixon to Trump*. New York: Ecco, 2020.

California Department of Finance. "Historical Census Populations of California, 1850–2010," https://dof.ca.gov/reports/demographic-reports/.

Camacho, Alicia Schmidt. *Migrant Imaginaries: Latino Cultural Politics in the U.S.-Mexico Borderlands*. New York: New York University Press, 2008.

Camarillo, Albert. *Chicanos in a Changing Society: From Mexican Pueblos to American Barrios in Santa Barbara and Southern California, 1848–1930*. Cambridge: Harvard University Press, 1979.

Cardoso, Lawrence A. *Mexican Emigration to the United States, 1897–1931*. Tucson: University of Arizona Press, 1980.

Carpenter, Virginia L. "The Valencia in Placentia." *Biblio-Cal Notes*, Vol. 8, No. 1 (Spring 1975): 13–17.

Carpio, Genevieve. *Collisions at the Crossroads: How Place and Mobility Make Race*. Oakland: University of California Press, 2019.

Carpio, Genevieve. "Unexpected Allies: David C. Marcus, Civil Rights, and the Mexican American Legal Landscape of Southern California." *Annual Review of the Casden Institute for the Study of the Jewish Role in American Life* 9 (2012): 1–32.

Carrillo, Bessie M.H. "Old Days in San Juan Capistrano." *Orange County History Series*, Vol. 1 (1931).

Chandler, Alfred D., Jr. *The Visible Hand: The Managerial Revolution in American Business.* Cambridge: The Belknap Press of the Harvard University Press, 1977.

Chapman University. *A History of Key Structures in the Cypress Street Neighborhood.* Orange, CA: Chapman University, 2007.

Chapman University. *Recollections of the Cypress Street Neighborhood.* Orange, CA: Chapman University, 2006.

Chavez, Linda. *An Unlikely Conservative.* New York: Basic Books, 2002.

Cocoltchos, Christopher Nicholas. "The Invisible Empire and the Search for the Orderly Community: The Ku Klux Klan in Anaheim, California." Shawn Lay ed. *The Invisible Empire in the West: Toward a New Historical Appraisal of the Ku Klux Klan of the 1920s.* Urbana: University of Illinois Press, 2004, 97–120.

Cogut, Ted and Conger, Bill. *History of Arizona' s Clifton-Morenci Mining District: A Personal Approach.* Vol. 1. Thatcher, AZ: Mining History, 1999.

Cohen, Deborah. *Braceros: Migrant Citizens and Transnational Subjects in the Postwar United States and Mexico.* Chapel Hill: University of North Carolina Press, 2011.

Cohen, Lizabeth. *A Consumers' Republic: The Politics of Mass Consumption in Postwar America.* New York: Knopf, 2003.

Cohen, Lizabeth. *Making a New Deal: Industrial Workers in Chicago, 1919–1939.* New York: Cambridge University Press, 1991.

Contreras, Eduardo. *Latinos and the Liberal City: Politics and Protest in San Francisco.* Philadelphia: University of Pennsylvania Press, 2019.

Cox, Kevin R. "Revisiting 'the City as a Growth Machine.'" *Cambridge Journal of Regions, Economy and Society* 10, No. 3 (November 2017): 391–405.

Cox, Oliver Cromwell. *Caste, Class, & Race: A Study in Social Dynamics.* New York: Doubleday, 1948.

Cramer, Esther R. ed. *A Hundred Years of Yesterdays: A Centennial History of the People of Orange County and Their Communities.* Santa Ana: The Orange County Centennial, 1988.

Cramer, Esther R. *La Habra: The Pass Through the Hills.* Fullerton: Sultana Press, 1969.

Cronon, William. *Nature's Metropolis: Chicago and the Great West.* New York: W.W. Norton, 1991.

Dávila, Arlene. *Latinos Inc.: The Marketing and Making of a People.* Berkeley: University of California Press, 2001.

de la Torre Aguirre, Margie. *LULAC Project: Patriots with Civil Rights.* Yorba Linda, CA: Abrazo Productions, 2009.

De León, Arnoldo. *In Re Ricardo Rodriguez: An Attempt at Chicano Disenfranchisement.* San Antonio, TX: Caravel Press, 1979.

Delgado, Richard, Juan F. Perea, and Jean Stefancic, eds. *Latinos and the Law: Cases and Materials.* St. Paul: Thomson/West, 2008.

Deverell, William. *Whitewashed Adobe: The Rise of Los Angeles and the Remaking of Its Mexican Past.* Berkeley: University of California Press, 2004.

Deverell, William and Greg Hise, eds. *A Companion to Los Angeles.* Malden, MA: Wiley Blackwell, 2010.

Diaz, David R. and Rodolfo D. Torres, eds. *Latino Urbanism: The Politics of Planning, Policy, and Redevelopment.* New York: New York University Press, 2012.

Díaz, George T. *Border Contraband: A History of Smuggling Across the Rio Grande.* Austin: University of Texas Press, 2015.

Dinius, Oliver J. and Angela Vergara, eds. *Company Towns in the Americas: Landscape, Power, and Working-Class Communities.* Athens: University of Georgia Press, 2011.

Dochuk, Darren. *From Bible Belt to Sunbelt: Plain-Folk Religion, Grassroots Politics, and the Rise of Evangelical Conservatism*. New York: W.W. Norton, 2012.

Donato, Ruben. *The Other Struggle for Equal Schools: Mexican Americans During the Civil Rights Era*. New York: State University of New York Press, 1997.

Donato, Rubén and Jarrod Hanson. *The Other American Dilemma: Schools, Mexicans, and the Nature of Jim Crow, 1912–1953*. Albany: State University of New York Press, 2021.

Dudziak, Mary L. *Cold War Civil Rights: Race and the Image of American Democracy*. Princeton: Princeton University Press, 2000.

Dunbar-Ortiz, Roxanne. *Not a Nation of Immigrants: Settler Colonialism White Supremacy, and a History of Erasure and Exclusion*. Boston: Beacon Press, 2021.

Epting, Charles. *The New Deal in Orange County California*. Charleston, SC: History Press, 2014.

Epting, Charles, ed. *Orange County Pioneers: Oral Histories from the Works Progress Administration*. Charleston, SC: History Press, 2014.

Esparza, Jesús Jesse. *Raza Schools: The Fight for Latino Educational Autonomy in a West Texas Borderlands Town*. Norman: University of Oklahoma Press, 2023.

Espinoza, Dionne, María Eugenia Cotera, and Maylei Blackwell, eds. *Chicana Movidas: New Narratives of Activism and Feminism in the Movement Era*. Austin: University of Texas Press, 2018.

Farmer, Jared. *Trees in Paradise: A California History*. New York: W.W. Norton, 2013.

Fernández-Armesto, Felipe. *Our America: A Hispanic History of the United States*. New York: W.W. Norton, 2014.

Fernández, Johanna. *The Young Lords: A Radical History*. Chapel Hill: University of North Carolina Press, 2020.

Flamming, Douglas. *Bound for Freedom: Black Los Angeles in Jim Crow America*. Berkeley: University of California Press, 2005.

Flores, Ruben. *Backroads Pragmatists: Mexico's Melting Pot and Civil Rights in the United States*. Philadelphia: University of Pennsylvania Press, 2014.

Foley, Neil. *Quest for Equality: The Failed Promise of Black-Brown Solidarity*. Cambridge, MA: Harvard University Press, 2010.

Foucault, Michel. *Discipline and Punish: The Birth of the Prison*. New York: Pantheon Books, 1977.

Friis, J. Leo. *Orange County Through Four Centuries*. Santa Ana: Pioneer Press, 1965.

Gaddis, John Lewis. *The Landscape of History: How Historians Map the Past*. Oxford: Oxford University Press, 2022.

Galarza, Ernesto. *Merchants of Labor: The Mexican Bracero Story*. San Jose, CA: McNally and Loftin, 1964.

García, David G. *Strategies of Segregation: Race, Residence, and the Struggle for Educational Equality*. Berkeley: University of California Press, 2018.

García, David G., Tara J. Yosso, and Frank P Barajas. "'A Few of the Brightest, Cleanest Mexican Children': School Segregation as a Form of Mundane Racism in Oxnard, California, 1900–1940." *Harvard Educational Review* 82, No. 1 (Spring 2012): 1–25.

García, Ignacio M. *Chicanismo: The Forging of a Militant Ethos*. Tucson, AZ: University of Arizona Press, 1997.

García, Ignacio M. *Viva Kennedy: Mexican Americans in Search of Camelot*. College Station, TX: Texas A&M University Press, 2000.

García, Ignacio M. *White But Not Equal: Mexican Americans, Jury Discrimination, and the Supreme Court*. Tucson: University of Arizona Press, 2009.

García, Mario T. *The Chicano Generation: Testimonios of the Movement*. Oakland: University of California Press, 2015.

García, Mario T. *The Making of a Mexican American Mayor: Raymond L. Telles of El Paso and the Origins of Latino Political Power*. Tucson: University of Arizona Press, 2018.

García, Mario T. *Mexican Americans: Leadership, Ideology, and Identity, 1930–1960*. New Haven: Yale University Press, 1989.

García, Mario T. and Sal Castro. *Blowout: Sal Castro and the Chicano Struggle for Educational Justice*. Chapel Hill: University of North Carolina Press, 2011.

Garcia, Mary. *Santa Ana's Logan Barrio: Its History, Story, and Families*. Santa Ana, CA: Santa Ana Historical Preservation Society, 2007.

Garcia, Matt. *A World of Its Own: Race, Labor, and Citrus in the Making of Greater Los Angeles, 1900–1970*. Chapel Hill: University of North Carolina Press, 2002.

Gibson, Pamela. "Early California on Rios Street." *Orange Countiana* 4 (1988): 15–20.

Gibson, Wayne Dell. *Tomas Yorba's Santa Ana Viejo, 1769–1847*. Santa Ana, CA: Santa Ana College Foundation Press, 1976.

Gilmore, Ruth Wilson. *Golden Gulag: Prisons, Surplus, Crisis, and Opposition in a Globalizing California*. Berkeley: University of California Press, 2007.

Gómez, Laura A. *Inventing Latinos: A New History of American Racism*. New York: The New Press, 2020.

Gómez, Laura A. *Manifest Destinies: The Making of the Mexican American Race*. New York: New York University Press, 2007.

Gómez, Laura A. "Mendez v. Westminster, 1945–1947." Lilia Fernandez ed. *50 Events that Shaped Latino History: An Encyclopedia of the American Mosaic*. 2 vol. Goleta, CA: Greenwood, 2018, 417–34.

Gonzales, David-James. "El Cine Yost and the Power of Place for Mexican Migrants in Orange County, California, 1930–1990." *Journal of American Ethnic History* 39, No. 4 (Summer 2020): 42–59.

Gonzales, David-James. "Mendez v. Westminster, 1945–1947." Lilia Fernandez ed. *50 Events that Shaped Latino History: An Encyclopedia of the American Mosaic*. 2 vol. Goleta, CA: Greenwood, 2018, 417–34.

Gonzales, David-James. "Mexican Americans and the Long Fight Against Segregation in the Southwest." Michael C. LeMay ed. *The U.S.-Mexico Border: A Reference Handbook*. Santa Barbara: ABC-CLIO, 2022, 129–35.

Gonzales, David-James. "Placing the et al. Back in *Mendez v. Westminster*: Hector Tarango and the Mexican American Movement to End Segregation in the Social and Political Borderlands of Orange County." *American Studies* 56, No. 2 (January 2017): 31–52.

González, Erualdo R. *Latino City: Urban Planning, Politics, and the Grassroots*. New York: Routledge, 2017.

González, Gilbert G. *Chicano Education in the Era of Segregation*. Cranbury, NJ: Associated University Presses, 1990.

González, Gilbert G. *Culture of Empire: American Writers, Mexico, and Mexican Immigrants, 1880–1930*. Austin: University of Texas Press, 2004.

González, Gilbert G. *Labor and Community: Mexican Citrus Worker Villages in a Southern California County, 1900–1950*. Urbana: University of Illinois Press, 1994.

González, Gilbert G. *Mexican Consuls and Labor Organizing: Imperial Politics in the American Southwest*. Austin: University of Texas Press, 1999.

González, Gilbert G. "The 'Mexican Problem': Empire, Public Policy, and the Education of Mexican Immigrants." *Aztlan: A Journal of Chicano Studies* 26, No. 2 (Fall 2001): 199–207.

González, Gilbert G. "Segregation of Mexican Children in a Southern California City: The Legacy of Expansionism and the American Southwest." *The Western Historical Quarterly* 16, No. 1 (January 1985): 55–76.

González, Jerry. *In Search of the Mexican Beverly Hills: Latino Suburbanization in Postwar Los Angeles*. New Brunswick: Rutgers University Press, 2017.

Gonzalez, Juan. *Harvest of Empire: A History of Latinos in America*. Second Revised and Updated Edition. New York: Penguin, 2022.

Goodman, Adam. *The Deportation Machine: America's Long History of Expelling Immigrants*. Princeton: Princeton University Press, 2020.

Gordon, Linda. *The Great Arizona Orphan Abduction*. Cambridge, MA: Harvard University Press, 1999.

Gottdiener, Mark. *The Social Production of Urban Space*. Second Edition. Austin: University of Texas Press, 1985.

Gottdiener, Mark, Ray Hutchison, and Michael T. Ryan. *The New Urban Sociology*. 5th ed. New York: Routledge, 2015.

Greiner, Clemens and Patrick Sakdapolrak. "Translocality: Concepts, Applications and Emerging Research Perspectives. *Geography Compass* 7, No. 5 (2013): 373–84.

Griswold del Castillo, Richard. *World War II and Mexican American Civil Rights*. Austin: University of Texas Press, 2008.

Guerin-Gonzales, Camille. *Mexican Workers and American Dreams: Immigration, Repatriation, and California Farm Labor, 1900–1939*. New Brunswick: Rutgers University Press, 1994.

Guglielmo, Thomas A. "Fighting for Caucasian Rights: Mexicans, Mexican Americans, and the Transnational Struggle for Civil Rights in World War II Texas." *The Journal of American History* 92, No. 4 (March 2006): 1212–37.

Gutiérrez, David G. *Walls and Mirrors: Mexican Americans, Mexican Immigrants, and the Politics of Ethnicity*. Berkeley: University of California Press, 1995.

Gutiérrez, Laura D. "'Trains of Misery': Repatriate Voices and Responses in Northern Mexico During the Great Depression." *Journal of American Ethnic History* 39, No. 4 (Summer 2020): 13–26.

Haas, Britt. *Fighting Authoritarianism: American Youth Activism in the 1930s*. New York: Fordham University Press, Empire State Editions, 2018.

Haas, Lisbeth. "The Bracero in Orange County: A Workforce for Economic Transition." *Working Papers in U.S.-Mexican Studies*. Vol. 29. University of California, San Diego (1981), 1–54.

Haas, Lisbeth. *Conquests and Historical Identities in California, 1769–1936*. Berkeley: University of California Press, 1996.

Hall, Jacquelyn Dowd. "The Long Civil Rights Movement and the Political Uses of the Past." *The Journal of American History* 91, No. 4 (March 1, 2005): 1233–63.

Hannah-Jones, Nikole, Caitlin Roper, Ilena Silverman, and Jake Silverstein, eds. *The 1619 Project: A New Origin Story*. New York: One World, 2021.

Harris, Cheryl I. "Whiteness as Property." *Harvard Law Review* 106, No. 8 (June 1993): 1707–91.

Hayes-Bautista, David E, Marco Antonio Firebaugh, Cynthia L. Chamberlin, and Christina Gamboa. "Reginaldo Francisco del Valle: UCLA's Forgotten Forefather." *Southern California Quarterly* 88, No. 1 (Spring 2006): 1–35.

Hernandez, Jose Amaro. *Mutual Aid for Survival: The Case of the Mexican American*. Malabar, FL: Robert E. Krieger Publishing, 1983.

Hernández, José Angel. *Mexican American Colonization During the Nineteenth Century*. New York: Cambridge University Press, 2012.

Hernández, Kelly Lyttle. *Migra! A History of the U.S. Border Patrol*. Berkeley: University of California Press, 2010.

Herod, Andrew. *Labor Geographies: Workers and the Landscapes of Capitalism*. New York: The Guilford Press, 2001.

Herod, Andrew. "Social Engineering Through Spatial Engineering: Company Towns and the Geographical Imagination." Dinius and Vergara eds. *Company Towns in the Americas: Landscape, Power, and Working-Class Communities*. Athens: University of Georgia Press, 2011, 21–44.

Higgs, Robert. "Landless by Law: Japanese Immigrants in California Agriculture to 1942." *The Journal of Economic History* 38, No. 1 (March 1978): 205–25.

Higham, John. *Strangers in the Land: Patterns of American Nativism, 1860–1925*. New York: Atheneum, 1988.

Hinojosa, Felipe. *Apostles of Change: Latino Radical Politics, Church Occupations, and the Fight to Save the Barrio*. Austin: University of Texas Press, 2021.

Hirsch, Arnold R. " 'Containment on the Home Front: Race and Federal Housing Policy from the New Deal to the Cold War." *Journal of Urban History* 26, No. 2 (January 2000): 158–89.

Hirsch, Arnold R. *Making the Second Ghetto: Race and Housing in Chicago, 1940–1960*. Cambridge: Cambridge University Press, 1983.

Hirsch, Arnold R. "With or Without Jim Crow: Black Residential Segregation in the United States." Hirsch and Raymond A. Mohl eds. *Urban Policy in Twentieth-Century America*. New Brunswick: Rutgers University Press, 1993, 65–99.

Hoffman, Abraham. *Unwanted Mexican Americans in the Great Depression: Repatriation Pressures, 1929–1939*. Tucson: University of Arizona Press, 1974.

HoSang, Daniel Martinez. *Racial Propositions: Ballot Initiatives and the Making of Postwar California*. Berkeley: University of California Press, 2010.

Hull, Osman Ransom and Irving R. Melbo. *Forward in the Fundamentals of Education*. Inglewood, CA: 1941.

Hull, Osman Ransom and Willard Stanley Ford. *Survey of the Los Angeles City Schools*. Los Angeles: Published for the L.A. Board of Education by Wolfer Print, 1934.

Hurtado, Albert L. *Indian Survival on the California Frontier*. New Haven: Yale University Press, 1988.

Ichioka, Yuji. "Japanese Immigrant Response to the 1920 California Alien Land Law." *Agricultural History* 58, No. 2 (April 1984): 157–78.

Jackson, Kenneth. *Crabgrass Frontier: The Suburbanization of the United States*. New York: Oxford University Press, 1985.

Japanese American National Museum. *Los Angeles's Boyle Heights*. Charleston, SC: Arcadia Publishing, 2005.

Jenkins, Destin and Justin Leroy, eds. *Histories of Racial Capitalism*. New York: Columbia University Press, 2021.

Jenks, Hillary. "Seasoned Long Enough in Concentration: Suburbanization and Transnational Citizenship in Southern California's South Bay." *Journal of Urban History* 40, No. 1 (2014): 6–30.

Jepsen, Chris. "OC History: The Willard Smith Era." *County Connection*. May 2019.

Johnson, Benjamin. "The Cosmic Race in Texas: Racial Fusion, White Supremacy and Civil Rights Politics." *The Journal of American History* 98, No. 2 (September 2001): 404–19.

Johnson, Walter. *The Broken Heart of America: St. Louis and the Violent History of the United States*. New York: Basic Books, 2020.

Kang, Deborah. *The INS on the Line: Making Immigration Law on the US-Mexico Border, 1917–1954*. New York: Oxford University Press, 2017.

Katznelson, Ira. *When Affirmative Action Was White: An Untold History of Racial Inequality in Twentieth Century America*. New York: W.W. Norton, 2005.

Kelley, Robin D.G. *Race Rebels: Culture, Politics, and the Black Working Class*. New York: The Free Press, 1994.

Kim, Jessica M. *Imperial Metropolis: Los Angeles, Mexico, and the Borderlands of American Empire, 1865–1941*. Chapel Hill: University of North Carolina Press, 2019.

Kling, Rob, Spenser Olin, and Mark Poster, eds. *Postsuburban California: The Transformation of Orange County Since World War II*. Berkeley: University of California Press, 1991.

Kolchin, Peter. "Whiteness Studies: The New History of Race in America." *The Journal of American History* 89, No. 1 (June 2002): 154–73.

Kopelson, Gene. "'Ya Basta?!' Ronald Reagan's 1966 Success with Mexican American Voters." *California History* 91, No. 4 (Winter 2014): 31–42.

Kraszewski, Miguel. "Juan Flores in San Juan Capistrano." *Orange Countiana* 12 (2016): 21–30.

Krochmal, Max. *Blue Texas: The Making of a Multiracial Democratic Coalition in the Civil Rights Era*. Chapel Hill: University of North Carolina Press, 2016.

Kropp, Phoebe S. *California Vieja: Culture and Memory in a Modern American Place*. Berkeley: University of California Press, 2006.

Kruse, Kevin. *White Flight: Atlanta and the Making of Modern Conservatism*. Princeton: Princeton University Press, 2005.

Kurashige, Scott. *The Shifting Grounds of Race: Black and Japanese Americans in the Making of Multiethnic Los Angeles*. Princeton: Princeton University Press, 2010.

Lamb, Karl A. *As Orange County Goes: Twelve California Families and the Future of American Politics*. New York: W.W. Norton, 1974.

Lassiter, Matthew D. *The Silent Majority: Suburban Politics in the Sunbelt South*. Princeton: Princeton University Press, 2006.

Lassiter, Matthew D. and Christopher Niedt. "Suburban Diversity in Postwar America." *Journal of Urban History* 39, No. 3 (2013): 3–14.

Lassiter, Matthew D. and Joseph Crespino, eds. *The Myth of Southern Exceptionalism*. New York: Oxford University Press, 2010.

Laszlo, Pierre. *Citrus: A History*. Chicago: University of Chicago Press, 2007.

Le Goff, Jacques. *History and Memory*. Translated by Steven Rendall and Elizabeth Claman. New York: Columbia University Press, 1992.

Lee, Erika. *America for Americans: A History of Xenophobia in the United States*. New York: Basic Books, 2019.

Lee, Erika. *At America's Gates: Chinese Immigration During the Exclusion Era, 1882–1943*. Chapel Hill: University of North Carolina Press, 2003.

Lee, Sonia Song-Ha. *Building a Latino Civil Rights Movement: Puerto Ricans, African Americans, and the Pursuit of Racial Justice in New York City*. Chapel Hill: University of North Carolina Press, 2014.

Leong, Karen J. "'A Distinct and Antagonistic Race': Constructions of Chinese Manhood in the Exclusionist Debates, 1869–78." Donna R. Gabaccia and Vicki Ruiz eds. *American Dreaming, Global Realities: Rethinking U.S. Immigration History*. Urbana: University of Illinois Press, 2006, 131–48.

Leong, Nancy. "Racial Capitalism." *Harvard Law Review* 126, No. 8 (June 2013): 2151–226.

Lew-Williams, Beth. *The Chinese Must Go: Violence, Exclusion, and the Making of the Alien in America*. Cambridge, MA: Harvard University Press, 2018.

Lewinnek, Elaine, Gustavo Arellano, and Thuy Vo Dang. *A People's Guide to Orange County*. Oakland: University of California Press, 2022.

Lillard, Richard G., ed. *Letters from the Orange Empire by G. Harold Powell*. Los Angeles: Historical Society of Southern California, 1990.

Lim, Julian. *Porous Borders: Multiracial Migrations and the Law in the U.S.-Mexico Borderlands*. Chapel Hill: University of North Carolina Press, 2017.

Lin, Patricia. "Perspectives on the Chinese in Nineteenth-Century Orange County." *Journal of Orange County Studies* 3, No. 4 (Fall 1989/Spring 1990): 28–36.

Lipsitz, George. *How Racism Takes Place*. Philadelphia: Temple University Press, 2011.

Lipsitz, George. *The Possessive Investment in Whiteness: How White People Profit from Identity Politics*. Philadelphia: Temple University Press, 2006.

Logan, John R. and Harvey Molotch. *Urban Fortunes: The Political Economy of Place*. Berkeley: University of California Press, 1987.

Lopez, Ian Haney. *White by Law: The Legal Construction of Race*. New York: New York University Press, 2006.Lowe, Lisa. *Immigrant Acts: On Asian American Cultural Politics*. Durham, NC: Duke University Press, 1996.

Lowitt, Richard. *The New Deal and the American West*. Norman: University of Oklahoma Press, 1984.

Loza, Mireya. *Defiant Braceros: How Migrant Workers Fought for Racial, Sexual, and Political Freedom*. Chapel Hill: University of North Carolina Press, 2016.

Luibhéid, Eithne. *Entry Denied: Controlling Sexuality at the Border*. Minneapolis, MN: University of Minnesota Press, 2002.

MacArthur, Mildred Yorba. *Orange County Under Spain, Mexico, and the United States*. Los Angeles: Dawson's Book Shop, 1968.

Macias, Anthony. *Mexican American Mojo: Popular Music, Dance, and Urban Culture in Los Angeles*. Durham, NC: Duke University Press, 2008.

Madley, Benjamin. *An American Genocide: The United States and the California Indian Catastrophe*. New Haven: Yale University Press, 2017.

Maiorana, Juliette. "Birth of the Mexican Problem: Oil in Mexico, U.S. Social Sciences, and Transnational Labor, 1917–1920." *The Western Historical Quarterly* 53, No. 3 (Autumn 2022): 245–65.

Marable, Manning. *How Capitalism Underdeveloped Black America*. Cambridge: South End Press, 1983.

Marquez, Benjamin. *Constructing Identities in Mexican American Political Organizations*. Austin: University of Texas Press, 2003.

Massey, Douglas S. and Nancy A. Denton. *American Apartheid: Segregation and the Making of the Underclass*. Cambridge, MA: Harvard University Press, 1998.

Maza, Sarah. *Thinking About History*. Chicago: University of Chicago Press, 2017.

Mboti, Nyasha. *Apartheid Studies: A Manifesto*. Trenton: Africa World Press, 2023.

Mboti, Nyasha. "Circuits of Apartheid: A Plea for Apartheid Studies." *Glimpse* 20 (2019): 15–70.

McCormick, Jennifer. "*Mendez v. Westminster*: Domestic Forces Underlying the Fight for School Desegregation." *Journal of American Ethnic History* 39, No. 1 (2019): 5–34.

McGirr, Lisa. *Suburban Warrior: The Origins of the New American Right*. Princeton, NJ: Princeton University Press, 2001.

McKiernan-González, John. *Fevered Measures: Public Health and Race at the Texas-Mexico Border, 1848–1942*. Durham, NC: Duke University Press, 2012.

McWilliams, Carey. *Brothers Under the Skin*. Revised Edition. Boston: Little, Brown, 1951.

McWilliams, Carey. *The Education of Carey McWilliams*. New York: Simon & Schuster, 1979.

McWilliams, Carey. *Factories in the Field: The Story of Migratory Farm Labor in California*. First California Paperback Printing. Berkeley, CA: University of California Press, 2000.

McWilliams, Carey. "Is Your Name Gonzales." *The Nation* 164 (March 5, 1947), 302–3.

McWilliams, Carey. *A Mask for Privilege: Anti-Semitism in America*. Boston, Little, Brown, 1948.

McWilliams, Carey. *North from Mexico: The Spanish Speaking People of the United States*. New York: Greenwood Press, 1968.

McWilliams, Carey. *Prejudice Japanese-Americans: Symbol of Racial Intolerance*. Boston: Little, Brown, 1944.

McWilliams, Carey. *Southern California: An Island on the Land*. Layton, UT: Gibbs Smith, 1946.

McWilliams, Carey. "Spectrum of Segregation." *Survey Graphic* (January 1947).

Meadows, Don. "The House of Bernardo Yorba." *Orange County History Series* 4, No. 1 (1963).

Meadows, Don. "The March of Portolá." Thomas B. Talbert ed. *Historical Volume and Reference Works: Orange County*, Vol. 1. Whittier, CA: Historical Publishers, 1963, 33–44.

Melamed, Jodi. "Racial Capitalism." *Critical Ethnic Studies* 1, No. 1 (Spring 2015): 76–85.

Melching, Richard. "The Activities of the Ku Klux Klan in Anaheim, California, 1923–1925." *Southern California Quarterly* 56, No. 2 (Summer 1974): 175–96.

Mellinger, Phil. "'The Men Have Become Organizers': Labor Conflict and Unionization in the Mexican Mining Communities of Arizona, 1900–1915." *Western Historical Quarterly* 23 (Fall 1992): 323–47.

Mendoza, Valerie M. "Beverly Guzman Gallegos's Testimonio." *American Studies* 56, No. 2 (January 2017): 53–62.

Milkovich, Barbara Ann. "Fullerton, Orange County, California: The Struggle for Local Control." *Southern California Quarterly* 48, No. 4 (Winter 1996): 301–22.

Miller, Marilyn Grace. *Rise and Fall of the Cosmic Race: The Cult of Mestizaje in Latin America*. Austin: University of Texas Press, 2004.

Mills, Charles W. *The Racial Contract*. 25th Anniversary Edition. Ithaca: Cornell University Press, 2022.

Molina, Natalia. *Fit to Be Citizens: Public Health and Race in Los Angeles, 1879–1939*. Berkeley: University of California Press, 2006.

Molina, Natalia. *How Race Is Made in America: Immigration, Citizenship, and the Historical Power of Racial Scripts*. Berkeley: University of California Press, 2014.

Molina, Natalia, Daniel Martinez HoSang, and Ramón A. Gutiérrez, eds. *Relational Formations of Race: Theory, Method, and Practice*. Oakland: University of California Press, 2019.

Molotch, Harvey. "The City as a Growth Machine: Toward a Political Economy of Place." *American Journal of Sociology* 82, No. 2 (September 1976): 309–32.

Monkkonen, Eric H. *America Becomes Urban: The Development of U.S. Cities and Towns, 1780–1980*. Berkeley: University of California Press, 1988.

Monroy, Douglas. *Rebirth: Mexican Los Angeles from the Great Migration to the Great Depression*. Berkeley: University of California Press, 1999.

Monroy, Douglas. *Thrown Among Strangers: The Making of Mexican Culture in Frontier California*. Berkeley: University of California Press, 1990.

Montejano, David. *Anglos and Mexicans in the Making of Texas*. Austin: University of Texas Press, 1987.

Mora, G. Cristina. *Making Hispanics: How Activists, Bureaucrats and Media Constructed a New American*. Chicago: University of Chicago Press, 2014.

Morales, Aurora Levins. *The History of Latinos in West Oakland: Community Narratives*. Berkeley, CA: Latino History Project, 2000.

Moreno, Carlos R. "*Mendez v. Westminster* and School Desegregation." *California Legal History* 14 (2019): 93–105.

Moses, Vincent. "'The Orange-Grower Is Not a Farmer': G. Harold Powell, Riverside Orchardists, and the Coming of Industrial Agriculture, 1893–1930." *California History*. 74, No. 1 (Spring 1995): 22–37.

Munemitsu, Janice. *The Kindness of Color: The Story of Two Families and Mendez, et al. v. Westminster, the 1947 Desegregation of California Public Schools*. Self-published, 2021.

Munemitsu, Janice. "Munemitsu Farms." *Walk the Farm*, https://www.walkthefarm. org/munemitsu-farms. Accessed January 30, 2024.

Muñoz, Carlos, Jr. *Youth, Identity, Power: The Chicano Movement*. New York: Verso, 1989.

Muñoz, Laura K. "*Romo v. Laird*: Mexican American Segregation and the Politics of Belonging in Arizona." *Western Legal History: The Journal of the Ninth Judicial Circuit Historical Society* 26 (2013): 97–132.

Needham, Andrew and Allen Dieterich-Ward. "Beyond the Metropolis: Metropolitan Growth and Regional Transformation in Postwar America." *Journal of Urban History* 35, No. 7 (2009): 943–69.

Ngai, Mae M. *Impossible Subjects: Illegal Aliens and the Making of Modern America*. Princeton, NJ: Princeton University Press, 2004.

Nguyen, Phuong Tran. *Becoming Refugee American: The Politics of Rescue in Little Saigon*. Urbana: University of Illinois Press, 2017.

Nickerson, Michelle and Darren Dochuk, eds. *Sunbelt Rising: The Politics of Space, Place, and Region*. Philadelphia: University of Pennsylvania Press, 2011.

Nicolaides, Becky M. *My Blue Heaven: Life and Politics in the Working-Class Suburbs of Los Angeles, 1920–1965*. Chicago: University of Chicago Press, 2002.

Nicolaides, Becky M. "Suburbia and the Sunbelt." *OAH Magazine of History* (October 2003).

Nicolaides, Becky M. and Andrew Wiese, eds. *The Suburb Reader*. New York: Routledge, 2006.

O'Brien, Robert. *Survey on Mexicans and Crime in Southern California, 1926–1927*. Claremont: Lawson Roberts Publishing Company, 1928.

Olden, Danielle R. *Racial Uncertainties: Mexican Americans, School Desegregation, and the Making of Race in Post-Civil Rights America*. Oakland: University of California Press, 2022.

Orange County Historical Society. *Orange County History Series*. Vol. 1. Santa Ana, CA: Press of the Santa Ana High School and Junior College, 1931.

Orenstein, Dara. "Void for Vagueness." *Pacific Historical Review* 74, No. 3 (August 2005): 367–408.

Orozco, Cynthia E. *Agent of Change: Adela Sloss-Vento*. Austin: University of Texas Press, 2020.

Orozco, Cynthia E. "Ladies LULAC." *Handbook of Texas*. Austin: Texas State Historical Association, 1995.

Orozco, Cynthia E. *No Mexicans, Women, or Dogs Allowed: The Rise of the Mexican American Civil Rights Movement*. Austin: University of Texas Press, 2009.

Ortiz, Paul. *An African American and Latinx History of the United States*. Boston, MA: Beacon Press, 2018.

Padilla, Jose Luis Castro. "Before *Brown v. Board of Education*: Paul J. McCormick, the *Mendez v. Westminster* Decision, and Its Religious-Social Context." *U.S. Catholic Historian* 41, No. 4 (Fall 2023): 79–98.

Palacios, Agustín. "Multicultural Vasconcelos: The Optimistic, and at Times Willful, Misreading of *La Raza Cosmica*." *Latino Studies* 15 (2017): 416–38.

Pascoe, Peggy. *What Comes Naturally: Miscegenation Law and the Making of Race in America*. New York: Oxford University Press, 2009.

Patton, James. *History of Clifton*. Greenlee County Chamber of Commerce. NP, 1977.

Pawel, Miriam. *The Browns of California: The Family Dynasty that Transformed a State and Shaped a Nation*. New York: Bloomsbury, 2018.

PBS American Experience. "Eyes on the Prize Series," http://www.pbs.org/wgbh/amex/eyesontheprize/about/fd.html. Accessed December 5, 2012.

Pearson, Stephen. "'The Last Bastion of Colonialism': Appalachian Settler Colonialism and Self-Indigenization." *American Indian Culture and Research Journal* 37, No. 2 (2013): 165–84.

Perales, Monica. *Smeltertown: Making and Remembering a Southwest Border Community*. Chapel Hill: University of North Carolina Press, 2010.

Pfaelzer, Jean. *California, A Slave State*. New Haven: Yale University Press, 2023.

Pflueger, Donald H. *Charles C. Chapman: The Career of a Creative Californian, 1853–1944*. Los Angeles: Anderson, Ritchie, and Simon, 1976.

Phillips, Lester H. "Segregation in Education: A California Case Study." *Phylon* 10, No. 4 (1949): 407–13.

Piven, Frances Fox and Richard A. Cloward. *Poor People's Movements: Why They Succeed, How They Fail*. New York: Vintage Books, 1979.

Power, Garrett. "Apartheid Baltimore Style: the Residential Segregation Ordinances of 1910–1913." *Maryland Law Review* 42, No. 2 (1982): 289–328.

Powers, Jeanne M. and Lirio Patton. "Between Mendez and Brown: Gonzales v. Sheely (1951) and the Legal Campaign Against Segregation." *Law & Social Inquiry* 33, No. 1 (Winter 2008): 127–71.

Pritchard, Robert L. "Orange County During the Depressed Thirties: A Study in Twentieth Century California Local History." *Southern California Quarterly* 50, No. 2 (June 1968): 191–207.

Pulley, Tom. "Early Citrus Culture in Orange County." *County Courier: Official Publication of the Orange County Historical Society* 36, No. 4 (April 2006): 2–4.

Quill Pen Club. *Rawhide and Orange Blossoms: Stories and Sketches of Early Orange County*. Santa Ana, CA: Pioneer Press, 1967.

Quintana, Maria L. *Contracting Freedom: Race, Empire, and U.S. Guestworker Programs*. Philadelphia: University of Pennsylvania Press, 2022.

Quiroz, Anthony, ed. *Leaders of the Mexican American Generation: Bibliographical Essays*. Boulder: University Press of Colorado, 2015.

Rakove, Jack N., ed. *The Annotated U.S. Constitution and Declaration of Independence*. Cambridge, MA: The Belknap Press of Harvard University Press, 2009.

Ramirez, Henry M. *A Chicano in the White House: The Nixon No One Knew*. Self-published, 2013.

Ramírez, Marla A. "Gendered Banishment: Rewriting Mexican Repatriation Through a Transgenerational Oral History Methodology." *Latino Studies* 20 (2022): 306–33.

Ramos, Lisa Y. "Dismantling Segregation Together: Interconnections Between Mendez v. Westminster (1946) and Brown v. Board of Education (1954) School Segregation Cases." *Equity & Excellence in Education* 37, No. 3 (2004): 247–54.

Ramsey, Merle and Mabel Ramsey. *Pioneer Days of Laguna Beach*. Laguna Beach, CA: Hastie Printers, 1967.

Ramsey, Merle and Mabel Ramsey. *This Was Mission Country, Orange County, California*. Laguna Beach, CA: Mission Printing, 1973.

Reisler, Mark. *By the Sweat of Their Brow: Mexican Immigrant Labor in the United States, 1900–1940*. Westport: Greenwood Press, 1976.

Resendez, Andrés. *The Other Slavery: The Uncovered Story of Indian Enslavement in America*. New York: Houghton Mifflin Harcourt, 2016.

Richardson, Peter. *American Prophet: The Life and Work of Carey McWilliams*. Oakland: University of California Press, 2019.

Robbie, Sandra. *Mendez vs. Westminster [Video recording]: For All the Children/Para Todos los Ninos*. Huntington Beach, CA: KOCE-TV Foundation, 2002.

Roberts, Dorothy. "Who May Give Birth to Citizens? Reproduction, Eugenics, and Immigration." Juan F. Perea ed. *Immigrants Out! The New Nativism and Anti-Immigrant Impulse in the U.S*. New York: New York University Press, 1997, 205–22.

Robinson, Cedric. *Black Marxism: The Making of the Black Radical Tradition*. London: Zed Press, 1983.

Robinson, W.W. *The Old Spanish and Mexican Ranchos of Orange County*. Los Angeles, CA: Title Insurance and Trust Company, 1950.

Roche, Jeff, ed. *The Political Culture of the New West*. Lawrence: University of Kansas Press, 2008.

Rodney, Walter. *How Europe Underdeveloped Africa*. London: Bogle-L'Ouverture Publications, 1972.

Rodríguez, Clara E. *Changing Race: Latinos, the Census, and the History of Ethnicity in the United States*. New York: New York University Press, 2000.

Roediger, David R. *The Wages of Whiteness: Race and the Making of the American Working Class*. New York: Verso, 1991.

Roediger, David R. and Elizabeth D. Esch. *The Production of Difference: Race and the Management of Labor in U.S. History*. New York: Oxford University Press, 2012.

Romero, Robert Chao and Luis Fernando Fernandez. "*Doss v. Bernal*: Ending Mexican Apartheid in Orange County." *CSRC Research Report*. No. 14 (February 2012).

Romo, Ricardo. *East Los Angeles: History of a Barrio*. Austin: Texas University Press, 1983.

Rosales, F. Arturo. *Chicano!: The History of the Mexican American Civil Rights Movement*. Houston: Arte Público Press, 1997.

Rosales, Steven. "Fighting the Peace at Home: Mexican American Veterans and the 1944 GI Bill of Rights." *Pacific Historical Review* 80, No. 4 (2011): 597–627.

Rosas, Abigail. *South Central Is Home: Race and the Power of Community Investment in Los Angeles*. Stanford: Stanford University Press, 2019.

Rosas, Ana Elizabeth. *Abrazando el Espíritu: Bracero Families Confront the US-Mexico Border*. Berkeley, CA: University of California Press, 2014.

Rose, Margaret. "Gender and Civic Activism in Mexican American Barrios in California: The Community Service Organization, 1947–1962." Joanne Meyerowitz ed. *Not June Cleaver: Women and Gender in Postwar America, 1945–1960*. Philadelphia: Temple University Press, 1994, 177–200.

Rothstein, Richard. *The Color of Law: A Forgotten History of How Our Government Segregated America*. New York: Liveright, 2017.

Rowland, Donald. "Jose Antonio Yorba." *Orange Countiana* 8 (2012): 3–16.

Ruiz, Vicki L. *Cannery Women, Cannery Lives: Mexican Women, Unionization, and the California Food Processing Industry, 1930–1950*. Albuquerque: University of New Mexico Press, 1987.

Ruiz, Vicki L. *From Out of the Shadows: Mexican Women in Twentieth Century America*. New York: Oxford University Press, 1998.

Ruiz, Vicki L. "South by Southwest: Mexican Americans and Segregated Schooling, 1900–1950." *OAH Magazine of History* 15, No. 2 (Winter 2001): 23–27.

Sackman, Douglas Cazaux. *Orange Empire: California and the Fruits of Eden*. Berkeley: University of California Press, 2007.

Salzer, George. *Rancho Los Alamitos*. Ramona, CA: Acoma Books, 1975.

San Miguel Jr., Guadalupe. *Chicana/o Struggles for Education: Activism in the Community*. Houston: University of Houston—Center for Mexican American Studies, 2013.

San Miguel Jr., Guadalupe. *In the Midst of Radicalism: Mexican American Moderates During the Chicano Movement, 1960–1978*. Norman: Oklahoma University Press, 2022.

San Miguel Jr., Guadalupe. *Let All of Them Take Heed": Mexican Americans and the Campaign for Educational Equality in Texas, 1910–1981*. College Station: Texas A&M University Press, 1987.

Sánchez, George J. *Becoming Mexican American: Ethnicity, Culture and Identity in Chicano Los Angeles, 1900–1945*. New York: Oxford University Press, 1993.

Sánchez, George J., ed. *Beyond Alliances: The Jewish Role in Reshaping the Racial Landscape of Southern California*. West Lafayette: Purdue University Press, 2012.

Sánchez, George J. *Boyle Heights: How a Los Angeles Neighborhood Became the Future of American Democracy*. Oakland: University of California Press, 2022.

Sánchez, George J. "What's Good for Boyle Heights Is Good for the Jews: Creating Multiracialism on the Eastside During the 1950s." *American Quarterly* 56, No. 3 (September 2004): 633–61.

Santillan, Richard and Federico A. Subervi-Vélez. "Latino Participation in Republican Party Politics in California." Bryan O. Jackson and Michael B. Preston eds. *Racial and Ethnic Politics in California*. Berkeley: IGS Press, 1991, 307–15.

Santillán, Richard A., Susan C. Luévano, Luis F. Fernández, and Angelina F. Veyna, eds. *Mexican American Baseball in Orange County*. Images of Baseball Series. Charleston, SC: Arcadia Publishing, 2013.

Saxton, Alexander. *The Indispensable Enemy: Labor and the Anti-Chinese Movement in California*. Berkeley: University of California Press, 1975.

Scott, James C. *Weapons of the Weak: Everyday Forms of Peasant Resistance*. New Haven: Yale University Press, 1985.

Self, Robert O. *American Babylon: Race and Struggle for Postwar Oakland*. Princeton: Princeton University Press, 2003.

Shah, Nyan. *Contagious Divides: Epidemics and Race in San Francisco's Chinatown*. Berkeley: University of California Press, 2001.

Shaw, Joy C. "Foreshadowing *Brown v. Board*: The 1946 Case of Mendez v. Westminster." *The California Supreme Court Historical Society Newsletter* (Autumn/Winter 2004): 1–12.

Sklar, Martin J. *The Corporate Reconstruction of American Capitalism, 1890–1916: The Market, the Law, and Politics*. Cambridge: Cambridge University Press, 1988.

Sleeper, James. "How Orange County Got Its Name." Esther R. Cramer ed. *A Hundred Years of Yesterdays: A Centennial History of the People of Orange County and Their Communities* . Santa Ana: The Orange County Centennial, 1988.

Sleeper, James. *Orange County Almanac of Historical Oddities*. Third Edition, 1889–1986. New York: OCUSA Press, 1986.

Sleeper, James. "Oranges Helped County Get Its Start." *Santa Ana Register*. November 17, 1968.

Sleeper, James. *Rancho Mission Viejo: "Where History Is Still Happening*. Santa Margarita, CA: Santa Margarita Company, 1985.

Sleeper, James. "Two Tales of the Dragon: The Night They Burned Chinatown." *Orange County Illustrated*, June 1970, 30–33.

Slotkin, Richard. *Regeneration Through Violence: They Mythology of the American Frontier. 1600–1860*. Norman: University of Oklahoma Press, 1973.

Squire, Vicki, ed. *The Contested Politics of Mobility: Borderzones and Irregularity*. New York: Routledge, 2011.

St. John, Rachel. *Line in the Sand: A History of the Western U.S.-Mexico Border*. Princeton: Princeton University Press, 2011.

Stavans, Illan. *José Vasconcelos: The Prophet of Race*. New Brunswick: Rutgers University Press, 2011.

Stephenson, Terry E. "The First Settlers." *Orange Countiana* 10 (2014).

Street, Richard Steven. *Beasts of the Field: A Narrative History of California Farmworkers, 1769–1913*. Stanford: Stanford University Press, 2004.

Strum, Philippa. *Mendez v. Westminster: School Desegregation and Mexican-American Rights*. Lawrence: University Press of Kansas, 2010.

Sugrue, Thomas J. *The Origins of the Urban Crisis: Race and Inequality in Postwar Detroit*. Princeton: Princeton University Press, 1996.

Sugrue, Thomas J. *Sweet Land of Liberty: The Forgotten Struggle for Civil Rights in the North*. New York: Random House, 2008.

Summers Sandoval, Tomás F., Jr. *Latinos at the Golden Gate: Creating Community and Identity in San Francisco*. Chapel Hill: University of North Carolina Press, 2013.

Tang, Annie. "The Munemitsu Legacy." *Pacific Citizen*, December 18, 2020, https://www.pacificcitizen.org/the-munemitsu-legacy/.

Taylor, Keeanga-Yamahtta. *Race for Profit: How Banks and the Real Estate Industry Undermined Black Homeownership*. Chapel Hill: University of North Carolina Press, 2019.

Tellez, Michelle. *Border Women and the Community of Maclovio Rojas: Autonomy in the Spaces of Neoliberal Neglect*. Tucson: University of Arizona Press, 2021.

Theoharis, Jeanne. "Introduction." Theoharis and Komozi Woodard eds. *Freedom North: Black Freedom Struggles Outside the South, 1940–1980*. New York: Palgrave Macmillan, 2003, 1–16.

Theoharis, Jeanne. *A More Beautiful and Terrible History: The Uses and Misuses of Civil Rights History*. Boston: Beacon Press, 2018.

Thompson, Gabriel. *America's Social Arsonist: Fred Ross and Grassroots Organizing in the Twentieth Century*. Berkeley: University of California Press, 2016.

Tichenor, Daniel J. *Dividing Lines: The Politics of Immigration Control in America*. Princeton: Princeton University Press, 2002.

Tilly, Charles and Lesley J. Wood. *Social Movements, 1768–2012*. Third Edition. Boulder: Paradigm Publishers, 2013.

Tobey, Ronald and Charles Wetherell. "The Citrus Industry and the Revolution of Corporate Capitalism in Southern California." *California History* 74, No. 1 (Spring 1995): 6–21.

Tokunaga, Yu. *Transborder Los Angeles: An Unknown Transpacific History of Japanese Mexican Relations*. Oakland: University of California Press, 2022.

Torres-Rouff, David. "Becoming Mexican: Segregated Schools and Social Scientists in Southern California, 1913–1946." *Southern California Quarterly* 94, No. 1 (Spring 2012): 93–130.

Trouillot, Michel-Rolph. *Silencing the Past: Power and the Production of History*. Boston: Beacon Press, 1995.

Trounstine, Jessica. *Segregation by Design: Local Politics and Inequality in American Cities*. Cambridge: Cambridge University Press, 2018.

Valencia, Richard R. *Chicano Students and the Courts: The Mexican American Legal Struggle for Educational Equality*. New York: New York University Press, 2008.

Valerio-Jimenéz, Omar. *Remembering Conquest: Mexican Americans, Memory, and Citizenship*. Chapel Hill: University of North Carolina Press, 2024.

Vargas, Zaragosa. *Crucible of Struggle: A History of Mexican Americans from Colonial Times to the Present Era*. New York: Oxford University Press, 2011.

Vargas, Zaragosa. *Labor Rights are Civil Rights: Mexican American Workers in the Twentieth Century America*. Princeton: Princeton University Press, 2005.

Varzally, Allison. *Making a Non-White America: Californians Coloring Outside Ethnic Lines, 1925–1955*. Berkeley: University of California Press, 2008.

Varzally, Allison. "Romantic Crossings: Making Love, Family, and Non-Whiteness in California, 1925–1950." *Journal of American Ethnic History* 23, No. 1 (Fall 2003), 3–54.

Vasconcelos, José. *La raza cósmica*. Madrid: Agencia Mundial de Librería, 1925.

Vasquez, Enriqueta L. *The Women of La Raza: An Epic History of Chicana/Mexican American Peoples*. East Hampton, CT: El Grito del Norte, 2016.

Vela, Albert V. *Tracks to the Westminster Barrio: 1902–1960s*. East Hampton, CT: Diocito Publishing Company, 2017.

Walker, Doris. *Orange County: A Centennial Celebration*. Houston: Pioneer Publications, 1989.

Wanzer-Serrano, Darrel. *The New York Young Lords and the Struggle for Liberation*. Philadelphia: Temple University Press, 2015.

Weber, Devra. *Dark Sweat, White Gold: California Farm Workers, Cotton, and the New Deal*. Berkeley: University of California Press, 1994.

Weise, Julie. *Corazón de Dixie: Mexicanos in the US South Since 1910*. Chapel Hill: University of North Carolina Press, 2015.

White, Hayden. *The Content of the Form: Narrative Discourse and Historical Representation*. Baltimore: Johns Hopkins University Press, 1987.

Wilson, Bobby. *America's Johannesburg: Industrialization and Racial Transformation in Birmingham*. Lanham, MD: Rowman & Littlefield, 2000.

Wilson, Steven H. "Brown over 'Other White': Mexican Americans' Legal Arguments and Litigation Strategy in School Desegregation Lawsuits." *Law and History Review* 21, No. 1 (Spring 2003): 145–94.

Wollenberg, Charles. *All Deliberate Speed: Segregation and Exclusion in California Schools, 1855–1975*. Berkeley: University of California Press, 1976.

Yarsinske, Amy Waters. *All for One & One for All: A Celebration of 75 Years of the League of United Latin American Citizens (LULAC)*. Virginia Beach, VA: Donning Company Publishers, 2004.

Zunz, Olivier. *Making America Corporate, 1870–1920*. Chicago: University of Chicago Press, 1990.

Dissertations and Theses

Apodaca, Linda Maria. "They Kept the Home Fires Burning: Mexican-American Women and Social Change." PhD dissertation, University of California, Irvine, 1994.

Bermudez, Nadine. "*Mendez et al. v. the Westminster School District et al.*: Mexican American Female Activism in the Age of *De Jure* Segregation." PhD dissertation, University of California, Los Angeles, 2015.

Broadbent, Elizabeth. "The Distribution of Mexican Population in the United States." PhD dissertation, University of Chicago, 1941.

Carey, Gabriele Gonder. "From Hinterlands to Metropolis: The Origins of Land Use Planning in Orange County, California, 1925–1950." PhD dissertation, University of California, Riverside, 1997.

Cocoltchos, Christopher Nicholas. "The Invisible Government and the Viable Community: The Ku Klux Klan in Orange County, California During the 1920s." PhD dissertation, University of California, Los Angeles, 1979.

Engle, Clara Huber. "The Orange County Citrus Strike, 1936: Historical Analysis and Social Conflict." MA thesis. California State University, Fullerton, 1975.

Gonzales, David-James. "Battling Mexican Apartheid in Orange County, California: Race, Place, and Politics, 1920–1950." PhD dissertation, University of Southern California, 2017.

Haas, Lisbeth. "The Barrios of Santa Ana: Community, Class, and Urbanization, 1850–1947." PhD dissertation, University of California, Irvine, 1985.

Hayden, Jessie. "The La Habra Experiment in Mexican Social Education." MA thesis, Claremont Colleges, 1934.

Jensen, James Maurice. "The Mexican-American in an Orange County Community." MA thesis, Claremont Graduate School, December 1947.

Leis, Ward. "The Status of Education for Mexican Children in Four Border States." MA thesis, University of Southern California, 1931.

Liang, Amanda Marie. "Inland Empire Schools and *Mendez v. Westminster*." MA thesis, University of California, Riverside, 2012.

Milkovich, Barbara Ann. "Townbuilders of Orange County: A Study of Four Southern California Cities, 1857–1931." PhD dissertation, University of California, Irvine, 1995.

Ocegueda, Mark Anthony. "Sol y Sombra: San Bernardino's Mexican Community, 1880–1960." PhD dissertation, University of California, Irvine, 2017.

Paule, Dorothea Jean. "The German Settlement at Anaheim." MA thesis, University of Southern California, 1952.

Peters, Mary M. "The Segregation of Mexican American Children in the Elementary Schools of California—Its Legal and Administrative Aspects." MA thesis, University of California, Los Angeles, 1948.

Reccow, Louis. "The Orange County Citrus Strike of 1935–36: The 'Forgotten People' in Revolt." PhD dissertation, University of Southern California, 1972.

Treff, Simon Ludwig. "The Education of Mexican Children in Orange County." MS thesis, University of Southern California, 1934.

Whitten, Chester. "An Experimental Study of the Comparison of 'Formal' and 'Progressive' Methods of Teaching Mexican Children." MA thesis, University of Southern California, 1939.

Williamson, Paul Garland. "Labor in the California Citrus Industry." MA thesis, University of California, 1947.

INDEX

For the benefit of digital users, indexed terms that span two pages (e.g., 52–53) may, on occasion, appear on only one of those pages.

Figures are indicated by an italic *f* following the page number.